PATCHWORK LEVIATHAN

Patchwork Leviathan

Pockets of
Bureaucratic
Effectiveness
in Developing
States

Erin Metz McDonnell

PRINCETON UNIVERSITY PRESS
PRINCETON AND OXFORD

Copyright © 2020 by Princeton University Press

Requests for permission to reproduce material from this work
should be sent to permissions@press.princeton.edu

Published by Princeton University Press
41 William Street, Princeton, New Jersey 08540
6 Oxford Street, Woodstock, Oxfordshire OX20 1TR

press.princeton.edu

All Rights Reserved

ISBN 978-0-691-19735-7 (cloth)
ISBN (pbk.) 978-0-691-19736-4
ISBN (e-book) 978-0-691-20006-4

British Library Cataloging-in-Publication Data is available

Editorial: Meagan Levinson and Jaqueline Delaney
Production: Erin Suydam
Publicity: Nathalie Levine (U.S.) and Kathryn Stevens (U.K.)

Portions of this text were published previously in McDonnell, Erin Metz. (2017). "Patchwork
Leviathan: How Pockets of Bureaucratic Governance Flourish within Institutionally Diverse
Developing States." *American Sociological Review* 82(3): 476–510.

This book has been composed in Adobe Text and Gotham

Printed on acid-free paper ∞

Printed in the United States of America

10 9 8 7 6 5 4 3 2 1

For Vicki Schultz, my mom.
And Terry, my love.
There are not words enough to say
what your love and support have meant.

CONTENTS

Preface   ix

Acknowledgments   xiii

Abbreviations   xvii

1   Introduction: Patchwork Leviathans   1

2   Recruitment: Clustering Distinctiveness   26

3   Cultivation: Clustered Distinctiveness, Interstitial Experience, and the
    Lived Foundations of the Bureaucratic Ethos   53

4   Protection: Coping with and Remaking Disruptive Environments   84

5   Introducing Comparison Cases: Patchwork Leviathans in Comparative
    and Historical Perspective   104

6   Beyond Autonomy: Elite Attention and Pathways to Shelter from
    Neopatrimonial Influence   135

7   Dual Habitus and Founding Cadres: The Sociological Foundations of
    How Discretion Is Oriented to Organizational Achievement   165

8   Long-Term Outcomes in Pockets of Effectiveness   187

Conclusion   202

Methodological Appendix   229

Notes   237

References   255

Index   275

PREFACE

On December 8, 2000, I stood under a corrugated tin roof watching the con-tested U.S. presidential election play out on a flickering little black and white television set in Cape Coast, Ghana. Clustered shoulder to shoulder with nearly a dozen of my Ghanaian neighbors, we were rapt by the political drama of hanging chads, close recounts in Florida, and the news that the Supreme Court would have to decide the U.S. election. It was what U.S. southerners call a "hot mess." Just the previous day Ghana had conducted nationwide elections, and the contrast could not have been starker. For the first time in twenty years, Ghanaians had voted a new head of state into power, with a new ruling party, in a process widely deemed free and fair. Next to me, Ko-bena clicked his tongue and nudged my shoulder with a smile, 'Eh *obrunyi*, all this time your people are coming here to tell us how we should do democ-racy. We should rather go there and show you how it is done!' He proudly stuck out his thumb, still visibly marked with the black indelible ink from thumbprint voting.

That moment has stayed with me through the years, a reminder of how much thinking about African countries is grounded in a stereotypical trope that paints Africans not as a potential source of solutions, but rather as the passive recipients of help, thereby erasing their own agency. In *How to Write About Africa*, Binyavanga Wainaina's biting satire reminds us that "Africa is to be pitied, worshipped or dominated." We might also add: Africa is to be *saved*, to be *fixed* … and not by Africans. Wainaina satirically advocates depicting the entire continent as a single country, full of untamed jungles, and lavishing attention on Africans' nakedness, their suffering, and their helplessness.

Instead, this is a book about the Africa that remains too rarely seen: pro-fessional Ghanaians in suits, their successes, and their ingenuity. It is set amid tall concrete and glass buildings fronting heavily trafficked roads in Accra, Ghana. The work those professionals do is inextricably entangled with the full range of life experiences comprising modern Ghana. Some of the officials grew up living in mud dwellings; others have one or two parents with a Ph.D. They worry about how the decisions they make will affect the growth of the boom-ing cell phone industry, high-end banking, and commercial businesses, but also how they will affect subsistence farmers, petty traders, and smallholders in Ghana's cocoa industry. This will be a story of those Ghanaian public servants in their suits, imperfect and real human beings working late into the night in heated discussions about how to solve problems facing their country, whether they are using radio engineering equipment to monitor the airwaves or running sophisticated econometric models to figure out how a policy might impact inflation. And so, I will go against Wainaina's satirical advice: "Never have a picture of a well-adjusted African on the cover of your book, or in it."

This book is not only about Ghana, but it seems appropriate to begin in Ghana because it was my experience there that led to this project. Having lived in Ghana for some time before I went to graduate school, I often found myself frustrated both by what was written about Africa and the stories that were conspicuous in their absence. So heavy was the focus on negatives— from AIDS to state corruption—that if I had only known about Africa through the scholarship I read, I would have assumed everything was doomed. The Ghana I had experienced was nowhere to be found. I felt frustrated even with scholarship doing the important work of analyzing Western complicity in Africa's developmental trajectory by pointing to the influence of colonialism and neocolonial corporate domination. Such work felt fatalistic, suggesting that not only was everything doomed, but Africa's hand had been dealt long ago, and there was nothing contemporary Africans could do about it.

Recently perceptions of Africa have begun to shift; however, the pernicious assumption that nothing works in Africa still runs incredibly deep. As Chimamanda Ngozi Adichie beautifully reminds us, there is "the danger of a single story" about Africa, one that is steeped in Afro-pessimism. When American undergraduate students read my work on Ghana, what do they say they learn? They say: "I was really surprised that some things are working well in Ghana. I never knew that." Sadly, those American undergraduates are not alone. At a conference, I had the pleasure of talking to a Kenyan economist about my book. I explained that I was analyzing highly effective pockets within states and enthusiastically mentioned that the Kenya Tea Development Authority was one of the cases in my book. She looked briefly shocked and then gushed, "You have to tell Kenyans this. We need to hear that. We usually don't think about anyone saying any part of our government works well."

It would be impossible to write this book without disclosing my dirty little secret: I love bureaucracy. I admire the drive to give order to the complexity of regularly encountered tasks. Every time I move through an airport, my poor husband has to listen to me remark on ways that it could be better ordered. When I hold a service position within my university or academic discipline, I create spreadsheets and forms and records of what worked previously, leaving the position with more formalized institutional memory than I found it. In popular Western discourse, bureaucracy often gets blamed whenever anything done by a large formal organization displeases us. In so doing, we throw the baby out with the bathwater, so focused on exaggerated moments of "red tape" that we become oblivious to all the good bureaucracy does for us daily.

However, this book's interest in the bureaucratic ethos comes from Ghanaian public servants at the heart of its story and the citizens they serve, not only from me, or Max Weber, or sociological theory. If you speak with everyday Ghanaians, from civil servants in offices to taxi drivers and tomato sellers on the street, the craving for more effective government administration is a frequent topic of discussion. The desire for better, more honest, more effective government is not something imported. However, that very local impetus for more effective administration has to confront a world that is not entirely of Ghanaians' making. Ghanaian public servants must navigate a world order of states patterned on the Western experience, administered by large formal and complex organizations divided into discrete jurisdictions by ministerial portfolios. That is not to say that Western administration is normatively superior, nor that Africans might not have developed a more ingenious system of administration had colonialism not imposed Western-style state organization. But unfortunately, Ghanaian bureaucrats do not get to operate in counterfactual realities; they have only the world as it currently is. Given the world order of large formal administrative states, Ghanaian public servants have worked to cultivate the bureaucratic ethos as a means of enabling that more honest and effective government to which they aspire.

In choosing to focus on what works well within state administrations that are otherwise typically considered weak, the book will, by necessity, pay less attention to other important topics already familiar to scholars of the Global South. Colonialism was certainly extractive and often violent, disrupting and remaking local social institutions in ways that have had lasting effects. Neocolonial forms of oppression exist. Contemporary multinational corporations, foreign aid, and international NGOs do both harm and good. (Neo)patrimonialism is a complex issue. Power, gender, religion, and ethnicity influence states, and vice versa. Entire books could be (and have been) devoted to any one of those topics in order to enable the deft analytic attention they require to give a balanced accounting, and I refer interested readers to excellent existing work on those topics.

I am aware that there are risks in writing about relatively high-performing state agencies in non-Western states, and I have tried to keep those concerns in mind while writing this book. There are moments where comparisons and contrasts are analytically necessary—between high- and low-performers within the same non-Western state and between the organizational environment in non-Western and Western states. I have tried to illuminate enough of a contrast so that readers who have never lived outside of the West can understand what is so noteworthy about the exceptional performance of the organizations highlighted throughout this book. At the same time, I have tried to manage such contrasts with an awareness of the dangers of appearing ethno-centric or reinforcing negative stereotypes of public servants generally in the Global South. I am also mindful that scholars may bring their own very different disciplinary perspectives to the reading, with some disposed to believe that any negative representation of Ghanaian public servants is a form of neo-colonial Western domination, while others cannot be convinced that there is a single civil servant in the Ghanaian state who is not taking bribes—both conversations I have actually had.

Mindful of these challenges, I have let the empirical data be my guide. In what follows it is clear that I respect the work these officials are doing, however I do my best not to romanticize the organizations I study, but to faithfully bring to life their daily working lives, the challenges they encounter, and how they grapple with those challenges. In the field, I talked to public servants, ate lunch with them, observed while "loitering with intent" in their places of work, and endeavored as much as possible within the limits of my own field positionality to understand the world as they see it and experience it. I have sought to provide a detailed account of the innermost workings of a non-Western state, including some august corridors of state power that are often off-limits. I want the book to feel accessible to students, insightful to scholars and practitioners, but most of all, I want it to feel accurate to the Ghanaians inside these niches who shared their time and stories.

As Ghanaian scholar Francis Dodoo observed, American sociology has woefully neglected Africa. Happily, that is beginning to change. Theories about the human social condition should be built on observations from a wide variety of contexts, including those outside the United States and Europe. We have things to learn from public servants in highly effective niches of states in the Global South, for they have found solutions to seemingly intractable problems that impinge on the well-being of millions of people.

ACKNOWLEDGMENTS

First and foremost, I am grateful to the more than 100 Ghanaian public servants and private individuals who generously shared their time and insight with the warm hospitality for which Ghanaians are justifiably famous. I am especially indebted to Dr. Joseph Ayee of the University of Legon. Dr. Ayee's sterling reputation as a researcher and his gracious letter of introduction facilitated my access into many offices of government. Daniel Pepprah and Eubank Arthur provided invaluable research assistance. For nearly twenty years, Rebecca Yeboah, Nii Martey Larbie, Hannah Quartey, and Victor Bannerman-Chedid have educated me on life in Ghana, helped build my local language skills, shared innumerable meals, and cared for me like family. My life in Ghana would never be the same without you.

Everyone should be fortunate enough to have an advisor like Jim Mahoney. From the earliest rough dispatches from the field through finished writing, I have benefitted enormously from Jim's intellectual breadth and generosity, showcased in his ability to engage an idea on its own terms, to identify, and then polish the kernels of potential even when they are still formative. I also remain deeply indebted to the intellectual generosity of my dissertation committee members Wendy Griswold, Bruce Carruthers, and Carol Heimer, whose expertise in culture and organizations profoundly shaped the project. Monica Prasad and Ann Orloff also contributed insight and encouragement on the project. I am also grateful to Chas Camic for cultivating my inchoate love of Weber. Chas's encouragement, keen insight, and encyclopedic knowledge have continued to contribute to my scholarly development through emailed missives dissecting charismatic authority and the iron cage. Though he was never a formal advisor, he has been a true mentor.

The initial Ghanaian fieldwork for this project would not have been possible without generous funding from the National Science Foundation (Doctoral Dissertation Improvement Grant #0728059), as well as research fellowships from Northwestern University's Department of Sociology and Program of African Studies. This project has also benefitted from a Weinberg Dissertation Writing Fellowship from Northwestern University and funding from the Kellogg Institute for International Studies and the Institute for Scholarship in the Liberal Arts at the University of Notre Dame.

The project and book have benefitted from comments from colleagues, and whatever errors or shortcomings remain are wholly mine. Garron Hansen has been a remarkable thought partner, sharing his time and frank experiences working as a development practitioner; our conversations were instrumental in pushing me to think about the practical implications of my work for development. Julia Strauss, Michael Roll, and David Leonard were incredibly gracious with their case expertise in the Salt Inspectorate, NAFDAC, and KTDA, respectively, and corresponded several times when I had questions. If you haven't read their books, you should run out for a copy now. My thinking benefitted enormously from discussions with the fabulous trio of development sociologists at Brown University, Nitsan Chorev, Andrew Shrank, and Patrick Heller, who each at various times over coffee or a meal have talked through ideas, pointed out omissions, and pushed me to think through new facets of the question. I have also benefitted from conversations with Ann Swidler over the years, including a memorable Tuesday afternoon ASA presentation slot to which I had thought no one would come.

I feel fortunate that Art Stinchcombe thoughtfully commented on the earliest versions of this project. His love of sociological approaches to organizations was infectious. Over many walks to the library, Art taught me to think ambitiously and write with a clarity that does not fear being later proven wrong. I have aspired to live up to his wisdom "I'd rather be wrong than vague. Being wrong advances knowledge." I am so fortunate to have outstanding colleagues at the University of Notre Dame who supported me through this process and provided insightful feedback on my writing. Two different chapters received thoughtful and detailed critique from my brilliant colleagues in writing group, which at times variously included Jessica Collett, Jennifer Jones, Amy Langenkamp, Elizabeth McClintock, Abi Ocobock, and Calvin Zimmerman. Special thanks also to Ann Mische and Tamara Kay: from winter writing retreats to weekly check-ins and writing feedback, I cannot imagine this process without the encouragement and guidance you have so generously shared with me in our book writers' group. I'm also thankful for comments from Betsey Brada, Salo Coslovsky, Michaela DeSoucey, Barry Eidlin, Maggie Frye, David Gibson, Bright Gyamfi, Geoff Harkness, Jenn Lena, Omar Lizardo, John Levi Martin, Damon Mayrl, Terence McDonnell, Daniel Morrison, Lisa Mueller, Paul Ocobock, Erin Rehel, Naunihal Singh, Dustin Stoltz, Matthias vom Hau, and Christina Wolbrecht. I have been fortunate to work with incredible graduate students who provided both research assistance and manuscript feedback, including Abigail Jorgensen, Luiz Vilaça, and Jake Dillabaugh. In particular, Luiz went through Brazilian archives for civil service records, and translated Portuguese materials for the Brazilian case. I'm grateful to Meagan Levinson at Princeton, who really understood the project and was an enthusiastic supporter from our earliest meeting. I'm also indebted to the tremendous anonymous referees, who were intellectually generous, understood the heart of the book, and offered thoughtful insights and developmental criticisms to strengthen and clarify it.

I also received helpful feedback during invited presentations of this material at the University of Wisconsin-Madison Economic Change & Development Seminar, Stanford University Business School's Organizational Behavior Seminar, University of Chicago's Social Theory & Evidence Workshop, Duke University's Department of Sociology, the Development & Governance Seminar at the Watson Institute of Brown University, the Comparative-Historical Social Science workshop at the Buffett Center for International Studies of Northwestern University, the Interdisciplinary Committee on Organizational Studies at the Ross School of Business at the University of Michigan, the Rotman School of Management at the University of Toronto, and the University of Notre Dame's Culture Workshop and Africa Working Group. Of these many intellectual opportunities over the years, several particularly stand out. It was enormously helpful to discuss my ideas with Jesper Sørensen and Sara Soule, thanks to their on-the-ground experience in African private-sector organizational capacity building. After my presentation at Chicago, Cheol-Sung Lee, John Levi Martin, Kim Hoang, and Marco Garrido joined me for an incredibly intellectually engaging dinner and provided valuable insights into my project. At Rotman, Sarah Kaplan, director of their Institute for Gender and the Economy, helpfully pushed me to talk through the practical implications of my study for organizational cultural change more broadly through the lens of how corporations could be more gender inclusive. That conversation stayed with me and fomented into a section of the conclusion explicitly tackling that question. I am grateful to all the professors and graduate students who asked questions that shaped my thinking, even though I cannot thank them all individually.

Beyond the words and ideas, others provided critical support to me in the process of writing. There were times I thought I only still loved this project because I had a severe case of Stockholm syndrome. I'm eternally grateful to the friends, colleagues, and mentors whose support helped me persist. I grew up working class and in an environment where it was not a foregone conclusion that everyone would go to college, so special thanks to Mrs. Karl, Mrs. Blandford, and Mrs. Ruxton, teachers who taught me a love of writing, and instilled the confidence to pursue it. I feel so fortunate to have Rory McVeigh as a colleague, who over years has always been willing to sit down and share professional experience and scholarly insight. I cannot imagine this book coming to completion without Dan Myer's "chipping and binging" talk, which completely reformed how I write. JJ and Alexandra Wright were an endless source of support, love, and encouragement. Instrumental music from the JJ Wright Trio and Yo-Yo Ma became the Skinner box of my productivity. Just hearing a cello now makes me want to type.

Most of all, I am grateful for my family. I'm grateful to my mom Vicki Schultz, who raised me to believe that I was capable of anything if I put my mind to it. I could never have asked for a better mother. I'm so thankful for my kids, who fill my heart with sunshine. Liam and Mara loved and supported me through the long and arduous task of writing this book. Mara brought me flowers and filled my soul with sunshine through her koala hugs. Liam gave me an Egyptian spell for "restore order" and "protect." I hope every book writer in the throes of frantic final edits has a ten-year-old son who is observant, thoughtful, and knows a bit of Egyptian magic courtesy of Rick Riordan.

Finally, I am eternally grateful to my brilliant academic spouse Terence McDonnell, who is my first sounding board and my tireless cheerleader. In the most intense periods of writing this book, Terry really put the "man" in feminism. So that I could write on weekends and evenings, he did long hours solo parenting our children, cooked meals, ran errands, and shouldered the lion's share of housework. At one point I despaired about critiquing development practice, observing "at the end of the day they can say at least a few people's lives are actually better off. Whose life will be better off when I finish this book?" to which he immediately quipped "Mine! My life will be better off when you finish this book." So here is to making at least one life better.

ABBREVIATIONS

ADR Alternative Dispute Resolution, legal mediation

BNDE/BNDES Brazil's National Bank of Economic Development, the acronym coming from the Portuguese Banco Nacional de Desenvolvimento Econômico, updated in 1982 to Banco Nacional de Desenvolvimento Econômico e Social

CDC Commonwealth Development Corporation

DASP Departamento Administrativo do Serviço Público (Administrative Department of Public Service)

FDA Food and Drug Administration (United States)

FRE Fund for Economic Rehabilitation (Brazil)

KTDA Kenya Tea Development Authority

MITI Ministry of Trade and Industry (Japan)

MOFEP Ministry of Finance and Economic Planning (Ghana), also colloquially called "Ministry of Finance"

NAFDAC Nigeria's National Agency for Food and Drug Administration and Control

NCA National Communications Authority (Ghana)

NGO Non-Governmental Organization

PARD Policy Analysis and Research Division (Ghana)

PTF Petroleum Trust Fund (Nigeria)

USDA United States Department of Agriculture

PATCHWORK LEVIATHAN

1

Introduction: Patchwork Leviathans

When the [bureaucratic] office is fully developed, official activity demands the
full working capacity of the official .... Formerly the normal state of affairs was
the reverse: Official business was discharged as a secondary activity.
—MAX WEBER[1]

People all around the world desire a more effective state, one that uses public
resources wisely to improve the well-being of citizens. Unfortunately, well-
funded and well-intended efforts to improve the human condition often fail
because many states are unable to administer effectively. This lack of administrative capacity cannot be solved with one more international training workshop teaching skills such as cost-benefit analysis. In Western countries, bureaucracy is practically a four-letter word, but among those who study states
outside the West, there is an emerging consensus that states fail not because
they have too much bureaucracy, but because they have too little.[2]

Particularly scarce in the social landscape of many countries is what Max
Weber called the bureaucratic *ethos*: characteristic tendencies to perceive,
think, decide, and act in ways driven by an orientation to achieving the organization's goals. The bureaucratic ethos captures a profound transformation of
social attachments that the epigraph alludes to, whereby people identify with
their job as "a focus of ethical commitment and duty"[3] that transcends other
social commitments while people are at work. However, in Ghana, and states
like it, the personal and professional spheres are not neatly separated. Work
is embedded in a patrimonial social order that places less value on individual

achievement, abstract rules, and impersonal universalism, and correspondingly more value on social solidarity, partiality, and particularism, with strong moral obligations to nurture social relationships by taking special care of other in-group members, like friends, kin, coethnics, or classmates.

Scholars often use the term *neopatrimonialism* to refer to situations where patrimonial practices and orientations suffuse legal-rational institutions, especially the globally imposed legal-rational structure of large formal organizations comprising the central administrative state.[4] Neopatrimonialism has become a catch-all pejorative used to encapsulate all the developmental short-comings of African countries. The label has been applied to politicians and civil servants using state resources to shore up their power within particular groups (political clientelism), giving government jobs to reward supporters (patronage), and illegally appropriating public resources for private benefit (corruption).[5] In line with this understanding, scholarship often explores how neopatrimonial logics shape the prevailing sense of legitimate social power, emphasizing their predominance and continued influence in places like Ghana.[6] Forms of clientelism, patronage, and corruption exist in all societies, including the United States; however, they become reified and seemingly insurmountable development obstacles under the label of neopatrimonialism.[7]

This is not another book about corruption and neopatrimonialism in African states. The stereotypical image of dysfunctional public service implied by the idea of a neopatrimonial state tells only part of the story. Monolithically dysfunctional state administrations are the exception, not the rule—albeit the exception that has long captured popular and academic attention.[8] Rather, many seemingly weak state "leviathans" are instead patchworked: Cobbled together from scarce available resources, they have a wide range of internal variation in organizational capacities sewn loosely together into the semblance of unity. This book is built upon a striking empirical observation with theoretical implications for how we conceptualize states and state capacity: Amid general organizational weakness and neopatrimonial politics, there are a few spectacularly effective state agencies dedicating their full working capacity to the routine satisfaction of organizational goals in the public interest—subcultural niches of the bureaucratic ethos that manage to thrive against impressive odds. *This is their story.*

A Day in the Life of One Bureaucratic Niche

Even at 10:00 p.m. on this particular night in late December, the lights are still ablaze in the Policy Analysis and Research Division (PARD) of the Ghanaian Ministry of Finance and Economic Planning. PARD is just one of several effective bureaucratic niches I observed within the Ghanaian state. PARD is racing a deadline to prepare the country's budget for the next fiscal year, that essential task of statehood that has so fascinated legions of social scientists. The budget encodes the priorities of the whole state and enables their execution; the budget is famously "the skeleton of the state stripped of all misleading ideologies."[9] It is not clear from the formal organizational chart that PARD would be heavily involved in this task; nevertheless this most essential task must be done, and done well, and so PARD has risen to the occasion. Usually the first to arrive and the last to leave, PARD has been a whirl of activity since before 6:00 a.m. As the experienced senior members collaborate on the arduous task of the fiscal tables, younger members have been "chasing" all day. "Chasing" is a colloquialism for physically going out to units throughout the state to ask, beg, cajole, and sometimes just do their work for them in order to obtain the data essential to completing the nation's budget—which, on paper, is supposed to be effortlessly and routinely available to the ministry. But PARD is painfully aware that they cannot take a foundation of bureaucratic orientation for granted: They cannot assume the routine and timely completion of other state organizations' tasks.

Kojo is a recent college graduate and new to PARD. He reflects with surprise how dedicated these few officials are, so far outside of the expected norm of civil servants as lazy and uninterested. Kojo remarks, "People go home as late as maybe, as sometimes 3:00 a.m. *Serious.* And people don't even sleep because they are working towards something. They have a deadline." Indeed, as the deadline for the budget draws near, some PARD members will sleep the night in their offices rather than waste time travelling to their homes on the outskirts of the city.

Around 10:00 p.m., the PARD team is only just wrapping up and quietly discussing where to pick up again tomorrow. The Ministry of Finance and Economic Planning building has an interior, central courtyard that opens all the way up to the sky, with walkways around this interior on every floor. This construction provides a much-needed breeze to those offices that are not air-conditioned. Mr. Kwesi Mensah, PARD's director, joins me on the balcony around the building's interior courtyard. From our vantage point on one of the highest floors, nearly every office is visible. A handful of lights still burn bright, illuminating a few civil servants still at their desks, typing away at this late hour.

'Still a few lights on,' I observe. Mr. Mensah leans on the railing and methodically points to each of the lighted rooms, naming each inhabitant without hesitation, and his or her department. One is a member of the budget division who used to work for PARD. In another, he notes the Multi-Donor Budget Support team, clustered around a desk deep in conversation and oblivious to the late hour. There is a pregnant pause, then, without taking his eyes off those few lighted offices, Mr. Mensah remarks, 'As for those people, they are like us. They come early, they stay late until the work is done.'

This simple proclamation spoke volumes about the ethos, challenges, and *distinctiveness* of being a civil servant who is oriented towards organizational achievement in a social context like Ghana. In Ghana, staying late is a radical badge of commitment to the organization, particularly when lesser levels of devotion are not only tolerated but normative. By contrast, in other parts of the Ghanaian state the second half of the epigraph is clearly visible: Official business is still quite often discharged second to a host of other personal obligations. Kofi observes, "If you sit by the wayside, you see people by 3:00 [in the afternoon] who take their bags and go home. You'd see people who come to work as late as 10:00 a.m." Keeping strict working hours is less of a priority, and even when physically present at work, not all government workers are pursuing official business as their primary activity. Many merely pass time, overcrowded into small offices amid towering piles of unorganized paperwork. Some sleep at their desks through the afternoon heat. Gesturing to a different part of the ministries buildings, Patience explains, "Over here, I've seen people have extra things outside work that they do, other businesses elsewhere. They don't mind. They just come in, hang around for a while, and then leave."

These are not the personal failings of a few bad apples, but widespread responses to public servants' challenging structural positions and an ethos of disenchantment that may date all the way back to the colonial period.[10] Some officials lack computers to do their work or are waiting for materials to arrive before they can begin a task. Others are just tired or disaffected and know how difficult it is to get punished for dereliction of duty. It is not uncommon for public servants to come late or slip out before official closing time, neglecting formal work to attend to obligations to friends or informal jobs augmenting their meager salaries. Some civil servants may leverage public office for private gain, often at the expense of organizational goals and the public interest, including bribery, patronage, nepotism, and budgetary theft. These examples capture the stereotypical characterization of state officials in contemporary developing countries, featuring low morale and scant productivity.

Given the administrative culture that predominates elsewhere throughout the state, the organizational practices within PARD are a distinctive organizational subculture. Membership in this radical subculture was not flaunted; rather the camaraderie of difference was expressed quietly and inadvertently—the lights were only on as a necessary consequence of working late. Based on prior literature that suggests civil servants in developing countries lack commitment, are ineffectual, or corrupt, one would hardly expect to find a small band of officials working late into the night, inscribing the state's priorities, and shouldering the lion's share of the work of the fiscal state.

Big Questions and Overarching Argument

This account of PARD introduces the empirical puzzle motivating the book: In a context where corruption and ineffectiveness are not only tolerated but expected of civil servants, how do groups like PARD manage to become so uncharacteristically oriented to achieving the organization's goals and serving the public interest? Or more simply: Why are some parts within the state highly effective while others are not? Answering these questions has wide-ranging empirical and theoretical significance for those who care about state-building and development.

PARD and the other effective state niches examined throughout this book pose an incredible empirical puzzle for the billion-dollar development industry. Those niches have managed to conquer a seemingly intractable problem: cultivating impersonal, effective, organizationally oriented administration in contexts where the bureaucratic ethos is most needed and most elusive. Current scholarship on states and development agrees broadly on two things. First, state organizational capacity in low-income countries is essential to the success of many other developmental efforts.[11] Second, we have little idea how to engender state organizational capacity. Efforts to build states' organizational capacity are notoriously prone to failure. In the last decade, the World Bank alone has spent over $16 billion USD trying to build or reform state capacity, mostly in low-income countries—with little success. Development organizations have scored impressive improvements in infrastructural or engineering projects, but practitioners now increasingly recognize that "building capabilities of human systems—including that human system called 'the state'—has proven much more difficult."[12] External actors have limited ability to impose complicated changes that actually alter people's daily practices.[13] Reform efforts sometimes change the letter of the law—a thin external veneer—but fail to change the animating *spirit* of daily practice, resulting in a bureaucratic façade familiar in many developing states, with superficial compliance layered over inner chaos that haunts reform efforts.

Scholarship on states typically proceeds as though the capacity of the administrative state can be captured as a feature of the state as a whole.[14] Surveys of state capacity and corruption alike tend to focus on questions of degree and frequency—how corrupt are officials? How often do officials seek a bribe? However, in many countries, being asked about the frequency of bribery in "the state" is almost nonsensical, because the answer would be something like "very often" at the Customs authority and "almost never" at PARD or the Ghanaian Commercial Courts, and the average of those does not capture the most important contours of social reality. It is as though we have all been engaged in a great debate about shades of violet, and failed to observe that many states are actually concentrated clusters of blue in a field of red.

This book argues that variation in capacity and ethos within central state administration is not merely irrelevant noise to be ignored: It is a significant empirical reality conditioning the organizational sociology of political bodies. Distinctively effective niches within the state, like PARD, may be uncommon and often overlooked, *but they are not idiosyncratic.* This book will argue that such patchworking is the hallmark structure of states in the midrange of capacity between the extremes of failed or strong states that have dominated scholarship. In predominantly neopatrimonial states from early twentieth-century China to contemporary Ghana and Nigeria, the bureaucratic ethos has flourished within concentrated niches of the state. Their structural position is *interstitial,* social niches entangled within a larger institutional field, distinct-yet-embedded subsystems characterized by practices inconsistent with—though not necessarily subversive to—those of the dominant, neopatrimonial institutional field. These interstitial niches are, effectively, *bureaucratic subcultures*—loosely bounded numerical minority groups within a predominant majority. Like other subcultures, such niches are characterized by "a set of modal beliefs, values, norms, and customs associated with a relatively distinct social subsystem (a set of interpersonal networks and institutions) existing within a larger social system and culture."[15]

My overarching argument centers on clustered distinctiveness: Where the human, cognitive, and material resources of doing bureaucracy are rare, it matters critically *how they are distributed.* Sufficient discretion, especially over personnel, enables *clustering* a critical mass of proto-bureaucratic resources, resulting in camaraderie born of similarity and synergies of concentration that are impossible when such scarce resources are spread thinly throughout the state (see Figure 1.1). Strong symbolic boundaries differentiating "us" from "them" increase identification with the subculture and lead to *cultivation,* as niche insiders increasingly identify with and conform to the standards that typify their distinctive work group. The small-group culture coheres around that which insiders have in common, and the practices that make them maximally distinctive from the contrasting "spoiled identity"[16] of public servants broadly—that is, they identify with impersonal and effective organizational practices that contrast sharply with the ineffectual or corrupt practices of the larger environment. Such clustering and cultivation ultimately produce a shared sense of *distinctiveness* vis-à-vis the larger administrative environment.

Detailed, qualitative insight into the inner workings of states such as Ghana are incredibly uncommon, and this perspective illuminates an iterative and endogenous change process of organizational culture. Niches do not simply recruit the "right" people—that is, people with fully formed ideal typical bureaucratic ethos. Rather niches recruit right-enough people, people whose prior experience, habits, and professional orientations have some incomplete

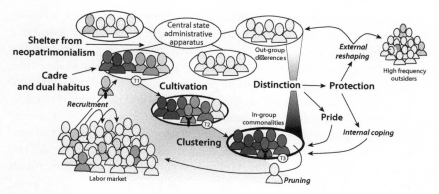

FIGURE 1.1. Theoretical overview of clustering distinctiveness.

and imperfect overlap with the bureaucratic ethos. Those imperfect foundations become the material upon which cultivation draws to further clarify the subcultural organizational practices and enhance their distinctiveness from the larger neopatrimonial administrative culture that predominates in the state broadly. Over time these many small iterative steps come to be consolidated into a new organizational identity, a widely shared understanding both within and beyond these niches that they operate in a very distinctive way.

Lived experience within a niche fosters habits of practice, which operate as a robust *alternative foundation* for action. Lived experience reinforced within the close-knit interpersonal environment of the interstitial niche thereby enables the establishment of distinctive strategies for action that are alternatives to familiar neopatrimonial practices. However, such distinctiveness vis-à-vis the environment also comes at a cost: Because niches operate under different "rules of the game" from the prevailing neopatrimonial environment, niches expend great effort to *protect* themselves from interruptions (both incidental and intentional) that can disrupt their ability to complete organizational goals. Operating as a bureaucratic interstice is like trying to play chess where everyone else is playing a different game, you have to whittle the pieces yourself, precious few potential players have ever seen the game before, and the playing area is prone to disruptive bursts of wind.

If clustering distinctiveness through recruitment, cultivation, and protection is how the bureaucratic ethos gets consolidated and manages to thrive interstitially despite an inhospitable environment, how then does the earliest foundation of distinctiveness first emerge? Stripped down to its simplest elements, two factors explain the initial emergence of pockets of the bureaucratic ethos: shelter from neopatrimonialism and a minimum critical mass of proto-bureaucratic distinctiveness. Shelter from neopatrimonial logics influencing hiring or operational decisions is essential for an interstitial niche to emerge, because such shelter enables the possibility of new practices emerging that are at odds with the predominant neopatrimonial means of ordering social conduct and power. Beyond the formal organizational autonomy or active elite sponsorship that has dominated prior scholarship, shelter from neopatrimonial influence can also be provided by merely willing or inattentive elites and informal means to obtain operational and personnel discretion.

Organizational orientation then takes hold in a sufficiently protected niche of the state in which a small cluster of people possess what I call *dual habitus*,[17] lived experience in the local environment *and* in the habits and practices of doing formal bureaucracy, which constitutes a sufficiently robust alternative to locally prevalent neopatrimonial practices.[18] If we look at the earliest moments of clustered distinctiveness, we find the smallest unit of social action: a small group. Organizations that became effective niches of the bureaucratic ethos began with founding *clustered cadres*, small and tightly knit corps of senior staff with strong proto-bureaucratic dual habitus. Those clustered cadres were the grit around which the pearl of organizational clustered distinctiveness would grow.

Empirically, most people in the clustered cadres within successful niches obtained that dual habitus through a very distinctive educational profile: a first degree from a local university and an advanced or professional degree from a university abroad. Attending a flagship local university builds local elite social and cultural capital essential for navigating the local environment, and ensures that actors are perceived by others as authentically local such that their ideas are not labeled as too cosmopolitan and thereby discounted as out of touch with local conditions and concerns. Then, an intermediate amount of time abroad for advanced education endows officials with sufficient lived experience where formal organization and the bureaucratic ethos are commonplace, giving them "tacit knowledge" or "knowledge 'how,'"[19] the accretions of repeated lived, practical experiences that cultivate a sensibility or disposition, a taste for, and tendency toward bureaucratic practices. Interstitial insiders with dual habitus thereby draw on a large repertoire of practical knowledge of *doing bureaucracy* grounded in their lived experience of the bureaucratic ethos elsewhere while remaining exquisitely sensitive to local tastes and grounded practicalities. Thus, these niches have succeeded where Western reformers failed because of the effort and ingenuity of a distinctive subset of local actors who had a foot in both institutional worlds, whose dual habitus enabled them to innovate organizational practices oriented to abstract organizational goals that were also well-fitted to local cultural and institutional environments.

This argument offers a sociological answer to why some parts of the state act effectively in the public interest when and where most do not. This answer illuminates how the interstitial structural position is particularly fruitful for cultivating a small-group organizational culture around the bureaucratic ethos. It offers meso- and microlevel insight into the daily practices of officials, nested within organizational contexts, whose conduct aggregates up to "the state." It draws on advances in organizational and cultural sociologies to unpack the theoretical black box of how states discipline officials, identifying sociological foundations for how the orientations, understandings, and practices of bureaucratic conduct emerge, are shared, and stabilize within groups. Interstitial bureaucracy thereby examines the microfoundations of a canonical institution—bureaucracy—calling attention to the social and cultural elements of institutions that are embodied in the bureaucratic *ethos*.

A Weberian ethos is "an ensemble of purposes and ideals within a given code of conduct but also ways and means of comporting oneself within a given 'life-order.'"[20] A *bureaucratic* ethos is then the characteristic tendencies to perceive, think, decide, and act in particular ways driven by an orientation to the characteristics of bureaucracy, including impersonal administration, commitment to the purposes of the office, and achieving the organization's goals. Comporting oneself according to the bureaucratic ethos is not an inevitable outcome but rather a "moral and ethical achievement ... represent[ing] the product of particular ethical techniques and practices through which individuals develop the disposition and capacity to conduct themselves according to the ethos of the bureaucratic office," a process dependent on the "contingent and often fragile achievements of that socially organized sphere of moral existence."[21] For public-sector organizations, the content of organizational mission includes an aspect of public service, and so correspondingly the ethos of orientation to organizational mission encompasses public service. The bureaucratic ethos is conceptually distinct from related organizational outcomes such as effectiveness (accomplishing goals) or efficiency (accomplishing goals while conserving resources expended). For example, organizations could be very effective at racketeering or drawing rents from corrupt practices, neither of which would fit the definition of accomplishing publicly stated organizational goals; such organizations may have some sort of ethos but it is not a bureaucratic ethos. However, empirically in the cases analyzed throughout this book the bureaucratic ethos was strongly correlated with organizational effectiveness. Being oriented to accomplishing an organization's stated mission is a critical precursor to deploying human effort in pursuit of those explicit, collective, formal organizational goals.

Orientation to abstract collective organizational goals is an oddity in the long purview of history, an achievement to be unpacked rather than taken for granted because of its presumed rationality.[22] Orientation to organizational goals was revolutionary, compared to historically prior organizational forms, because it radically depersonalized administration. Instead of personal economic interest or network ties motivating work in prebendalism or patrimonialism, bureaucratic officials were oriented to achieving goals on behalf of abstract collectives—the organization, "state," or "the people." From paperwork to rules and meritocracy, those characteristics were means for cultivating the bureaucratic ethos and reorienting individual action to collective goals. Ultimately then, bureaucracy inures not in the characteristic existence of "paperwork" but in what paperwork aims to accomplish: separation of personal and professional spheres, increased transparency, and more effective goal achievement based on analysis of documented patterns. Without the bureaucratic ethos, characteristic bureaucratic features like paperwork often fail to achieve the ends of rational, predictable, effective administration, instead becoming red tape that can be leveraged into a bribe. Conversely, in high-variation environments like Ghana, characteristics that appear nonbureaucratic can actually support the bureaucratic ethos and ultimately achieve rational, predictable, effective, and depersonalized administration.

Advanced industrialized nations are so accustomed to the bureaucratic ethos that citizens often take for granted that bureaucracy will function— almost like clockwork without a keeper—and seem only aware of bureaucracy when it fails to work well. *Patchwork Leviathan* reminds us that in other times and places, functional bureaucracy is a fragile, active project entangled with dominant and often inimical local conditions. This work significantly advances understanding of the organizational foundations of state capacity, and in turn the social foundations of institutions like bureaucracy. It also counters the logic of inevitability that sometimes pervades accounts of institutional change broadly. Too often, we assume modes of rationality and modernity are natural, and therefore overlook the effort and commitment it took to bring them into being and continue to cultivate them.

Attention to the bureaucratic ethos thereby brings us to a fresh answer for why well-funded cosmopolitan organizational reform efforts fail: They do not account for the social foundations of *doing bureaucracy*. Bureaucracy is not merely a simple set of new rules to be enacted, but a cultural practice instantiated in thousands of large and small behaviors and interactions. Those moments of conscious, deliberative, decisions where something like impersonal rationality might be exercised are inextricably entangled with a larger foundation of habits and inclinations that shape daily behavior. Ultimately, *Patchwork Leviathan* argues that the administration of the *office* may be carried out, as Weber famously asserted, according to "general rules, which are more or less stable, more or less exhaustive, and which can be learned,"[23] but the bureaucratic ethos upon which that administration depends cannot. Every contingency of a business relationship cannot be enumerated in a written contract; therefore, contracts depend critically on myriad unspoken, noncontractual elements.[24] Similarly, bureaucracy includes explicit rules and features of administration, but also myriad implicit habits, practices, and inclinations that together comprise the bureaucratic ethos. The reason top-down reforms fail is that the bureaucratic ethos cannot be effectively and exhaustively enumerated such that it can be transmitted by mandate. Rather, *it must be lived to be learned.*

Theory Building in the Midrange: Data, Cases, and Comparisons

This book offers an uncommonly close look at the inner workings of non-Western states, analyzing effective statecraft in institutionally challenging environments, thereby casting new light on the nature of state-building and organizational change more broadly. Prior scholarship and popular media attention have mostly focused on the extremes of state functioning, from developmental darlings like Singapore to states that are so "predatory" or "failed" that they scarcely deserve the label "state." Instead, Ghana belongs to a large range of understudied states around the world and throughout history, states whose administrative abilities fall in the midrange.

Ghana gained independence from the British in 1957, the first formerly colonized Sub-Saharan African country to do so. The organization of the administrative state in many parts of Sub-Saharan Africa is a legacy of a colonial state, a Western export whose principal purpose was to regulate and extract value from the natural resources and labor of local peoples. Ghana is just the sort of midrange case that has been neglected in conventional research. The organizations of the Ghanaian administrative state span a wide range: Some approximate the stereotypical image of "third world" civil service mentioned previously, while a few have outstanding reputations for working effectively in the public's interest.

Today, this ethnically diverse country enjoys a reputation as a vibrant democracy and state that, while not without faults, is relatively strong compared to other postcolonial African nations. Ghana is nestled in the middle of numerical measurements of state capacity globally,[25] and generally considered among the best-governed mainland African countries.[26] Over its five decades of statehood, Ghana has regularly confronted many of the same economic and political challenges that typically plague African states, but has often grappled with those challenges more successfully than many other African countries. After Independence, in a pattern common to many African states, economic, social, and political optimism quickly deteriorated into a series of coups and economic hardships.[27] In 1981 Jerry Rawlings seized power, ruling as a populist one-party authoritarian who imposed sweeping structural adjustments, then as democratic reforms swept the continent in the 1990s, as Ghana's democratic president until 2000.[28] Ghana is a presidential republic that formally has a multiparty system, although in practice two parties have dominated the political scene since democratization in 1992. Ghana is now arguably one of the most vibrant African democracies, with an active civil society and several changes of party control through free and fair elections.

High ethnic diversity has posed difficulties for many African states. However, despite Ghana being the twelfth most ethnically diverse country in the world, ethnicity is relatively depoliticized, there is no history of interethnic war, many citizens speak multiple Ghanaian languages, and interethnic marriage is relatively common.[29] Ghanaians have a richly deserved reputation for hospitality, which is a point of national pride,[30] and generalized social trust is among the highest in Africa.[31] Like elsewhere on the continent, demographically more than half the Ghanaian population is younger than twenty-five years old, and the country has become increasingly urbanized, with more than half the population now dwelling in cities.[32] Roughly three-quarters of the population are Christian, 17 percent are Muslim, alongside traditional spiritualists, atheists, and others. Like many African nations, its economy is largely dependent on natural resources, extraction, and agriculture. Within an ecologically diverse landmass roughly the size of Oregon, gold and cocoa have long been mainstays of the Ghanaian economy, with offshore oil more recently coming into production.

Based on interviews with a wide range of expert observers of the Ghanaian state, I selected four niches of the central state about which there was expert consensus that they were unusually effective and honest. The Policy Analysis and Research Division, introduced earlier, was one such unit. Similarly, the Ghana Commercial Courts were making waves for tackling a higher case load with a quicker time to case completion than any other court system in Ghana, all with incredibly high satisfaction from litigants and an ironclad reputation for integrity. The Bank of Ghana was widely lauded as a whole, with particularly strong regard for the Monetary Policy Analysis and Financial Stability Department (Monetary Policy Analysis for short), which had contributed to decreasing inflation, and increasing transparency by making unprecedented amounts of data available. Similarly, the National Communications Authority had attracted attention for playing a more active role in shepherding the new, but booming, telecommunications sector of the Ghanaian economy, with the Spectrum and Frequency Management units particularly well regarded for impartial and effective regulation of the airwaves. The qualitative data from Ghana are based on over 100 interviews with public servants and expert observers, supplemented with ethnographic observations, over a year and a half of direct fieldwork, and embedded within expertise from nearly twenty years of work on Ghana. Double quotation marks indicate recorded verbatim transcriptions, and material enclosed in single quotes is from field notes or interview notes taken at the time (see Methodological Appendix).

However, bureaucratic interstices are not unique to Ghana: This book argues that patchworking is an overlooked but characteristic structural feature of many other contemporary and historical states. The first part of the book develops a framework based on detailed qualitative fieldwork with multiple organizations in Ghana. The second part then analyzes how the framework applies beyond Ghana, deepening the theoretical framework through comparative historical analysis of primary and secondary source materials from four comparison cases, drawn from different government functions, in different states around the world, at different periods of time in the last hundred years. In contemporary Nigeria, amid turbulent politics rife with corruption—and while facing targeted vandalism, arson, and kidnapping attacks—the National Agency for Food and Drug Administration and Control (NAFDAC) halved the rate of counterfeit drugs in circulation, emerging as the agency with by far the strongest public reputation for effectiveness. In mid-twentieth-century Kenya, amid the infamous ethnicized neopatrimonialism of the Independence era—and despite dire proclamations by the World Bank that the project was doomed to failure—the Kenya Tea Development Authority (KTDA) increased the quantity of production fifty-fold and improved quality to command above-world-market prices. In mid-twentieth-century Brazil, while the state generally was a haphazard administrative quagmire held together by institutionalized patronage, the National Bank of Economic Development (BNDE) emerged as a pocket of effectiveness—more technocratic, effective, and efficient than private banks within the Brazilian economy. Furthermore, some of today's global superpowers were in the past very similarly structured as patchworked leviathans, with a few distinctively successful agencies amid more generalized organizational weakness. As early twentieth-century post-dynastic China descended into warlordism, the Chinese Salt Inspectorate escaped corruption and local capture, increasing net revenues by 747 percent in the first ten years and almost single-handedly keeping the fragile state afloat.

A case study of a single agency is always vulnerable to fixating on features, practices, or events that seem logically important but that may be idiosyncratic or spurious. Therefore, the argument of *Patchwork Leviathan* is focused and refined through multiple axes of comparison. The second part of the book employs multiple comparisons among success cases across a wide range of diversity in geography, time frame, and state function, in order to identify the features of bureaucratic subcultural niches that transcend particular contexts. Beyond the comparisons across positive cases, each positive case is paired with a failed or control case that was otherwise maximally similar. Within Ghana, I conducted abbreviated fieldwork with control cases selected within the same organization as the positive cases. For example, as a control for the Ghana Commercial Courts, I conducted fieldwork in another High Court (see Appendix Table A.2).

The comparison cases enable excellent within-case paired contrasts to gain additional analytic leverage, because several are organizations that either replaced or were transformed from functionally similar but ineffectual organizations. When KTDA was formed in 1964, just a year after Kenyan independence, it took over functions previously performed by the colonial Special Crops Development Authority. Similarly, the Salt Inspectorate assumed tax collection functions previously performed by the moribund and ineffectual *Yanwu Shu* salt tax collection agency. NAFDAC has an even closer within-case comparison: NAFDAC was constituted in 1993, a new institutionalization that assumed the mandate for food and drug safety, which had long languished under the ineffectual Directorate of Food and Drug Administration and Control (established in 1974). However, even upon its institutional reincarnation in 1993, NAFDAC continued to struggle organizationally until the early 2000s when it rapidly emerged as the most trusted and effective state agency in Nigeria. Similarly, BNDE was formed in 1953 but struggled in its early years, emerging as a strong organization in the late 1950s. Thus, the contrasts in the expanded cases set seek to minimize variation between positive and contrast cases to the fullest extent possible, by comparing successful cases to themselves or to an analogous organization in the same environment, focusing on the period of time just before their emergence as pockets of bureaucratic effectiveness to minimize temporal period effects that might confound findings.

The analysis focuses on features that were common among positive cases but absent in paired controls. Finding any commonalities among positive cases is noteworthy because the selected positive cases are very heterogeneous, with large variation in their time period, country context, and state function. Conversely, each paired control case is as maximally similar as possible, which affords sharper contrast to the elements that differentiate each positive case from its control. Maximizing the heterogeneity among the positive cases and minimizing the heterogeneity within each paired contrast thereby affords greater confidence that the commonalities found among positive cases but absent in controls explain the variation in outcomes.

What Patchworking Tells Us about Leviathan

Identifying interstitial niches as the crèche of the bureaucratic ethos in neopatrimonial contexts has various implications for the broader literature on states, state capacity, and state formation. *Patchwork Leviathan* calls attention to institutional variation as a foundational feature of the organizational sociology of the administrative state. This may be particularly true in many so-called developing countries, but may also apply more widely. Broadly, it suggests scholars reconceptualize states as patchworked composites of fractious subunits that may differ vastly in foundational organizational capacities and the institutional rules of the game guiding their actions.[33] The consequences of variation within state administrative structures are typically overlooked by a particularly influential body of development work, which is enmeshed in the convenient shorthand fiction that "the state" is a single, homogenous entity. This assumption is then woven into cross-national analyses because the most frequently used indicators—such as the World Bank's worldwide governance indicators (WGI)—may disaggregate governance into different conceptual elements, like "rule of law" or "control of corruption," but all measure governance as a uniform quality of the state as a whole—the shades of lavender mentioned earlier.[34] Important advances in sociological scholarship extolling the developmental virtues of Weberian bureaucracy have similarly analyzed the quality and extent of bureaucracy as a uniform feature of the state. This notion that "the state" has a monolithic character is misleading. Scholars' focus on inequalities of bureaucratic administration *between* states has overlooked tremendous variation *within* states. The difference in "corruption" between Ghana's best- and worst-rated state agencies approximates the difference between "the state" of Belgium (WGI=1.50) and Mozambique (WGI=−0.396), spanning the chasm of so-called developed and developing worlds (see Figure 1.2).

In drawing attention to institutional variation *within* central state administration, this book joins a growing scholarly movement arguing that states are not unitary but instead "sprawling, complex concatenations" of agents and agencies enacting the work of governing.[35] *Patchwork Leviathan* differs critically from prior work on variation within states by examining variation in

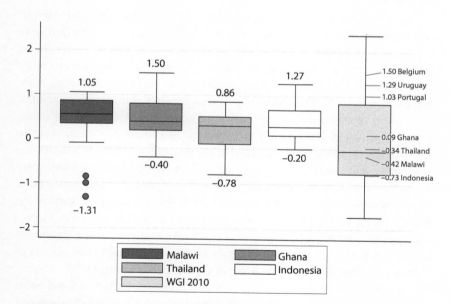

FIGURE 1.2. Control of corruption rating for ministries within selected states vs. global range of country-level Worldwide Governance Indicator (WGI). *Data Source:* Worldwide Governance Indicators (2010) and World Bank Governance and Anti-Corruption (GAC) Diagnostic Surveys (1999–2007)

organizational orientation and capacity *among* different parts of the central state administrative apparatus. Burgeoning interest in "subnational variation"—largely by political scientists working outside the West—analyzes variation in organizational capacities, but focuses on variation across geographic locations and scales within national boundaries, for example, comparing performance among regional governments.[36] Other work—largely by political sociologists focusing on the United States and Europe—analyzes variation among central state agencies, but instead of focusing on varied organizational capacities, this work sees institutional variation as a matter of agencies pursuing varied and sometimes conflicting goals that exist because agencies are "charged with distinct functions."[37] For example, state counseling departments prioritize "protecting the children" while accounting departments focus on "keeping the money stream flowing."[38] This reflects a presumption, built into much of Western organizational theory, that individuals will identify with and align their efforts to their office—in other words, it presumes the bureaucratic ethos. My account differs importantly from prior works by analyzing the causes and consequences of more foundational institutional variation in neopatrimonial and bureaucratic orientations, illuminating the social foundations of the bureaucratic ethos, which orients officials towards that most individually irrational activity: giving their full working capacity to accomplishing organizational goals on behalf of an abstract collective, "the public."

As "leviathan" in the title suggests, this book joins the canonical dialogue on the nature of states, which has been largely based on premodern European state-building[39] and American political development,[40] thereby advancing understanding of contemporary non-Western states.[41] The bureaucratic ethos is at the heart of a number of big questions about states that have long interested scholars, including state strength, state capacity, administrative reform, corruption, governance quality, collective action problems, and the emergence of prosocial cooperation in networks. *Patchwork Leviathan* seeks to uncover the origins of orientations that channel officials' efforts towards the work of the state and thereby constitute the human foundation of state capacity. In its focus on bureaucratic development in niches of the state, this book offers a substantially different view of state building and administrative reform from those previously advanced. Examining how the interstitial structural position facilitates cultivation of the bureaucratic ethos is a significant contribution to what Skocpol has characterized as the unfinished agenda of bringing the state back in: how states discipline public servants.[42]

Disciplining state agents is as elusive as it is essential. Conventional political science answers to disciplining officials are grounded in principal-agency theory, wherein discipline depends on systems enabling mass monitoring so that the "principal"—often a manager theoretically acting on behalf of the public—can enforce agents' compliance with the principal's desires. Based on principal-agent theories, many international organizational reforms aim to enhance monitoring, but such efforts often fail because the would-be monitors themselves are complicit.[43] Moreover, such principal-based monitoring reforms often have perverse effects, reducing the morale and intrinsic commitment to integrity in other would-be honest officials.[44]

Conversely, *Patchwork Leviathan* fleshes out the sociological underpinnings of *how state officials discipline themselves and others*. It thereby joins a small but growing group of scholars arguing that state officials can be surprisingly diligent and principled in the execution of their tasks, reclaiming bureaucracy and bureaucrats from their pejorative associations.[45] Interstitial bureaucracy advances understanding of how actors within states engage in productive work to shape the meaning and purpose of the state and its resources. In so doing, it contributes to new agendas examining states as organizations continuously (re)making claims to legitimacy.[46] It identifies organizational and cultural foundations for how understandings and practices emerge, are shared, and stabilize within groups. This is consonant with recent institutional and organizational research seeking to "inhabit" institutions, situating institutions not within the unspecified ether, but within human actors engaged in specific contexts.[47]

Seeking a Better Answer for Why Some Agencies Succeed While Others Fail

Several existing theories, although not explicitly focused on high-functioning niches of the state, might offer potential alternative explanations to the question "why do some agencies succeed when so many others struggle?" The dominant explanation for why some state administrative reforms succeed has focused on "executive will": top-down reform instigated by the head of state.[48] Such accounts tend to overestimate executive will, treating it either tacitly or explicitly as both necessary and sufficient for administrative reform, a sort of *deus ex machina* account in which the mechanics of that fundamental transformation remain unclear. Crucially, executive will also fails to explain the cases at hand: All of the Ghanaian success cases arose without active presidential sponsorship. (See Methodological Appendix Table A.2 for a table overview of all eight selected and eight control cases and their values on these alternative explanations.) I argue prior scholarship has overestimated the importance of executive will because executive will is particularly legible—the formation of new agencies under active presidential protection always attracts notice. However, the comparative analysis in this book clarifies that presidential sponsorship is only one of several means to foster a highly effective state niche, and indeed, a means with some distinctive drawbacks for long-term durability. Executive will is neither necessary *nor* sufficient as an explanation for why some agencies succeed against the odds. This is good news for a great many states because often where the need for reform is most acute, political will at the top is either absent or sporadic due to a revolving door of power.

Two other potential alternative explanations each see the organizational function as the primary determinant of organizational integrity and effectiveness, though for different reasons. Corruption theories center on how certain administrative functions—especially policing, taxation, and customs—allow officials lightly monitored access to revenue and monopoly control over imposition of fees or access to needed resources, enhancing opportunities for "corrupt" practices like bribery.[49] This story is persuasive as an explanation for where the bureaucratic ethos is lacking and accords well with observed patterns: Across a variety of contemporary states around the world, traffic police, tax, and customs authorities almost universally appear at the top of any list of the most corrupt public organizations.[50] Critically, the converse is not true: There is not one central state ministry or agency that consistently appears among the most *trusted* public organizations.[51]

Others might expect the most effective and efficient state administrative functions would be those—like central banks and ministries of finance—that are more connected to the global economy and cosmopolitan institutions like foreign donors, the International Monetary Fund, and the World Bank. This intuition too does not accord well with observed patterns. Customs authorities are manifestly deeply connected to global trade flows, and they impinge on capitalist interests, yet both in Ghana and globally, customs is among the most corrupt state agencies.[52] Ghana's Ministry of Finance as a whole was not particularly well regarded; but *within* the ministry PARD, a group with little contact with global capitalism, was a standout success. Globally, finance ministries were regarded as among the most corrupt state agencies in Benin, Ecuador, Ghana, Madagascar, and Zambia, though their central banks are well-regarded. The opposite was true in Burundi, Guinea, Indonesia, and Slovakia, where central banks were among the worst-reputed public agencies, while in Thailand both organizations were poorly regarded.[53]

The Ghanaian and comparison cases are further evidence that function is not an essential explanation for the emergence or location of a pocket of effectiveness. Identified niches emerged in numerous different sectors, ranging from regulation to commercial law to fiscal policy. Counterintuitively, a surprising number of cases emerged within sectors that are thought to be structurally *vulnerable* to bribery. Development banking is particularly vulnerable to high-end corruption whereby political elites attempt to sway the dispersal of loans towards political supporters rather than the evaluation of econometric criteria and national interest. Taxation, justice, and regulation—respectively, the sectors of the Salt Inspectorate, Ghana Commercial Courts, and both NAFDAC and Ghana's Spectrum and Frequency Management—are sectors frequently identified as having high structural vulnerability to bribery and corruption because wealthy outsiders may seek to suborn lone officials responsible for administering the costly legal penalties (for an overview of sectoral vulnerability to bribery for all the selected and control cases, see the Methodological appendix).[54]

Ultimately, all function-based accounts for why some agencies succeed while others fail suffer the same critical flaw: *the most effective and trusted ministries vary widely* from one nation to the next. This does not mean that the organizational task is irrelevant; organizational function may still confer some proportional effects that could be more or less conducive to clustering distinctiveness, but this is clearly not an outcome that can be explained exclusively by organizational function. The within-case contrasts are further evidence that sector is not an essential explanation for the emergence of a pocket of effectiveness, because the ineffectual predecessors of NAFDAC and the Salt Inspectorate worked in the same sector with the same constituents. Function-based accounts alone also cannot account for the timing of changes in effectiveness within agencies: for example, Nigeria had a Food and Drug Administration famous for ineffectiveness for years before the same agency in the same sector was transformed into the most trusted and effective public agency in the state. Exposure to global forces and capitalist interests may be one pathway to greater organizational effectiveness, but empirical patterns suggest it is neither necessary nor sufficient: Organizations in state functions with high-level exposure fail to become highly effective, others with low-level exposure demonstrate uncommonly strong capacities, and still others change from ineffective to effective while performing the same function.

Another potential alternative explanation for why some agencies succeed claims that state organizations' ability to make independent decisions in the interest of a broad public depends on the group affiliations of personnel, particularly whether officials remain strongly identified with social groups of origin.[55] Research on African politics has long been concerned with how states are affected by the extent to which officials remain beholden to ethnic groups. States operate in an arena of competing domestic power sources including religion, family, tribes, and political parties "in which multiple sets of rules struggle for predominance."[56] A concentration of officials from the same social group who remain principally loyal to that outside identity may undermine organizational capacity through nepotism—favoring group membership over merit in hiring—and suborning the organization's broad mission to serve the identity group's goals. However, as with corruption theories, the group affiliations perspective may explain why some organizations with demographic concentrations fall prey to nepotism, but not why other organizations work diligently in the public interest. Importantly, there is no clear pattern differentiating staff demographics within high-performing Ghanaian niches from those elsewhere within the Ghanaian state. Participants in both selected and control cases roughly approximate college graduates in Ghana generally, spanning a wide range of common Ghanaian life circumstances—from extreme rural poverty to well-off urbanites, representing a diverse cross-section of Ghana's regions and ethnicities (see methodological appendix for details).

Importantly, the influence of group affiliations depends not only on the strength of attachments to outside social groups, but also on the weakness of attachments to the working group. If organizations are weak or lack a distinctive identity, they may be unable to counterbalance external social identity attachments. Conversely, professions and working groups with strong organizational identity and significant esprit de corps can socialize newcomers, reorienting officials to incorporate work as a significant identity.[57] *Patchwork Leviathan* argues that significant esprit de corps is itself an accomplishment of organizational cultural work and one of the characteristic, distinguishing features of interstitial niches.

Ultimately, those prior theories are attractive in their parsimony, but they fail to explain the observed empirical patterns. Understanding why some agencies succeed, where and when so many peer agencies have failed, requires a new set of explanations. Scholars have increasingly become interested in analyzing well-performing organizations in adverse environments where most government organizations are ineffectual or corrupt,[58] often labeled "pockets of effectiveness" or "islands of integrity."[59] Most of this work is based on case studies of single agencies,[60] although increasingly a few feature comparisons among agencies within the same country.[61] These scholars broadly agree that existing theories focused on analyzing public service failures are inadequate to explain why some public agencies succeed against impressive odds.

Prior work on relatively successful state organizations has produced some seemingly conflicting findings: for example, whether pockets of effectiveness require autonomy *from* political elites,[62] or the active sponsorship *of* political elites;[63] whether increased salary is necessary or sufficient;[64] and whether (or how) a charismatic or "great" organizational leader matters.[65] This book's coupling of rich micro-level detail with meso-level comparisons is an important step toward the further theoretical development of this body of literature. I prefer the term interstitial "niche" to emphasize the dynamic tension of entanglement, of being embedded-yet-distinct that underscores how distinctiveness is an active and ongoing accomplishment, rather than a given or natural endowment of the topography, as implied by a term like "island." The language of niche is also importantly ambiguous as to the scale, applying equally well to groups where the boundaries of excellence are coterminous with the whole formal organization, such as the entire Brazilian National Development Bank (BNDE), as well as for those, like PARD, that are a subgroup of a larger organization. However, in deference to the prevailing terminology, I use the terms *bureaucratic niche*, *interstitial niche*, and *pocket of effectiveness* interchangeably throughout the text.

Prior studies of these uncommonly effective state agencies frequently observe that such pockets of effectiveness tend to have unusually strong pride in their work, strong organizational identification, corporatist ethos, and an "organizational mystique" wherein employees "internalized the organization's goals and saw themselves as vital contributors to its accomplishments,"[66] in short, what I would characterize as a subculture of the bureaucratic ethos. Prior work points to the importance of these organizational cultures, but most are based on arm's length analysis and therefore acknowledge that they cannot address the crucial question of how such uncommon performance orientation becomes embedded in organizations.[67] Ultimately, much like the prior macro-political work on states that highlighted the unresolved question of how states discipline officials, this body of work too points to the origins of organizational orientation as one of the great unresolved questions of state-building. That is precisely the crucial question this book tackles.

Overview of the Book

In the chapters that follow, *Patchwork Leviathan* addresses these questions through an empirically rich comparative analysis examining the small-group processes and organizational features foundational to such pockets of effectiveness. I begin by constructing an organizational and cultural explanation for how these state niches work, how they manage to succeed against the odds, which synthesizes sociological and political insights with cutting-edge research from cognitive science, network analysis, organizational studies, and social psychology. Drawing on this detailed insight into how these niches operate, grounded in the qualitative Ghanaian data, the second half of the book then takes up the question of how such niches initially begin, drawing the Ghanaian data into greater dialogue with the international comparison cases.

Chapter 2 argues that niches are built by *clustering distinctiveness*, drawing together particular types of people who are otherwise rare in the larger environment. First, this requires filtering out the influence of patronage politics, reducing the importance of networks on hiring decisions that leave employees more beholden to their patron than to their position. Second, it requires active selection. Selection entails finding, attracting, and recruiting a rare human resource: people who have motivations, inclinations, practices, and skill sets that provide a foundation for building a rational, impersonal administration oriented towards achieving the organization's goals, rather than advancing the benefits of themselves and their networks. Unfortunately, these dispositions—such as "incorruptibility" and "hard work"—are both rare and difficult to discern without personal knowledge or observation, which creates high search costs. In the face of environmental challenges, the chapter highlights the intensive recruitment process of employees across the Ghanaian niches, including selection strategies, probationary periods, and recruiting from already professionalized environments. Those intensive and highly interpersonal recruitment processes create a sense within recruits that they are special and have been chosen—specifically, chosen for particular characteristics like incorruptibility and hard work, which others in the niche also share. Clustering a critical mass of those scarce resources with a shared sense of commonality enables new organizational possibilities, fostering in-group identification, dedication, and enhanced effort, culminating in a subculture of the bureaucratic ethos—a cultivation process that the next chapter addresses.

Chapter 3 analyzes how niches cultivate their personnel. It is not enough to merely select the best people available in the environment, because in these environments people with a *fully developed* bureaucratic ethos are exceedingly rare. In addition to selection effects, there are considerable *influence* effects of the small-group culture: the lived daily experience of working in such a clustered environment cultivates a group style centered on the elements participants have in common. The elusive bureaucratic ethos is forged from the varied proto-bureaucratic experiences of those selected individuals clustered together in the niche. This chapter analyzes how newcomers adapt to incorporation into the niche and adjust their daily practices, conforming with what they observe are the characteristic ways of the working group. The interstitial structural position enhanced niche insiders' perception that they were a small subculture—tightly socially connected to others within but with large perceived differences to nearby outsiders. The contrast of perceived commonalities within, and differences outside, the working group forged commitment to the ways of comportment distinguishing the working group, which were in turn the foundation of the corporatist ethos and the bureaucratic orientation.

Chapter 4 argues that interstitial niches face ample environmental challenges and therefore engage in considerable work to protect themselves. Even when niches concentrate distinctive staff whose prior experiences are well-aligned with the organizational goals, and whose knowledge of, and commitment to, bureaucratic comportment have been strengthened by participation within the small-group culture, niches still operate in environments that are tremendously inhospitable to their aims, offering both unintentional disruptions and active interference. Because scholars typically do not think of parts of the state as being so much at odds with the surrounding institutional environment, we have not given enough attention to the considerable organizational effort that high-performing niches must put into coping with that environment. This chapter analyzes the organizational strategies that niches employ to ensure that their ability to regularly and effectively accomplish their organizational goals is not negatively affected by their environment. Organizational responses include *internal coping mechanisms* and *external projects of reshaping*. Internal coping mechanisms are ways in which the highly effective niches modify processes and practices within their work group to mitigate vulnerabilities to outside interference.

Having used the rich qualitative Ghanaian data to examine how these unusually effective niches actually work, how they manage to discipline their members and increasingly converge around a small-group culture of the bureaucratic ethos through clustering distinctiveness, chapter 5 then seeks to peel back the earliest seeds of that clustered distinctiveness. Chapter 5 introduces the comparison cases, which confirm the importance of recruitment, cultivation, and protection, while also shedding light on subtle variations in how those mechanics play out in different environments. The comparison cases provide additional analytic leverage from within-case contrasts in cases that were formerly ineffectual but that rapidly transformed into pockets of effectiveness. The chapter concludes with theoretical observations that emerge about the onset of a bureaucratic ethos, moving the book towards the more vexing theoretical question of how bureaucratic niches *first* emerge. These insights include 1) whether niches appear upon the formation of a new organization or result from reforms to an existing organization; 2) the speed of change; and 3) the scale of niches.

Chapter 6 pushes further on the question of initial emergence by analyzing the conditions under which parts of the administrative state obtain sufficient protection from neopatrimonial pressures to inculcate a highly effective niche within the administrative state. The conceptual focus on protection from neopatrimonial pressures broadens a theoretical discussion that has been too strongly focused on elite interests while reconciling seemingly discrepant arguments about whether highly effective niches require autonomy from political elites or, conversely, the active sponsorship of political elites. The chapter develops a four-part typology of political elite interest-alignment with organizational goals, which includes the elite sponsorship that has captured prior attention but also draws attention to two typically overlooked conditions that are also capable of fostering effective niches: merely interested elites and inattentive elites. The framework engages a larger pantheon of work on state capacity, including work by Charles Tilly and Daniel Carpenter.

Chapter 7 then asks the crucial question: Why do organizations use the potential for difference afforded by operational discretion to pursue abstract

public goals of organizational achievement, bucking prevailing neopatrimonial patterns? Building on Bourdieu's idea of habitus—habits, practices, and
orientations to which people become accustomed by virtue of lived experience and immersion in a particular social world – the chapter develops the
idea of actors with *dual habitus*. Appreciating how institutionally fruitful innovations can emerge from dual habitus helps make sense of an important
empirical observation: Most Ghanaian niches became centers of excellence
when they were populated by a critical mass of Ghanaians who had local first
degrees that endowed them with valuable social and cultural capital, coupled
with lived experience abroad of a medium duration, often through advanced
foreign education. These Ghanaians had acquired implicit skills of, and taste
for, formal organizational practice while still remaining connected to local
Ghanaian cultural practices and networks. The same pattern holds true for
the international comparison cases. The chapter concludes by observing that
these organizations were not so much transformed by singular leaders but
rather by clustered cadres: small and tightly knit corps of senior staff with
strong proto-bureaucratic habitus who were hand-picked for their commitment to the organizational mission. Those clustered cadres were the foundation that socially legitimated, modeled, and spread distinctive practices
throughout the social niche.

Chapter 8 gives readers a sense of what happened to the cases in the longer term. I think it is an intellectual strength that the main findings and arguments of the book often raise a host of new questions for readers, including
whether these niches of bureaucratic effectiveness can become seeds from
which greater administrative capacity could spread throughout the state. Unfortunately, such questions are beyond the scope of the data and the particular comparative design of the book to answer. However, the chapter engages
that curiosity by describing what happened to the positive cases in the book
over the longer term. Examining the outcomes observed in the selected cases
sheds some speculative light on whether the bureaucratic ethos can survive
the departure of the niche founder, and sketches a range of possible outcomes
for whether niches can scale up or possibly even diffuse more broadly. The
cases collectively illuminate some of the promise and pitfalls of interstitiality
as a force for organizational reform more broadly throughout the state.

The conclusion examines how *Patchwork Leviathan* extends and reimag-
ines a long scholarly tradition of state-building based on the European state
experience, including ways the framework may help scholars fill in some of
the mechanics of early European state-building that have been less well documented in the historical record because they affected public servants rather
than elites. The conclusion also highlights contributions to the field of development sociology. It points toward a fruitful new framework that opens new
avenues of research for *configurational* approaches to understanding state ca-

pacity, interrogating the developmental consequences for where and how state capacity is situated within the varied administrative apparatus of central states. It also highlights how the framework of the book may be of interest to organizational scholars more broadly, including identifying how the framework might also apply to private-sector organizations.

The conclusion also discusses implications for development practitioners, including potential ways that global development practice might be changed in light of the book's arguments, including potential efforts to systematically attempt to foster pockets of effectiveness as a means of enhancing state administrative capacity. The chapter concludes by suggesting that the book's findings about the challenges of top-down institutional change and the importance of lived experience lay the foundation for a cognitive turn within institutional development scholarship that takes cognitive science more seriously in the way development interventions are designed.

2

Recruitment: Clustering Distinctiveness

Kofi joined PARD fresh from Ghana's flagship university with an economics degree. He flashes a disarming smile when recounting how he first came to work in the civil service. Kofi explains, "When I joined the civil service ... someone told me, you know how much you'll be paid? Can you live on one million cedis [approximately $105 USD] at the end of every month? So, I think about it and I was like, oh, one million is no money." He pauses briefly before continuing, "But I also wanted to develop my career ... I wanted that experience, exactly about what I had studied in school. So, I said, 'Well, I don't mind. I'm not thinking about money now. Let's just get the experience.'" Kofi's account is emblematic of the ambiguous position of government employment in contemporary Ghana, where government employment has both real enticements and significant drawbacks. Nearly all interstitial insiders reported working there *despite the salary*. How then do these highly effective niches find and recruit people who contribute to deepening the organizational performance orientation within the niche?

In contemporary Ghana, the civil service has a somewhat tarnished reputation, especially compared to its heyday in the late colonial and early Independence period, when the civil service was regarded as a sought-after and respected post to which highly educated people aspired because it was one of the few well-paying and stable formal employment opportunities.[1] Today, the perspective is more mixed. Civil service positions are still valued as stable jobs, and remain particularly attractive to poor rural graduates who are using educational credentials to move out of subsistence agriculture into formal employment but whose cultural and social capital may exclude them from more lucrative private-sector employment. For example, one participant grew up as a shepherd boy in the far north with parents who had no money and little interest in schooling, and only went to school through an accidental encounter with the local Catholic catechist. Another came from a region of "cattle and coconut" and had to negotiate with extended family to sell cattle in order to go to school. Yet within the bureaucratic niches studied in this book, members from very humble backgrounds work side by side with Ghanaians from more privileged backgrounds. One niche insider has a father with a university degree and a mother with teacher training. Another explains, "My mother has a first degree in history and English. My daddy has an MBA in finance."[2] Some government posts still manage to also attract upper-class educated Ghanaians.

In 2010, two-thirds of men and women in Ghana were economically active. Among economically active adults, the vast majority of Ghanaians are employed in private, informal work, mostly small-scale farming, trading, and artisanal manufacturing.[3] Only one-quarter of Ghanaian men and 8.2 percent of women were engaged in formal wage employment. Civil and public service each account for 13.7 percent of the total labor market, compared to formal private-sector employment at 18.9 percent.[4] Government work in Ghana offers the stability of the formal sector, but with only modest pay, on par with other forms of informal employment. Average hourly earnings (GH¢) in public administration (0.78) were approximately half the average hourly earnings in the financial services sector (1.54), slightly behind earnings for mining (.80) and education (.87) while only slightly ahead of those working in hotels and restaurants (.64) and traders (.59).[5] In the years before the study, nominal income rates rose in the public sector. According to government statistics, public-sector basic monthly public pay surpassed one-dollar-a-day in 2003 and reached $49 USD in 2006. However, in most years the basic monthly public-sector pay was only fractionally higher than the national minimum wage.[6] Despite growing nominal incomes, government wages remained considerably lower than private-sector wages, such that in 2006 the average government worker received a wage that was only 68 percent that of what a private-sector worker earned.[7] As shown in Table 2.1, public-sector employment still offers some advantages relative to employment in civil society or the formal private sector. More government workers have contracts, paid vacation, paid sick leave, and pensions. The bulk of government employees work fewer hours and receive lower pay, but at the upper-middle and highest levels of government compensation can be competitive.

The government's position in the labor market poses structural challenges to recruitment that are deepened by the need to filter out the influence of patronage politics, reducing the importance of networks on hiring decisions that leave employees more beholden to their patron than to their position.

TABLE 2.1. Are Government Jobs Attractive in Ghana? Pay, Hours, and Benefits by Formal Sector

	Public sector	Civil society	Private sector
Contract	79%	63%	45%
Paid vacation	86%	65%	48%
Paid sick leave	86%	73%	48%
Medical care	45%	50%	33%
Pensions	87%	53%	31%
Training	20%	30%	9%
Hours worked			
Annual pay			

Author's Calculations, Ghana Living Standards Survey 5 (2008).
Note: Public sector includes civil service and other public service but excludes parastatals; civil society includes NGO and international organizations but excludes cooperatives.

From Ghana to Guinea, from Bangladesh to Bolivia, scholars of development increasingly agree that the root cause of government ineffectiveness is too little bureaucracy, not too much.[8] This book clarifies that observation: The problem is not merely that the human, cognitive, and material resources of bureaucracy are rare in many poor countries around the world. Where they are rare, it matters critically *how they are distributed*. This chapter argues that the organizational orientation of highly effective niches within otherwise institutionally fractious or weak environments depends critically on recruitment that *clusters together* people with particular types of proto-bureaucratic experiences and orientations. The challenge is that such people are relatively rare in the labor pool of many countries and recruiting them into government positions is sometimes challenging.

Recruitment is challenging for interstitial niches, and not only because of the tenuous position of government employment in the larger labor market. Bureaucratic niches must attempt to identify more than the abstract types of knowledge that are typically visible on a resume. Niche insiders face the additional environmental challenge of trying to actively identify difficult-to-discern practices, orientations, and dispositions that have elective affinities for doing effective, impersonal organizational work. Selection entails finding, attracting, and recruiting a rare human resource: people who have the skill sets but also the motivations, inclinations, and practices that provide a foundation for building a rational, impersonal administration oriented towards achieving the organization's goals rather than advancing the benefits of themselves and their networks. When niche insiders talk about these aspects, they often conceive of them as personal characteristics—like "incorruptible" and "hardworking." However, scholars know from culture and cognition studies that what people label a personal characteristic is not actually an innate genetic feature, nor necessarily the result of a conscious and deliberative choice to be incorruptible, but rather a label used to signal people who frequently evidence a set of habituated practices. Such tacit practices and orientations have elective affinities for the bureaucratic ethos. For brevity, I will call these practices, habits, and orientations *proto-bureaucratic schema*. Proto-bureaucratic schema are both rare in the local environment and difficult to discern without personal knowledge or observation, which creates high search costs.

There are, of course, different experiences for different people in any country. However, in broad strokes, U.S. organizations recruit from a pool of workers who are generally already accustomed to performing tasks in a timely manner, prizing efficiency, responding to external incentives, and maximizing productivity. This is what neoinstitutionalists meant when observing that myths of rationality and the collective good are presumed to be "built into modern societies and personalities as very general values" such that "the building blocks for organizations come to be littered around the societal landscape; it takes only a little entrepreneurial energy to assemble them into a structure."[9] The broader social environment in the United States has shaped future workers in ways that are incredibly helpful for formal organizations, offloading what would otherwise be considerable social effort. That is true not only for one's own employees, but also a reasonable assumption to make about the workers from other firms with which one has to interact.

Therefore, in many advanced economies, recruiting someone with a high baseline of skills, practices, and orientations that are organizationally beneficial is a bit like shooting fish in a barrel—what organizational scholars sometimes call the "density of administrative competence."[10] James March, an eminent organizational scholar, famously argued that the practices, abilities, orientations, and values that help managers succeed in large formal organizations are so common in American labor pools that applicants are "nearly indistinguishable" according to such characteristics.[11] Because those organizationally beneficial practices and schema were so prevalent in the pool of applicants, measures of executives' skills and values did little to predict which executives would have more successful careers. That is not, however, because organizationally beneficial practices and orientations do not matter. March quipped, "It is hard to tell the difference between two different light bulbs also; but if you take all light bulbs away, it is difficult to read in the dark."[12]

In other words, within environments where the bureaucratic ethos is widespread, as neoinstitutionalists presumed, those building blocks of organization are indeed helpfully strewn throughout society. However, in Ghana the orientations, habits, and dispositions that constitute the "building blocks" of impersonal, rational, bureaucratic organization are not readily "littered around the societal landscape," nor easily brought together with little entrepreneurial effort. In many countries the experiences, practices, and proto-bureaucratic schema for enacting formal organization are less common and more dispersed (see Figure 2.1). Even powerful, autonomous, and well-funded state agencies cannot control the skills and tacit socio-organizational schema of the labor pool, which are mostly shaped by factors beyond their immediate control—at least in the short term—from cultural habitus to the quality of schooling. Potential recruits vary in the extent to which they possess subject-relevant technical skills, which are typically explicit knowledges such as econometrics or how to use Excel® software. But potential recruits also vary in the extent to which they possess proto-bureaucratic schema, which are often more implicit dispositions and practices.

By comparison, within overwhelmingly neopatrimonial environments, finding someone with proto-bureaucratic schema is more like searching for a needle in a haystack. Even if found, those rare proto-bureaucratic individuals who enter the civil service are often isolated and spread thinly throughout the service, perhaps in the hope that, like the proverbial little Dutch boy who single-handedly plugged the leaks to hold back the flood waters, each in their own area might be able to hold together the leaky behemoth of the state. However, more often than not, those isolated individuals instead find themselves quickly exhausted.[13] They often leave the civil service or, if they remain, are disheartened and reduce their efforts as they learn from repeated struggles with their environment that their lone actions are ineffectual.

Between dominantly bureaucratic and dominantly neopatrimonial labor pools are numerous societies with sometimes extreme variation in the availability and distribution of both explicit educational knowledges and proto-bureaucratic schema. Within societies in that institutionally bricolaged midrange, a modest number of potential recruits possess relevant explicit technical knowledge and often-implicit proto-bureaucratic dispositions. The availability of such human resources is neither so rare as to make clustering nearly impossible, nor so plentiful as to make clustering effortlessly inevitable. However, moderate availability itself is not sufficient without *clustering*, because even in such midrange labor pools, if the proto-bureaucratic recruits are thinly dispersed, each faces the same overwhelming challenges that frustrate individual effort described previously. Where those proto-bureaucratic schema are comparatively uncommon, bringing them together requires overcoming structural

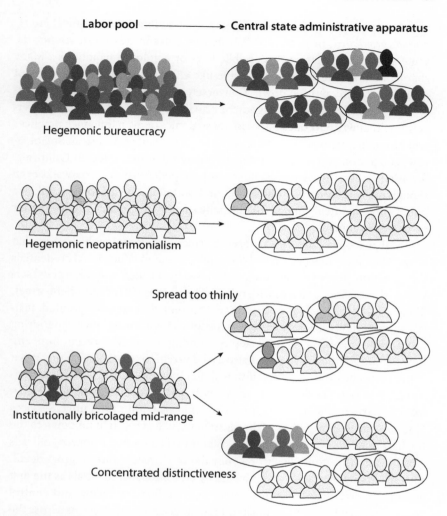

FIGURE 2.1. Proto-bureaucratic concentration in labor pool and clustering within state.

obstacles and takes organizational effort. Clustering a critical mass of those scarce resources enables new organizational possibilities, which, as the next chapter will argue, fosters in-group identification, dedication, and enhanced effort, culminating in a subculture of the bureaucratic ethos.

Credential Matching and the Social Topography of Patronage Pressure

Rules are important to understand because they shape human behavior and, in particular, help coordinate social action. Elinor Ostrom, winner of the Nobel Prize for economics, argues that rules are "shared understandings by actors about *enforced* prescriptions concerning what actions (or outcomes) are *required, prohibited,* or *permitted*."[14] Note that rules in this sense are not the same as written codes, such as public laws or employee handbooks. Many shared understandings that have a rule-like effect on social behavior are not actually explicitly written down. Conversely, there are many explicitly written rules of which people are ignorant or willfully ignore in their daily interactions. That written codes often do not structure or even influence practices will be familiar to many who have served on a council of American Sociological Association sections, but there are many other examples: in California, for instance, it is illegal for cars not to stop for pedestrians at crosswalks even though many ignore the prohibition,[15] in London it is illegal to be drunk in a pub,[16] while in Michigan it is still officially a felony to commit adultery or for divorcées to cohabit.[17]

In Ghana, one of the widely observed rules of government hiring was that a candidate must meet or exceed the explicitly stated educational credentials for a position. This understanding was shared by the highest-ranking civil servant to the lowliest, and also widely held by everyday Ghanaians on the street. This rule was so deeply ingrained that it possessed a taken-for-granted quality. In interviews, I asked various questions about hiring, including hiring procedures in general, step-by-step recounting of the most recent hire, and how people got their own jobs. I also asked variations on the question "What could someone do to get hired if they didn't meet the stated educational criteria?" This last question, more than any other, produced genuine *befuddlement* in participants, from high-ranking officials within the Public Services Commission and the Office of the Head of Civil Service right on down to the lowliest public servant interviewed. When I asked human resources officials within various state bodies to recount the most recent hire in great detail, they inevitably mentioned winnowing by educational credentials as the first action. This was true in both selected high-performing niches and control cases—an issue I will return to later. Indeed, in all my interactions across the many bodies of the Ghanaian state, I was unable to find someone who did not possess the explicitly stated educational credentials for their paid public or civil service position.

CREDENTIALS-MATCHING AS POTENTIALLY MASKING AND LEGITIMATING PATRONAGE

Credentials-matching as a rule—in the sense of a widely shared understanding that is enforced—does not, of course, mean that Ghana is a meritocratic paradise. First, it is possible that people may have been hired for a position without the stated credentials somewhere within the state and I did not encounter them. Moreover, even though credentials-matching is a widespread rule, patronage hiring can still have a significant presence within and along-side credentials-matching. We can get a sense of a more typical process of recruitment outside the successful niches by examining some earlier employment experiences from the Ghanaian respondents. One respondent describes how he came by his first job as a young man: "A guy who taught me chemistry. So, I bumped into him and so he needed somebody to help him and he was appointed in the Office of the President. [As though speaking for second person] 'If I don't mind, I should come and help him.' So, I thought it was – a young man, a young boy, I thought it was interesting. So, I went and helped for almost two years." Another explains, "I was having trouble finding a job, so my mother's friend told me I should come for a job." I probe, asking whether there had been a formal application, an interview, or an examination at the Public Services Commission. The participant responds, "No, that was it. I just brought my application to the man and I had a job." Another describes his earliest position as an unpaid position in the private sector that he also obtained through personal connections, "My, the boss there, he was like a family friend. And he said, 'Oh, it's wasteful for you to stay at home doing nothing. Just come there for like an internship.' So I went there without a pay or anything. Like kind of killing myself a bit."

In the above examples, the candidates *did* possess the explicitly stated credentials for the positions they obtained. However, the candidates make clear that their educational performance was not the primary *reason* they obtained the job. Critically, meeting a stated credential type is a *categorical* distinction, whether it entails meeting the stated level (e.g., secondary school vs. bachelor's degree) or field (e.g., economics vs. literature). Meeting a categorical condition may subdivide an applicant pool into those who do and do not meet the categorical requirement, but credential matching itself does not array potential candidates into an ordered list that might insert more mechanical objectivity in place of subjective evaluation of candidates. Interpersonal connections may predominate where credential matching does not sufficiently limit the applicant pool—as in the hiring examples above, for example, where stated qualifications are vague, few, or commonly held by many people. Assistant positions, as in the example of the Office of the President above, typically only specify secondary school completion or any undergraduate degree. Similarly, unpaid positions frequently have no advertisement and therefore no explicitly stated requirements. Therefore, the use of interpersonal connections did not violate the rule of credentials in those unpaid posts, even if such unpaid positions may routinely act as stepping-stones to full-pay positions.

Vague, broad, or commonly held credentials create a situation in which matching stated credentials does little to winnow the applicant pool and thereby enables interpersonal connections to play a relatively stronger role.

Some public-sector job advertisements specify only general requirements—such as a bachelor's degree in any field—or seek credentials that are relatively common. For example, a Ghanaian official in the Human Resources department explained, "If we want an HR officer, we ask that you have a bachelor's degree in Human Resource, or the social sciences, and that you have had some experience. So, that is the basic points you have to satisfy that." Here again, the basic rule of meeting credentials had to be satisfied, but compared to a narrowly defined degree field—like electrical engineering—specifying only a bachelor's degree in any social science is relatively broad. Because many powerful families are multiply privileged, having social influence and economic wealth almost ensures the children of privilege a college degree of some sort. Therefore, an applicant pool that is only barely limited by broad credential requirements will likely to be dominated by candidates who *also* have influential interpersonal relationships.

CREDENTIALS-MATCHING AS SUBSECTING THE LOCAL LABOR POOL

The rule of credentials also provides insight into the further segmentation of the local labor market. Some agencies, and some jobs within agencies, would have more explicit and rare credential requirements even if job postings were crafted by a benign meritocratic overlord, reflecting genuine variation in the operational skills demanded of positions. In contexts where credentials-matching is a widely shared social understanding *even among would-be patronage seekers*, some positions or agencies will benefit from a social topography of credentials that create within-country variations in the extent to which the relevant labor pool is plentiful, contains high-social-influence candidates with low-quality skills, and are exposed to professionalization influences that provide lived proto-bureaucratic experiences.

Selection effects at the level of credential pools mean that not all corresponding labor markets will be equally likely to contain candidates with highly influential social networks. This is partially a function of the numbers of graduates with a given credential. If Ghana's flagship University of Legon graduates 1000 people with an English degree but only 200 with an engineering degree, then even if there were no selection effects and the proportion of influence-peddlers was equally distributed, there would still be absolutely more influence-peddling candidates in the larger pool. But, of course, influence-peddlers themselves make strategic choices about fields of study. As many American students can imagine, few students suffer all the way through to a degree in organic chemistry merely because they were looking for a low-effort way to ride the coattails of an influential family member. Highly connected candidates with low skills and low interest in professional development are likely to select out of such a credential pool. To the extent that socially influential youth select into majors where the perceived effort is high, the candidates in such a pool are likely to be *both* high in social connections and high in merit and professional orientation.[18]

Different credential pools also correspond to different work sectors after graduation. Sectors further vary in the extent to which they are *professionalized*. Professionalization is a useful analogous form of social discipline that has many similarities to bureaucratic comportment, which makes lived experience in a relatively highly professionalized occupation a useful experiential foundation for building bureaucratic comportment. Where rationalizing myths are not part of the widespread social habitus, state-builders instead appropriate other forms of social disciplining that habituate individuals to working towards collective goals;[19] in contemporary poor states, one of the foremost examples is sufficiently professionalized occupations.[20] Participating in a professionalized occupation makes members accustomed to identifying with and orienting to advancing the status of an abstract collective that transcends face-to-face contacts. Professionalization also promotes seeking nonfinancial "professional" status rewards.[21] Individuals thereby acquire "orientations which transcend individual rational-instrumental behavior," a necessary foundation for institution-building,[22] by participating in a sufficiently professionalized occupation. Economics, engineering, and law are all considered highly professionalized fields within Ghana, endowing the Ghanaian niches with advantageous baseline pools.[23]

Nonfinancial Incentives

Middle management is the mascot of hegemonic bureaucracy, which is born, as Max Weber observed, of "office holding as a vocation,"[24] entailing a secure and predictable "career" with "a system of 'promotion' according to seniority or to achievement or both."[25] However, such iconic middle managers are largely absent in Ghana's interstices. Middle management's stable bureaucratic career is possible only insomuch as that career provides reasonable financial security.[26] The harsh fiscal reality for many low-income countries is that official salaries cannot compete with business and international NGOs.[27]

Instead, the professionals attracted to working in the Ghanaian niches tended to come from two different demographic clusters: (1) youth drawn to experience and exposure, who could tolerate low pay because of familial support and intend to leverage experiences into a more financially secure position in the future; (2) older, established professionals from private practice or abroad with sufficient financial security, drawn to the prestige of working at the pinnacle of their profession, exercising significant influence, or making a patriotic gift of their service to the state. By contrast, few highly skilled mid-life Ghanaians could afford to make the same tradeoffs because they are expected to provide for dependents, including extended kin, creating considerable social pressure to avoid low-paying government work.

The modal older niche member entered public service later, at higher levels of authority, and aspired to advance within the system to its highest levels. For example, one Commercial Court justice noted, "[Where will I be in] five years? Whew. I'm already a high court judge for four years now, so probably five years, nine years, I'll be at the Court of Appeal." Because older members were already near the professional pinnacle, they saw upper-echelon promotion within public service as offering more of what drew them to service in the first place—a means to achieve even more professional distinction and influence—and foresaw no difficulty accomplishing the goal. And as the penultimate chapter shows, time would prove the Commercial Court justices correct in their promotion prospects. A number of them also had significant prior experience in private-sector work, and sufficient savings to enable them to take on professionally interesting work despite the lower pay. One high-ranking official at NCA explained why promotions to leadership were important for him. "There is a big gap between incomes on this side and on that side. So, anybody who feels unappreciated is going to work on private side. I have done that part already for a good ten years, twelve years. So, there is nothing new for me."

Attracting the brightest young graduates presents a distinct challenge in a resource-scarce environment. Yet, relative to the rest of the public service, these niches manage to attract high-quality university graduates. Younger members were explicitly aware of the finance–experience tradeoff. Like Kofi's explanation at the beginning of the chapter, Kobena notes, "Well, the ministry is not all about the money but the exposure is huge. And people that we see right now in very top positions around Ghana ... most have started from ministries or Ministry of Finance. So, it's like a trade-off now. I'm giving up something, money, a lot of money, to get exposure." The director consciously cultivates beneficial exposure, creating great affection and loyalty among younger staff. Kobena continues:

> And every meeting that goes on in the country that has Ministry of Finance involved, whether a minister there or not, my colleagues and I can enter the meeting.... We go to every place, and that is the exposure we have. That is the privilege we have. And the good thing is our boss not only wants to have the knowledge, but he diffuses it.... He pushes, "Hey, my people, call people at PARD, tell them to come."

Young members willingly forgo higher short-term salaries, seeing the interstice as a long-term investment in experience and exposure that will later open up more lucrative careers beyond the civil service. When I asked PARD's youngest members where they saw themselves in five years, only one considered remaining in the civil service. Most anticipated leveraging their high-profile experience into graduate education, international NGOs, or private-sector positions.

Older and younger members share a belief that the work itself is valuable —to someone beyond themselves—and personally or professionally interesting. Implemented policy ideas originating from PARD staff were a source of pride and conversation, including the cell phone tax and a new tracking system for paying government contractors, which insiders interpreted as valuable and tangible contributions to the nation. Whether a communications engineer at the NCA, a Commercial Court justice, or a newly hired Junior Economics Officer at PARD, respondents describe their work as something that gives them an opportunity to practice their profession and education at the highest levels. Thema says she enjoys the job because of "the quality of the work you get." Daniel echoes that the primary benefits are "the ability to personally influence important decisions. And the nature of the work itself."

Nonpecuniary Motivations and Recruit Selection Effects

Somewhat paradoxically, niches simultaneously filter patronage and select for professionalized candidates by offering work that is unusually demanding with no extra financial benefits. Niches offer personally costly, high-time, high-effort work. For example, those who work in the field monitoring units at the National Communications Authority have to travel regularly to remote, sometimes undesirable locations. Francis, a high-ranking official in the field units, explains: "We're going to count the whole spectrum from the lowest frequency that we issue to the highest ... So, what we do is we have the equipment and we move from place to place. And then, we monitor the whole spectrum ... We ship you from here to the maybe the border." Sedu, another NCA monitoring official, recounts his recent trip: "We are less than sixty covering the whole country. It's demanding. But we are trying our best to do something. So, like, for instance, the last three weeks I was Upper East. From Accra, I had gone to Upper East, where I got to cover all of the services on the way to Upper East." I have taken a bus from Accra to the Upper East, and even the direct route is roughly twenty hours of travel time. Many of the places they travel have scant and humble lodging options. Those costs are balanced principally by benefits that do not attract all applicants equally: engaging in high-impact work and (typically nonpecuniary) status rewards. The cumulative structure of costs and benefits tends to disproportionately attract profession-oriented candidates and selects out applicants merely seeking stable government jobs, which can be had with less effort elsewhere.

How Organizational Practices Can Filter Patronage and Attract Talent

State organizations confront a varied social topography of relative patronage pressures, a structural position largely outside of their control. Conjointly, these structural factors may exert a probabilistic effect on the likelihood of a pocket of effectiveness emerging within a particular area of the state. However, such explanations alone cannot explain how distinctiveness comes to be clustered. PARD and the Bank of Ghana recruit from the same general labor pool of economists as a great many other public agencies with less sterling reputations. The Ghanaian Commercial Courts recruit from the same general labor pool—the Ghanaian Bar Association and existing lower-court judges— as do other high courts with reputations for sloth, inefficiency, or corruption. What do highly successful public organizations in Ghana do *organizationally* to filter out the effects of patronage or attract candidates who possess both the explicit educational skills and tacit organizationally beneficial proto-bureaucratic schema?

The Bank of Ghana is an illustrative example because it enjoys the most sterling reputation for merit-based hiring of any central state organization, according to my interviews with dozens of key observers of the state. When I asked expert observers of the state to recommend a group, agency, or organization that they thought stood out for being the most effective in the state, the Bank of Ghana was the first organization respondents suggested, without hesitation. Several expert observers also suggested that within the Bank of Ghana, they were particularly impressed with the Monetary Policy Analysis Department—which provided research to the prestigious Monetary Policy Committee that set monetary policy for the country.

Members of the Monetary Policy Analysis Department recalled their recruitment and interview procedure as a grueling, nerve-wracking process. At the time, the Bank of Ghana had three rounds of interviews through which applicants had to pass, and applicants were culled from consideration at each stage. Before interviews were scheduled, bank officials made a "long list" of candidates for consideration. Division directors often added candidates into the pool based on recommendations from senior economics professors at the nation's flagship university, the University of Ghana at Legon. A high-ranking official who has been with the bank for decades explains, "Some people thought, let's bring them straight from school, so they aren't corrupted, and subject them to supervision discipline." In addition, staff within the bank's Human Resources (HR) department are responsible for sorting through all the applications sent directly to the bank, including both responses to published public advertisements and a large file of ongoing unsolicited applications. Unsolicited applications not sent in response to a specific advertisement are filed according to educational credentials. As evidence of how prestigious and sought-after public service at the bank is, other than High Court justices, the Bank of Ghana was the only organization to report receiving unsolicited applications—applications from job seekers that were not sent in response to a specific job advertisement.

When a position became available, HR staff pulled the file of applications with the matching required degree—for example, at least a first degree in economics. According to Mr. Essien, a bank member with 30 years of experience, due to the large number of filed applications, low-level HR staff pulled files "essentially at random" from the relevant drawer. Some of those staff then narrowed down the stack of applications, primarily based on prior experience and educational credentials. The list would be sorted to prefer those with particular degrees, for example economics, finance, or accounting depending on the position, and then further sorted to put those with "firsts" or "upper second" qualifications on their degree to the top of the list. Thus, the hundreds of applications the bank receives were narrowed to a single long list. After that point, candidates were not added to the list, only winnowed down. From this long list, HR called applicants in for the first round of interviews with HR officials from the bank.

Applicants who passed the HR department interviews then confronted the daunting Management Committee for evaluation. The Management Committee was a diverse group of top-level managers, including the heads of most of the divisions within the bank. At that stage, applicants were asked to defend their thesis, whether first-degree or advanced-degree holders. Rebecca and Selasi, two younger members of the Monetary Policy Analysis Department, describe being surprised by how their thesis work was questioned rigorously, including delving into details. Selasi shook his wrist and snapped his fingers in a classically emphatic Ghanaian gesture, exclaiming: 'They will really grill you! You will find yourself sweating.' Applicants were called on to discuss translating theories they had trained in, or ideas from their specific thesis, into practical considerations for the central bank. Heads of departments, who were proximate to the target position and conducted the questioning, were technical experts in their relative fields. The Management Committee members all exercised veto powers, so again at this stage in the hiring sequence some applicants were sorted out.

For those who passed the grueling interview by the Management Committee, there was a final-round interview before the highest governing body in the bank: the Board.[28] When Monetary Policy Analysis members recalled their experience coming before the Board in their interview, their tone of voice and demeanor changed. Rebecca's face lit up. Selasi tried to convey the mingled sense of thrill and terror he felt when facing the members of the Board for the first time. It is as though they are describing meeting a greatly admired celebrity. The Board of the central bank included the governor himself as well as deputy governors, other representatives from within the bank, and at least two outside representatives nominated by the Ministry of Finance. So, for students who spent their education eagerly training to be practitioners of economics and finance, the members of the Board of the Bank of Ghana are, indeed, celebrities of a sort. The governor at the time of my interviews, Dr. Paul Acquah, was regarded among young Ghanaian economists at the bank with the nerdy reverence reserved for Stephen Hawking and the enthusiasm accorded Beyoncé. At this stage, the governor personally presented each candidate's merits and defended each candidate's selection to the Board, and the Board—including the governor—would actively question candidates.[29]

Candidates who make it through the three rounds of selection describe their job offer with a sense of accomplishment. In defending their thesis work to some of the foremost economics practitioners in their country, they cultivate a sense that the quality of their work was responsible for their job selection. In expressing an understanding that all of those around them in the Monetary Policy Analysis Department also went through a similarly rigorous process, the subcultural members come to view each other through a distinctly corporatist orientation, much like soldiers who have survived a particularly difficult mission together.

How Organizational Recruitment Procedures Can Filter Patronage

Dominant social practices are powerful in social life because they assume a taken-for-granted character. People presume, sometimes without actively considering, that the behaviors of others will follow the taken-for-granted social practices. In this sense, patronage hiring can be a pervasive practice that is enacted by many in a taken-for-granted manner even if particular individuals might vocalize opposition if they were asked. In such contexts, if meritocracy is to have a chance, it is important to identify organizational procedures that can filter patronage, or reduce the ability of actors both inside and outside of the organization to hire based primarily on social connections to powerful people.

When I asked Mr. Essien, a longtime Bank of Ghana official, about the possibility of influencing the hiring process, he scoffed, "What are they going to do? Daddy can't dash [bribe] all those people. No, it can't be done." Why? The recruitment process for the Bank of Ghana has several organizational features that stymie potential efforts to use patronage social networks to influence the hiring process. First, hiring is the cumulative choice of a relatively large number of people with uncommonly diverse social backgrounds. The previously described hiring process at the bank was an intensely multilevel process, such that the final hire was the cumulative result of choices made across different levels within the bank. Consequently, the hiring decision incorporated social actors with vastly different social networks: People from the lowliest HR intern, who pulled the applications "at random" from the drawer, to the powerful governor of the bank himself had a hand in the process.

It also included organizationally proximate recruitment authority, especially by comparison to standard recruitment in the civil service. According to a former deputy director, the Bank of Ghana had, since its inception, included the director of the division seeking to recruit in the recruitment and interview process. Concurrently with the ability of multilevel decision-making to frustrate patronage and nepotism, the organizational proximity may further influence meritocratic hiring through professional interdependence. Vesting authority with proximate organizational actors tends to incentivize more merit-based hiring: The more immediate the recruiter is to the position being hired, the more the future work outputs of the recruiter depend on the quality of the person being recruited. By comparison, if a "big man" atop the organization hires a personal connection to be staffed within a large formal organization, that patronage hire will have less of a discernible and immediate effect on the daily experience or outcomes of the big man. Contingent on being in an organizational system that rewards operational performance to some extent, greater proximity and interdependency mean the recruiter more acutely and personally bears some of the costs of recruiting a less professionally able candidate through nepotism.

Within the bank's multilevel recruitment process, there is only one point of entry into consideration—candidates are only added into the initial pool for consideration before HR begins the first stage of evaluation—but there are multiple *veto points*. Across a wide range of organizational decisions, having more people who can veto or say "no" to a decision tends to converge on decisions that are cautious, risk-averse, and more rational.[30] Within the bank hiring process, those veto points are held by people from different social backgrounds and different positions within the organization. I argue that, organizationally, veto points distributed across multiple levels of an organization by different groups reduce the potential for both nepotism (favoritism from an insider) and corruption (influence from an outsider).

Multiple veto points multiply the number of actors who must be influenced to accept a candidate on a basis other than that which is readily visible from the application package. Consider how much easier is the process of influencing hiring where one person has authority over who is hired: Patronage seekers need only find the social or financial capital to influence one person. Moreover, when those multiple veto points are also spread across different levels of the organizational hierarchy, they not only multiply the sheer number of actors involved, but also diversify the *status* of involved actors and, by extension, the nature and composition of those actors' personal networks. This makes the process both qualitatively and quantitatively more difficult to influence, and I argue correspondingly reduces the ability of outside actors to corrupt the process. Ultimately then, a multilevel process with veto points throughout helps to filter outside influence and simultaneously reduces the ability of organizational insiders to exercise nepotism.

Conversely, multiple entry points—where an actor can insert a candidate into the pool for consideration—increase the ability of internal actors to practice nepotism, particularly those located at sequentially later stages of the recruitment process. A prior regime at the National Communications Authority highlights this vulnerability. On paper, the NCA had then, and still has now, a procedure for recruitment in which initial narrowing is done by lower-level officials, whereby upper-level political appointees are only involved in the last stage of selection, and typically only for hiring higher-level managers. Though the process as explicitly codified on paper has fewer overall levels than that of the Bank of Ghana, it is conceptually similar. However, organizational procedures depend critically on whether written codes actually structure people's behavior, particularly that of powerful agents within the organization from whom others take behavioral cues. Employees cautiously noted that the former director was often known to insert favored candidates into consideration in the final round of evaluation, subverting the formal recruitment process. The former NCA serves as a cautionary tale not only of having late entry points, but more importantly, of how tenuous formal written codes are in largely neopatrimonial contexts. Neopatrimonial habitus disposes officials to taking their behavioral cues not from employee handbooks, but rather from powerful players at the top of the social status hierarchy. When that former director left and a new director was appointed, the behavior changed because the new director was widely understood to support objective merit-based hiring. According to HR officials, the new director never tried to insert a new candidate into the last recruitment interview.

"Because Once You Say NCA, Instead of Posting Their Resume, They Will Come Here Personally"

Other organizations within Ghana may not have the same level of resources or discretion over hiring procedures enjoyed by the central bank. However, some pockets of effectiveness deploy relatively simple and inexpensive tactics to similarly interrupt the ability of outsiders to influence the hiring process. In the midst of describing the most recent external job search, Collins—a Human Resources official in the NCA—explains, "Before the interview, we didn't disclose our identity. We said a firm in the public sector. We didn't say that it was NCA that was recruiting." If the sector is deemed relevant to the position, the external advert will also specify that the position is in the communications sector. I confirm that the advertisement did not specifically mention NCA, and then ask him why. He explains:

> COLLINS: Well, in Ghana—how long have you been here?
>
> AUTHOR: I've been coming since 2000. But tell me anyway.
>
> COLLINS: You know our culture ... there's a lot of personal contacts. Oh, my brother is here and they are recruiting, so I'll go and see my brother to help you get a job. Some of them even go to a member of Parliament and get a letter that says, "Please consider this candidate for me," even though he might not be qualified or he might be qualified. So, to avoid all those pressures that will come to bear on us in HR, we decided that a public-sector organization is recruiting, blah, blah, blah. So, nobody knew.
>
> AUTHOR: How long has that been a policy?
>
> COLLINS: It's not a policy, per se. We want to avoid such a pressure. Because once you say NCA, instead of posting their resume, they will come here, personally, and they will say, "We want to see the Human Resources manager." They will come and tell you I need a job and it would take all my time. So, to avoid those things, we say a public-sector organization.

Collins explains this is not an official policy, but rather a practice employed in a few of the public-sector organizations, but not all, "I couldn't say when it started. But it is—mostly it is to reduce undue influence on the people who make the decisions." Note that Collins frames the unspecified agency as a tactic to frustrate patronage influence—an explicit framing he volunteers unprompted from me, merely in response to a benign question asking him to walk me step by step through the most recent hire. Collins is clearly consciously and deliberately aware that efforts to use interpersonal connections to influence hiring are part of "our culture," which is to say, widely shared understandings of how things are typically done.

The Bank of Ghana frustrates would-be efforts to exert external influence in hiring through multilevel interviews that multiply the quantity and social heterogeneity of decision-makers. The NCA does not have as many sequential rounds of interviews at different levels; however, they intentionally withhold information about the hiring organization in a functionally analogous organizational move to frustrate patronage efforts. The Bank of Ghana has enjoyed a long-standing and widely held reputation for merit-based hiring.

That understanding itself also acts to dampen external efforts to influence hiring, because would-be patronage seekers understand that their normal strategies will be ineffectual, and possibly even damaging, if employed within the bank. As a result, when people within the bank are asked to reflect on the hiring procedures, they tend to spontaneously frame the procedures as merit-seeking: the best way to find the best candidate. Bank officials rarely explicitly and consciously think of their procedures as simultaneously frustrating patronage. By contrast, NCA as an organization had a relatively new and fragile reputation for merit at the time the research for this book was conducted. Correspondingly, NCA officials were more explicitly conscious of framing their organizational hiring practices as intentional efforts to frustrate patronage.

Assessing Reputations for Proto-bureaucratic Schema

Of course, it is not enough to merely frustrate patronage seekers. In order to concentrate distinctiveness, niches seek to actively acquire people who are skilled and credentialed in the explicit knowledge of the relevant field, but who also exhibit dispositions that are favorable to the organization effectively accomplishing goals in the public interest. Those proto-bureaucratic dispositions, however, are not only relatively uncommon and unevenly distributed throughout the labor pool. They are also very difficult to discern at a distance, not easily legible on someone's resume or cover letter.

How then do niches solve the high search costs? Typically, they activate "weak ties" in professional interpersonal networks to seek relevant reputational information.[31] As I will argue later, this both directly facilitates selection of candidates, and also critically reshapes how officials understand the primary cause for their selection towards more meritocratic ideals. Recruits identify a reputation for various proto-bureaucratic orientations—such as "merit," "hard work," or "integrity"—as the proximal cause of their hiring, the condition that differentiated them from the rest of the applicants. With that understanding in mind, they tend to orient themselves towards acting within the organization in ways that accord with that reputation for merit, hard work, or integrity.

Reputational Assessing in the Founding of the Ghana Commercial Courts

The founding of the Ghanaian Commercial Courts illustrates how an influential founder used interpersonal networks to evaluate reputations of potential recruits, thereby addressing the challenging costs of searching for proto-bureaucratic tendencies. Justice Kwame Bannerman, a founding justice at the

Commercial Courts, explains the process: "In Ghana you, the Judicial Service doesn't advertise. I mean, if it's staff. But for judges they don't advertise. Normally, what you do is to put in the application and then hope that they will invite you." Similarly, when I ask another founding judge, Justice Emmanuel Kwarteng, how he came to be at the Commercial Courts, Kwarteng responded simply, "Well, I was selected by the chief justice." When I prompt, he elaborates:

> JUSTICE KWARTENG: I was called to the head office. And the chief justice told me he wants to bring me to Accra. [Short pause] To be part of the judges that he has selected for the commercial court.
> AUTHOR: Okay. And did you know anything until you were called to the ... [trails off as he begins speaking]?
> JUSTICE KWARTENG: No, eh I ehh, I didn't know. He just called me. What he said was that he wanted, he had his own criteria, and he wanted judges of good quality to be in the Commercial Court. And so, what he used, the term he used was "carefully selected judges." Those are the terms. That, that those are the words that he used— "carefully selected judges"—to manage the commercial courts. And that gave me some provenance, you know, among the acolytes.

Justice Bannerman shows a similar awareness that those selected were carefully chosen, as he elaborates, "When the previous Chief Justice [George Kingsley Acquah] was there, the one who actually set up the court, this court was *his* baby." Sandra Cofie, a solicitor of the Supreme Courts of both England and Ghana was closely involved in the judicial reform project for the Judicial Services. Cofie publicly observed that Chief Justice Acquah had a well-deserved reputation as a judicial reformer, whose personal reputation for, and commitment to, judicial integrity was essential to the establishment of the Commercial Courts.[32] Justice Bannerman details his awareness that the influential chief justice was personally involved in selection, as well as some of those difficult-to-discern traits that the chief justice sought:

> JUSTICE BANNERMAN: In the course of the selection of the, the judges, I don't know, but the chief justice did his own investigation. They do it without you knowing. They check your background, they pull and see all sorts of things about judges. Some may be true, some may not be true. So, they put their ear to the ground and [pause] investigate ... Given the nature of their cases, you want people who will be able to [pause] put their foot down. Right is right, wrong is wrong. I guess that is what worked at the background of those who are, who did their choice in terms of the judges who are brought here. Even in terms of the staff who were brought here.

One justice had worked previously with the Revenue Commissioners—a precursor to what was later called the Serious Fraud Office, with oversight of the revenue collection agencies—and later with the Commission on Human Rights and Administrative Justice (CHRAJ), a corruption watchdog agency that itself had a very strong reputation. That background signaled someone who had experience with commercial law through past involvement with the revenue agencies, but also someone with a well-tested commitment to ethics. Even so, the chief justice reached out to a high-ranking official who had been able to personally observe the candidate when they worked together at CHRAJ.

This reputation-based evaluation also extended to staff. Justices who worked closer to Accra recommended staff that they had worked with, whom they knew to be "honest and hardworking." Justice Bannerman explains, "Because you need to know, you need to work with somebody you trust. That's the first thing. It's better to work with somebody you *know* and *trust* rather than to get a new person you don't know and whose behavior and attitude you don't know." Esther was a high-ranking nonjudicial official who supervised staff at the Commercial Courts. She explains, "They were looking for someone we can trust to be the registrar of the commercial court. We didn't want any people with—people who were troublesome." Esther had worked for judicial services for decades prior to the appointment. She also had previous experience working in the complaints unit, the equivalent of Internal Affairs, responsible for investigating allegations of misconduct, which afforded opportunities to observe how she would respond to ethically challenging situations.

Thus, clustered distinctiveness within the Commercial Courts arose first by the influential chief justice intentionally selecting people with reputations for proto-bureaucratic tendencies, including the staff. Several courtroom staff were discussing their hiring. Aku and Solomon had both worked previously elsewhere in the judicial system. Aku explains how she was curious about why she had been selected for the new court when so many others around her had not, so she began asking around. Solomon listens to the exchange nodding silently before confirming his own awareness that their selection was the result of seeking information about their work reputations from those around them:

> AKU: We don't know but what I learned, those of us who were in the system, I think they investigated our background and something before we were brought here.
>
> AUTHOR: So, how—what were they looking for in your background?
>
> AKU: I wouldn't know, but that was what I was told.
>
> AUTHOR: That they investigate—so you were actually told when you were selected?

AKU: They didn't state it in the letter, but I asked the criteria. Because we were many there [at the other court], so how come they picked some? By recommendation? I don't know how. So I asked.

AUTHOR: Did you also hear something like that, that they had investigated your background or —

AKU: Upon recommendation of some people, they picked.

SOLOMON: Maybe you might not know. But people around you.

Like those court staff, evaluation of reputation extended all the way down to the scopists of the Commercial Courts, who prepare and format official court proceedings records. David is a scopist. It is also evident within a few minutes of meeting him that David is also someone who is aspirational and professionally oriented. When asked where they see themselves in five years, the scopists from the comparison case gave relatively lackluster responses, hoping perhaps to be promoted to the next level but also content to remain here. By contrast, David responded, "I am working towards going back to school. My aim is to be a lawyer one day, my projection is that in eight years I will be a lawyer. But it isn't man who proposes, God proposes but asks we aim high." He exudes enthusiasm for the work, speaking with zeal and at great length about the intricacies of his daily scopist tasks. Before being assigned to the newly formed Commercial Courts, David personally met the chief justice as part of an advanced training course for scopists, in which David distinguished himself and the chief justice personally gave David a raise.

Reputation through Observation: Trial and Poaching

Difficult-to-discern proto-bureaucratic dispositions could also be assessed through direct observation. Because civil service laws make dismissing officials difficult, observation in advance of hiring usually involved (1) poaching from elsewhere after observing an official from afar and (2) temporary or trial employment, including national service and informal internships. Like the Commercial Courts, PARD also faced considerable search costs in their efforts to identify and recruit staff who were both technically qualified and possessed difficult-to-discern proto-bureaucratic dispositions. A number of current PARD officers were recruited after doing national service, affording a year for them to acculturate and be evaluated before niche insiders had to decide whether to move to officially hire them as civil servants. Mr. Mensah, the current PARD director, had himself initially been posted elsewhere within the Ministry of Finance for his national service. He went abroad to get a master's degree. While abroad, he met with several high-ranking ministry officials, including one from the then newly formed PARD. Mr. Mensah recalls, "When we started chatting, he said, 'Oh, we have a unit in Policy Analysis

Division that is money credit and banking desk, that is, that nobody is occupying ... So, they asked me to think seriously about [it] if I come back whether, if I wanted to join them in PARD." After completing his courses abroad in Europe, Mr. Mensah returned to his original position outside of PARD:

> MR. MENSAH: When I came back, the then Acting Chief Director Technical [of PARD] started, started giving me a lot of work to do.
> AUTHOR: At your [other ministry] desk?
> MR. MENSAH: Out of, *outside* my [other ministry] desk.
> AUTHOR: So he was giving you additional work?
> MR. MENSAH: Additional work to do, yeah: write-ups, pulling me to meetings, ummm, and he finally said that he thinks I should be transferred to PARD.

Giving Mr. Mensah additional work to do completely outside of his official job position allowed PARD's then-acting chief director technical to observe firsthand Mr. Mensah's orientation to work, and the caliber of what he could produce. Indeed, being willing to complete work that is manifestly outside of one's official duties for someone who is not one's actual supervisor is itself a clever means of assessing whether someone is hardworking, eager, and intrinsically interested in the work. Fifteen years after Mr. Mensah went through an informal trial period before being taken into PARD from his position elsewhere, PARD would still occasionally "poach" officers from elsewhere within the Ministry of Finance. As it had with Mr. Mensah, recruiting within the ministry provided an informal probationary period during which they could observe for those difficult-to-discern proto-bureaucratic orientations.

For example, Adjoa was a young member who joined PARD only recently. She describes a parallel process for her move into PARD. Adjoa began in another unit within MOFEP but, "when I got there, it was like there was nothing there and it was like I come to work I don't do anything. So, it's like I keep moving on like going to people asking about what's good in other divisions and I found myself in other divisions." Adjoa eventually met a senior official who suggested she was a good fit for PARD. Although Adjoa did not explicitly reflect on the link, as later chapters will show, PARD prizes people who take initiative and find work to do even when nothing has been assigned to them. Adjoa's eager searching for more work to do commended her, providing evidence of the very quasi-bureaucratic disposition that PARD prizes, including a strong work ethic and a professional orientation. Adjoa explains that the senior ministry official then brokered an informal connection to PARD: "He showed my CV to the director of the division. And then the director also called me—he asked me a couple of questions." Her next comment evidences the carefulness with which interstitial niches go about acquiring other internal human resources: Careful to be politically tactful, people worked behind the scenes to gain the chief director's permission reassigning her to PARD. Adjoa recalls, "And then he [PARD's director] said he was not the one who brought me to this ministry. I have to go and see the chief director." Adjoa was afraid of talking to the chief director herself, and stalled. Eventually, she explains, "I talked to this particular person and then he said, I should bring my CV, then he went and talked to the chief director, then he said, 'Chief, move her.'"

Perceptions of Recruitment Affects Orientation

Recruits were honored to feel personally chosen, but importantly, because of the relatively small scale of all these niches, they regularly encountered those responsible for selecting them and felt a sense of reciprocal obligation. Sociologist William Sewell has famously argued that social change is possible within relatively powerful social structures when people transpose schemas to new situations; Bourdieu similarly reflects on how habitus facilitates "analogical transfers of schemes permitting the solution of similarly shaped problems."[33] When a schema is transposed to a seemingly analogous situation, the new situation may differ in subtle but important ways with sometimes unpredictable or unintended consequences for outcomes. I argue that these kinds of "high touch" intentional selections within a predominantly neopatrimonial social order are a case of analogous transposition of neopatrimonial schema. The momentum of familiar neopatrimonial practices of interpersonal relationship maintenance and an orientation toward pleasing a patron were bent toward a proto-meritocratic orientation because the selection process suggested to recruits that accomplishing the organization's official goals would be most pleasing. The plow of meritocracy was thereby yoked to the oxen of neopatrimonialism.

The two justices we met earlier explain how the sense of having been intentionally chosen by a particular person created expectations that influenced their sense of their job. Justice Kwarteng explains that the sense of having been chosen created high external expectations for the judges to live up to: "Well ['enyy'—a drawn out nasal sound Ghanaians use to signal resignation]. I mean it is natural, when your boss says that this group of people were carefully, have been carefully selected. I mean it's natural that it would, ehh, I mean people will look at these carefully selected judges with some bubble eyes, and thinking that they are some something." Justice Bannerman similarly articulates a sense that there was grumbling, even jealousy, felt by those who had not been selected for the new court.[34] Justice Bannerman also expresses a sense of having to act in a way that would not disappoint those who selected him, articulating a sense of interpersonal obligation that is characteristic in neopatrimonial habitus, but that orientation has become attached not merely to a singular patron, but to a system:

> JUSTICE BANNERMAN: When the previous chief justice was there, the one who actually set up the court, this court was *his* baby, actually, if you like. And [four-second pause]. As it, as it were, the other court and the other judges, all of them have their eyes here, and there was a question as to why did you pick these people and not me? Somebody who say, "I have been a high court judge for six, seven years; I should have been there [at the Commercial Courts]. Why did you pick these young … [trails off]?" And invariably, quite of, a lot of us were quite young as compared to other high court judges. So, there was initial murmuring and, about the mode of selection. So, once we are here, we think that we should not do anything that will make those who brought us here get disappointed.
>
> AUTHOR: Even though the justice himself is no longer [having died in 2007]?
>
> JUSTICE BANNERMAN: Yes. But, the system is there. Even though he himself is no longer, the system is there. Even the Supreme Court judges, the Court of Appeal judges, they all have their eyes on the Commercial Court. They want to see how the system performs. And therefore it's, I see that it's my duty to make sure that the system works, the system of which I am part and parcel of works. If it failed, I, I would feel very bad, and I would have disappointed those who set up the, the system.

Justice Bannerman touches briefly on concerns about explicitly violating practices and expectations common in the broader administrative environment, particularly the sense of seniority as an entitlement to promotion that is a dominant sentiment in the administrative apparatus broadly. The entangled presumption of seniority and promotion—seemingly such a classic feature of Weberian bureaucracy—is felt quite strongly as a constraint by the interstitial niches. For example, one of the senior officials in the Ministry of Finance explained that for a long time PARD had only an "unofficial head." When I ask what it means for someone to be the unofficial head, the ministry official explains, "I said unofficial head because most of the time everything that concerned PARD was passed through him by the minister, or the deputy ministers. But they never gave him a letter that, 'You are the head' [chuckles]." When I ask why an official head was not directly appointed, the official explained that there were several other people within the ministry at the time who had more seniority; therefore the most appropriate person for the job could not be promoted to officially head PARD without inciting problems.

So, for slightly more than five years in the 1990s, to avoid offending more senior officials, PARD technically had no head whatsoever. The ministry official recalls, "He was, yeah, nobody, there was no the acting head. There was no *official* head. At *all* ... Nobody was officially appointed." The Commercial Courts were one of the few in which the expectation of seniority was flagrantly and publicly flaunted in the selection of the judges—something that further underscored their selection as meaningful, special, and grounded in logics that were distinctive from the prevailing business as usual.

Conclusion

This chapter illuminates some of the issues that make recruitment challenging for highly effective niches of the Ghanaian administrative state. I've argued that Ghanaian niches recruit within an environment where it is widely understood that selected applicants must have the stated credentials. Where such credentials requirements are vague or very common, credentials-matching does little to narrow the pool. However, where credentials are specific and relatively rare, especially when obtaining the credential itself is challenging, credentials-matching can reduce the relative number of people in the respective labor pool that could seek a job through influential interpersonal connections. Some structural factors further help shift the overall composition of the pool from which niches recruit: offering unusually demanding work with no extra financial compensation tends to skew applicants towards those with some professional and public service motivations.

Niches also employ intentional organizational practices to filter patronage seekers and select for recruits interested in achieving the organization's aims. The recruitment process is structured to frustrate external would-be influencers' access to recruitment decision-makers, for example, because decision-makers are too numerous and diverse (as in the Bank of Ghana) or were kept anonymous (as in the NCA). Niches face substantial search costs when attempting to assess difficult-to-discern proto-bureaucratic dispositions. They address these search costs by relying on either firsthand observation through temporary employment or reputational assessments through "weak ties" interpersonal networks.[35] The modal example would be asking a well-respected college professor (whom the recruiter knows from her own schooling) to relay the professor's firsthand knowledge about promising students in the graduating class (whom the recruiter does not personally know). Note that obtaining information through such weak ties is substantially different from direct recruitment of close ties such as coethnics or family, which is typically associated with conventional patronage. The process of recruitment influenced recruits' perceptions of *why* they were recruited—underscoring that new niche members were recruited for job-related abilities and orientation towards accomplishing organizational goals—which in turn shaped their orientation while on the job. Recruits felt honored and personally chosen. Because of the relatively small scale of all these niches, they then regularly encountered those responsible for selecting them and felt a sense of reciprocal obligation to perform according to the selectors' expectations of them.

Scholars who study the administrative apparatus of developmental states have observed—sometimes only in passing—that particularly effective states possess a discernible esprit de corps, a shared sense of pride, belonging, loyalty, and cohesiveness within a group.[36] The detailed qualitative data of this chapter help flesh out the sociological foundations through which distinctive selection procedures cultivate a shared sense of esprit de corps, both through internalized interpersonal obligations and expectations for performance that others projected onto them. Niche discretion over personnel selection emphasized work-related reasons for hiring as a shared experience of membership. The conditions of job recruitment structure attention and interpretation of what constitutes success, both consciously and tacitly. Patronage hires feel beholden to a patron, and therefore orient work conduct to maintaining those relationships rather than achieving any particular organizational objective. By contrast, when niche insiders perceive a shared experience of being hired for work-related skill, it engenders an orientation to defining personal success as excelling at work-related tasks. The combination of esprit de corps and reorientation to succeeding at work tasks thereby further cultivates the bureaucratic ethos and deepens identification with practices that typify the niche—a cultivation process that the next chapter addresses.

3

Cultivation: Clustered Distinctiveness, Interstitial Experience, and the Lived Foundations of the Bureaucratic Ethos

Bureaucracy is often a black box of rules, wrapped in tautological or quasi-functionalist language such that "proper bureaucracy" itself "generates norms of comportment for state functionaries and, in doing so, channels their actions away from individualistic and predatory practices."[1] Impersonal norms of comportment are a pivotal reorientation of individual practices deserving careful scholarly attention. However, conventional explanations of bureaucracy are clear on *what* happens but deceptively thin on *how* the transition happens: "This it does by putting into place abstract and clearly specified rules and ensuring that functionaries' decisions are guided by such rules, rather than by their own private interests."[2] How are agents able to institute a set of abstracted rules that are contrary to existing popular practices? Even if abstracted rules are created, why would anyone comply?

Both low-income and wealthy Western countries are replete with examples of rules that exist on the books but have little or no impact on daily practice.[3] Amid fanfare from shareholders, American corporations formally adopt stock repurchase programs or long-term incentive plans for CEOs, but many never actually implement the officially adopted plans.[4] Formerly communist countries officially adopted free-market policies for state-owned enterprises, but long continued to prop up unprofitable ventures.[5] In Britain, it is illegal for pub owners to "knowingly permit drunkenness," and yet a glance around London would suggest that rule does little to curb the thirst of pub-goers.[6] Rules alone seem an ineffective way to change familiar habits, even in environments where people are already generally oriented towards rules-following. Indeed, following the rules *simply because they are the rules* is itself evidence of a fairly advanced bureaucratic habitus. So, if the mere existence of rules cannot explain the cultivation of bureaucratic comportment, how does the bureaucratic ethos emerge?

This chapter will argue that the bureaucratic ethos emerges as part of an iterative consolidation of small-group organizational culture around the characteristics, orientations, and practices that niche members share in common, and which make the niche distinctive from the surrounding environment. In other words, it is grounded in lived experience, emulation, and repeated practice that affords the tacit knowledge of *doing* bureaucracy. The administration of the *office* may be carried out (as Weber observes) according to "general rules, which are more or less stable, more or less exhaustive, and which can be learned."[7] But paradoxically, this book suggests that the bureaucratic ethos upon which that administration depends cannot. Just as every contingency of a business relationship cannot be enumerated in a written contract, so that contracts depend on unspoken, noncontractual elements,[8] bureaucracy includes *rules* and *features* of administration, but also myriad *practices* that together comprise the bureaucratic ethos. One reason top-down reforms fail is that the bureaucratic ethos cannot be effectively and exhaustively enumerated such that it can be transmitted by mandate. Rather, *it must be lived to be learned.*

This chapter analyzes the sociological structural position of the Ghanaian cases and discusses how that structural position of feeling like a small subculture—tightly socially connected to others within, but with large perceived differences to those that surround you—is particularly fruitful for forging the bureaucratic orientation, including the foundation of the corporatist ethos grounded in identification with, and commitment to, the working group. The chapter then briefly discusses how the consequences of that distinctive structural positioning is resonant with recent network theory on the effects of homogenous networks and decades of laboratory-based social psychological experiments on identification and group effort.

Toward a More Sociological Conceptualization of State Officials: From Principal-Agency to the Influence Effects of Small-Group Acculturation

A body of work known as "principal-agent" theory argues that most organizational functionaries (or "agents") are driven by their own narrow self-interests, which often conflict with the interests of the "principal," which might be the business owner, or for government organizations may be the minister, president, or even the public interest broadly. This perspective believes self-interested agents must be controlled through monitoring, sanctioning, or incentivizing their behavior to better align with the principal's interests. Principal-agent models have the benefit of being elegantly simple and capable of generating concrete predictions that are operationalizable and empirically testable in a wide array of situations from automobile insurance to corruption in ancient China.[9] However, I argue this theory takes an incredibly optimistic view of elites' capacity to design systems. Expanding the use of quantitative metrics to measure performance and offer incentives has resulted primarily in a stunning set of examples of perverse incentives and unintended consequences. To cite merely one example, efforts intended to monitor and encourage quality teaching by holding teachers accountable to student evaluation scores instead contributes to fewer assignments and greater grade inflation with little discernible connection to quality instruction.[10]

More importantly, believing workers will act in the public interest only because, and when, they are being monitored is an incredibly impoverished view of workers' social motivations. Principal-agent models informed by self-interest maximization may help explain why some public officials are corrupt, but like other explanations of corruption, they tell us very little about positive deviance: why some public servants strive against challenges, pursue the public interest, and go above and beyond the call of duty.[11] Instead, I argue the critical realignment to the bureaucratic ethos oriented to accomplishing organizational goals occurs as organizational structures and small-group sociological dynamics interact to produce a strong identification with the group and an increasingly ordered sense of what it means to be a "good" member of that group.

In relatively small group settings, the people who comprise the group can make a world of difference. Our social experience of a group is partly determined by the kinds of people who have chosen to join—this is what social scientists call a *selection effect*. For example, the kinds of people who join a quilting group are different than those who are drawn to a Hell's Angels motorbike gang, and those two social settings will be quite different because of it. But once people are relatively durable members of a social setting, they will also be changed and shaped by it: this is called an *influence effect*. When there is a systematic difference in the kinds of people who are opting into a particular situation, especially if there is a critical mass of unusually distinctive behaviors, it will tend to shape the group culture, which in turn influences how members behave and think of themselves. For example, we know from studies of American adolescents that young people are more likely to engage in delinquent, deviant behaviors when they are part of dense, cohesive friendship groups with others who are deviant.[12]

Clustering a critical mass of people with unusually distinctive behaviors can transform a small-group subculture. For example, imagine the classroom dynamics in a spring semester course where 30 percent of the class were seniors taking it as a pass-fail elective. I can tell you from experience: it is pretty rough for everyone involved. Over time the initial inclination toward disengagement from that 30 percent of students spreads to other students who might otherwise have been moderately inclined to participate. Eventually, only the most eager students remain active, and even they are frustrated. There is little that even an inspiring professor can do to counteract the general malaise that pervades a class dominated by disengaged and unprepared students.

Conversely, the best class I ever taught started with a critical mass of students who had previously taken classes with me and so began on the first day eager, highly prepared, and actively participating. Their behaviors had a pronounced effect on the rest of the class as well: because it was not just one easily snubbed "nerd" but rather multiple students, their distinctive behavior was the most readily observable set of practices in the classroom. That set of practices became the example others emulated. Soon more than three-quarters of the class spoke every class period, and the quality of assignments was unlike anything I have seen before or since. Both the initially peripheral and initially eager students were transformed by the environment throughout the semester. A cluster of distinctive practices within the social environment influenced other students to participate further, emulating the practices they observed in others and converging on a set of distinctive ways of comporting themselves within that particular classroom, a distinctive student ethos, if you will.

Appreciating the sociological foundation of clustered distinctiveness thereby helps illuminate an alternative explanation for how the bureaucratic ethos emerges: iteratively, as a small group with overlapping distinctiveness influences each other and converges on a shared set of practices. This chapter argues that it is not enough to merely select the best people available in the environment, because in these environments people with a fully developed bureaucratic ethos are exceedingly rare. As the Introduction pointed out, niches cannot simply recruit the "right" people—that is, people with fully formed ideal typical bureaucratic ethos. Instead, as the prior chapter showed, niches recruit right-enough people, people whose prior experience, habits, and professional orientations have some incomplete and imperfect overlap with the bureaucratic ethos. The overlap and shared core of those imperfect foundations become the material upon which cultivation draws to further clarify the local subcultural organizational practices and enhance niche distinctiveness vis-à-vis the neopatrimonial administrative culture that predominates in the state broadly. Only over time do these many small iterative steps come to be consolidated into a widely shared understanding both within and outside that the niche operates in a way that is very distinctive.

Ultimately then, in addition to selection effects, there are considerable *influence* effects of the small-group culture: The lived daily experience of working in such a clustered environment cultivates a group style centered on the elements participants have in common. The elusive bureaucratic ethos is forged from the varied proto-bureaucratic experiences of those selected individuals clustered together in the niche. This chapter draws on interview and ethnographic observations from the Ghanaian cases, particularly focused on analysis of how newcomers adapt to incorporation into the niche and adjust their daily practices, conforming with what they observe are the characteristic ways of the working group.

Learning by Emulation: On Seeing and Doing

The newer and younger members of niches are particularly aware of learning about how to act within the niche by observing senior members. Kojo was doing his national service at PARD—something like a postcollege internship assigned by the state. He was young, so he still lived at home with his parents, both of whom were relatively well educated. When I ask him about the general reputation of civil servants he is initially reticent. He begins to answer several times, each time lapsing into lengthy pauses. When I prompt him further, he eventually articulates his understanding of the public stereotype:

AUTHOR: You don't have to be shy, you can just be frank.

KOJO: They take a lot of presents, I wouldn't say bribe. But if you want to really, if you want somebody to do something for you, people think that because it goes through a lot of bureaucracy and, most people because the pay is low, it's like, they have no option but to work here. So people don't really, people think, people think the civil, the public service [vocal stalls] they don't really have a good reputation outside.

Kojo articulates a public reputation wherein civil servants are underpaid and prone to accepting gifts. He also implies that civil servants are underqualified, only working in public service because they have no other option. The early part of his response was laced throughout with hesitations and vocal stalls. However, immediately after admitting that public servants do not have a good reputation overall, he launches into a full-throated defense based on his experience after arriving at PARD:

KOJO: But when I came in, I thought it was wrong because I saw that those who work, work, and those who don't, you can, you can make yourself invisible here. But people who work, give full duty to their work. And it's true because when you come in the evening, that is when you realize, even around nine, ten [at night], people are still in their offices, especially those, the heads, working. During the day they go to a lot of meetings so they have to sit down and work. So people who work, work.

As he describes his own personal experience, notice that Kojo does not completely refute the general public stereotype as false. Rather, he builds in a categorical distinction between those who conform to that negative public stereotype—who make themselves invisible and do little—and a different type of people: "people who work." He then reflects on an example that directly contradicts the public stereotype, one drawn from his observations of his superiors: that the heads of the department stay in their offices working until nine or ten at night. By contrast, this intensive symbolic boundary marking was not present in control cases.[13] In control cases public servants were more likely to talk of themselves as "part of the system." When participants in the control cases acknowledged the negative public reputations of public servants, they did not assert a distinction but rather appealed to the many (and legitimate) structural constraints that made it difficult to be more effective.

Francis, a manager at NCA, articulates a similar categorical distinction, noting that when it came time to assign work, his superior would selectively assign tasks, "Because maybe he wants it to be done in a certain way, he wants it to meet a certain time. So, those would sit back, those who were working would work. You understand." Francis notes that the distinction is not merely interpersonal, but maps onto different working groups or ministries, "I will just say that because like here, you come anytime and find people still at their desks. But other ministries, some places you go 12:30 is lunch. I mean, forget it. Even if you meet a person they tell you 'it's my lunchtime' but my division was not like that."

The contrast between prevailing stereotypes and interstitial practices can sometimes present difficult or delicate challenges for interstitial insiders. Thanks to the relatively small size of niches and the relatively high interpersonal interaction among members, newcomers to the niche learn to navigate those delicate social challenges by observing and emulating established members:

KOJO: People think that, "Ah, they go to work, they go to work very late and close very early. They don't have anything to do. If you want them to do something for them, you have to give them a present or something before they'll do something for you." So it's like a whole lot of stuff, and because, you know that, people think they [civil servants] are corrupt.

But, once I came in here because even when, if we have something doing for people, they give us, we don't take it. Especially my boss. He doesn't even like, because sometimes it's like, even after doing the work for them, people think they'll maybe need you again. So they'll want to give you maybe a dash [small monetary gift] or present.

But Mr. [Mensah] would tell you no. He's okay. What he enjoys doing is doing his work. He enjoys accomplishing his work, and as long as he's finished that, he's going, he's achieved his aim, and that's it. So, it's like, when you come into the system, especially at Ministry of Finance and experience it different from how people see it.

Kojo articulates a significant struggle that members of the niche face in navigating their interstitial position: Outside the interstice gift-giving is culturally acceptable, and refusal could cause offense, but within the interstitial organizational culture people do not accept gifts for services rendered. Avoiding the situation is not as simple as not seeking a bribe, because outsiders who are unfamiliar with the niche's reputation approach the interaction expecting to give a bribe. Niche members may not seek a "present," but the outsiders actively offer one, creating a delicate social situation that interstitial insiders have to navigate.

Notice that declining a bribe is a learned behavior. This is a point too often overlooked: Anticorruption campaigns operate on the belief that refusing a bribe depends only on rationally convincing civil servants they should not want it, and thereby overlook the critical importance of learning how to decline a bribe. Many of the characteristic interstitial practices are not directly in conflict with expectations outside the niche, but some are. When niche practices clash with external practices and expectations, niche members learn through observation how to navigate those potentially uneasy social interactions, and newcomers are particularly oriented towards learning by emulating the observed practices of high-ranking experienced members. Kojo's experience and reflections are characteristic of the young members of PARD.

The expectations of unfamiliar outsiders may set up a situation in which the practices within the niche are in direct conflict with the practices outside of it. However, interactions with outsiders are not always, or only, deleterious for cultivating the distinctive niche practices. Novice outsiders may pose challenges, but perennial outsiders who have frequent, recurrent interactions with the niche can actually reinforce the niche's distinctive practices. Perennial outsiders who interact frequently develop a sense of the niche's distinctive reputation, which cultivates a set of different expectations frequent outsiders then impose on future interactions with niche insiders. This mechanism is evident in the reflections of Bright, another relatively young member of

PARD who, unlike Kojo, is an official civil servant not merely doing national service. His reflections closely parallel Kojo's:

> BRIGHT: I think the thing is our director and [Akosua], you know, they, they work really hard and you know they go to a lot of places so. And if I'm associated with them, it's, you know, people kind of tend to expect you work as hard or you, you, you produce as much. So that you know, because you're working with these people and they are really good at what they do.

Here Bright also articulates a form of learning by emulating superiors, focused on diligence and work ethic. Notice that Bright's explanation suggests another mechanism through which newer members of the niche come to identify with distinctive interstitial characteristics, like unusual work ethics: as *ascribed* characteristics. That is, when niche insiders like Mr. Mensah and Akosua interact frequently with the same outsiders, those outsiders build an understanding of the distinguishing characteristics that typify the niche (in this example, working hard). Outsiders ascribe those characteristics to the niche. Younger members are aware that those ascriptive typifications create expectations that apply to them. Thus, perennial outsiders reinforce the niche's distinctive practices by reinforcing the ascriptive identity associated with the niche—essentially, perennial outsiders formulate a schema for interacting with the niche that structures their assumptions and practices when engaging niche insiders, and the presumptions structuring those interactions can then have feedback effects affirming distinctive characteristics, especially for newer niche members.

Staff at the Commercial Courts likewise articulate how ascriptive typifications held by outsiders shape their behavior. When I ask Aku, a staff member, about the reputation of a judicial servant in the Commercial Courts, she replies without hesitation, "They think we are not corrupt." Solomon, another court staff member eagerly agrees, "Yeah." When I ask if there is anything else, Aku adds, "And maybe we are efficient." Beatrice, a court reporter, explains how those expectations held by outsiders shape their interactions, putting pressure on staff to conform to the ascriptive typifications outsiders hold of them:

> BEATRICE: For instance, they come to a motion, for an order to be typed. They don't even wait for the next day because they really need the order to be typed, maybe some injunction or something ... [trails off] they don't come the next day. So, you have to do it for them and make sure—it should be ready within the day for them.
>
> AUTHOR: And the way that lawyers are acting with you—like, "I really want it today," is that also how they would interact with you in other high courts?

BEATRICE: No, the thing is, they heard Commercial Courts established to speedy up and things, and it is fully automated. So, since they know it is fully automated, we have all the facilities here needed. And they put pressure on you.

Commercial law attorneys are a set of perennial outsiders who interact frequently with the Commercial Court judges and staff. They, and their business clients, are a significant external coalition with an interest in swift administration of justice.[14] Note that this positive feedback loop through the ascriptive identity assumptions of perennial outsiders is enabled by the clustered distinctiveness of the interstitial niche. If only a few bureaucratically inclined individuals were scattered throughout the service, it would be difficult for outsiders to learn to identify the set of distinctive characteristics that deviated from business as usual in the larger environment, and more difficult still to know when they should be applied. Outsiders would instead tend to apply their conventional schema of interaction grounded in their neopatrimonial habitus. Clustering distinctiveness makes the shared traits more legible to outsiders, which facilitates the development of alternative schema and templates for interaction among perennial outsiders. Simultaneously, clustered distinctiveness enables perennial outsiders to readily understand when that alternative template for interaction should apply.

Boundary Marking

TIME AS A (LEARNED) SYMBOLIC BOUNDARY

Emulation contributes to a convergence of practice, but also to the perception of similarity among members of the niche, highlighting awareness of the characteristics and practices niche insiders have in common. Boundary marking increases awareness of the dimensions on which the niche differs from the larger environment, simultaneously socially constructing categorical distinction and specifying its content. Symbolic boundaries are distinctions people use to differentiate and categorize, which can include attitudes, practices, manners, "habits of thought," preferences, tastes, as well as "temporal, spatial, and visual cognitive" distinctions.[15] By attributing particular qualities to insiders and juxtaposing them with outsiders, symbolic boundaries become the tools with which people impose order on the social world and understand themselves in relation to others, not as an individual but as a member within a system of groups, each with particular characteristics.[16] Emulation and symbolic boundary marking in concert thereby contribute to members' perception that the working group is an entity—a social abstraction to which characteristics may be attributed, and which is more than the mere sum of its individual members.[17]

Recall to mind the vignette from the opening of the book where Mr. Mensah—director of PARD—leaned on the balcony late at night, and quietly named the occupant of each other office alight despite the late hour before pronouncing "as for them, they are like us." For nearly all of the interstitial insiders, time was the most significant symbolic boundary that demarcated the difference between "us" and "them," between interstitial insiders and outsiders. All four of the Ghanaian interstitial niches expressed a near-universal emphasis on forms of time urgency, like "punctuality" and "timeliness," as well as time stewardship, including "work ethic" and "productivity." These sentiments echoed from the lowest-paid clerk at the Commercial Courts to the director of the National Communications Authority. As Bright explains:

> BRIGHT: I personally think that PARD is set apart from other divisions while I'm not saying that just because I'm in the division. Because most of the time, in you are within the ministry, PARD's staff would be some of the first to come to work and some of the last to leave. And you know, our director is, he's always talking about punctuality and you know and hard work and that kind of stuff.

Bright, a relative newcomer on temporary appointment, describes how his evolving attention to time is grounded in emulation, learning about practices that define belonging to the niche through observation—PARD staff are "some of the first to come to work"—as well as explicit instruction from established members—"our director, he's is always talking about punctuality." Notice also however, that his observation of defining characteristics of insiders is inextricably intertwined with observation of the social distance to outsiders, imbued with greater significance as simultaneously defining the content of what "we" have in common as an axis of difference from others.

Often people take their cultural beliefs about time for granted, like water to a fish. Unless those time expectations are violated, we rarely consider them consciously, instead naturalizing our own time culture as axiomatically good, right, and universal. However, as many international travelers know, the practices and orientations towards time vary vastly cross-culturally, both between and within nations. Levine, a prominent social psychologist of time, astutely observes "time talks, with an accent." Some cultures or groups of people display greater or lesser time urgency, which includes concern with clock time, but also speed in eating, speaking, walking, driving, as well as other practices that support time orientation, including scheduling, making lists, and feeling anxious about waiting.[18]

For Americans accustomed to greater time urgency, it can be mind boggling to travel to places like Ghana or Brazil, where the pace of life is slower, tasks may be put off until the next day whenever possible, and events are not beholden to clock time but rather "events begin and end when, by mutual consensus, participants 'feel' the time is right."[19] Levine recounts his amazement at observing students wander unabashedly into class more than an hour late for a two-hour class. Whereas white middle-class Americans may consider it quite rude to show up late for a party, in Mexico it is quite rude to show up for a party precisely at its stated start time, an embarrassment that might occasion teasing from others and scorn from hosts, who would be still setting up. By mutual unspoken agreement, guests are instead expected to arrive fifteen to fifty minutes after the stated time.[20] Precise synchronous coordination is challenging in such time cultures, and not even the foolhardy expect that all parties will show up for a 1:00 p.m. appointment at 1:00 p.m.

Explicitly considering broad cross-cultural differences in time culture can thereby highlight how astonishing, distinctive, and boundary-defining time culture is for Ghanaian interstitial bureaucratic niches. After receiving clearance to study PARD from the highest levels of the Ministry of Finance and Economic Planning, I came to the ministry to meet with the director of PARD, and to explain my program of research to him. When I next returned, I received a detailed interview schedule in which almost every person from PARD had volunteered for a precise one-hour interview window—an act of scheduling that was itself a noteworthy indicator of time urgency. But more remarkable still: everyone who had signed up reported for their interview time slot precisely on time or five minutes early. For those who have not lived or travelled outside the United States and Western Europe, perhaps that example sounds like unremarkable business as usual in any large formal organization. However, the example likely stands out to people with extensive experience living and working in various African countries. I cannot emphasize how rare such organized coherent timeliness is within a Ghanaian context where jokes about being "on African time" allow people several hours' casual leeway on any appointment time. These Ghanaian civil servants exhibited a kind of clockwork timeliness more stereotypically associated with German engineers.

Interstitial insiders were exquisitely aware of a distinctive orientation to time as a defining feature of what made them different from outsiders. The vast majority of the members of these four organizational units evoked aspects of time when asked to explain what advice they might give a newcomer to their group, or in response to questions about what made their group distinctive. Respondents referenced aspects of time orientation to sharpen categorical distinctions between themselves and civil servants generally. Insiders articulated a social boundary between "us" and "them" grounded in concern for being "on time" (routine punctuality and long-term deadlines), for economizing time (productivity), and for being good stewards of time (work ethic). Kofi invokes time stewardship in his characterization of civil servant stereotypes: "People think that civil servants are a group of people who just come to work, sit around, wait till it's 5:00, or even at 3:00, take their bags, go home, come to work, sit around, do some work … If you sit by the wayside, you see people by 3:00 who take their bags and go home. You'd see people who come to work as late as 10:00 a.m." Patience similarly notes, "Over here [gesturing to a different part of the ministries buildings], I've seen people have extra things outside work that they do, other businesses elsewhere. They don't mind. They just come in, hang around for a while, and then leave."

My interviewees did not object to this characterization of the civil service generally; rather, they objected to being painted with the same brush. Kofi echoes this sentiment later in the interview, re-enacting a typical conversation with a friend who is surprised by the late hours he works, "So, you call somebody and 'oh, are you still in the office? You're civil service, what are you still doing in the office at this time?' So, they think that there's nothing that should keep you in the office after 5:00. But there's a lot that would keep you in the office till daybreak." Kojo explains that work can be particularly intense when they are preparing the budgets to go to Parliament, "People go home as late as maybe as something 3:00 a.m. Serious. And people don't even sleep because they are working toward something, they have a deadline … And when you are lazy you can't be in our division."

TIME CULTURE AS LEARNED

The particular time culture that characterizes the interstice is learned, both implicitly through observation and emulation, and explicitly through instruction. Senior members of PARD, for example, describe explicitly introducing some of the newer junior officers to the time-oriented work culture. One respondent explains that some newcomers to the division initially have problems with "work time." When I ask for clarification, he continues:

> GIDEON: Not that they don't work hard, it's the time they come to work.
> AUTHOR: They don't come to work on time?
> GIDEON: Maybe 8:30 or 9:00. And they will say that it's too far away from here. I would tell them well [pause] leave sort of early to get here.

To time-urgent Americans, leaving early may seem obvious. But it is important to be aware of the ways in which the social structure in an environment may enable—or constrain—time orientation. Until the proliferation of technologies capable of telling time to the minute, social manners around promptness could not exist. In some places, private timepieces are still rare, and public clocks are both rare and inaccurate. Work is largely informal, and so even traffic patterns are less predictable. Few people have private vehicles, so most Ghanaian civil servants are at the mercy of tro-tros. Tro-tros do not leave the station on a set clock schedule, but rather only depart whenever they are full to capacity. One could arrive at the transport park the same time as yesterday, only to discover that today a full tro-tro just departed. Depending on the popularity of the route, one might wait an hour for another to fill and depart. Those structural challenges may stymie the punctuality of even time-urgent Americans living in Ghana.

It is therefore widely accepted in most Ghanaian settings that even if punctuality were desirable, arriving on time is largely beyond the individual's control. By emphasizing that new recruits should take care to leave early in order to assure they will arrive on time, Gideon is therefore somewhat radical, both suggesting that punctuality is important and that it is an achievable personal responsibility of each interstitial insider.

Gideon connects his advice to a logic that is already familiar and sensible, even to people who have not yet acclimated to the interstitial subculture: cultivating a good reputation with the group leaders. Gideon explains, "You know, there are senior officers around who are watching you. Okay, so if you come to work late, it looks bad. People are watching you ... So I tell them, it's better for you to come to work early." Similarly, PARD's director Mr. Mensah explains that he regularly visits all the offices that house PARD staff. "In fact, every day I go to some office. We have just about four offices. We have just about four offices, so it's not difficult at *all* [chuckles] ... to get there." He visits at different times throughout the day, but notes: "For instance, sometimes you see people don't come to work early ... Any time that I come very early I deliberately go there to see who are there. And then I start telling them that I've, that you people—all of them—don't come to work early."

Timeliness is also reinforced in the NCA. Collins makes clear the work that established niche insiders do to continually affirm that different standards are expected within the niche so that people do not slip back into other habitual time dispositions. Collins explains that there is a sheet for signing in and out at NCA (such sheets are a common practice across most government ministries and agencies). However, unlike many other locations, at NCA someone—Collins—looks at those logs regularly and follows up. Like Mr. Mensah, he begins with informal social discipline: "We give people verbal warning, and then we talk to them. So, we take it serious. And if people are leaving before 5:00, we also talk to people. But mostly after they have been spoken to, they don't commit such offense, again." Like Gideon above, Collins too is familiar with the many structural explanations for lateness. When I ask if he gets pressure or push back from people when he enforces the time standards Collins responds, "Yeah, yeah [giggles]. When you speak to them, they give such excuses. My child was sick, I had to rush the child to the hospital, the traffic was very heavy, ahhhh I had to go somewhere else." But even in cases where good planning could be frustrated by conditions beyond anyone's control, he asserts personal responsibility for at least calling to alert your supervisor. Collins observes that most people "tend to reform" if they have been spoken to even once, something he attributes to the small size of the organization, which facilitates named interpersonal interaction—a feature that later in the chapter we will observe again about the Commercial Court staff:

> COLLINS: If, let's say, lateness is persistent, then we will give you a query. But most people when you speak to them on one occasion, they tend to reform. Probably because we are a small organization [laughs]. But big organizations encounter such problems.
>
> AUTHOR: So, what do you mean "probably because we're a small organization"? How does that help them reform?
>
> COLLINS: Because they know we are watching them. We are observing them, when they come in and when they come out. So, I know that [the person in] my next office is late today. I could ask why. But if it's a big organizations, people—ehh [voice trails off] the loss of identity.
>
> AUTHOR: But if you, yourself, were not checking the logs and speaking to people who were late or leaving early, what would happen?
>
> COLLINS: Then it would become the norm for people to be late.
>
> AUTHOR: So, you are sort of the thing standing between timeliness and not timeliness. So, what happens if we get another person in your position who doesn't care?
>
> COLLINS: Then people will take the time they come in for granted. Once they know that we are observant and we are taking note of that, they come.

I am struck by the unhesitant, matter-of-fact statement that if Collins were not checking the logs "then it would become the norm for people to be late." Collins' admission of the crucial *personal* role played in consistently underscoring the importance of time is a stark reminder that the mere presence of the social technology of sign-in sheets is insufficient to cultivate a social practice of timeliness. A sign-in sheet alone may be enough in a different social environment, where time consciousness was a more widespread part of the prevailing habitus and people were accustomed to following rules because rules-following itself was both a virtue and a habit. Conversely, in the prevailing Ghanaian habitus the workers were *capable* of orienting to time, but many did so primarily when it was reinforced through face-to-face interpersonal connection. Ultimately then, dense interpersonal interactions within these relatively small-scale niches facilitated emulation of, and explicit instruction by, established senior members, which helped cultivate distinctive practices of time orientation, from a distinctive concern with being "on time" to the stewardship of time implied by discussions of being "hard working" or "efficient."

DISTINCTIVE TECHNOLOGIES AS BOUNDARY MARKING

Several of the Ghanaian cases involve particular innovative technologies, to which observers partly attribute the distinctive successes of the group. For example, upon their establishment, the Commercial Courts insisted on alternative dispute resolution (ADR) prior to trial, in which the litigants meet for mediation before courtroom hearings. ADR is a legal practice that has diffused globally; it was not innovated within the Ghanaian Commercial Courts. However, the Commercial Courts were the first to adopt the practice within Ghana—meaning that they took a risk implementing a practice that was unfamiliar to local clients. Indeed, the justices uniformly note that initially, lawyers and their clients resisted ADR because it was unfamiliar and in a legal context in which justices still wear the formal powdered wigs of the English legal system, mediation felt less "official."

The justices adopted ADR because they saw it as a key tool to achieve their organizational mandate—expediently resolving cases. Justices imposed mandatory ADR even over objections of their key constituents: commercial lawyers and their clients. ADR was therefore a doubly risky gambit because it might not work as intended and it risked riling powerful outsiders. Early on clients tolerated the ADR—which they disliked—in order to access the expedient judicial expertise available at the Commercial Courts. Initially, to counteract skepticism about the officialness of ADR, the presiding justices themselves acted as the ADR mediator between litigants. Justices report that most users eventually came to favor ADR after experiencing it and discovering firsthand that mediation could arrive at satisfactory outcomes with full legal weight even faster than through courtroom hearings. Justice Kwarteng looks at the statistics the court has produced on time to completion of business, noting that "the average time of the completion for the mediation, cases of mediation, is three months. And then the average time for cases that go to trial is six months." Six months is incredibly fast, especially by African standards, but ADR leads to case resolution at an unheard-of speed. The justices' goal-oriented risky gambit paid off. It enabled them to satisfy their organizational mandate, and they were able to convert skeptical outsiders. The practice became so popular, with a strong external coalition in support, that a National ADR directorate was established, and nearly 300 mediators were trained, with the goal of expanding the program to all courts nationwide, an expansion addressed more fully in the penultimate chapter.[21]

The Bank of Ghana has the most technologically elaborate monitoring system I observed in any of the central state agencies. The difference in the formality of the bank is palpable from the moment you set foot into the building, where everyone must pass through revolving tubes that admit one person at a time, and only move when an employee swipes a badge. This distinctive technology simultaneously underscores the seriousness of the bank's task and is a formal mechanism to monitor and encourage timeliness. Daniel explained that the bank introduced formal "time management" training in 1993. Nii, another Monetary Policy Analysis member, explains the system, whereby they must "badge" in by swiping their bank identification card through a series of electronic readers to get from the front atrium to their office, "We just log in, and that's it. But somewhere, somewhere somebody knows at what time you entered the bank. Somebody somewhere knows at what time you checked out of the bank. And it's an indicator of time management in the bank."

Public-sector employees are generally more risk averse; therefore they tend to prefer the status quo over a risky gambit.[22] Any new and untested organizational innovation or technology represents a gamble with unknown odds, and uncertain payoff. In a challenging environment like Ghana, if a civil servant keeps doing what has always been done, and keeps getting lackluster results, there are myriad plausible external constraints to blame. However, if a civil servant does something novel and fails, he calls down focused blame upon himself. Therefore, introducing locally novel practices and organizational technologies is a distinctive boundary-marking act in and of itself. Above and beyond any technical benefits derived from the novel technology or practice, instituting novel practices that are oriented to achieving the organization's mandate underscores and affirms the boundary between the interstice and the larger neopatrimonial environment.

PRUNING POOR PERFORMERS: A BOUNDARY MARKER WITH DUAL BENEFITS

Defining the body of members who comprise the interstices includes not only who joins through recruitment, but also who is made to exit. The concentration of rare proto-bureaucratic socio-organizational orientations is further defended by pruning niche insiders who fail to conform to the distinctive comportment of the niche. Like instituting novel organizational practices or technologies, pruning poor performers within the niche simultaneously has direct technical benefits for improving performance, but also important indirect benefits of brightening the symbolic boundaries that demarcate the niche as a distinctive place within which different practices and expectations prevail. Pruning poor performers is another way that interstitial niches differentiate themselves from business as usual in the larger environment.

Within the prevailing administrative state culture, even disciplining a public servant for being late, leaving early, or failing to complete work was relatively rare. Contrasting to the lackadaisical attitude in other courts, one Commercial Court staff member explains, "I think that authorities here, too, are a bit strict." When asked to elaborate, the staffer points out ways that leaders exercise their authority to discipline staff and hold them accountable, "You don't have to leave before the closing time. When you are late [arriving] too, at times, you'll be called. As a warning." But in the other courts, things are different. With warmth and laughter in her voice, she explains "As the judge there is not around, the staff too may go home. But here you have to wait for the normal time."

Legal provisions and cultural norms make it exceedingly difficult to terminate a civil servant. Reassignment within the civil service does not violate the extensive legal labor protections, but is remarkably rare, violating dominant administrative norms. Such an action therefore draws particular attention and awareness from others in the organization. Staff within the Commercial Courts were widely aware of a case of someone who had been transferred outside of the Commercial Courts for failing to conform to the courts' expectations for timeliness and work conduct. Similarly, younger members of PARD were aware that someone had been transferred out of the ministry for failing to meet the niche's standards for timeliness, productivity, and work quality, something they took as a sign of how "serious" work was at PARD. PARD's director Mr. Mensah explains:

MR. MENSAH: I had an economics officer here. Ummm, and I, I, something happened, I said I will not be able to work with the person, and the person got transferred, outside the ministry.

AUTHOR: Really? I didn't know economics officers were transferred out.

MR. MENSAH: I didn't, I didn't say that the person should be transferred outside the ministry. But I said I will not be able to work with the person here, in the division.

AUTHOR: How much leverage do you have if someone is not working out, to have them transferred? At what level does it have to reach before you have to have someone transferred out of the unit or you'll carry them along as dead weight?

MR. MENSAH: That is, umm, it is a very difficult decision to make. Ummm. There are a few situations where I have had to talk about it. I have talked to the officers involved that I, I don't see their contribution to the division. And I know some of them have not been very happy. But, ummm, there are one or two of them that have improved, since. One of them, one of them, as I said, one of them, that was an extreme case, that was an extreme case and umm, I had to tell management that I can't work with that person again.

I probe in response to Mr. Mensah's characterization that it was an extreme case, asking whether by that he meant a case of fraud. He clarifies that it wasn't fraud; rather "I didn't see the person's contribution to the, to the division. So I decided I would not be able to work with that person." Taken together, his description conveys an environment that expects to have to teach newcomers to get accustomed to different ways of being and acting, that reinforces those expectations through informal interpersonal exchanges and increasingly formal organizational mechanisms. But when people repeatedly fail to conform to expectations and do not respond when sanctioned, the leadership of the niche is willing to take what by conventional Ghanaian standards are extreme measures: having someone formally and officially transferred out of the unit.

Transferring a poor performer may seem unremarkable to those with private-sector experience in the West, where job insecurity is typical. But Ghanaian participants underscored the rarity of transferring a civil servant for poor performance. Interstitial insiders animatedly recalled this transfer as an "event," a cautionary tale in the collective imagination, particularly for new members. Interviewees retelling the event underscored it as a marker that the department was distinctive and "serious." Commercial Court support staffers were similarly impressed by their own similar cautionary tale about a problematic staffer being transferred for failure to conform to expectations for punctuality and performance.

In other words, transferring poor-performing members is itself a distinctive organizational technology that is explicitly oriented to achieving the organization's goals and contradistinct to the prevailing neopatrimonial practices of the broader environment. Neopatrimonialism is foremost about maintaining social relationships, cultivating a network of individuals with whom you have reciprocal ties of social obligation. The logic of neopatrimonialism emphasizes reciprocal loyalty, rather than considerations of productivity or efficiency. Only in an environment where one cares more about accomplishing the organizational mandate than about interpersonal loyalty would it be sensible to upset expectations by firing or transferring someone who is unproductive.

The further concentration of proto-bureaucratic orientation within the niche occurs by changing the composition of the membership—for example, eliminating an insider who does not display the expected comportment (a selection effect)—and by thickening, concentrating, and organizing the proto-bureaucratic schema of remaining members (an influence effect). Pruning thereby improves productivity directly through selection, but also influences remaining members by further distinguishing niches from business as usual in the surrounding milieu, where punishment for poor productivity was unthinkable. As the comparison cases later in the book will show, high-profile dismissals for underperformance or corruption are a common feature of distinctively high-performing niches.

Cultivating Members When Selection Effects Are Low

Some of the support staff at the Commercial Courts provide an illustrative example of how an interstice can habituate even reluctant members—that is, those who may not have personally selected into the environment, and whose starting practices and orientations are somewhat farther from those of the niche. But even for such members, routine participation within the interstice increases awareness of what practices are legitimate among insiders, and the symbolic boundaries that differentiate them from other groups.

As the second chapter described, many of the Commercial Court support staff were selected for, but they themselves did not select into the new courts. Influential people staffing the new courts sought out reputational information on the staff, but unlike most other interstitial insiders, many of the support staff who were already within the judicial system did not intentionally seek employment at the newly forming Commercial Courts. Nor were they highly professionalized lawyers handpicked by the chief justice, like the justices themselves. Solomon and Aku previously worked within the Judicial Services before coming to the Commercial Courts. I ask Aku how she came to the Commercial Courts. Aku explains, "I was just given a letter to come." Solomon confirms, "Because we were in the system already so we were just given the letter to transfer."

The support staff were selected because they demonstrated more proto-bureaucratic tendencies than other staff who were *not* chosen for the Commercial Courts. Yet they demonstrated less proto-bureaucratic orientation than the justices or most professional officials in the other interstitial niches, evident even in the way they discuss work below. The support staff are therefore a telling case of how the interstitial niche can cultivate even reluctant insiders. The niche cultivated the comportment of these staff through (1) experienced ascriptive expectations from perennial outsiders, (2) a built environment that limited distraction and enhanced supervision, (3) people in powerful positions both modeled proto-bureaucratic orientations and disciplined others for failure to follow suit, and (4) an organization of work that enhanced small-group interpersonal supervision, social modeling, and reduced possibilities for shirking.

Staff repeatedly emphasize the *work itself* places demands on them. For example, Beatrice explains:

BEATRICE: That is, here if you leave early, the next day the work will be waiting for you. And if you come the next day, it piles up. So, since you don't want the workload to be piled on you, I think you have to stay and do—finish the day's work. If you are not able to finish and maybe it is left with a little, you come the next day early and then you continue before the court starts.

Although staff focus their expression on the work itself, there are indications that the motivation is grounded in social obligations to other team members, though they have some trouble expressing this, suggesting it is a largely tacit foundation. I ask how they adjust if one member of the team is away, whether it will slow down the others:

> AKU: No [long pause]. If he's not there, you will have to do it anyway. So, it's like the work will be too much on her. No, it will not be like she cannot do that—it will maybe keep her from doing it her own work.

When I then ask how they feel if they have to be away from the others, Solomon quickly replies, "I feel bad." I ask Solomon whether he would feel badly because the absence or inconvenience would be openly discussed, "So, even if she doesn't say anything to you at all?" All three of them quickly and emphatically respond "yes." Here again is an instance in which an orientation widely available in the typical Ghanaian habitus—a profound sense of reciprocal obligation to people with social interdependencies—intersects with this particular organization of work to bend that habitus toward proto-bureaucratic tendencies.

For reluctant insiders who enter the niche with relatively less proto-bureaucratic orientations, there is some indication that monitoring—which principal-agent theorists consider so crucial—does play a role in their comportment. But principal-agency theory often advocates for arm's length monitoring, where perhaps even a single principal is able to monitor a large volume of agents through, for example, technology. That sort of distant and technologically mediated monitoring, however, can backfire by creating an environment where agents attempt to game the system. Conversely, in the articulation of these Ghanaian civil servants, notice that the issue is not merely monitoring itself. Rather, the staff reflect an internalized sense of the possibility of being monitored not merely in the abstract but by particular named individuals in a close-knit social group of both peers and superiors, coupled with lived experiences and interactions that enhance the perception that those observing you have different standards and greater willingness to enforce those standards.

The physical building—which was specially constructed for the Commercial Courts—was often mentioned as something that made the Commercial Courts different from other High Courts. Staffers explain that in the other courts, for example, someone in their position would have to exit the court building and walk to another building to take a record to the typist. That built environment creates many legitimate reasons for a staffer not to be present at her desk, which makes it harder for a judge or supervisor to monitor. Once someone is out of the building on the pretense of transferring a file, there is little to keep her from just going home, and even if her long absence were noted, there are plenty of plausible excuses.

By contrast, the costs and opportunities for being away from duty without cause were much more limited in the Commercial Courts, due to the physical construction the building and the different social organization of work, whereby each justice had staff specially assigned to him or her rather than relying on the centralized pool. Each justice had a team composed of one of each "type" of support staff—typist, clerk, and so on—who were physically located within that courtroom. Staff were thereby physically and socially close with the justices—and the justices themselves had strong proto-bureaucratic tendencies, which included a willingness to discipline for failure to conform to the judge's expectations (something relatively rare in the broader environment). In explaining why they thought work in the Commercial Courts was different than in the other High Courts, Aku observed:

AKU: I think that authorities here, too, are a bit strict.
SOLOMON: Strict, yes.
BEATRICE: Yes.
AKU: You don't have to leave before the closing time.
AUTHOR: Okay.
AKU: When you are late too, at times, you'll be called. As a warning.
AUTHOR: But in the other courts, they don't mind? If you come late, no one really ... [trails off as Aku begins speaking]?
AKU: No, not that they don't mind. [Starts, hesitates, smiling sound "herm"] They do, but it's not like here.
SOLOMON: Here we are confined so definitely you can be checked. But ehhh, over there, you see, that is the particular thing. [Heartily laughing and giggling.]
AUTHOR: So, there things are all spread out. So, no one can really check you?
SOLOMON: [Smiling sound in his voice] Yeah. You see? [Giggles] Hehehe.
AKU: Like, Fast Track, for instance, the registrar is here, and the staff are here [hands apart]. So if someone picks her bag and she's going, the registrar will not see her. Maybe unless he decides to come around to check. But here the man, he is sitting up there. When you are going he will see you. If he doesn't see, maybe the administrator will see you. *And we are not many here too, so they know all of us* [emphasis added].

Aku notes it is "not that they don't mind" lateness in the regular high courts. The staff convey an understanding that at the other high courts, there is a formal sense of the ideal but coupled with a tacit permissiveness—a widespread acceptance that the ideal will not be met and is not worth defending.

The staff raise both built environment and threat of social sanction in their discussion. But this barely articulated difference suggests it is also something more. That is, it is not merely the physical built environment, nor merely the threat of sanction, but even for reluctant insiders, the foundation of their behavior change is a barely articulable sense that the acceptable ways of being in the Commercial Court are different, that what is acceptable elsewhere is not acceptable here. The built environment affords few excuses for dereliction, and many opportunities to be observed by others. The team structure means that being derelict will inconvenience their close friends and disappoint the judge. Staff felt that those in leadership positions—who have an oversized role in shaping the practices that others emulate and take cues from—were actually willing to defend their high expectations for staff comportment. Staff know that they will be held accountable for failures and also praised for successes. Aku shyly explains, "Actually, every end of year, [the justice] she calls us in and she congratulates us for having the work to be done successfully. She congratulates us and then say we are improving."

Pride in Comparison

All four Ghanaian cases displayed continual boundary work demarcating the interstitial subculture, within which different practices and logics dominated. Each instance of demarcating a distinction had the effect of brightening symbolic boundaries, making them more visible and legible to insiders—and sometimes to outsiders as well—contributing to the aggregation of a shared understanding about what made niche insiders distinctive. Each dimension of symbolic boundary maintenance had the effect of thickening symbolic boundaries—that is, that the schematic distinctions between "us" and "them" come to have more types of content—which in turn accentuated felt social distance between insiders and outsiders.

However, it was not merely that they felt *different* from outsiders. The source and dimension of their difference invoked positive emotional response. Although always cautious to be tactful in their interactions with outsiders, interstitial insiders felt *proud* because, by comparison, they perceived themselves to be better or more important than outsiders. Talk of pride in comparison reinforced distinctiveness and encouraged positive identification with the niche, affording a positive identity imbued with meaningfulness. This echoes Phillip Selznick's observation that within some organizations, there was a culture around the organizational mission that bound members together and enhanced their pride in and identification with the organization: "Organizations become institutions as they are infused with value, that is, prized not as tools alone but as sources of direct personal gratification and vehicles of group integrity. This infusion produces a distinct identity for the organization."[23]

Niche insiders' fervor for both the content and process of their work is a stark contrast to the conventional views of bureaucracy. Bureaucracy has long been associated with drudgery, alienation, and diminution of ingenuity—the "iron cage" of modernity. Weber, speaking of bureaucratic administrators, opined, "it is still more horrible to think that the world could one day be filled with nothing but those little cogs, little men clinging to little jobs and striving towards bigger ones." [24] But where the bureaucratic ethos is rare, it can be a source of fierce pride. Interstitial niches express pride in their unit, the work they do, and how they do it.

Participants in all four cases spontaneously mentioned explicit pride in their work. Communication engineers at NCA saw themselves as integral to the nation's communication system, bridging policy and practice, and keeping watch for abuses. Justice Hannah Quartey recalled that since she was a little girl, she dreamed of serving her country as a judge. Several Commercial Court support staff likewise said they felt honored to be selected for the new Commercial Courts rather than the regular courts. By contrast, those in comparison groups rarely mentioned pride in their work.

Members of these niches expressed pride in their unit, and in particular, in the importance of the work that they did. Rather than viewing themselves dispiritedly as "cogs," members described PARD as "the engine of the ministry," "the heart tremor," or "the backbone of the ministry." Each of these expressions frame their work as a dynamic force within the ministry, and a core, central aspect of the work performed in the ministry. Two workers, interviewed separately, echo similar sentiments about the vibrancy and centrality of their unit within the work of the ministry:

PATIENCE: For us, I think, more often, they say this ministry, the best place to be is PARD. Because PARD is the heart tremor. That's what I heard. PARD is involved in just about everything that goes on in the ministry. So, for us, people get to go, we always get to go to meetings, we are always involved in a lot of things. We always get to do a lot of training. Okay, we're involved in just about everything.

YAO: When it comes to PARD, policy analysis and research, I think it's a very vibrant place. Well ... you're always working, running around because it's sort of backbone of the ministry. And everything that comes to the ministry has to go through PARD.

The pride that insiders feel is both substantive—they feel they do important work for the country—but also relative. Their sense of self and accomplishment is heightened by stark contrast to the reputation of civil servants generally. The reputation of civil servants generally is not merely different, but a "spoiled" identity.[25]

It is evident that niche insiders are both keenly aware of the negative reputation of civil servants generally, and also discomforted by that reputation. Like Kojo earlier, the staff at the Commercial Court hesitated and struggled to discuss it. After first describing the reputation of a judicial servant at the Commercial Court being "not corrupt" and "efficient," I ask:

> AUTHOR: What is the reputation of a judicial servant in general?
> AKU: [Short nasal laugh with drawn-out end] Hermmmm.
>
> SOLOMON: [Chuckles on the edge of amusement and discomfort] Heh-heh-heh.

Twelve seconds pass from the end of my question before Beatrice ventures a response, and like Kojo her response is full of hesitations, stalls, and pauses.

> BEATRICE: I don't know [short pause]. I don't know but most of the time when you tell somebody you work at the judicial service, the person look at you in a certain. [Inhales loudly through nose. Short pause.] But I cannot say in one word. They look at you [short pause]. Either maybe you have money, I don't know.

It takes several attempts at encouragement before Beatrice clarifies, "[Herm] These days, that is, people think maybe we are corrupt in general." But she clarifies with some exasperation: "When they talk about this thing, then it beats my mind, yes, that somebody would be corrupt." When I ask how the staff might be involved in corruption, Aku explains, "They think maybe you want somebody to type something for you and the person will let her give her something before she types." Beatrice adds, "Before she do the work which she's supposed to do." But quickly Beatrice clarifies, "The commercial court, we don't." Solomon also immediately echoes her position, explaining, "That is why we are special. We don't."

Group pride in comparison to others evokes an explicitly subcultural mechanism, that perceived difference between subculture and mainstream reinforces boundaries, group solidarity, and cohesion. The comparison to the spoiled identity of civil servants generally cultivates a sense, as Solomon describes, that by contradistinction they are *special*. Recall the insiders above who articulated sharp distinctions between their experience within the interstitial niche and the stereotypical reputation of public servants generally. Solomon, who previously worked in the court system, similarly invoked that contrast: "So far commercial court and they seem much efficient. There's no one lazy." Perhaps paradoxically, this implies that these bureaucratic subcultures may feed off the mediocrity of others to fuel their own hyper-performance.

Amplifying Commonalities and Maximizing Distinctiveness: Theoretical Reflections on How the Interstitial Structure Cultivates a Group Style around the Bureaucratic Ethos

This section theorizes how cultivation within niches results in a dominant group style that converges on the bureaucratic ethos, as well as why members strongly identify with and conform their comportment to become more prototypical of that group style. The sociological structural position of the Ghanaian cases cultivates the feeling of a rare and positively distinguished subculture—tightly socially connected to others within but with large perceived differences to those surrounding them. That structural positioning is particularly fruitful for forging commitment to the working group.[26] The strong identification with the working group, and convergence on a particular group style of comportment, is in turn the foundation of the bureaucratic ethos, that distinctive orientation to accomplishing the organization's goals in a timely and routine manner.

Attachment to the group and its mission are established through camaraderie of distinction typical of situations in which a subculture feels itself a numerical minority. Social psychologists interested in identity have long observed that people tend to identify strongly with identity groups that are "optimally distinctive": neither too large nor too small, thereby balancing people's dual desires for inclusion and distinctiveness.[27] The size and structural position of interstitial niches afford optimal distinctiveness. Prior research demonstrates that members of optimally distinctive groups strongly identify with their groups, forming powerful bonds of attachment.[28] This is also coherent with sociological research finding that group identification is particularly intensive for members who perceive their groups to be a numerical minority, whether identifying with a minority racial group,[29] women in the male-dominated French champagne industry,[30] people who take virginity pledges,[31] or small musical fan communities.[32]

Moderate-sized groups with strong identification and frequent interaction —such as interstitial niches—tend to foster a discernible *group style*, or "recurrent patterns of interaction that arise from a group's shared assumptions about what constitutes good or adequate participation in the group setting."[33] Once clustered together, niche members experience a centripetal force, whereby group style tends to amplify commonalities, converging on a shared

set of habits, tastes, practices, and tendencies.[34] Through iterative and repeated interactions, individual members discover shared commonalities,
learn from, and are influenced by, each other. Regular interaction within a
bounded social space reinforces behavior, presentation of self, comportment, judgment, and appropriate or valued practices, which collectively
comprise the group style. Conscious instruction—including status rewards
and sanctions—combines with observation and emulation to continuously
redefine and encourage convergence on a set of practices and styles of comportment that typify the niche. A relatively stable group style thereby emerges
through interaction over time. For Ghanaian civil servants in interstitial niches,
repeated lived experience within the niche comes to comprise a largely un-
conscious group style keyed to the office, a network of associations influencing perception, evaluation, and action.[35] The commonalities among the niche,
which get amplified through repeated social interaction, aggregate into a style
of comportment oriented towards accomplishing the organization's goals
while eschewing neopatrimonial influences.

Beyond what they have in common with each other, the group style of
structurally *interstitial* social groups is simultaneously shaped by what distin-
guishes them from the larger environment. Beyond the within-group centripetal tendencies, numerical minority groups may also feel a sort of magnetic
repulsion that subtly and multiply presses the group's conception of their defining characteristics away from characteristics that typify relevant outgroups
in the local environment. Not all social groups have this oppositional dynamic
as a strong feature of their collective sense of self, in which describing what
(or who) they are *not* is almost as important as describing what they are.
Distinct-yet-embedded, interstitial groups are exquisitely aware of a felt sense
of difference from a particular external comparator group. Theoretically, the
external comparator group may be real persons or a stereotypical abstraction
or a combination of both.

As the data above show, empirically the comparator group for interstitial
niches was the "spoiled" identity of public servants generally, which was a
sort of stereotypical antithesis of the bureaucratic ethos. Niche insiders are
nearly universal in their emphasis: We are *not* like stereotypical civil servants. We are not like them over there. We do not come to work late. We do
not leave early. We do not take long lunches. We are not lazy. The negative
interpretation of the surrounding environment creates a sort of social polar-
ity, which subtly encourages the group to converge not only on that which
they have in common, but also on that which makes them maximally distinct
from the most salient comparison groups. It might thereby be accurate to
say that interstitial niches converge on quasi-bureaucratic comportment simultaneously *despite* the surrounding neopatrimonial environment, *and because of it.*[36]

This identity position influences behavior of existing and new members. Decades of prior lab research demonstrates that people alter their behavior as a result of strongly felt positive identification with an optimally distinctive numerical minority group. Members come to consider themselves typical of the group, and describe themselves using characteristics that are reflective of the group.[37] Group members find it cognitively easier to think of themselves in ways that typify the group, and conversely, more difficult to think of themselves in ways that differ from the group.[38] This affects their behaviors and presentation of self, as members "alter the self to be more consistent with the group prototype ... group members can change their behavior or appearance or adopt the beliefs and attitudes that are typical of the group."[39] Both amplifying commonalities within the group and maximizing distinctiveness to outsiders, niche members alter comportment to become more prototypical of the group, which "involves both a shift toward the in-group prototype and a shift away from the out-group prototype."[40] The intensive identification and coherence are considerably more pronounced within numerical minority groups than those that are numerical majorities.[41] Outsiders also perceive members of numerical minority groups to be more similar to each other.[42] Therefore, as the discussion of ascriptive identity earlier in the chapter demonstrates, interactions with outsiders also reinforce individual convergence on characteristics that typify the group. The tendency to conform behavior to a predominant group style in optimally distinctive groups thereby helps explain how interstices of sufficient size and establishment can assimilate new members, even those who were not fully ideal candidates before joining the niche.

There is one important caveat that may not be obvious: These mechanics do not require that all interstitial insiders have a deep, enduring, and conscious dedication to some core characteristic such as "incorruptibility" when they first join the niche. This occurs not necessarily out of a conscious grand plan that anyone holds for the niche or themselves personally—for example, to "be incorruptible." Indeed, with the possible exception of justices at the Commercial Courts, there is little evidence that interstitial insiders initially consciously sought to join niches *explicitly because* they were actively seeking to work in a corruption-free environment. Rather, I argue interstitial bureaucracy is a case of what scholars have termed "partially deliberate matching," in which there are both selection and influence effects that culminate in the clustering of distinctiveness.[43] When people make decisions about where to work or whom to befriend, they cannot know, let alone actively consider, all the potential conditions that might affect their choice.[44] Instead, people tend to make deliberate choices about a few very important characteristics. Even though we deliberately match on a few high-priority characteristics, we are nevertheless also exposed to a variety of other attitudes, preferences, and practices beyond those we considered, and our future behavior may be strongly influenced by those unanticipated and not-consciously sought aspects, which can include practices of eschewing corruption.[45]

Small Size, Big Work, and the Neurological Effects of Experienced Efficacy

A highly cohesive, strongly identified, numerically small, and close-knit group with a group style centered on the bureaucratic ethos enables the group to accomplish small wins. Niche insiders express a taste for practicing their profession at the highest levels and for doing work they believe consequential. Bureaucratic interstices both cultivate that taste and are one of the few places in the local environment that can satisfy that taste. Interstitial insiders take pride in being actively involved in creating something they have acquired skills and a taste for, deepening attachment to the group and esprit de corps among niche insiders. This section will argue that those collectively enabled small wins are an essential component of their cultivation, habituating niche insiders to persist even in the face of predictable and unpredictable challenges from the larger environment. The relatively moderate scale of niches allows members to directly observe how their actions affect consequential outcomes. Thereby, individuals realize that their day-to-day efforts make a difference in their local environment. Niche members can see the direct connection between their efforts and many small successes accomplished by the niche. This section will argue that experience is incredibly consequential, drawing on decades of laboratory research in cognitive science that finds experiencing the efficacy of one's actions in the face of challenges is powerful enough to actually rewire the brain and confer enduring resiliency when confronting subsequent challenges.

These cognitive and neurological insights can also help make sense of the conventional stereotype of public service in countries like Ghana, where the stereotypical image of "lazy" civil servants who do little is perhaps the result of prolonged exposure to what cognitive science calls learned helplessness. There is little else that saps motivation and effort more than the belief that nothing you can do will make any difference. Indeed, this intuition spawned a huge research tradition in cognitive psychology, starting in the 1960s with laboratory experiments administering shocks to animals in a variety of escapable and inescapable situations. Early work with animals using shocks discovered, almost by accident, that animals who had initial exposures to situations in which nothing the animals did could stop the shocks would then passively endure shocks later—even when the situation had changed and escape should have been easy.[46] This came to be called "learned helplessness."

Later work demonstrated that learned helplessness occurred in humans as well. People who were exposed first to an inescapable loud noise would later fail to act even when put in a situation where their actions *could* help them avoid the noise simply by sliding a knob on a box. The effect applied to people's sense of efficacy in problem-solving, too: People who were first tasked with solving puzzles that were—unbeknownst to them—unsolvable were later incapable of finding a solution when given solvable puzzles.[47] Importantly, subsequent research affirmed that such enduring effects of learned helplessness were "trans-situational," that is, they persisted even when later tasks and environments were different from the setting where helplessness was first experienced.[48]

Critically, initial experience with *efficacy* also had profound and lasting changes to behavior. People or animals who experienced an early trial in which their actions *could* affect the negative outcome were remarkably resilient, even when later placed in negative situations that were (unbeknownst to them) inescapable. Perhaps the most dramatic example of this comes from animal trials with rats. Rats who experienced efficacy first—that is, they could escape electric shocks by pressing a lever—were later exposed to inescapable shocks. Rats who had first learned their own actions mattered would continue to struggle to solve the problem without giving up—*even throughout 200 consecutive exposures to now-inescapable shocks*. Early experience with their own efficacy had, in effect, "immunized" those rats from learned helplessness—or as researchers would later discover, had taught those rats "learned mastery."[49]

This research suggests that lived exposure to even a few small "wins" within the bureaucratic niche may be enough to give its members resiliency to persist in the face of the many environmental challenges they frequently encounter. Lab research suggests that even succeeding about half of the time can be enough to protect people from learned helplessness in the face of failure.[50] Like learned helplessness, learned mastery is also trans-situational: People with learned mastery will go on to approach even very different adverse situations as though they can positively affect the outcomes.[51]

Later technological advances in neuroscience would confirm that both helplessness and mastery experiences can have profound effects on the circuitry of the brain itself. A common neuroscience observation is that "neurons that fire together wire together." When participants simultaneously experienced a stressful situation *and* discovered that their actions mattered, proteins formed a new response circuit in the brain. Effectively, this circuit wired together the part of the brain that experienced stress and the part of the brain that acted as though all problems could be solved.[52] This new brain circuit led the brain to be "biased to initially react to aversive events as if they

[were] controllable, thereby prolonging the duration of active responding."[53] In summary, decades of laboratory psychology experiments and recent neuroscience find that early experiences of efficacy in the face of challenges literally construct new circuits in the brain, resulting in increased resiliency across a wide range of future challenges, which illuminates why it is so important for individuals within interstitial niches to observe that their efforts can lead to successes, however small.

Conclusion: Lived Experience as the Social Foundation of the Bureaucratic Ethos

Too often efforts to reform public sectors involve top-down sweeping campaigns that aim to change familiar behaviors by pure edict alone, or at best by appealing to abstract logic. Instead, this chapter makes a case for the importance of tacit knowledge of *how* to do bureaucracy. There do not need to be particular moments of heroic and conscious commitment to grand ideals for this to happen. Evidence from niche insiders suggests that they converge on bureaucratic comportment in part because they are habituated to it through regular daily practice—as one might gain skill in any type of new practice. Repeated lived experience within the niche socializes and habituates insiders, enabling them to comport in niche-typical ways with less intensive or intentional effort.

Central to its power to enact lasting behavioral change among its membership is the idea that bureaucratic niches afford a rich lived experience of what *to do,* often distinguished from the surrounding organizational environment as a negative model of what not to do. Mental models that are grounded in personal lived experience combine together a rich array of information, allowing people to navigate familiar social situations effortlessly and with little conscious thought. This is particularly true of positive models—that is, those we wish to replicate as a template for future action[54]—and models that are grounded in our own lived experience rather than abstract models diffused from elsewhere. Drawing on a positive model grounded in lived experience gives access to more information with less effort, because so much of the thinking, experimentation, and effort has already been accomplished. If a young father can recall his own positive, warm, involved father as a role model to emulate, it is much more likely that the new father will also become positive, warm, and involved.[55] His own life experiences are *prescriptive*—his schema of fatherhood is richly populated with particular positive practices that he can emulate, whether consciously or unconsciously. And because his understanding is grounded in lived experience, his mental model encompasses the fullness of the relevant experience and context. It is considerably harder for people to figure out what *to* do on the basis of only negative models of what *not* to do. Condemning certain practices in the abstract—like accepting bribes or being lazy—offers only a thin and incomplete template for action, without affording a schema for alternative practices grounded in the same robust foundation of lived experience.

Interstitial group style emerges through repeated interactions both within and outside of the group, a continual process of clarifying that amplifies commonalities, particularly along vectors that maximize distinctiveness from relevant external comparison groups. Here, the initial endowment selects for proto-bureaucratic qualities. Then intense day-to-day interactions within the niche further amplify those proto-bureaucratic commonalities, while felt distinctions from the larger neopatrimonial environment sharpen differences, shaping the group style in ways that maximize distinctions. These experiences aggregate into an increasingly ordered schema as group participation routinely reaffirms a proscriptive and prescriptive bureaucratic logic—oriented to achieving the organizational mandate—contradistinguished from neopatrimonial logics. That which interstitial insiders have in common, and which makes them maximally distinct from outsiders, is the style of comportment oriented towards accomplishing the organization's goals in a timely and effective manner while eschewing neopatrimonial influences. Among other things, experience within the interstitial niche provides crucial firsthand exposure to *how* to be "not corrupt," in which people learn new practices through observation and emulate those practices within a similar context to which they were learned, developing an increasingly ordered and defined schema for bureaucratic comportment.

That lived experience with a body of practice orientated to accomplishing the organization's goals is how interstitial insiders come to be imbued with the bureaucratic *ethos*. Niche members strongly identify with, and feel an ethical commitment to, the office that transcends everyday commitments to kith and kin. They have distinctive ways of doing and being in the office that are oriented toward achieving rational, predictable, effective, and depersonalized administration. Deep reading of Weber's work highlights the centrality of ethos as the core animating force of bureaucracy. The bureaucratic ethos embodied the distinctively modern transformation of social attachments, whereby one's job became an affectively laden identity category, unreflexively commanding commitment. At the heart of bureaucrats' "distinctive and independent comportment" was an orientation to the office as "a focus of ethical commitment and duty, autonomous of and superior to the holder's extra-official ties to kith, kin, class, or conscience."[56] Thus, the distinctive comportment, the group style, that comes to characterize the interstice *is* the bureaucratic ethos: characteristic tendencies to perceive the world, think, decide, act, and appear in ways driven by an orientation to the organization's goals.

4

Protection: Coping with and Remaking Disruptive Environments

When I ask Patience—one of the junior members of PARD—about the biggest challenge he regularly faces in his day-to-day work, he doesn't hesitate. Patience leans forward, his hands animatedly illustrating his frustration: "There's a problem when you are going for data … Maybe they don't recognize the agency involved and they just go about it anyhow, they go like, 'come back later for it.'" He is speaking fast, his voice pitches up, and he flicks his hand and snaps his fingers in a common Ghanaian gesture of incredulity, "And go back and they still don't have it … Because when you have a deadline, I have to present something, I need that data to work with."

Patience needs access to data to which he is officially entitled. Completing his duties depends critically on accessing that data. But the data is produced and held by other ministries and agencies outside of PARD. According to the organizational diagrams and formal rules, the data should simply be routinely transferred to PARD. However, actually obtaining the data instead takes considerable time and ingenuity. The problem of getting outsiders to turn over needed data is so common that PARD and other niches have a term for it: "chasing." Within PARD, almost anyone you ask has an exasperated laugh and a story to share about chasing. Yet what masquerades as insider vernacular also highlights the shared understanding of the kinds of conduct that differentiate "us" from "them," drawing attention to the large and small ways that their position of being distinctive-yet-embedded poses constant challenges to the niche's ability to get their work done. This chapter analyzes how actors within high-functioning niches cope with being embedded in disruptive and often highly unpredictable environments.

The analysis thus far has shown how niches cluster staff whose prior experiences are well-aligned with the organizational goals, and whose knowledge of, and commitment to, bureaucratic comportment has been strengthened by participation within the small-group culture. The Introduction observed metaphorically that operating as a bureaucratic interstice is like trying to play chess where everyone else is playing a different game, you have to whittle the pieces yourself, precious few potential players have ever seen the game before, and the playing area is prone to disruptive bursts of wind. This chapter examines then how those niches grapple with the environmental winds, that is, how these effective niches operate in environments that are tremendously inhospitable to their aims, replete with unintentional disruptions and active interference. Because scholars typically do not think of parts of the state as being so at odds with the surrounding institutional environment, we have not previously given enough attention to the considerable organizational effort that high-performing niches must put into coping with their external environment. This chapter analyzes the organizational strategies that niches employ to mitigate environmental disruptions to their ability to regularly and effectively accomplish their organizational goals.

The environmental challenges, for reasons detailed below, are often beyond the niche's immediate control, and niches cannot exit unfavorable situations by extracting themselves from interdependencies with other state agencies. Therefore, niches respond to the challenges of being inextricably bound to an unfavorable environment through a combination of *internal coping mechanisms* and *external projects of remaking*. Internal coping mechanisms are ways the highly effective niches modify processes and practices within their work group to mitigate vulnerabilities to outside interference. The successful niches respond to their environmental uncertainty by modifying their internal work practices, for example, by building in intentional redundancy —an organizational practice that seems inefficient from the perspective of Western organizational scholars, but which is highly adaptive to the turbulent environment within which these niches operate. Alternatively, niches will sometimes unite their collective effort behind a project to reshape the external social environment. External projects of remaking are enabled because distinctiveness marks the niche as a space of difference, cueing outsiders that different expectations may apply. Clustered niche insiders share the burden of disciplining outsiders and support each other through the sometimes-exhausting work of doing so.

Setting the Stage: Disruptive Environments

The same clustered distinctiveness that fosters insider identification and dedication—even the shared insider humor of jokes about "chasing"—also poses particular challenges. Recall that American companies recruit workers who, thanks to a highly rationalized habitus, have spent their lives accustomed to performing tasks in a timely manner, prizing efficiency, responding to abstract external incentives, and learning to measure and maximize. Most people in such environments rightly assume that, while on the job, new recruits will act primarily to succeed at their assigned tasks, operating under a relatively rationalized habitus that predisposes how they will conduct themselves at work. Moreover, any one person's ability to succeed at their job is facilitated by the fact that the vast array of coworkers, producers, clients, and others with whom workers have to interact to accomplish their jobs share broadly similar dispositions to work. This makes many routine business interactions relatively easy and predictable. Although, of course, dysfunctional organizational environments and unmotivated workers exist to some extent everywhere, the shared rationalized habitus generally facilitates a lot of formal organization in ways that Westerners and scholars typically take for granted. If an American lawyer is scheduled for court, the judge can be fairly sure she will show up. If a subunit within a larger American organization is formally required to routinely provide information to another subunit, people can typically take it for granted that coordination will take place.

By contrast, bureaucratic interstices in Ghana are surrounded by an *adverse* environment. The bureaucratic ethos is relatively less common in the lived habitus of most Ghanaians. This not only makes recruitment a challenging task for interstitial niches: It also means that even after they have managed to identify and recruit those rare people, their daily organizational life is still inextricably entangled with an array of outsiders who operate under widely varying expectations and practices. The environment, far from being helpful, poses instead both predictable disruptions and unforeseen challenges that threaten the niche's ability to routinely, predictably, and effectively accomplish organizational goals.

The larger administrative, cultural, and epidemiological context can raise a host of disruptions that interrupt personnel availability without warning. That such disruptions will occur is anticipated, but when they will strike is unpredictable. Interstitial niches are embedded in the larger administrative system of the Ghanaian state, which poses particular disruptions. For example, "secondment" is a form of requisitioning staff, temporarily transferring a staff member to another unit either within or outside of the ministry, that is fairly common within the Ghanaian state. Such secondment typically facilitates a joint project between ministries, or patches a gap in another ministry's

skill set. Secondment is usually short term, for example, spanning the duration of a modest project, but can be a longer-term arrangement. Often secondment between organizations or ministries will be facilitated by one minister
approaching his counterpart to request staff assistance. Thus, the arrangement is agreed upon and sanctioned by high-status "big men" in the government, which makes any resistance difficult for departments from whom staff
are requisitioned.

One day at PARD I arrived to meet someone only to find him on his way
out the door. This struck me as odd, because punctuality for meetings was a
distinguishing hallmark for PARD. I apologized, suggesting that perhaps I
had misunderstood when he had said he would be available. He replied, 'No,
I thought I would be here today, but the word has just come from the minister. I've been seconded to another ministry, so I'll be away for a bit. But when
the big men tell you to go, what can you do?' Because interstices enjoyed
quiet reputations for efficiency and competence that, *while plentiful within
the niche, was rare elsewhere*, they were frequently targets for secondment
from outsiders who needed to borrow the abilities of the interstice.

Beyond challenges from embeddedness in the state, interstices are also
embedded in larger social and epidemiological systems that can disrupt personnel availability without warning. The Ghanaian epidemiological system
is characterized by a variety of tropical illnesses—including typhoid fever,
yellow fever, and malaria—that can strike suddenly causing prolonged sick
leave, threatening workers' health and productivity. The larger sociocultural
system within which interstitial niches operate likewise presents locally distinctive threats to personnel reliability. Notable examples are the elaborate,
time-consuming, Ghanaian funeral customs. Kinship is an important social
institution in the life of Ghanaians, typically the foremost means of structuring their sense of belonging, and the principal social safety net in hard times.
In Western countries "family" typically refers to nuclear family—your parents
and siblings, or your partner and children. For many Americans, the sense of
mutual belonging and obligation to family drops off sharply between those
core nuclear family relationships and more distant uncles or cousins.

By contrast, in Ghana family or kin embraces a much wider set of extended kin, and maintaining those relationships is much more central to one's
sense of belonging and status in a wider community. Because the obligations
are deeper and encompass a wider range of relations, funerals are frequent
and socially important obligations in the life of Ghanaians.[1] Ritualized events
for reaffirming ties can be especially important for Ghanaians who have mi-
grated to urban centers for formal sector employment. Ghanaians paid a
monetary wage are elite by comparison to rural relatives who may still be
subsistence farmers. As such, civil servants working in the capital city of
Accra not only derive social connection and legitimation from funerals but

may also feel an obligation to display and share their financial success with rural relations.

Upon the death of a kinsman, an official may be called away on little notice for up to several weeks to organize and celebrate funerary rites. These can be particularly time consuming for the death of a close kinsman or a family head (*abusua panyin*). Funeral events are held in the family's village of origin, potentially requiring a bus ride up to twenty-four hours away from the capital where officials work. While doing fieldwork with the frequency monitoring units, one day I noticed an official I had not seen before. After I greeted her, she explained, "I have been out of the office for about a month. I lost my mom so I was out. I just came this week." Even though interstitial niches cluster together and cultivate hard-working and dedicated staff, those staff are still subject to social obligations, sickness, or administrative whims that can cause them to be absent from work without prior warning. These disruptions are predictably unpredictable: Niches can anticipate *that* such personnel disruptions will occur, but cannot plan when, how often, or who will be affected.

How then do niches impose predictability and manage to be productive in such a disruptive environment? Because of these challenges, arising from the interstitial structural position they confront, niches spend greater organizational effort mitigating basic vulnerabilities compared to Western organizations or poor-performing local peers. Niches cope with environmental challenges by modifying internal practices and engaging in longer-term projects remaking their physical and social surrounds.

Internal Responses to Managing Problematic Embeddedness

A great many of the challenges that bureaucratic niches confront in their day-to-day work arise from macro-social factors beyond niches' immediate control. Deep-seeded cultural practices around funerals are a prototypical example of such an external disruption that is large and diffuse. For the most part, niches grapple with these large, diffuse external challenges to their stability by modifying their internal organizational practices to cope with the uncertainty. Niches employ organizational practices that allow them to absorb the uncertainty while mitigating its effect on their ability to regularly and predictably accomplish their work. In contrast to one-size-fits-all global "best practices" so often advocated by cosmopolitan reformers, the specific content of internal organizational responses is perhaps as varied as the diverse local challenges that interstices confront. Yet all the adaptations shared the core characteristic of targeting particular challenging local conditions with solutions that were relatively uncommon in the local environment. As such, those adaptations both directly enhanced the effectiveness of the niche, and simultaneously further underscored its distinctiveness.

CHASING AS CODE SWITCHING

Interstitial insiders are explicitly cognizant of much of the culture work they do to protect the vulnerable position of being embedded in a larger administrative culture that is often subversive to interstitial practices. Niches are particularly vulnerable to upstream outsider interactions, when the niche's work *depends on* inputs received from outsiders. This is particularly acute for PARD and Monetary Policy Analysis whose principal focus is analyzing vast and variable data that are almost all produced outside the niche. Kojo, a PARD member, describes the regular problem of acquiring data from an external source:

> KOJO: I wanted data from GETFund [Ghana Educational Trust Fund].
> I was sending them a fax; I was chasing on it, so I could do some
> end-of-year poverty expenditure calculations. I was chasing them
> on it.
> AUTHOR: So how were you chasing it?
> KOJO: I called them yesterday. Like the person is not in ... I should call
> around this time, called again [pause] and then they were like I
> should call later maybe.

PARD's core mandate is analysis, critically dependent on externally produced data. Kojo repeatedly attempts to acquire data to which he was officially entitled and is exasperated that the dilatory outsider will affect the timely completion of PARD's duties. Similarly recall Patience, whose chasing opened up this chapter. Patience tacitly distinguished between interstitial insiders and outsiders, even seeming affronted because the outsider didn't recognize that PARD worked differently and therefore handled the request with typical sluggish apathy: "They just go about it anyhow."

So tightly coupled are the ideas of getting data from outside the unit and the effortful practice of acquiring it that PARD insiders often employ the term "chasing" to address either issue—effectively equating outside acquisition with effortful acquisition. For example, shortly after Kojo described "chasing" as a series of efforts to pursue the data by calling repeatedly, I ask him to consider his routine, core duties, and estimate how often he finds he needs to rely on information from outside PARD to complete those tasks. Kojo replies, "90 percent I'm chasing."

Internal coping mechanisms can mitigate vulnerability from interorganizational dependencies. When confronted with situations where they have to engage outsiders on whom they depend, interstitial insiders "code switch," altering their practices, language, and presentation of self to fit to the predominant "rules of the game" outside of the niche. For example, when confronted with a lackadaisical outsider holding needed data, PARD insiders like Kojo or Patience will "chase." But what they actually *do* to chase the data shows their dual cultural competency, not only in the distinctive culture within the niche, but also in the predominant culture and modes of interaction outside of it. When chasing, niche insiders switch from interstitial practices to externally valued practices by appealing to interpersonal obligations and social connections. For example, when I ask Kojo what he ultimately does to get the data he needs, Kojo explains that he gets it "By going there personally ... When I go there, the people gather information if you want it very, like, early. Then, if you want it, if you want to do something with that data as soon as possible, then you have to go there so you can quicken the process." Kojo will physically go and sit in the office of the person who possesses the data, waiting for it to be available and revisiting as often as needed. Paperwork or official requests command little attention within the organizational culture of the Ghanaian administrative state more broadly, and certainly not axiomatically. Conversely, even within the broader Ghanaian social environment, neglecting someone who has come to visit would feel terribly rude.

Apart from physically visiting when chasing data, junior officers within PARD also reported relying on interpersonal networks to improve the quality and hasten the speed of work from outsiders. Many younger officials would first reach out through elite educational networks from the university. Kojo and other young officials appealed to friends from the university, trying to find some classmates within the data-generating organization to see if some social contact can intervene on their behalf. If niche insiders cannot find a university contact or if interpersonal appeals fail, young PARD officials appeal to "big man" social capital respected in the larger administrative environment. They did this either by asking PARD's more high-ranking director to intervene, or through strategic framing of their requests to outsiders. In an attempt to get outsiders to prioritize work for PARD, officials would frame their request to emphasize that the work was required by important figures, like the minister of finance. The minister of finance is widely recognized, even among Ghanaians on the street, as a very influential and important person. Monetary Policy Analysis officials likewise would emphasize that the governor of the bank himself was requesting these figures, similarly facilitating access to needed materials not by emphasizing abstract bureaucratic rules officially granting access, but rather relying on the symbolic stature of the governor as a "big man" in the broader social status hierarchy.

Insiders fluidly engage with the larger administrative culture, "code switching" vernaculars, cultural capital, and interaction strategies. Seemingly without conscious intent or reflection, some respondents dropped from the highly erudite English typically used in the office into thickly accented "pidgin" English to replay these exchanges, verbally marking the transition from one ethos into another.[2] Niche insiders were so adept at code switching they even did it with me at times. For example, in Ghana what Americans would call "high school" is typically called "secondary school" because of the British history. Yet when I, with my evident American accent, ask, "Where did you do your secondary school?" Kobena, like several other interstitial insiders, smoothly replies, "I went to Adisadel high school." He pauses a fraction of a second, perhaps realizing that I have framed the question in the conventional Ghanaian terms, then adds, "Yeah we call it secondary school here, but it's high school out there."

Code switching is not unique to Ghanaian interstitial insiders. Indeed, code switching may be characteristic among those who occupy interstitial positions generally, as their structural between-ness results in endlessly oscillating between two worlds with two different and often irreconcilable codes of conduct. Elijah Anderson, for example, famously described code switching among the inner-city black Philadelphia residents he studied, as they altered their speech, behavior, and presentation of self to navigate the social world. Anderson discusses code switching using the vernacular that people in the community employ to distinguish between what they call "decent" and "street" ways of comporting oneself:

> The same family is likely to have members who are strongly oriented toward decency and civility, whereas other members are oriented toward the street—and to all that it implies. There is also a great deal of "code switching": a person may behave according to either set of rules, depending on the situation. Decent people, especially young people, often put a premium on the ability to code-switch. They share many of the middle-class values of the wider white society but know that the open display of such values carries little weight on the street.[3]

Like the Ghanaian interstitial bureaucrats, Anderson's "decent" youth find themselves constantly switching between two distinct ways of presenting themselves depending on the demands of the situation, sometimes hiding their interstitial comportment and instead using language, dress, body style, and interactions that convey their fluency in the modes of cultural interaction common to, and valued in, the larger surrounding environment.

People accustomed to organizational life in Western countries may feel an impulse to view chasing as a "problem," evidence of inefficiency that should somehow be fixed. It is true that interstitial insiders find chasing a frustrating, though common, experience. It is also true that many of the insiders would be glad to have to do less chasing. But as decades of failed organizational reform efforts have demonstrated, intentionally re-engineering organizational culture to cause large shifts in the daily practices of masses of civil servants is almost never successful. The conditions that create the need for chasing are unlikely to change any time soon. So instead of asking how *should* these organizations be functioning in a more ideal world, I argue it is much more fruitful to learn from how these successful niches actually *are* functioning well despite the challenging environment. Instead of a "problem" or an "inefficiency" that requires fixing, chasing is an organizational practice that is extremely adaptive to the immutable conditions of the local environment.

COMPENSATORY COMPETENCE: INSOURCING AND DOING FOR OTHERS

It is not uncommon to encounter officials elsewhere within the state who are unhelpful, not from a lack of desire, but because they are not equipped with the skills needed to perform the task. I encountered this myself while trying to track down comprehensive listings of all civil servants since Independence. The national archives contained public records of all civil servants for the earliest years, but nothing contemporary. I visited the Office of the Head of Civil Service to see if perhaps they had their own organizational archives that might contain the more-recent files. I found a very helpful official, who responded to my question by saying that he had a list of everyone who was now a civil servant, which was 'kept in the excel.' Heartened, I responded, 'Oh! Is it in a file in Microsoft Excel® on the computer?' He responded in the affirmative, but then looked embarrassed as he noted that although it was his job to maintain this file, he had never been trained in the program and had no idea how to use it. I ultimately spent two hours that afternoon showing the official everything I knew about operating Excel and answering any questions he had to the best of my ability. It is worth noting that he was an eager and quick student.

Interstices routinely encounter challenges acquiring needed information, files, paperwork, data, and other resources from outside units because those units are unable or unmotivated. Beyond chasing, interstitial insiders would instead sometimes offer unofficial voluntary assistance on outside work to ensure it was done promptly and well, particularly when a skills-gap seemed to be impeding progress. Yao recounts seeking data PARD needed, and not unexpectedly, access was not progressing as he hoped. He therefore used his analytic and computer skills to help the outside unit manage their data though this was not part of PARD's duties. Yao recalls, "They conducted a survey on, it was on health workers, okay? And I helped them with some of the compilation of some of the data. And I had to print something out to help them and pull up some data at the censuses secretariat."

Sometimes this compensatory competence takes the form of voluntary assistance to others, such that the niche still relies on the outputs of some external organization, but niche insiders effectively help the external units complete their formal organizational tasks in order to facilitate PARD's access to those needed outputs. Other times units may reduce external dependencies by creating a parallel system within their own organization to produce the output or perform the service in-house. Because the officials of PARD and Monetary Policy Analysis have highly flexible and fungible skills in data analysis and management, their human capital translates well into intermittently doing for outsiders when the outsiders either cannot or will not do for themselves. By contrast, when confronting similar uncertainty about the quality and timeliness of an external service on whom they depended, the courts are less able to intermittently and flexibly do for others. Instead, the Commercial Courts routinized compensatory competence by substituting that external dependency for an analogous in-house service— what is sometimes called "insourcing."[4]

In many ways, compared to PARD or the Monetary Policy Analysis Department, the courts are in an organizationally stronger position: Courts are in a position of power over the litigants and lawyers who come before them, and have the formal ability to discipline those actors. Recall that the most frequent contact with outsiders are "upstream" dependencies for PARD or Monetary Policy Analysis. By contrast, the Commercial Courts' most frequent outsiders were "downstream," dependent on the rulings the court produces. Yet there are still dependencies that all courts face, because the administration of justice is exquisitely tied up in the creation and processing of paperwork documenting each step of the proceedings. Moving, storing, and retrieving court papers are not skills that justices themselves can readily or efficiently do for others. Failures in the external systems that move, store, and retrieve court papers can be catastrophic for the administration of justice within courtrooms. For example, courts in the country of Niger were consistently bogged down by their dependency on an ineffective postal service to deliver summonses, such that some cases before the court were decades old, having been rescheduled repeatedly when the mail did not reach the recipients.[5]

Outside of the Ghana Commercial Courts, the other Accra high courts at the time relied on a cabinet pool of support staff that served all the justices, including secretaries, court reporters who transcribed the spoken content of the courtroom into text, and scopists who edited those court proceedings into legal format. Justice Kwarteng notes, "One of the features that differentiates this court from the other ones is that all of the, all of the judges have their own secretary and that it's sort of a tight-knit pool, the use of scopists." The Commercial Court justices made a decision to replicate the services normally performed by the shared cabinet pool within the Commercial Court itself, because they realized early on that reliance on the external cabinet pool was likely to substantially impede their efforts at swift administration of justice. Justice Kwarteng explains, invoking that familiar interstitial problem of chasing: "We realized that it was going to ensure efficiency as compared to a system where there is a cabinet pool serving all judges and the scopist would have to go and chase their records, their documents from the cabinet pool."

Ultimately, the way the Commercial Court insourced the production and management of court documents differed in form from the "doing for others" that PARD utilized, but both are means of managing embeddedness in their larger environment by substituting reliable competence within the niche for the less predictable competence and expediency found outside of it.

ADAPTIVE REDUNDANCY INSTEAD OF DISCRETE JURISDICTIONS

Recall that the local Ghanaian environment posed threats to personnel stability that were difficult to anticipate, whether the death of a kinsman or unexpected secondment to another ministry. The niches were somewhat small in size to begin with, and their ability to be effective was highly dependent on relatively rare people who had been further cultivated through lived experience. There was no crowd of competent alternatives waiting to step in if someone was called away. As such, personnel disruption was not merely a *frequent* problem posed by their embeddedness in the larger environment, it also had a *high impact* on niches' ability to continue their work unimpeded. Perhaps because of the frequency and centrality of this challenge, all of the niches employed a practice that is uncommon, bordering on nonsensical, from a conventional Western organizational perspective: Niches employed adaptive redundancy.

Redundancy has a self-evidently negative association in Western organizational wisdom. Western organizational scholars do not call something "redundant" to praise it. Zero redundancy would seem to be the hallmark of efficiency for which all eager managers should aim, yielding a lean, streamlined organization. Based on established bureaucracy, scholars have long asserted specialization and discrete jurisdictions in the division of labor promote orderly and efficient conduct. In this conventional view, each official covers her—and only her—jurisdiction. Workers are not substitutable. Thus, in an effort to conform to the appearance of states globally, states like Ghana seek to create discrete jurisdictions both at the organizational level of ministerial portfolios, but also at the individual level of workers.

This seemingly über-bureaucratic characteristic of discrete jurisdictions characterizes the Budget Division of the Ministry of Finance. However, it proved problematic rather than efficient. In the Budget Division, each worker was assigned to a "desk" corresponding to a portfolio of other government units whose budget and spending they oversee. Yet the seemingly rational efficiency of discrete jurisdiction makes it considerably more difficult to reliably and predictably complete work, especially when confronted with the disruptions inherent in the larger environment. When a budget official is away from his desk due to illness or funeral preparations, no one else in the office knows enough about the current state of his portfolio to seamlessly step in. If a representative from another ministry comes in need of assistance from the missing budget officer, the supplicant may linger by the empty desk unaware until informed by an office mate that the budget officer had been out of the office for some time. Although other budget officers may be hospitable— hospitality is a source of national pride in Ghana[6]—there is little assistance anyone else can give. Budget colleagues may sympathize with the supplicant's frustration; however, they typically cannot say exactly when the absent officer will return, nor manage the budgetary disbursement in his absence.

Redundancy seems anathema to effectiveness in conventional Western organizational wisdom, yet redundancy is highly adaptive to the local context in Ghana. Adaptive redundancy was present in all four cases of interstitial bureaucracy in Ghana but lacking in control cases like the Budget Division. Redundancy here means work was actively managed so that each individual or subunit paired with another who was nearly identical in skills and project knowledge, thereby able to substitute immediately in case of an absence.[7] An external observer might view this overlap as fundamentally *unbureaucratic*. It defies the taken-for-granted wisdom of organizations, such that you will not find that strategy recommended by organizational textbooks or management consultants.[8] But this is bureaucracy at its finest: a strategic, routinized response to context, oriented to that core, defining feature of bureaucracy—the routine satisfaction of organizational goals. Paradoxically, redundancy enables that essence of Weberian bureaucracy, that "methodical provision is made for the regular and continuous fulfillment of these duties,"[9] within interstices entangled in the predominant neopatrimonial power structure.

INDIVIDUAL REDUNDANCY

Interstices responded to these conditions of personnel insecurity by cultivating intensive jurisdictional redundancy. In PARD and the Monetary Policy Analysis Department redundancy existed at the level of individual workers: Each official partnered with others who replicated both the skill sets and the up-to-date project knowledge required to complete the work. They had regular meetings to keep informed on all aspects of the partner's work to stay abreast of project knowledge so that either could at a moment's notice pick up their partner's work if needed. In the Monetary Policy Analysis Department, this redundancy was a taken-for-granted aspect of the daily work routine. Patrick's response was typical:

> PATRICK: The way things are organized here in this unit, I can do about two different guys' duties. So, they, it's been structured in such a way that if I'm not there, someone can easily just jump in my shoes. And if

he is not there, I can easily just jump ... so I could just go in there and work on procedure as normally as possible.

The redundancy Patrick from Monetary Policy Analysis articulates is remarkably similar to the solution that PARD developed. PARD's director explains that they have intentionally set up their work plan to ensure that as many people as possible are informed on all the projects, better assuring that "nobody will be indispensable" to the completion of the work:

MR. MENSAH: We've done our work plan and the work schedule in such a way that we have someone who is a lead person in a unit. Then we have one or two other people who also work within the same unit.

AUTHOR: Is everyone mutually exclusive, like, if you're in the tax unit you're not in also one of the other units?

MR. MENSAH: That is the opposite. That is, that is what I mean by if we get one who is a lead unit in one unit and then you have about two, three other people. Then the lead person in this unit will be second-in-command in another unit. So then somebody will then be the lead person in that other unit with about three or four other people. And, we have tried to set it up in that way so that ummm, nobody will be indispensable ... everybody should know what is happening in all the units.

The intentional, adaptive redundancy of the Monetary Policy Analysis Department and PARD includes similar skill sets and also project knowledge. Pairs or teams meet regularly to keep each other abreast of specific developments as work progresses so that others possess not only the intellectual ability but also the project knowledge to "just jump" and hit the ground running. I quickly became sensitized to how important and also taken for granted such adaptive redundancy was among all the interstitial niches. For example, like Patrick, Patience describes what would happen if he were unable to report for work at PARD:

PATIENCE: I have other colleagues, so if I'm not there, they just have to fill in for me, so they'll do extra work.

AUTHOR: So there are others who know how to do every element of your job somehow?

PATIENCE: Just about, yeah. If, maybe there's about ten. Maybe about— actively involved about six [people]. Then there's another person who's also actively involved in all the six [areas] I do as well.

Esther describes a similar system at the Commercial Courts for the registry staff she oversees. After discussing challenges, I ask how they cope if someone is unexpectedly away. She replies:

ESTHER: We cope by—those in the registry have been trained in such a way that at least each person does two or more things. So, he has two or more schedules. So if one person is, has to stay away for some reason, the others will chip in and help. So everybody does something else apart from the normal schedule he or she has.

UNIT REDUNDANCY

The Commercial Courts and Spectrum & Frequency Management also employed intentional redundancy; however, they employed redundancy at the level of working units rather than individuals. For example, beyond the staff redundancy described by Esther, the Commercial Courts were composed of six courtrooms, each with its own justice and dedicated courtroom staff. Each courtroom subunit had near-perfect replication of skill sets with the others. The regular high courts are also composed of multiple courtrooms; what distinguished the Commercial Courts from conventional High Courts was the additional redundancy of case-specific knowledge. Commercial Court Justices met regularly to keep each other abreast of the progress made on specific cases, including both progress in mediations and courtroom proceedings. Similarly, Spectrum & Frequency Management at the National Communications Authority was organized according to functionally analogous units, each with the same set of capabilities, each capable of substituting for each other.

REDUNDANT ENGINEERING FOR HIGH
RELIABILITY AMID UNCERTAINTY

Although redundancy is practically a four-letter word in Western organizational scholarship and practice, redundancy enjoys a considerably different reputation among engineers. If you are an airplane passenger and something goes wrong with the rudder system midflight, you will be glad that the engineers designed the plane with multiple redundant systems capable of compensating for each other if one goes awry.[10] Indeed, intentionally redundant systems are prized by engineers when stakes are high and the system must function well in highly uncertain or adverse environments. For example, space shuttle parts must function well in the varying weather conditions around the launch site, and also in the extreme environment of space. The failure of a single part can have catastrophic consequences, which is why engineers typically design redundant systems capable of compensating if a critical part fails.[11] Redundancy limits the extent to which the failure of an individual component can affect the entire system. That is, redundant systems may not be efficient—in the sense of maximal benefit for minimal cost—but they are considerably more *reliable* and *flexible* in the face of unanticipated or highly variant conditions.[12] In other words, engineers prize mechanical redundancy under analogous conditions of uncertainty and high variability that characterize the *institutional* environment in Ghana.

Some scholarship on organizations has also appreciated that there are conditions under which redundancy is effective for organizations.[13] However, these works have been mostly marginalized within organizational studies against the mainstream of efficiency. Thirty years ago, W. Richard Scott, a famous organizational sociologist, observed that the increasing trend attempting to rationalize organizational systems by eliminating duplication failed to appreciate the benefits, noting that "redundancy and overlap [are] a repository of needed variety and heightened responsiveness," which then "safeguards against system component failure."[14] Critically, development scholarship and practice continue to be dominated by mainstream organizational scholarship, often reflecting the latest fads from Western corporations. Organizational scholarship on the benefits of redundancy has not influenced development scholarship and practice, even though high uncertainty and variability are widely recognized characteristics of the institutional environments many organizational reforms target.

Demarcated Distinctiveness Makes Possible External Projects of Reshaping

Interstices may also engage in longer-term projects to reshape their environment. The interstitial structural position of clustered distinctiveness enables challenging long-term projects to reshape their environment, particularly compared to when scarce proto-bureaucratic resources are scattered throughout the state like so many isolated eccentrics. Lawyers may forgo the effort of learning new practices to satisfy one isolated judge, unable to anticipate the judge operates according to unconventional practices, and uncertain of the next time that lone judge will preside over their case. In such a system, the proto-bureaucratic demands of an individual judge appear merely idiosyncratic and eccentric whims. By contrast, when clustered together, signals of distinctiveness demarcating the niche cue outsiders when alternative schema apply. Such cues can be behavioral or physical. Physically, the Commercial Courts' building was visually distinctive from the rest of the High Courts and stood literally apart. But the building alone would not be enough to cue lawyers that alternative schemas of practice apply within. That visual distinctiveness was underscored by concerted efforts by all the Commercial Court justices to enforce similarly high standards for lawyers' preparation and courtroom conduct. The demarcated distinctiveness makes it easier for lawyers to anticipate when alternative practices will apply. Clustering distinctiveness also affords economies of concentration, providing lawyers greater opportunities to learn and greater incentives to adopt different practices when in the Commercial Courts, such as punctuality and preparedness. A commercial lawyer cannot readily ignore concerted signals from all commercial law specialty courtrooms, which he can anticipate he will revisit regularly in the future.

Discipline means not merely negatively sanctioning, but discipline in the sense of teaching: training others into practices beneficial for the successful functioning of the interstitial niche. Disciplining interstitial outsiders were efforts to make niches' environments more predictable—a hallmark of bureaucratic administration. In many ways, the most important and also the most challenging projects of remaking are not efforts to remake the physical environment, but rather niches' efforts to remake their *social* environment. Interstitial insiders occupying positions accorded power in the larger system —Commercial Courts justices' legal authority or Spectrum and Frequency Management officers' regulatory authority—have more direct means of disciplining the environment than do groups like PARD and the Monetary Policy Analysis Department. The Commercial Courts and Spectrum and Frequency Management both enjoy official formal sanctioning power. They are also relatively advantaged by how their workflow intersects with interstitial outsiders: The National Communications Authority and Commercial Courts primarily interact with "downstream" outsiders who consume the niche's work outputs. For example, the National Communications Authority controls licensing and regulation of audible spectrum use rights, necessary for radio and cellular companies. Spectrum and Frequency Management themselves barely need to interact directly with outsiders at all. They utilize mobile technical equipment to collect their own data, limiting upstream dependencies. If the Spectrum and Frequency Management mobile monitoring units detect violations, they can pass the information along to others within the National Communications Authority who issue warnings, impose fines, and, for severe repeated transgressions, threaten licenses.

The relative position of power enables more ambitious social disciplining, especially in the face of resistance. To revisit an earlier example, upon founding, the Commercial Courts justices began a coordinated effort to remake their social environment by coercing all litigants who came before the Commercial Courts to go through mandatory "alternative dispute resolution" (ADR), where two parties meet for mediation before courtroom hearings. As I argued, the justices saw this as a tool central to their organizational mandate of expediently resolving a large number of cases. However, the practice was very unfamiliar within Ghana when first introduced and also contravened deeply held cultural expectations about proper and legitimate court practice, which centered on conspicuous formality. Justices reported that lawyers and clients initially resisted ADR because it was unfamiliar and ADR mediation felt less "official" even when the mediation was conducted by the presiding justice. However, the Commercial Courts quickly earned a reputation among lawyers and the business community for expedient, professional trials and expertise in commercial law. Justices leveraged this beneficial reputation to impose ADR over client objections. Justices reported that most users came to favor ADR after experiencing it. The statistics from the Judicial Service's *Annual Reports* document the success of ADR and other Commercial Courts organizational innovations: even in their first year, Commercial Courts handled a larger caseload with shorter time to resolution than comparable High Courts.[15]

Disciplining is not merely a single large battle to impose an unfamiliar formal legal practice like ADR. Disciplining is also dozens of everyday skirmishes in which justices disciplined daily practices affecting the niche's goals. While observing public court proceedings, I witnessed Commercial Court judges embarrass lawyers who arrived late, came with incomplete or incorrect paperwork, or who were not properly attired in black robes and white curled wigs per courtroom protocol. In response to one ill-prepared lawyer, Justice Hannah Quartey pointed her gavel at him and emphasized gravely, 'It won't happen again, yes?' If informal verbal discipline proved insufficient, justices could formally sanction lawyers. By contrast, in the comparison regular High Court, lawyers arrived late, unprepared, or dressed inappropriately, without sanction.

Niche distinctiveness cues outsiders that alternative schemas apply. Critically, clustering means that niche insiders share the burden of disciplining outsiders and support each other through the sometimes exhausting work of doing so. The frustration and futility of lone effort is illustrated by Justice Damoah in the control case, who was considered for the Commercial Courts but ultimately practiced in the regular High Courts.[16] Justice Damoah espoused identical desires for efficient, effective, and impartial judicial practice and yet was routinely frustrated in his efforts. While observing his courtroom, I watched Justice Damoah attempt to cajole late lawyers into coming on time next time. But his efforts were met with little more than sheepish smiles shared among the various lawyers present. After closing a long, hot day on the bench, Justice Damoah lamented how tiring it was to tell lawyers things that they should already know, while feeling sure in his heart that it likely was not going to make any difference. It is not merely that the sea of environmental threats overwhelms, for interstitial niches face the same waves. Clustered distinctiveness signals and incentivizes outsiders, while simultaneously distributing the burden of disciplining among insiders. A clustered, critical mass of distinctive members with strong internal identification can thereby engage processes of external change that would otherwise overwhelm individual efforts.

REVERSE COOPTATION

Another longer-term tactic managing interorganizational dependencies hints at one possible mechanism for diffusing the practices of interstitial bureaucracy outside of originating niches. Selznick's classic organizational study describes cooptation as "the process of absorbing new elements into the leadership or policy determining structure of an organization as a means of averting threats to its stability or existence,"[17] wherein organizations respond to threats by incorporating outsiders into their own leadership structure. By contrast, I observed interstices employ "reverse cooptation," sending niche insiders out into positions of leadership in outsider units positioned to disrupt the interstice.

We might think of compensatory competence as an ephemeral form of reverse cooptation, but reverse cooptation can be more significant and durable. PARD routinely depended on data from the ministry's Budget Division. Therefore, lack of expediency or quality in the Budget Division threatened PARD's productivity. Eventually, the ministry's leadership partitioned the Budget Division. Zakaria, a highly regarded and core member of PARD, was transferred to head one of the Budget units along with several junior PARD members. Although the *content* of budget work was different, I observed that the work *style* in the Budget unit staffed with former PARD members more closely resembled PARD than that of the other Budget unit. Furthermore, PARD and the reverse-coopted Budget unit remained connected through long-standing interpersonal relationships. The PARD director describes how Zakaria remained connected to PARD:

> MR. MENSAH: In fact [Zakaria] had been in the Policy Analysis Division all this time until about, about three or four months ago. *We* still consider him as a member of PARD in the diaspora [chuckles] because umm, he even seems to be reporting to me still because I had to convince him to leave Policy Analysis and go because we thought that will help us because he understands the issues. It will help us to coordinate better with the Budget Division.

Zakaria was not the only case of reverse cooptation. As I was conducting fieldwork, another high-ranking and experienced member of PARD with advanced international degrees was transferred into an influential position elsewhere within the ministry. Mr. Mensah explains "[Isaac] will be moving to [another division], because we think [that division] is a weak link. It's a weak link in the ministry." Mr. Mensah continues by reflecting on the operational costs and benefits of external cooptation, "So if he goes there, it will mean I'm losing my staff. But I've told the chief director that if they want us to train people to service the other divisions, so be it, I don't have any problem with it. But it would serve a good link, between [that division] and Policy Analysis

Division. So maybe it will make our work less strenuous if he goes." These examples of reverse cooptation suggest bureaucratic interstices potentially serve as sites within which individuals gain lived exposure to the benefits of Weberian-style bureaucracy, thereby augmenting the corps of bureaucratically experienced and oriented individuals, that scarcest of all bureaucratic resources.

Conclusion

It is intuitive to think that states lacking abundant resources should particularly prize efficiency—that is, squeezing the maximal benefit from every possible resource. From such a view, redundancy seems particularly abhorrent. That conclusion makes less sense if we view states as a fundamentally *human* system—with all of humans' social, psychological, and cognitive complexities. Even if efficiency were to be prized above all else, the efficiency of complex human systems should be measured not as an abstracted rational ideal that *could* be achieved if its workers were automatons, but rather as the optimal *actual* outcome that can be achieved taking into account the very humanness of the components. Effectiveness may be at odds with efficiency: Confronting an unwieldy environment prone to disruptions, the humans within seemingly "efficient" lean systems routinely fail, and have no excess capacity to compensate. Over time, we may then understand how people in such a situation could become demotivated and indeed, habituated to failure.

This chapter has drawn attention to how much organizational energy interstitial niches expend protecting themselves from environmental disruptions. Niches evidence creative and distinctively interstitial solutions to the perceived problems of their environment, coping through internal modifications that bend and blend conventional Ghanaian habitus with the distinctive culture within the niche, arriving at solutions that work well in the local environment but that might never occur to a cosmopolitan organizational consultant, such as chasing, code switching, and compensatory competence. In some cases, clustered distinctiveness also enabled niche members to attempt more ambitious external projects to remake their physical and social environment, for example Commercial Court justices disciplining commercial lawyers to conform to their particular expectations.

Considering the breadth of how niches protect themselves suggests that niches often go to great lengths to avoid standing out too much, or getting into explicit conflicts with outsiders. Recall from the book's introduction the account of PARD's director standing on the balcony, quietly pointing out the other offices with lights still burning bright well into the night. It was a profoundly quiet recognition. There was no active club of the members of various interstices. Interstitial insiders did not claim their accomplishments loudly and proudly for all to hear. Why? Calling attention to themselves risks raising the ire of other civil servants, who might then make the niche's work more difficult.

Scholars of work and organizations have long observed that workers socially control the "right" amount of work output one should produce; groups will sanction, mock, scorn, and abuse not only those who produce too little, but particularly those who *produce too much*.[18] This phenomenon of other workers resenting and disciplining high performers was well documented among early industrial assembly line workers who were paid by piece rates, and such high performers were therefore known as rate breakers.[19] The social stigma could be particularly painful and consequential. A star performer, earning more money than ever before and facing potential promotion to management, can nevertheless decide to quit the company because his fellow workers treat him with hostility and rejection, resulting in intolerable anxiety.[20] Even where workers are not paid by piece rates, decades of scholarship on labor indicate that workers will socially sanction high performers out of the sense that they are raising standards and, by comparison, are making the rest of the workers look worse.

I argue a similar tacit concern with being identified as rate breakers underscores how most interstitial niches typically approached the disruptive larger environment. In most instances, Ghanaian niches sought to minimize disruptions but did so in ways that minimized attention from the outside environment. The interstitial position is, perhaps by definition, precarious. This may be particularly true when the scale of the interstice is suborganizational, such as PARD within the Ministry of Finance and Economic Planning, rather than coterminous with formal organizational boundaries, such as the organization-wide reputation of the Bank of Ghana. The need for discrete, concealed, organizational excellence in the face of structural precarity may shed light on why the patchworked structure of states has received relatively little attention: By necessity, bureaucratic niches may not leave very externally legible traces of their rate breaking organizational success.

5

Introducing Comparison Cases: Patchwork Leviathans in Comparative and Historical Perspective

The rich data from Ghana have brought to life the inner workings of state-craft, analyzing how some public administrative organizations perform well in environments that are generally characterized by ineffectiveness. Better understanding *how* these organizations work is a critical task in and of itself for legions of scholars, development practitioners, and citizens hoping to understand how to make states more effective. More than 100 years of organizational research and theory make the argument that *how* organizations work is a substantial component of the explanation for *why* some organizations perform better than others. However, meso-level organizational insights have been absent in most work on non-Western states, which has instead tended to privilege macro-political factors. The detailed look inside the Ghanaian state has illuminated how doing the work of the state is accomplished, including otherwise hidden mechanics of how these niches work on a day-to-day basis to achieve what has seemed to be an otherwise intractable problem: cultivating the bureaucratic ethos and enabling relatively high levels of administrative capacity. The preceding chapters developed a framework for understanding how interstitial mechanics enable clustering, cultivating, and protecting distinctiveness centered on the bureaucratic ethos. One might wonder if the patchworking structure of the Ghanaian state—and those underlying interstitial mechanics—are unique to Ghana. To address that question, this chapter will introduce four comparison cases drawn from around the globe and across the last 100 years. Across a great range of heterogeneity in those cases, the chapter argues they were all patchwork leviathans, within which bureaucratic niches existed, flourishing through fundamentally similar underlying mechanics.

Examining this broader set of international comparative and historical cases helps identify the probable scope conditions for the book's analytic framework, suggesting that interstitial bureaucracy better captures the nature of statecraft where: (1) neopatrimonialism is the predominant means of organizing political power, engendering widespread assumptions that official positions will be used to enrich oneself and one's networks; (2) the bureaucratic ethos, including other forms of social disciplining upon which it may be built, is not routinely available in the social habitus; (3) but within which exist proto-bureaucratic human, cognitive, and material resources that are intermediate in their intensity, organization, and distribution. Such contexts of incomplete institutional dominance, wherein proto-bureaucratic elements are neither too high nor too low are conducive to the emergence of bureaucratic interstices.

Those theoretical scope conditions are surprisingly common. The midrange of incomplete institutional dominance particularly characterizes many contemporary formerly colonized, low-income states, which underwent decades of external coercion that incompletely transferred Western institutions, thereby weakening traditional institutions without fully supplanting them. Like Ghana, state administration in countries as diverse as Bolivia, Malawi, and Indonesia are characterized by a few distinctively excellent agencies amid many other ineffectual or corrupt ones.[1] Within those midrange contexts, as with Ghana, a few state agencies or departments are distinctively high-functioning, known for competent, impersonal administration in the public interest despite operating in adverse environments in which neopatrimonialism, patronage, and generally weak administration predominate. This chapter examines clustered distinctiveness and niches of bureaucratic strength within patchwork leviathans beyond Ghana, identifying broadly similar mechanics that underlie pockets of effectiveness despite different time periods, national contexts, functional tasks, and organizational scales, which cumulatively suggest that the framework helps explain bureaucratic niches beyond Ghana. The remainder of the book will utilize those comparisons in dialogue with the Ghanaian cases to further develop understanding of interstitial bureaucracy by examining variations that emerge as responses to different structures.

This chapter introduces the new comparative and historical cases, starting with a broad comparative overview and then giving each case narrative integrity so that readers can have a foundational sense of how the dynamics of that

TABLE 5.1. Overview of Comparative and Historical Cases

Agency	Location	Time period	Sector
National Agency for Food and Drug Administration and Control (NAFDAC)	Nigeria	Early 21st C	Pharmaceutical and food safety
Kenya Tea Development Authority (KTDA)	Kenya	Mid 20th C	Agricultural production & marketing
Brazilian National Bank of Economic Development (BNDE)	Brazil	Mid 20th C	Banking
Sino-Foreign Salt Inspectorate	China	Early 20th C	Tax administration

case are both similar and varied from those of other cases. In contemporary Nigeria, amid turbulent politics rife with corruption—and while facing targeted vandalism, arson, and kidnapping attacks—the National Agency for Food and Drug Administration and Control (NAFDAC) halved the rate of counterfeit drugs in circulation, emerging as the agency with by far the strongest public reputation for effectiveness. In mid-twentieth-century Kenya, amid the infamous ethnicized neopatrimonialism of the Independence era— and despite dire proclamations by the World Bank that the project was doomed to failure—the Kenya Tea Development Authority (KTDA) increased the quantity of production fifty-fold and improved quality to command above world-market prices. In mid-twentieth century Brazil, while the state generally was a haphazard administrative quagmire held together by institutionalized patronage, the Brazilian National Bank of Economic Development (BNDE) emerged as a pocket of effectiveness—not merely more effective and efficient than private banks within the Brazilian economy, but would go on to have a higher return on assets and income-per-employee than any other development bank globally, including the World Bank.

The first section of this chapter will demonstrate that the same interstitial organizational dynamics identified in the Ghanaian cases also help explain the uncommonly successful state agencies in neopatrimonial contexts situated throughout history and around the globe. Across considerable variation in time period, geography, and state function, these unexpectedly effective organizations possess similar *interstitial* mechanics: sufficient *operational discretion* to control personnel and rewards, enabling *clustering* of otherwise rare proto-bureaucratic resources to produce a subculture of bureaucracy that is *distinctive* from the surrounding institutional milieu. That distinctiveness promotes within-group identification and esprit de corps that further organizes and intensifies a group style oriented to the bureaucratic ethos among group members. Distinctiveness from the environment also necessitates organizational responses to *protect* the organization from environmental vulnerabilities, including internal coping mechanisms and more ambitious projects to reshape the external environment.

The comparison niches placed great emphasis on securing internal control over personnel recruitment, a foundational mechanism for clustering distinctive persons. When recruiting, niches sought both job-relevant substantive skills (traditional meritocracy) and difficult-to-discern proto-bureaucratic socio-organizational dispositions. Unfortunately, these elements—like "incorruptibility" and hard work—are relatively rare in the larger labor pool, and difficult to evaluate except by personal knowledge or observation. As chapter 2 observed, these conditions create high search costs. This may explain why prior knowledge of candidates is a comparatively common feature of recruitment within bureaucratic interstices, as it was in the Ghanaian cases, which used poaching, observing, or seeking deep reputational histories when selecting candidates.

Comparison cases likewise support the importance of niche-side active selection, utilizing firsthand observation or securing reputational information on difficult-to-discern organizational orientations. NAFDAC's reformist director, Dora Akunyili, handpicked her management team and balanced technical merit and "proven integrity and commitment to the NAFDAC mission."[2] Recruitment into KTDA balanced "an element of personal loyalty mixed in with a preponderance of objective merit."[3] Ironically, as chapter 2 argued, the seemingly nonbureaucratic practice of recruiting among known associates may be an essential aspect of interstitial bureaucracy, because direct observation or interpersonal knowledge may be the most effective way to manage search costs and discern rare and difficult-to-measure characteristics. At arm's length, it might be hard to tell organizationally oriented recruitment of known associates from more conventional patronage practices.

As in the Ghanaian cases, the comparative cases affirm that concentrating distinctiveness and cultivation is further enhanced by pruning niche insiders who fail to conform to the distinctive comportment of the niche. Pruning improved productivity by directly eliminating unproductive insiders, but also further distinguished niches from business as usual in the surrounding milieu, where punishment for poor productivity was rare. Both Karanja at KTDA and Akunyili at NAFDAC had particularly high-profile dismissals that drew attention for going against prevailing neopatrimonial rules by firing their own relatives. The Salt Inspectorate too had a reputation for dismissing corrupt officials without allowing them to save face. The total number of those purged in any of the observed cases is surprisingly small.[4] This suggests that a considerable portion of the total effect of staff purges comes not from the direct effect of culling unproductive or corrupt staff—that is, its selection effect—but rather through significant influence effects on the remaining staff. In a classically Goffmanian fashion, cultivation and pruning are socio-organizational techniques to redefine the situation,[5] which encourage both increased productivity and commitment to the niche.

Like the Ghanaian cases, the comparative cases worked hard to modify internal organizational responses and reshape the external environment to protect themselves from challenges and disruptions, whether bribe seeking and pilfering by local political elites for the Chinese Salt Inspectorate or President Vargas politically pressuring BNDE in staffing and loan decisions. Those challenges arose because niches were interstitially embedded in a larger environment with markedly different institutional "rules of the game" that could disrupt the routine functioning of the niche.

Twenty-First Century Nigeria: National Agency for Food and Drug Administration and Control (NAFDAC)

In the first decade of the twenty-first century, a new global leader in eradicating counterfeit drugs emerged in an unexpected place: Nigeria. Nigeria's sudden global prominence in this arena was surprising because in the 1990s Nigeria had gained notoriety for producing and trafficking fake products from machine parts to pharmaceuticals.[6] In 1990, thanks to lax standards and near nonenforcement, contaminated paracetamol pain relief syrup resulted in public scandal and the death of 109 children.[7] In 2001, nearly half of the drugs sold at official pharmacies did not meet testing standards, with some having too much active drug and some having none at all.[8] Counterfeiters would repackage a cheaper drug with different active ingredients to pass it off as a more expensive drug, for example selling an antidiabetic drug as one for hypertension, or selling paracetamol—a pain reliever—as the antimalarial drug Fansidar.[9] Sick people unknowingly taking the wrong drugs meant their illness persisted untreated, and in some cases they sickened and died.

But in the first decade of the twenty-first century, Nigeria's National Agency for Food and Drug Administration and Control (NAFDAC) underwent a rapid transformation, quickly emerging as one of the most trusted and effective government agencies in representative nationwide surveys.[10] The transformation of NAFDAC coincides with the appointment of Dora Akunyili as its director. Shortly after her appointment in 2001, NAFDAC reduced counterfeit drugs in circulation from 40–60 percent to only 16.7 percent. They reduced unregistered drugs from 68 percent to 19 percent, improved water sanitation to reduce cholera, and became the first African country to reach universal salt iodization.[11] These structural changes also shepherded a revitalization of Nigeria's pharmaceutical production industry, as other African nations lifted bans on Nigerian drugs that had been enacted out of fear of low quality standards and rampant counterfeiting.[12]

NAFDAC's remarkable organizational performance took place in an incredibly inhospitable environment. The Nigerian state at the time was rife with corruption and inefficiencies while also subject to political instability and military influence in politics. The Nigerian economy had been stagnant or falling since the 1980s, with an economy that was, in absolute terms, $20 billion USD smaller than Nigeria's economy in 1980 despite rapid population growth. Strikingly, the GDP per capita in 2000 remained below the average GDP per capita from the 1960s, the first decade of Nigerian independence (constant 2010 USD).[13] Financial pressures resulted in rampant underfunding of government agencies and a general administrative culture that was lax about work and permissive of corruption. Nigerians had grown accustomed to news stories of high-level officials misappropriating public money for personal gain. In 1999, after sixteen years of military rule, President Obasanjo was elected, who in 2001 appointed Dora Akunyili to head the foundering NAFDAC.

CLUSTERING THROUGH RECRUITMENT

After assuming leadership of the struggling NAFDAC, Akunyili—a pharmacist and professor—began to assess the organization, paying particular attention to personnel. To convert this lax, corrupt, and inefficient organization into one capable of going out into the field to combat counterfeiting, Akunyili realized "we needed a total change of attitude and, in fact, a cultural revolution throughout the organization."[14] Akunyili first recruited a handpicked team of special assistants around her, who worked tirelessly in the early period of her leadership. After observation, she selected two directors within the agency, but also brought in private-sector outsiders with proven records. She was explicitly looking for both the overt skills relevant to the job and also a proto-bureaucratic orientation to work: "in addition to merit, proven integrity and commitment to the NAFDAC mission were also important."[15]

Once her management team was established, Akunyili engaged in a very public purge, dismissing staff who were "corrupt," "incorrigible," "recalcitrant," or "lazy." Even though only 5 percent of the total staff were dismissed in the purge, it was a shock to the system, clearly drawing a symbolic boundary for the staff that remained about the kinds of practices that would not be tolerated, and the willingness to enforce. One insider referred to it as " 'an organizational cultural revolution.' "[16]

NAFDAC recruited new staff through a process that also explicitly highlighted merit, drawing another highly visible symbolic boundary between NAFDAC and the larger administrative milieu. For the first recruitment wave, notices posted publicly in newspapers garnered 3,000 applications. Later recruitments for frontline officials would see 35,000 applications. External consultants halved the applicant pool, and the remaining applicants took an aptitude test administered by an outside body. The most successful candidates on the aptitude test then interviewed for positions. The different external evaluators in the selection process thereby incorporated multiple differently situated veto players, analogous to the selection process at the Bank of Ghana. This both directly affected the caliber of candidates selected and also indirectly enhanced the symbolic boundary differentiating the "new" NAFDAC as one where tribalism and nepotism were no longer the principal means to employment.

CULTIVATION OF DISTINCTIVENESS

The purge and new selection procedures underscored that employment depended on competence and bureaucratic orientation. Staff orientation to the organization was further cultivated through training, both in-house and internationally. More than two dozen staff members went for international training every month through training grants. Most of the work in NAFDAC was carried out in teams. As in the Ghanaian cases, that structure afforded organizational slack for grappling with interruptions and provided opportunities for intense, recurrent face-to-face interactions among team members. Observers argue that this fostered "internal cooperation and collegiality" but was also a form of social monitoring and control because "at NAFDAC, internal whistle blowing is explicitly encouraged and rewarded if the case is confirmed."[17] In the reformed NAFDAC, officials were responsible for each other: Officials who engaged in corruption were dismissed along with colleagues who knew and abetted it with their silence.

An attention-grabbing event underscored for all the staff that this was not merely a rule on the books but one to which they would actually be held accountable. Akunyili's brother-in-law was a team leader in NAFDAC enforcement. A company reported that he had demanded and collected a bribe valued at several thousand U.S. dollars, then gone back for more, and assaulted the expatriate company manager when the manager refused to pay again. NAFDAC internally investigated the case and confirmed his guilt. Akunyili summarily dismissed him, taking a particularly poignant stand against nepotism. Among the staff, Akunyili notes, "It effectively put everybody on notice that there would be no sacred cows in the war against counterfeit medicines in Nigeria."[18]

Akunyili also introduced means of monitoring time to cut down on absenteeism and lateness, dismissing several employees for failure to conform to time expectations. Cultivation included not only punishments for wrongdoing, but also rewards for honesty and hard work. Because NAFDAC had the means to internally generate revenue, Akunyili created compensation packages and bonuses that encouraged workers to generate revenue through appropriate collection of legitimate costs, fines, and fees. Workers who caught counterfeiters or reported on the wrongdoing of colleagues were recognized, promoted, and financially rewarded. When a company reported how impressed they were that a team of NAFDAC inspectors in the field had refused the company's offer of free hotel accommodation and spending money, Akunyili saw that those inspectors were financially rewarded by NAFDAC upon their return.

PROTECTION

NAFDAC sought external grants and utilized internal revenues to engage in a significant effort to remake NAFDAC's physical infrastructure throughout Nigeria to better cope with the challenges of field-based work, including expanding laboratory and warehouse infrastructure. NAFDAC worked to reshape the social environment by disciplining outsiders relevant to their mission, encouraging them to adopt practices that were better aligned with NAFDAC's organizational interests. NAFDACs efforts to combat illicit trade was always their most risky effort to reshape the external environment, and there they had to rely almost entirely on coercion and force, seizing goods at strategic points.

NAFDAC carefully balanced its more dangerous efforts to combat highly organized, lucrative, and violent illicit trade with highly publicized gains in other domains, where the vested interests were less well organized and influential. Regulatory powers had been endowed by the law that formed NAFDAC in 1992 but had been little used. Under Akunyili, NAFDAC acted on its regulatory endowment, and also expanded its purview after 2001 to include water purity, herbal medicine producers, food labeling, and more. NAFDAC specified new regulations for water safety standards and then sought to reshape the practices of the vast corps of small-scale water producers. One of the first aggressive public campaigns of the new NAFDAC was a nationwide educational campaign that offered workshops to the many small-scale producers of "pure water" sachets (plastic bags of water sold inexpensively throughout much of West Africa).[19] NAFDAC found mostly willing partners in the many small-scale pure water producers, and the efforts drew widespread public-interest media accolades. Compared to the challenging task of battling illicit criminals getting wealthy from counterfeit drugs, with the pure water intervention NAFDAC was thereby able to score a highly visible victory with little resistance, shoring up public support for the organization. The successful pure water campaign then became a template for a similar effort to regulate traditional herbal medicines, working with producers to ensure herbal medicines were registered and labeled without unsupported claims about efficacy.

Mid-Twentieth-Century Kenya: The Kenya Tea Development Authority (KTDA)

In the mid-twentieth century, scholars and practitioners observed that " 'The Kenya Tea Development Authority is one of the most successful agricultural development programs in Sub-Saharan Africa.' "[20] In 1959, while tea production was still in the hands of white expatriate British producers, Kenyan tea prices were 14 percent below world market averages. Only two years after KTDA was established, Kenyan tea prices surpassed the global average price; by the early 1970s, Kenyan tea exports commanded the world's highest prices.[21] These tremendous quality gains occurred alongside fantastic expansion in scale. In the first thirty years of operation, KTDA expanded the hectares farmed fifty-fold, while the average farm size was still just under one acre of land. By incorporating more than 100,000 smallholder farmers into commercial export agriculture, KTDA also helped reduce rural poverty: the average income of KTDA farmers was more than triple that of other rural agricultural peasants.[22]

This surprising organizational success took place in a context of ethnicized political pressures. Kenya gained independence from the British in 1963 and rapidly emerged as a polity in which the benefits of statehood would be distributed based on ethnic membership. The state was riven by interethnic competition over which ethnic groups would get to benefit from its largesse.[23] Jomo Kenyatta, the first head of state, was from the largest ethnic group, the Kikuyu, who were 19.6 percent of the population.[24] The Kikuyu had been privileged by colonial administrators, and after Independence, Kenyatta continued to favor coethnics both symbolically and economically. Upon independence, Kenyatta claimed land from departing expatriate settlers and disproportionately distributed that land under the Million Acre Settlement Scheme to himself and his fellow Kikuyu.[25] Kikuyu provinces received more schools and teachers,[26] and more new road constructions.[27] Half to two-thirds of the loans issued by the government-owned Development Corporation went to Kikuyus.[28]

The broader environment created strong expectations of ethnic patronage, together with heightened interethnic suspicions. In post-Independence Kenya, "society expects that senior administrators will provide assistance to those from their home areas and applies a good deal of pressure toward that end.... Many [civil servants] will use junior staff appointments they control to satisfy the pressures of petitioners from their villages."[29] But staffing other coethnics also came with a price. Coethnics appointed through patronage often felt entitled to positions, and therefore gave only a minimum of effort. Moreover, managers known for appointing coethnics frequently found their authority undermined with others who did not share their ethnicity.

CLUSTERING THROUGH RECRUITMENT

Charles Karanja oversaw the emergence of the KTDA as a global leader in tea production. Karanja used personal connections to search for new recruits and influence new hires to conform to his organizational orientation. Of all the cases, Karanja most explicitly invokes a version of *mixed meritocracy*, whereby recruits have both personal connections to influential decision-makers—within or outside the organization—and objective merit for accomplishing the organization's stated mission. Particularly for senior management positions, personal influence could be important in helping a candidate get to the interview stage; however, the final hiring decision was made by a committee through a rigorous open interview not unlike the Bank of Ghana. Sequentially then, some level of interpersonal connections was an important base condition, but among those sufficiently well-connected, merit was the final and proximal cause of hiring. Organizational orientation was explicitly underscored by Karanja: "He was adamant, however, that his favors went no further than a chance at the job; to keep it, one had to perform."[30]

As we saw in NAFDAC and the Ghanaian cases, early upon assuming leadership, Karanja pruned officials who failed to meet his expectations or make timely progress on goals, underscoring the symbolic boundary between the organization and business as usual elsewhere within the state. Karanja was known by subordinates as someone quick to fire officials whose performance did not meet expectations, but like PARD's Mr. Mensah or NAFDAC's Akunyili, Karanja went to great lengths to advance the career of officials who were doing great work.[31] Importantly, within the highly ethnicized environment of Independence Kenya, Karanja "applied the principle as rigorously to his relatives and the politically connected as to those of other ethnic groups."[32] Like Akunyili, Karanja had several highly public firings that underscored for all the remaining employees the seriousness of performance: Karanja fired for poor performance two of his own sons, as well as the son of a high-ranking minister. The work of pruning poor performers or corrupt officials was not merely an initial purge. Instead, much like Collins tirelessly checking the NCA sign-in sheets to reinforce punctuality, "The price of a relatively uncorrupted KTDA was eternal vigilance by its general manager and its Accounting Department and ruthlessness in removing the offenders."[33]

CULTIVATION OF DISTINCTIVENESS

Karanja emphasized the distinctiveness of KTDA and began early cultivation of new staff by incorporating an observational period into the hiring process, by "training more people for jobs than he had openings and then making the promotions from among the best performers."[34] Readers will recall that observations during trial employment also occurred in the Ghanaian cases that hired national service members. As in Ghana, this observational period made visible both explicit skills and tacit organizational orientations that together contributed to people's ability to perform the task at hand. A trial period with explicit competition was a means to address challenges of evaluating merit —in the sense of the person who will perform best on the job—particularly in an environment where people cannot take for granted the set of practices and orientations that are core to the bureaucratic habitus, for which distant evaluation is particularly fraught.

More than any other organization, Karanja's KTDA made use of comparison and competition as mechanisms for cultivating an ethos of organizational achievement. KTDA included many different geographic locations that were organized into teams of functionally equivalent units. Gathering internal production data made exemplary performance legible and underscored that exemplary performance (rather than ethnicity or interpersonal connections) was central to success at KTDA. When KTDA expanded into factories, Karanja worked with his elite political connections to secure the right to access productivity information from private-sector factories in the same industry. His chief accountant then created a system to allow KTDA to compare the production process costs at all the KTDA factories to each other and to the private-sector data. Although market-like competition among functional equivalents rarely exists within government, Karanja leveraged the spirit of competition and reward to great effect: "As a result, vigorous competition was set off among managers, and the commercial agents began to modernize and improve their performance."[35]

PROTECTION

The early KTDA was embedded within a tensely ethnicized political environment. They could not wholly isolate themselves from those forces, foremost because the success of the KTDA required routine interaction with hosts of smallholder farmers in a variety of different regions. KTDA strategically modified its internal staffing procedures to cope with and mitigate the risk of disruption from the ethnicized political climate. Therefore, KTDA was careful to consider ethnicity in the selection of factory and management positions within KTDA, such that factory trainees were roughly proportionate to the ethnic group's share of the population in the local area. Sensitive to the need to work closely with local smallholder farmers, factory managers were usually of the same ethnicity as the surrounding growers.

As their revenues grew, KTDA engaged in more ambitious projects to re-shape their environment to facilitate their core organizational mission, both through physical infrastructural changes and disciplining key participants. At KTDA's behest, the government constructed and improved roads in tea growing areas.[36] KTDA also opened two schools that trained their staff and offered growers one-week short courses to train in tea production.[37]

KTDA's core mission required that they develop the capability to shep-herd the cooperation and shape the practices of a large and diverse body of peasant farmers. One of the early innovations was a form of Selznick-style cooptation, in which those with a capacity to disrupt the organizational func-tioning were brought into the leadership structure.[38] KTDA established tea committees, where registered growers in each subdistrict could elect repre-sentatives. Initially, the principal purpose of the committee was to ensure that important information from growers was heard by the KTDA, and that, in turn, they communicated KTDA policies to the growers in their district.[39] KTDA also enjoyed structural sources of power with which they could better coerce farmer compliance: For the first few decades of operation, KTDA was the only legal source of tea plants for and the only legal buyer of green leaf from smallholders.[40]

In a sense, the tea committees provided a kind of embedded autonomy for the KTDA, which Peter Evans has argued was so essential for the success of East Asian developmental states generally.[41] Committees ensured that vital information about the challenges of production, which was best known by producers, reached KTDA while also keeping the organization from capture by any one group. They also became important sounding boards for the de-velopment of new KTDA policies and practices, giving KTDA a way to test whether proposed changes would be acceptable to local growers and assure buy-in before committing to a new direction. Over time, the committees also acted as local liaisons for KTDA head office staff, helping to allocate new tea tree stumps, mobilize farmers, and even assist with enforcing KTDA regula-tions in their district.

Mid-twentieth Century Brazil: National Bank of Economic Development (BNDE)

Starting in the mid-twentieth century, the period of state-building under Pres-ident Getúlio Vargas (1930–1945; 1951–1954) and later Juscelino Kubitschek (1956–191961) was to Brazil what the New Deal was to the United States: a pe-riod of previously unprecedented expansion of state structures and capacities, particularly those state capacities to actively intervene to shape development.[42] Scholars of Brazil observe that during this period, much of the state was a dysfunctional quagmire, but a handful of agencies emerged that were "models of effectiveness."[43] Of those agencies, arguably the most important, influential, and unusually effective was the National Bank of Economic Development (BNDE).

At the time, BNDE was possibly the most ambitious development banking project attempted in a low-income country. BNDE was charged with the considerable task of correcting financial market failures by making credit available to hasten national economic development. Thus, BNDE is important not only for its success in accomplishing its own organizational mandate, but also because its organizational success was crucial for enabling the success of many other developmental ventures. Indeed, many attribute the impressive levels of economic growth Brazil achieved in the mid-twentieth century to the foundation of credit and technical advice provided by BNDE.[44] In the first twelve years of operation (1953–1964), administrative costs as a percentage of assets managed averaged 0.56 percent; at the same time, return on assets increased rapidly, from 3.9 percent in 1955 to 17.8 percent in 1961.[45] These measures indicate that even relatively early after its establishment, BNDE was both efficient and effective. BNDE has been the focus of more than a thousand scholarly articles,[46] and scholars of the twentieth-century Brazilian state have argued that at the time "No other Brazilian government entity has a stronger or better-deserved reputation for incorruptibility and honest administration than BNDE."[47]

BNDE became an exemplar of organizational success, both relative to other Brazilian banks and to development banks globally, despite environmental and sectoral challenges. At the onset of Vargas' presidency, the "public service was in a deteriorating and chaotic state."[48] At the time BNDE emerged as a pocket of excellence, the Brazilian state was generally a "bureaucratic morass" such that new projects "would have taken many months to meander through bureaucratic channels in one agency after another."[49] The state administration had become captured by the economic coalition of commercial exporters and landed elites.[50] Core aspects of staffing and managing state funds were handled in a "completely haphazard manner" exacerbated by the onset of a general economic depression.[51] The political environment in Brazil had long been defined by charismatic personalities rather than by parties clearly distinguished by ideological or programmatic differences. This was due in part to constitutional institutions that provided perverse incentives to court patronage rather than party discipline or programmatic development.[52] Therefore, the larger political environment was rife with pressure to shore up political support through the distribution of patronage positions within government.[53]

CLUSTERING THROUGH RECRUITMENT

Relatively early on, BNDE cultivated a distinctive reputation for "a first-class staff with a strong sense of mission."[54] The process of clustering distinctiveness began with a founding nucleus of distinctiveness: A strong organizational orientation and rational technocratic ethos first took hold within a small core of senior personnel with strong interpersonal ties and distinctive lived experiences in rationalized and technocratic environments prior to coming to BNDE. In 1953, when BNDE finally moved into its own building, it was still relatively small: The entire staff was composed of only 150 people, secretaries included.[55] Being numerically small, interpersonal interaction was high, and a relatively small number of distinctive people in key positions could have a significant effect on the organization.

From this distinctive nucleus, BNDE grew its personnel ranks slowly and selectively. BNDE drew a considerable number of its early recruits from among former members of the Administrative Department of Public Service (DASP).[56] DASP itself was one of the earliest "pockets of effectiveness" within the Brazilian state, officially tasked with administrative reform of the state and filled with a distinctive ethos that valued "neutral competence and scientific management."[57] During the early period of BNDE's personnel growth, most new staff joined through personal invitation from an existing BNDE insider, and those new recruits tended to come from the universities or from other agencies within the state—such as DASP, the Ministry of Foreign Affairs, or the Brazilian Institute of Geography and Statistics—that themselves had reputations for unusually high technical competency. BNDE leaders Campos, Paiva Teixeira, and others had preexisting relationships with those organizations, having worked within them previously, and they mobilized those networks to aid them in their search.[58] Whether by accident or design it is unknown, but this had the effect of simplifying the challenging search costs of targeting staff who were both technically competent and possessed pro-organizational orientations that are so difficult to assess from arm's reach. Then in 1956, BNDE management implemented the *concurso* competitive merit exam as a condition for recruitment.[59]

CULTIVATION OF DISTINCTIVENESS

Through the clustering of distinctive persons, early on BNDE created the structural position of feeling like a small subculture that was so prevalent among the Ghanaian cases as well, a convergence on a set of practices common among inside members but which also made them maximally distinctive from the most salient external comparison groups: civil servants of the state generally. BNDE developed an organizational identity around its adherence to "a technical-rational approach to economic decision-making" that sharply contrasted with the more political and personalistic environment that predominated elsewhere throughout the Brazilian administrative state.[60] As described in earlier chapters, this contrast encourages insiders to converge on perceived insider commonalities and also that which makes them maximally distinct from the most salient comparison groups. The contrast heightened a sense of "we-ness" among the relatively small group of insiders who initially comprised BNDE, reflected in the intense identification typical of members of numerical minority groups. Like the Ghanaian interstitial insiders described in the cultivation chapter, BNDE insiders were likewise characterized by "a strong group consciousness or esprit de corps."[61] BNDE came to be characterized by a distinctive culture of practice that was further cultivated both through everyday interaction among the tight-knit ranks of BNDE insiders and through explicit educational and travel experiences. BNDE technical staff worked very closely with each other. BNDE staff at the time recall that the frequent opportunities to work closely together "created strong and lasting bonds among the bank's small but growing staff."[62] These close interactions among insiders enabled learning by emulation, observed in the Ghanaian cases as well, resulting in a stronger shared understanding of the distinctive group style of BNDE, an internal sense of identification with mission, and an appreciation of their distinctiveness vis-à-vis business as usual elsewhere in Brazil.

Like Akunyili, the BNDE leadership made aggressive efforts to further train and develop the organizational orientation of its staff through training opportunities. These trainings had the explicit goal of enhancing their technical banking expertise—a number had university degrees as engineers or lawyers—but also indirectly exposed participants to environments where rational, technocratic, organizational-oriented thinking predominated. By providing such experiences, the early managers "hoped that, through building an expert staff, they would orient their own decision-making on loan requests."[63] In the early period, when funds were limited, the bank still secured funding to send some staff abroad to training courses on economic development and development banking sponsored by the United States and the United Nations, while others were able to attend international banking conferences.[64] Those employees who were not able to go abroad for international training and exposure cultivated both skills and organizational orientation through cooperative research and training arrangements BNDE forged with the Getulio Vargas Foundation (FGV)—an institution founded by Luis Simões Lopes, ardent fan of scientific management and founder of DASP.

PROTECTION

During a formative period in its history, BNDE enjoyed executive-level protection—from President Kubitschek—which helped its meteoric rise and establishment as a robust subculture of meritocracy within the Brazilian state. This protective relationship early in its organizational development afforded BNDE the opportunity not only to cultivate a robust internal organizational sense of identity, but also to establish formal organizational mechanisms for disciplining outsiders and to cultivate a strong positive reputation among external constituent groups. These would prove important later, when BNDE would find it needed protection *from* subsequent presidents—an issue addressed more fully in the next chapter.

In the Kubitschek era, several organizational features were established that gave BNDE greater abilities to discipline outside entities with which it had frequent interactions, including both upstream organizations whose co-operation was essential for BNDE's administration and loan recipients whose performance determined the success or failure of BNDE's lending portfolio. Because the national development plan mandated lending to private industry, not just public projects, the bank was exposed to pressures from private-sector clients, "modern firms able to deal with the bank on its own technical terms."[65]

BNDE was structurally positioned to discipline both public and private entities through its strategic position as a guarantor of and repository for international loans. A number of funds that were not legally under BNDE's operational purview were nevertheless deposited in BNDE, and BNDE served as a guarantor that the funds would be used in economic development projects.[66] Moreover, international loans at the time frequently required matching funds from a Brazilian source, which BNDE was in a position to offer. Therefore, other public and private entities came under the sphere of BNDE influence, such as the Ministry of Public Works seeking port dredging or the Ministry of Agriculture efforts to import agricultural machinery.[67] The financial dependency of other agencies allowed BNDE to apply performance criteria and enforce performance standards relative to plan goals as conditions for receiving subsequent disbursements.[68]

BNDE's influence on other state agencies came not only from its strategic financial position but also from organizational decisions that gave the BNDE leadership strategic roles in governance of other related organizations. This is yet another instance of reverse cooptation, where key members of an interstitial subculture were sent out into strategic positions in external organizations that might otherwise be structurally positioned to disrupt the functioning of the interstitial niche. During Kubitschek's presidency, the president of BNDE was put into leadership positions over several other related state organizations to better ensure their smooth coordination with BNDE. The BNDE president was always made the secretary-general of the Council of Development, which was responsible for development planning, and by law was also a member of the Superintendency of Money and Credit (SUMOC).[69]

Even as the bank solidified an "institutional personality" and external reputation for effective administration that applied strict econometric criteria to loan selection, its operational autonomy still required consistent defense against executive encroachment. Bank staff recall numerous incidents in which BNDE had to side-step ongoing efforts from post-Kubitschek presidents to use BNDE for political purposes outside of its economic development mandate. For example, in early 1961 when floods devastated northeastern Brazil, President Quadros sent a handwritten note to BNDE directing the bank to divert funds to help flood victims. Such a humanitarian use of funds was clearly at odds with the explicit legislative dictum on the use of BNDE funds, and even more so at odds with the now-established ethos of BNDE to fund projects with clear economic merit to stimulate broader economic development. Though compassionate to suffering, bank staff rallied against the diversion of funds away from the bank's core mission, and in response the bank's leadership refused the president's directive.[70]

Direct confrontation with the president would have been more difficult during the fledgling Vargas years. However, under the shelter from political pressure that Kubitschek's support afforded, BNDE developed a robust sense of organizational identity and cultivated a strong record of performance, with a great many direct and indirect beneficiaries of its effective and efficient administration of loans. Over time a constituency emerged within the private sector, civil society, and the public generally that defended BNDE's independence.[71] Much like how the symbolic power of Kenyan smallholder farmers afforded the KTDA greater leverage when disagreeing with the president, BNDE was emboldened by the growing constituency who saw firsthand the benefits of a rational, technocratic, and independent national development bank.

Early Twentieth-Century China: Sino-Foreign Salt Inspectorate

When the declining Qing dynasty finally fell in the early twentieth century, China's fledgling republic inherited a weak central state dominated by uncertainty, patronage, corruption, and warlord politics. Within this inhospitable context, a salt-taxing agency transformed from a lethargic bastion of patronage to arguably the most effective state agency, increasing net revenues by 747 percent in the first ten years and almost single-handedly keeping the fragile state afloat. The postdynastic government desperately needed revenue to combat regional warlords and stabilize its fragile hold on power. The state received a £25 million gold loan from six foreign governments, on the condition that salt tax revenues would service loan repayments.[72] The ineffectual existing salt tax agency, the *Yanwu Shu*, would be responsible for collecting salt revenues. A new organization, the Sino-Foreign Salt Inspectorate, was initially given a mandate only to transfer salt tax revenues to service the loan.

Almost immediately, and much to the surprise of nearly everyone, the Sino-Foreign Salt Inspectorate began recording unprecedented revenue increases.[73] In the first year, the quantity of taxable salt being legally transported or sold increased by two to fourfold. Later reforms cut down on rampant smuggling and under-reporting by transport merchants, expanding the quantity of taxable salt by as much as 30 to 50 percent per year while increasing revenue per unit.[74] The Salt Inspectorate increased revenues from $36 million USD to $72.5 million USD, with two-thirds of those gains arising from more efficient administration.[75] Early on, even after servicing the mandatory loan payments, the Inspectorate yielded a surplus of $52 million USD.[76]

This expansion of capabilities occurred in an administratively challenging context. The salt industry was shockingly illegible to the central state, lacking data and confounded by a dizzying array of local arrangements as to where, when, in what form, how often, how much, and by whom salt taxes would be collected.[77] Moreover, in disregard of official dictums, taxes often were paid in annual lump sums, frustrating efforts to correlate the volume of salt to revenue collected.[78] Payments were more determined by symbolic gestures than by rule of law. One report observed, "If it is desired to make a good show and pay in to the Salt Revenue Account a large sum, the assets are written up. If funds are required for other purposes, the assets are written down."[79] Without a nationally standardized system for weights and measurements, multiple measurement systems and often suspiciously inconsistent scales were simultaneously in use throughout the transport and taxation process. Overall, the atmosphere surrounding the neophyte Salt Inspectorate was not oriented toward the bureaucratic habitus, posing challenges to the Inspectorate's mission that seemed insurmountable.

The conventional organizational effects of these sectoral and environmental challenges were apparent within the *Yanwu Shu*. Absenteeism and collusion of salt tax employees were rife. The *Yanwu Shu* had paid for salt police to protect the salt works from bandits, which created local jobs but did little to curb the biggest source of smuggling. The first Foreign Chief Inspector, Sir Richard Dane, observed, "The salt is at present protected, though at too high a cost, against attacks by robbers, but practically no attempt is made to prevent frauds and evasions of the duty by the salt merchants themselves."[80] Estimates suggested that a majority of the smuggling that had so eroded revenues was not outright banditry, but rather merchants' representatives removing salt from licensed works or taking advantage of unstandardized weights to obfuscate the full amount of salt they transported, frequently with the collusion of local salt officials.[81] Absenteeism was also a common problem, even at the highest levels. Head officers of branch offices had not shown up to work for months, though they continued to collect uncommonly lavish salaries.[82] Salt Inspectorate reports found " 'The principle [*sic*] function of the checking offices was apparently to provide employment for the needy relatives of higher officials." Because high-ranking *Yanwu Shu* officials appropriated much of the salaries intended for district officials and salt police, officials stationed in the districts had to primarily rely on unofficial customary "commissions" they collected as a primary source of income.[83]

CLUSTERING THROUGH RECRUITMENT

The Salt Inspectorate was formed as a new organization in parallel to the existing *Yanwu Shu*, so rather than redefine the situation through an attention-getting corruption purge, the Inspectorate established a distinctive organizational culture from its founding. Concentrating merit was mostly achieved through the unwavering adherence to a merit-based entrance examination. The Inspectorate exam required a school degree and tested for skills in English, Chinese, math, and overall ability to read and write. Similar to NAFDAC and BNDE, strict reliance on the exam served to filter out patronage and increase the density of merit among new recruits. Moreover, the exam allowed Chinese officials to shift blame for violating local patronage norms onto the mechanical objectivity of the exam—merit exams had a long history in China —and onto foreign partners within the Inspectorate, who were not bound by local expectations. This shift in blame cut costs for local officials adopting a bureaucratic ethos by diminishing the effect of social shame for deviation from local norms.

Like NAFDAC, the Inspectorate's core tasks required dispersing staff throughout a large geographic expanse. The comparatively limited early twentieth-century communication and transportation technologies rendered those distances more challenging, both administratively and in the social life of officials. Such conditions seemingly posed challenges to staffing such positions. However, adverse conditions were also a fortuitous means of imposing selection effects on the pool of applicants: "Since those concerned with their careers had to move (and move frequently) to locations that ranked among the least desirable in all of China, the insufficiently committed tended to select themselves out."[84]

Personnel discretion was nearly complete. Although the reformed Salt Inspectorate took over the organizational duties of the former *Yanwu Shu* salt tax organization, it took none of its officials.[85] The Inspectorate directly recruited all of its foreign and Chinese staff and "adamantly resisted politically inspired appointments to the central office and the districts." It utilized control over its personnel to institute a mandatory exam for entry and promotion within the Salt Inspectorate. Although regulations stipulated that the minister of finance appoint the Chinese chief inspector, "in practice, the Inspectorate pressed for the appointment of an official expert in salt affairs, preferably from its own ranks."[86]

The structure of work and promotion at the Inspectorate meant that people selecting into its service were less likely to come from wealthy families with influential social networks, filtering out prime patronage candidates. Almost without exception, the only way to advance was to work up through the ranks. Such advancement required frequent postings rotated through undesirable, remote, rural district offices. Postings were physically arduous and considered beneath the Chinese upper classes. One report noted, "The efficient control of salt works necessitates much physical exertion and long hours in the sun in boats or on foot and on horseback; and the control of the storage and issue of salt from depots calls for the performance of mechanical duties (weighment of bags, careful counting of stacked tiers of bags etc.) which are evidently very distasteful to Chinese gentlemen."[87] Selecting out socioeconomic elites best positioned to exert patronage pressures shifted the balance in the Inspectorate's potential labor pool towards greater consideration of merit.

CULTIVATION OF DISTINCTIVENESS

The Salt Inspectorate rigorously pruned insiders who violated the characteristic comportment of the organization, further concentrating distinctiveness and simultaneously underscoring symbolic boundaries differentiating the Inspectorate from the larger environment. Pruning improved productivity by directly eliminating unproductive or "corrupt" insiders, and, as in other cases, also served as a strong symbolic boundary further distinguishing the niche from business as usual in the surrounding environment. Unlike most of the contemporaneous Chinese state, within the Inspectorate censure for poor productivity or corruption was swift and explicit, leaving no ambiguity to "save face." [88] Moreover, as with the cases of KTDA and NAFDAC, dismissals for poor performance or wrongdoing reached from the lowest ranks of rural officials up to the managerial ranks. [89] In a sample of 185 officials who had worked in the first 20 years of the reform administration, there were 14 cases of dismissal: 5 of those had served for 10 or more years, 1 had reached a managerial rank of assistant district commissioner, and 1 had previously received a distinguished service award. [90]

The concentrated distinctiveness of the Salt Inspectorate cultivated the behaviors, practices, expectations, and orientations of its staff. As with other cases, a strong sense of a distinctive organizational reputation emerged early on that was sharply distinct from the chaotic and patrimonial surrounding environment. The symbolic boundary between the Salt Inspectorate and other officials centered on its strong orientation to accomplishing the organization's mission. The Salt Inspectorate was known for "a highly motivated staff that internalized the Inspectorate's norms of bureaucratically determined neutrality, fairness, and technical competence."[91] As the influence of the central state eroded, typical Chinese officials had a reputation for leveraging their office for personal gain and disappearing at any sign of trouble. By contrast, Inspectorate officials developed a reputation for "dedication, steadfastness, and unwillingness to buckle to the pressure of local notables, marauding warlords, or the claims of family and friends."[92] Like the Ghanaian niches whose distinctive organizational identity was reinforced through interactions with influential outsiders, outsiders who repeatedly interacted with Inspectorate officials came to understand their distinctive reputation and act accordingly, cultivating a reinforcing cycle.

The Inspectorate had various symbolic boundaries demarcating its difference from the surrounding environment. It utilized a different pay scale than the Chinese government, which cultivated organizational distinction and "reinforced the organization's sense of separateness."[93] However, the Inspectorate delicately managed this different pay scale to avoid inciting resentment from other civil servants: The overall range from lowest to highest rank was nearly identical to that of the civil service. The external legibility of the similar pay *range* obfuscated internal differences in practice and distribution. In particular, the Inspectorate had a greater number of midrange scales and a reputation for promotion that meant low and midrank officials were better compensated in the Inspectorate than elsewhere in the Chinese state.[94]

The distinctive reputation of the Salt Inspectorate inspired fierce loyalty and identification among its members. Indeed, the language with which this allegiance is described is strongly reminiscent of the way Ghanaian interstitial insiders speak with fierce pride about the reputation of their organization and its role. Strauss argues: "Because bureaucratic, rule-oriented impersonalism so demarcated the Inspectorate and set off from the particularistic outside environment, Inspectorate administrators felt very strongly that their 'civil service traditions' were the heart and soul of the organization's distinctiveness and success."[95] Characteristic of a numerical minority group that feels itself beleaguered from the outside, Salt Inspectorate officials defended their distinctive organizational culture "with a tenacity bordering on the ferocious."[96]

PROTECTION

As with other cases, the Salt Inspectorate modified internal processes to cope with a disruptive environment. The Inspectorate rotated its staff through postings in different areas, thereby frustrating capture by local elite networks, promoting identification with the organization, and homogenizing organizational culture across inspectorate offices. Officials spent two-to-five years at a location, alternated with shorter tours of duty elsewhere. Even low-level support staff were frequently rotated, with only 7 percent of low-level staff remaining at one location for the duration of their service.[97] The Inspectorate strategically utilized regional outsiders and foreigners in roles and locations particularly prone to corruption, because outsiders lacked social ties that might reinforce expectations for patronage or exceptions to rule enforcement.[98]

The Inspectorate expanded its organizational jurisdiction to assume new duties that mitigated its dependencies on ineffectual partner organizations. Initially, the Inspectorate was only tasked with *transferring* salt revenues to service the foreign loan. Like the Ghanaian niches, however, the Inspectorate engaged in significant compensatory competence, unofficially expanding into new activities when partner organizations were too weak or unreliable. Within months the Inspectorate expanded operations to include *collecting* regional salt taxes, administering merit exams for Salt Police, and auditing district offices.[99] The Salt Inspectorate assumed control over where and how salt taxes would be collected, replacing the plethora of taxes enacted throughout transit—with all of the attendant "leaks" and opportunities for corruption—with a single consolidated tax at the point of production. In so doing, the Inspectorate extended its organizational reach into duties technically the jurisdiction of the *Yanwu Shu,* unofficially compensating where the *Yanwu Shu* was too organizationally weak to perform.[100] Like KTDA, the Inspectorate supplemented the weak technological capacity of private producers, developing technical improvements to salt evaporation production processes that raised the quality of salt produced.[101]

Beyond internal coping mechanisms, the Salt Inspectorate is noteworthy for ambitious efforts to remake the external environment to mitigate threats and discipline outsiders. Through construction projects, the Inspectorate physically remade infrastructure to optimize salt tax revenue collection and centralization. The Inspectorate closed small salt works to better consolidate control and relocated district offices closer to high-volume production areas.[102] Like KTDA, they built new roads to enable transport. Like NAFDAC, the Inspectorate incorporated previously external infrastructure—in this case, salt storage—into their purview by building salt storage depots and requiring that salt be deposited within 48 hours of manufacture.[103] These new depots were intentionally designed to frustrate merchants' illicit smuggling: Depots had only one entrance and exit, and the only key to the exit was held by Inspectorate officials. At key sites like Shantung where the new infrastructure was in place, "It is safe to say that since 1915 not a single excess bag of salt has been transported by a merchant from these works."[104] The $20 million USD spent on reorganization and new development projects were modest compared to the gains generated, such that "the initial expenditure more than paid for itself in one year of the reform administration."[105]

One of the Inspectorate's foremost disciplinary challenges was reshaping outsiders' long-standing practices, whereby reforms had to grapple with entrenched local power holders. Arguably the greatest point of contestation was the Inspectorate's desire to abolish hereditary monopoly transportation licenses (*yin*). Inspectorate leadership viewed free trade as the best organizational technology to achieve the mission of maximizing centralized tax receipts. However, this proposal conflicted with the economic interests of powerful regional elites as well as long-standing cultural tradition.

The Inspectorate cleverly took advantage of natural variation in the presence of entrenched local interests. In several areas wealthy *yin* merchants had fled during the 1911 revolution. In their absence, free salt transportation rights were granted to "any reputable agents," initially as an emergency measure.[106] The initial crisis afforded an opportunity to test the Inspectorate's favored free-trade system, which created new economic elites aligned with the agency's interests. Successful free-market sellers subsequently supported the Inspectorate in opposing efforts to reinstate monopoly licenses in those localities and created pressure to expand the system to new areas.[107]

New Insights from Comparisons

The addition of comparative and historical cases affirms many of the patterns observed in the Ghanaian cases and also draws out some new insights, including (1) a mission-focused organizational culture as a critical precursor to adopting innovative technologies to which organizational success is often subsequently attributed; (2) clarifying different paths in the onset of administrative distinctiveness, distinguishing cases where a strong bureaucratic ethos emerged upon founding or the reform of an existing organization; (3) clarifying that effective niches can be either coterminous with a large formal organization or a subunit, but in either case were relatively small at the time they became a highly effective niche; and (4) how external opposition may actually contribute to officials identifying more strongly with the organization and its mission.

ORGANIZATIONAL CULTURE AS A PRECURSOR
TO INNOVATIVE TECHNOLOGY ADAPTATION

The comparative cases illuminate how the specific content of internal organizational responses was as varied as the diverse local challenges interstices confront, yet they all shared the core characteristic of targeting particular local conditions and challenges with solutions that were relatively uncommon in the local environment. The use of uncommon solutions further underscored the niche's distinctiveness, in sharp contrast to one-size-fits-all global "best practices" often advocated in cosmopolitan reform efforts. When most government officials enjoyed lucrative patron-client relationships with local elites, the Salt Inspectorate instead frequently rotated official postings "to forestall incipient tendencies towards 'capture' by local elites."[108] The KTDA installed practices that seem the opposite on paper, but which were similar in responsiveness to their particular set of local environmental challenges. Within the intense racially and ethnically charged context of post-Independence Kenya, when Kikuyu favoritism was expected but resented, KTDA found it necessary to engage coethnic managers to work with the varied ethnic tea farmers, engendering trust and making visible demographically proportional hiring of management. Interstitial insiders drew on a depth of context-specific local knowledge to innovate distinctive practices that helped mitigate disruptions from the often unpredictable and sometimes inimical surrounding environment.

The Ghanaian cases mostly relied on internal changes to protect themselves from environmental uncertainties. Efforts to significantly reshape the physical environment or social practices beyond niche insiders were comparatively limited—Commercial Court justices imposing alternative dispute resolution (ADR) and disciplining lawyers into desired court practice are the foremost examples. By comparison, the longer time horizon of the comparative historical cases illuminates interstitial niches' efforts to remake the external environment both through social discipline and through more ambitious projects of physical remaking and infrastructural change.

Many of the historical cases of distinctively high-functioning niches involved some particularly innovative technologies or organizational policies, to which scholars studying the case in isolation often attribute the distinctive success of the organization. The Salt Inspectorate innovated new salt evaporation techniques to improve quality and built new depots to frustrate smuggling—engaging in some of the most ambitious efforts to *physically* remake the external environment to reduce uncertainties and facilitate the routine satisfaction of core organizational goals. NAFDAC hosted a series of unusually effective and well-received educational workshops for the public and small-scale pure water producers. KTDA built new factories and feeder roads, and developed new transportation containers made from locally grown sisal to reduce leaf damage in transport at a fraction of the cost of previously used shipping materials.[109]

This is where the logic of comparison across heterogeneous cases can illuminate foundational socio-organizational aspects that transcend cases and contexts. Across the diverse cases the *particular content* of technical solutions varied. However, what all the cases had in common was that niches selected locally novel procedures based on organizational goal-oriented logics, and not the prevailing logics of personal enrichment, political preference for particular groups, or nurturing clientelist relationships. Beyond direct technical benefits, utilizing distinctive goal-oriented technologies thereby further affirmed the boundary between the interstice and environment.

Public-sector employees are generally risk averse and tend to preserve the status quo over new practices that may go awry.[110] Untested organizational innovations or technologies are gambles with unknown odds and uncertain payoffs. Novel approaches are particularly risky where myriad environmental constraints can easily be blamed for lackluster results when merely continuing to pursue familiar practices. However, failing with a novel approach calls down focused blame. Therefore, introducing locally novel practices and organizational technologies is a boundary-marking act in and of itself. Above and beyond any technical benefits derived from the novel technology or practice, instituting novel practices that are oriented to achieving the organization's mandate underscores and affirms the boundary between the interstice and the larger neopatrimonial environment.

ONSET

As observed in the Introduction, cultivating a bureaucratic ethos that helps foster increased organizational capacity has seemed to be an intractable problem, stubbornly unchanged despite billions of dollars of donor aid targeting state capacity building. It has become something of a fashion lately to assert that ineffective or corrupt public-sector organizations cannot be reformed and therefore to pursue the creation of new agencies as a kind of blank slate. It is therefore substantively relevant for development practitioners, and of theoretical interest to scholars of organizational change more broadly, to understand how long it took for a case to emerge as a recognized pocket of effectiveness, and whether such pockets were the result of organizational reform or the founding of new organizations.

The cases demonstrate that effective niches may arise either upon the founding of a new state organization *or* as the transformation of an existing organization with a previously lackluster reputation. The Ghana Commercial Courts quickly acquired a strong reputation and impressive statistics on productivity within the first three years after founding. When existing organizations are transformed, the available cases suggest that a relatively quick and dramatic transformation is possible. A distinctively new sense of the organization may be palpable within six months and organizational performance indicators within a year or two. Akunyili assumed leadership of a NAFDAC that had existed for roughly a decade but accomplished little, but within a year of her stewardship there was a sense of a dramatically new direction in the organization.[111] The Chinese Sino-Foreign Salt Inspectorate is something of a hybrid case: It was created in parallel to the weak, corrupt *Yanwu Shu*, as a new organization performing an old task. The tension of being a separate organization and yet clearly overlapping administratively is even reflected in reports and scholarly accounts that sometimes refer to the Sino-Foreign Salt Inspectorate as the "reform administration." Its reincarnation coincided with its quick rise to organizational excellence, including the accomplishment of seemingly impossible tasks—like collecting salt tax at the point of production—and an impressive level of infrastructural reach.

Because subunits do not leave as detailed and disaggregated a record of their unit-level performance, it is more difficult to unambiguously date the onset of effectiveness. The highly technical mobile field monitoring units within Ghana's Spectrum and Frequency Management had long been dominated by professional engineers with rare credentials doing a generally inglorious but professionally interesting task with great care. There was a sense among the officials who had been there for some time that the field monitoring units had long been reputable. However, the National Communications Authority as a whole had a much more varying reputation for effectiveness that had suffered under a previous director with a penchant for patronage. Then the NCA's public image was rapidly transformed when Bernard Forson, a Ghanaian with thirty years of telecommunications experience in the United States, took over as director-general and began instituting a large number of new reforms.

The Monetary Policy Analysis Department of the Bank of Ghana was formed by then-governor Paul Acquah, drawing together some staff previously employed in research and policy elsewhere in the bank and recruiting new young economics graduates to join. Monetary Policy Analysis was well-regarded from its founding, and drew public attention because Acquah had a particular policy about information transparency that meant much of the unit's research work was publicly available on the bank's website.

SCALE & SIZE

The comparison cases have one curious difference from the Ghanaian cases: Entire agencies were identified as distinctively high functioning. In other words, in each one, the boundaries of the bureaucratic ethos coincided with the formal organizational boundaries. By contrast, the same was true only in the Bank of Ghana, where the entire organization was very well reputed. Instead, most of the Ghanaian cases were subunits within a larger organization: PARD and the monitoring units were respectively embedded within the formal organization of the Ministry of Finance and the National Communications Authority, larger organizations whose reputations for effectiveness varied across units and over time. The Commercial Courts were technically an administrative subunit of the High Courts, themselves under the Judicial Service. I do not believe, however, that Ghana is the only state where high-functioning niches exist as units within larger organizations. Rather, I think such subunit-level effectiveness may too often be overlooked. If effective subunits must pass the products of their labor on to another unit before the output is legible to the public, even contemporary outsiders may have a hard time differentiating performance. For example, a number of anticorruption agencies around the world have investigative but not prosecutorial powers. If an organizationally effective investigative unit has to pass its work on to an ineffective prosecutor, a public attuned to media-grabbing successful prosecutions may never know of the investigative prowess. Historically, discerning unusually high performance from a subunit may be even more difficult because its outputs are much less externally legible and leave few distinctive traces on the historical record.

Though the cases vary in scale—agency-wide or subunits within larger organizations—they were all relatively small in size at the time when cases emerged or were transformed to become highly effective niches: between 7 and 200 public servants. For example, in 1963 when founded, KTDA had 116 public servants, excluding farmer members, which grew to 156 by 1965.[112] The subunit niches were, understandably, smaller in size than the agency-wide cases. PARD was initially formed with just seven members, and developed a reputation as a pocket of effectiveness when it still had fewer than fifteen staff. The Monetary Policy Analysis Department within the Bank of Ghana was also comparably small in size at the time of its emergence as a recognized niche of excellence. The agency-wide niches were larger, though most were still relatively small for large formal organizations. For example, BNDE had approximately 150 members at the time when it emerged as a recognized pocket of effectiveness.

Understanding how the relatively small scale is theoretically beneficial for niche formation both illuminates some of the aspects of early niche formation and is also instructive for practitioners interested in learning practical lessons from these cases. First, a smaller scale is numerically advantageous for clustering distinctiveness, because a relatively small absolute number of people can constitute a relatively large percentage of the total relevant population, meaning it takes fewer distinctive people to establish a proto-bureaucratic organizational culture as the most visible mode of interacting. Second, within smaller organizations or subunits, a relatively large portion of the total organization are either in direct face-to-face interactions or are a few short network ties away from interactions with everyone else in the organization. Such structures are advantageous for the interpersonal diffusion of an ethic.

"IT JUST CAN'T BE DONE": THE SUBCULTURAL UNDERPINNINGS OF INTERNAL CULTIVATION BY EXTERNAL OPPOSITION

The comparison cases also cumulatively highlight a seemingly curious commonality: Many succeeded despite high-profile and vocal opposition, succeeded precisely in areas that well-informed critics argued were doomed to failure. Critics were sure that the Salt Inspectorate could never possibly successfully collect tax at the point of production because it was simply too administratively overwhelming and the proliferation of local interests against it too intractable, and yet succeed they did.

NAFDAC's work combating counterfeit and illicit drugs put them in conflict with lucrative criminal enterprises. As a result, NAFDAC faced not merely temptation to engage in corrupt acts, but outright danger for attempting to honestly complete the organization's tasks. Facilities were vandalized and set afire, while NAFDAC personnel attempting to do their jobs were threatened, assaulted, had family members kidnapped, and faced attempted assassinations.[113] NAFDAC became a paragon of honest and effective public service even though its employees faced personal harm for doing so, and amidst an environment wherein corruption and sloth were not merely tolerated, but expected of public officials. Those environmental and sector-based challenges make it all the more surprising that NAFDAC would emerge as a pocket of excellence and public trust within the Nigerian state.

Likewise, tax collection in early twentieth century China could also be outright dangerous. Tax collectors were sometimes physically threatened for carrying out their duties. In the aftermath of other reforms that upset traditional clientelistic orders, mobs beat collectors.[114] When another reform-minded tax official tried shipping tax revenues by steamer, "the [traditional transport] carters and junk men mobbed him, burned his official residence, and forced him to flee for his life."[115] Even the materiality of the sector and administrative environment were ill-suited to effective organization. The technologies for salt production and tax administration were outmoded, and the physical infrastructure was "deplorably neglected."[116] A report from the first year of the reform administration noted, "The depots are insecurely fenced and are more or less dilapidated" with storage facilities exposed to the elements.[117] Administrators in the central offices "had hardly ink to write with or paper to write on."[118]

At BNDE, development banking had acute sectoral challenges: Because development banks disburse large amounts of capital where it is scarce, the sector could have been particularly susceptible to political pressure to grant loans on the basis of the political connections of elites, rather than on the economic merits of the project. Indeed, for this reason, state-owned banks are typically less efficient than private banks, and more inclined to risky or economically unsound loans based on political motivations.[119] Moreover, the kind of large-scale, long-term infrastructural projects that BNDE was meant to target in the earliest years—like railroads and energy—were precisely those with long-term economic externalities that improve growth, but could leave BNDE doubly unsupported. They would be isolated from the executive branch because such projects lack short-term political benefits, but also left without significant external coalitions of public support, because such projects have large but diffuse benefits.[120] Given the local political environment and gen-eralized sectoral challenges, it was not at all clear at the outset that BNDE would succeed.

The Kenya Tea Development Authority was a surprising success for sev-eral reasons. First, it was a state-owned enterprise, and such enterprises have a history of failing cataclysmically. State-owned enterprises tend to fail in part because they are often riven between conflicting aims, tasked with being a productive enterprise while simultaneously trying to provide subsidized goods to producers or consumers, which renders the enterprise itself finan-cially instable.[121] State-owned enterprises in Africa have also been particularly vulnerable to becoming "patronage dumps," whereby political elites shore up support by finding low-skill jobs for supporters.

Second, tea is an incredibly technically demanding crop. Among other things, high-quality tea requires manual harvesting, relatively frequent man-ual weeding, and is agroclimatic-zone-dependent, only growing at certain altitudes and rainfall levels. Harvest requires technical finesse, careful trans-port to prevent damage, and because tea is very perishable, it has to get to processing within hours of plucking.[122] More challenging still, KTDA was going to have to oversee such difficult cultivation among scores of mostly un-educated smallholder peasants. This was no small task: "To make it a viable smallholder crop, KTDA had to determine the right size plots for smallhold-ers; develop a complex network for leaf collection and transport with tight scheduling; establish appropriate incentives, controls and payment systems for out-growers; determine the right size and location of factories; develop better tea plants; and set up an effective, disciplined extension service."[123] Tea had been introduced to Kenya only in the 1920s, and its production was the exclusive purview of white settlers until Independence.[124] Experienced experts in the World Bank initially refused to participate in the KTDA because they felt smallholder tea cultivation in an area with no prior history was surely doomed to failure because tea was a demanding and technical crop requiring strict quality control, systematic harvesting, and cautious transportation.[125]

Instead of saying that these groups succeeded *despite* the opposition, we might observe that they also succeeded *because* of it. Appreciating the subcultural social dynamics underpinning interstitial bureaucratic niches makes sense of this otherwise puzzling correlation between opposition and success. Within sociology, there is a classic recognition that conflict between groups can increase in-group cohesion.[126] From early twentieth-century anti-vice movements to contemporary virginity pledges and anti-abortion centers, researchers find that collective action and group cohesion can be enhanced by the perceived threat posed by other groups, especially groups seen as holding dissimilar or opposed values.[127] The perception of being beset by nearby outsiders can enhance attachment. For example, *foie gras* producers in France responded to rising animal rights activists in nearby European countries such that "foie gras has come to represent and demarcate French national patrimony, at least in part, because it is morally contentious elsewhere."[128] People identify most strongly with antivaccine stances when a small cluster of demographically and ideologically similar people live in close proximity to others who are demographically and ideologically different.[129] Similarly, Evangelicalism in America gained tremendous popularity in no small part because adherents felt themselves to be "embattled" vis-à-vis a larger secular American culture against which their beliefs had to be actively defended. Interactions with outsiders underscored the symbolic boundaries and clarified commonalities among Evangelicals through contrast: "Collective identities depend heavily for their existence on contrast and negation. Social groups know who they are in large measure by knowing who they are not. In-groups establish what it means to be 'in' primarily by contrasting with outgroups whose members are 'out.'"[130]

Conclusion

Thus far, the Ghanaian and comparative niches have demonstrated the concentration, deepening, and defense of clustered distinctiveness, which supports the flourishing of the bureaucratic ethos even in environments where it is rare and deviant. The heterogeneous comparison cases also contribute analytic leverage on the theoretically attractive but methodologically vexing question of how such clustered distinctiveness initially emerges in its earliest incarnation. This chapter has uncovered some aspects about the initial establishment of niches, including the observation that the initial emergence of a bureaucratic niche can occur either as a niche within a larger organization or agency-wide, and can occur either upon the founding of a new organization or the reform of a seemingly intransigent one.

Pockets of effectiveness that either replaced or were transformed from ineffectual organizations tasked with the same function—such as the 1990s NAFDAC, Vargas-era BNDE, and the *Yanwu Shu*—provide excellent within-case contrasts, demonstrating that profound changes to the organizational culture are possible within the relatively short period of a year or two. Those quick changes are encouraging news to development practitioners, reformist politicians, and organizationally oriented public servants who may hope to reform public-sector organizations to enhance their effectiveness. But perhaps more importantly, high-performing niches that replaced or were transformed from ineffectual organizations performing the same tasks in the same country just a few years apart minimize extraneous difference, and thereby enable attention to the few conditions whose timing accounts for that change, thereby shedding light on the earliest emergence of bureaucratic niches. The next two chapters leverage those within-case contrasts to analyze in greater detail the conditions under which the earliest clustered distinctiveness arises.

6

Beyond Autonomy: Elite Attention and Pathways to Shelter from Neopatrimonial Influence

Autonomy has long been a topic of interest in political sociology[1] and is some-times considered a sort of organizational silver bullet to reform ineffective public-sector organizations in low-income countries. However, formal orga-nizational autonomy is typically rare in most neopatrimonial states because it is at odds with the patronage needs of political elites. From Jacksonian-era America to many contemporary Latin American and African states, political elites often prefer to consolidate power by influencing agency goals and staff-ing decisions to reward supporters with valuable resources and employment.[2] Giving people jobs on the basis of political support may conflict with hiring on the basis of merit, so patronage hiring sometimes results in hiring people who are not even minimally qualified. When patronage interests completely overwhelm consideration of merit, organizations can become "patronage dumps" saturated with patronage employees.[3] Patronage hiring can have neg-ative effects on organizational orientation not only because it biases who is chosen and who is not, but also because among those hired, it orients atten-tion to interpersonal connections as the proximal cause of their hiring rather than merit or professional accomplishments. That orientation then tends to influence the way they make choices and behave on the job.

The political benefits of patronage hiring explain why it persists, even though it generally hampers organizational effectiveness.[4] From state-owned enterprises to government agencies, patronage dumps result in organizations that are inefficient, overstaffed, corrupt, costly, politicized, and ineffectual.[5] In such a context, even a few qualified and dedicated but isolated public servants can become despondent and ineffectual when surrounded by others whose principal interest is nurturing their relationship with their patron, rather than achieving the organization's goals.[6] A great many organizations become beholden to multiple, and sometimes conflicting, unofficial goals, like providing "jobs for the boys."[7] Numerous unofficial goals may lay waste to an organization's ability to achieve its core function: A state-owned energy enterprise also tasked with providing jobs to political supporters and offering subsidized electricity to appease voters may then ultimately fail to be effective, responsive, or financially sustainable. Bloated payrolls and political pressure to provide inexpensive electricity to garner favor with the electorate erodes the ability to be economically self-sustaining, and therefore the organization cannot keep up the maintenance of the power infrastructure and generating capacity—ultimately undermining its foundational ability to supply power.[8]

The Autonomy Debate: Protection
from Elites, *of* Elites, or *with* Elites?

Formal organizational autonomy is often seen as the antidote to patronage. Framing autonomy as the logical redress for politicalization is evident in many of the state reform trends that swept the globe in the late twentieth century. For example, the Bank of Ghana is both one of the most well-regarded organizations in the Ghanaian state and also one of the most formally *autonomous* organizations, which some see as the explanation for its success. During the 1990s, Ghana joined a global movement to strengthen central bank independence, responding to an international neoliberal wave that argued for buffering key decisions about the economy from the sometimes shortsighted political calculus of elected politicians (neopatrimonial or otherwise).[9] Yet the experience of the Bank of Ghana also highlights the cracks and contradictions in the concept of autonomy, which will be unpacked below. Though officially autonomous on paper, a long-standing bank official recalls that there was a period in its history when politicians were so eager to make state-owned enterprises succeed that political elites eager to capitalize on the bank's organizational effectiveness tasked the Ghanaian central bank with operating a sheep farm, fairly clear evidence the bank had acceded to the desires of political elites despite de facto autonomy. Interestingly, organizational records show that the Bank of Ghana has been granted formal legal autonomy no fewer than four times throughout its history, even when it had not officially had its formally autonomous status legally rescinded.

There are multiple and sometimes confusing ways that autonomy has been used in scholarship on states and organizations. Autonomy is typically defined as the absence of external control over an organization, such that all operational decisions are made within the organization. External constraints impinging on autonomy range from legal mandates, external control over funding, external control over personnel, or influence over policy choices.[10] There has been considerable discussion over autonomy from *whom*. Scholarship on state autonomy has variously debated whether agencies are autonomous from politicians, but also the "capture" of agencies, where agency decisions are influenced externally by capitalists, shared ethnicity, or social background.[11] Autonomy may be a formal, legal declaration or refer to practical, de facto autonomy. There is a tendency to assume formal declarations of organizational autonomy grant de facto autonomy. However, in practice organizations may have high formal autonomy but little practical autonomy or, conversely, organizations may appear legally to have low autonomy but in practice may exercise considerable internal control.[12]

The literature on state capacity, however, is far from any consensus that organizational autonomy—variously conceived—is an unmitigated boon to agencies' effectiveness. Instead, autonomy is something of a theoretical conundrum. From Weber onward, hierarchical coordination has classically been considered a critical organizational technology that enabled effective administration over large and complex tasks, including the governance of a state.[13] Scholars of developmental states have similarly argued that autonomy of state agencies from central administrative control was a source of inefficiency that reduced the coordinated effect of governance such that even if individual ministries were pursuing their organizational mandate in the public interest, it could result in an ineffective quagmire.[14] The right hand doesn't seem to know what the left is doing, resulting in parts of the state that issue contradictory or conflicting policies.

Conversely, observers of states in developing regions often note that in otherwise weak states, the most trusted and effective government organizations are often those that are formally autonomous agencies, which gives some institutional insulation from political pressures.[15] For example, increasing the autonomy of revenue agencies in Latin America improved public perceptions of fairness and increased total revenues collected.[16] Other scholars sketch something of a middle road, equating formal organizational autonomy with elite support because, they argue, in neopatrimonial contexts grants of formal autonomy only occur where interpersonal loyalty is assured, and true de facto discretion depends on political elites' consent.[17] Thus many have argued that significant organizational reforms to improve effectiveness cannot happen without executive will and significant "buy-in" from high-level political elites, without which organizations cannot secure discretion over personnel or shelter from neopatrimonial pressures.[18] For example, political elites with economic and political linkages to a particular industry—as was the case for dairy in Uganda and meat in Botswana—may take an active interest in fostering strength and increased capability in the state organizations that affect that industry.[19] Active executive sponsorship may be particularly intense when political elites face an existential threat to their power and see a state organization as the remedy to that threat.

However, even among those who argue that within institutionally weak states autonomous agencies tend to perform better than those of the central state, there is no clear agreement on *why* autonomous agencies seem to perform better. Some scholars interpret the relative success of autonomous state agencies as evidence that states should move away from conventional Weberian bureaucratic organization. Most prominently associated with "New Public Management,"[20] this body of scholarship equates bureaucracy with the very worst of its popular caricatures: unnecessary red tape, lack of motivation, a dizzying maze of rules and regulations that seem to work at cross-purposes or no purposes at all. Such scholars believe autonomy is associated with unusually effective agencies because autonomy allows those agencies to distance themselves from the bureaucratic morass that dominates the rest of the state.[21] These ideas have also influenced the increasing reliance on semi-autonomous agencies to enact central state governance even within advanced industrialized economies with states that are generally regarded as strong, like Finland, the Netherlands, Sweden, and the United Kingdom.[22]

Unfortunately, that interpretation is based on the faulty but widespread assumption that most states possess not merely bureaucratic trappings, but also the bureaucratic ethos, such that moving away from the state means moving away from bureaucratic ways of operating. DiMaggio and Powell famously declared that "the bureaucratization of the corporation and the state have been achieved."[23] Perhaps largely true in the West, this declaration neglects that which is common knowledge to citizens of low-income countries: All contemporary states have formal organizations performing administration, but not all state organizations embody the animating ethos of bureaucracy.

Instead, I argue that in contexts where neopatrimonialism predominates, any form of discretion or autonomy matters because it gives agencies insulation from the neopatrimonial status quo, enabling some agencies to carve out the possibility of a different way of doing things. In the context of neopatrimonialism, autonomy may enable change *toward the bureaucratic ethos*. Contrary to the erroneous presumption that organizations everywhere are already thoroughly bureaucratized, in many non-Western contexts the bureaucratic ethos *is* the deviant institution requiring protection to insulate it from the contrary practices of the patronage-based administrative milieu. The clustering and contradistinction from the larger neopatrimonial institutional field that characterize interstitial bureaucracy are only possible with sufficient organizational discretion, especially over personnel, tasks, and rewards (including status rewards).

The analysis particularly highlights the foundational importance of organizations having *personnel discretion,* that is, internal control over the hiring and firing of their own staff. To appreciate why discretion over personnel may help explain the empirical observation that "autonomous" agencies outperform conventional state administration, we need to revisit the insight that bureaucratically inclined and enabled people are the fundamental scarce resource for the construction and performance of bureaucracy in low-income weak states. This refocuses the broad multifaceted concept of autonomy onto the particular way it intersects with people: through the selection, hiring, distribution, and practical daily enskillment of humans. *Personnel* discretion is significant for understanding bureaucratic niches because locally held discretion over hiring can, in some circumstances, enable the emergence of hiring oriented to achieving organizational goals, even within state administrative cultures dominated by patronage.

This chapter argues that shelter from neopatrimonialism is a critical condition for the emergence of a pocket of effectiveness. The theoretical move to focus on shelter from neopatrimonialism helps resolve prior debates about autonomy and executive will, reframing these as functional substitutes. Below I use the term *autonomy* only to refer to formal legal declarations of organizational autonomy or semiautonomy. I employ the term *discretion* to indicate a relatively high degree of internalized control on a continuum of practical independence from extraorganizational influence. I focus particularly on relative freedom from the influence of high-level neopatrimonial political elites; unless otherwise qualified for brevity the term *elites* refers to this group. I develop a four-part typology of political elite interest alignment with organizational goals that draws attention to two typically overlooked conditions also capable of fostering bureaucratic niches—merely interested elites and inattentive elites—while integrating the clustering distinctiveness framework into a larger pantheon of work on states, including notable work by Charles Tilly and Daniel Carpenter. The chapter demonstrates how the typological framework of elite attention helps explain observed outcomes in the high-performing niches from Ghana, Nigeria, Kenya, Brazil, and China, using control and failed cases for contrast.

Because the Ghanaian cases are all drawn from the same state at the same time period, in effect the Ghanaian cases control for some important dynamics that may affect the process at the national and international levels. Expanding examination to cases with varying times and contexts gives theoretical purchase on how the mechanics of highly effective state niches are shaped by differences in scale, distinctive sectoral challenges, varying national contexts (especially of elite agendas), and world-historical timeline conditions. Thus the chapter aims to construct a broadly applicable theoretical explanation while also attending to variability, temporal dislocation, and unplanned events.

Elite (In)Attention and Shelter from Neopatrimonial Politicalization

Theoretically, I argue that shelter from neopatrimonial logics influencing hiring or operational decisions is essential for an interstitial niche to emerge, because such shelter enables the possibility of new practices that are at odds with the predominant neopatrimonial means of ordering social conduct and power. It is fruitful to shift the conceptual debate from autonomy to shelter from neopatrimonial logics because shelter from neopatrimonial influence does not require formal organizational autonomy, and conversely organizations with the same formal-legal autonomy can have widely varying levels and types of discretion in practice.[24] Formal organizational autonomy has too often been conflated with shelter from politicized decision making,[25] but disentangling the two can give analytic leverage on the seeming conflict between those who argue successful state organizations require autonomy from elites and those who argue just as forcefully that organizational success depends critically on active support of or working with political elites.

Autonomy advocates argue that organizational autonomy improves outcomes because it affords civil servants isolation from political or social pressures, particularly in environments that are generally organizationally weak or dominated by patronage politics.[26] But it is important to disentangle autonomy as a potential *means* from the ends of shelter from neopatrimonial politicalization, particularly because (1) de jure formal organizational autonomy does not always convey such shelter in practice and (2) formal organizational autonomy is only one means to obtain such shelter. Like formal autonomy from elites, the sponsorship of elites is presumed to act through the mechanism of sheltering decisions from neopatrimonial influence—"political leaders insulate the organisation from widespread patronage practices"[27]—because elites have taken a particular interest in the organization succeeding at its goals. Thus, reframing around shelter from neopatrimonial pressures helps resolve the seeming contradiction between autonomy *from* elites and sponsorship *of* elites: both are functional substitutes capable of providing shelter from neopatrimonial logics.

Reconceptualizing around shelter from neopatrimonial and patronage pressures highlights elite *attention* as a critical variable. The attention of political elites is a finite resource. This is acutely true in many low-income coun-

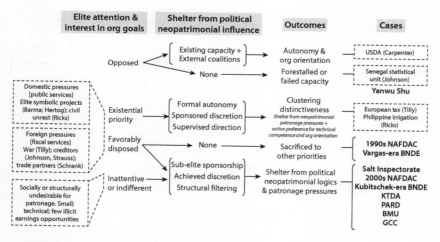

FIGURE 6.1. Elite attention and pathways to shelter from neopatrimonialism.

tries, where the volume and quality of data to make the sprawling administrative state legible, even to its own leaders, are relatively poor. The limitations of elite attention are a well-documented fact in organizational research,[28] but too often macro-political analyses of states seem to endow political elites with cognitively unrealistic omniscience. Instead a more cognitively and organizationally realistic view is that political elites have a finite number of state projects about which they can pay intensive attention. The two most legible forms of elite attention are both cases of intensive elite attention: active support or active opposition. However, if we take seriously the idea of limitations on elite attention, it highlights two other types of elite attention: Political elites may be merely favorably disposed—somewhat aware and tolerant but not supportive—or be inattentive and therefore unaware of some informal increases in organizational discretion over personnel and operations that occur endogenously within niches.

Figure 6.1 presents a framework focused on four ideal-typical forms of elite attention, differentiating whether and how each provides shelter from neopatrimonialism and clusters distinctiveness to yield organizational orientation. This reconciles seemingly discrepant findings by highlighting how *different types* of elite attention can provide functionally analogous shelter from neopatrimonial influences.[29] Among the cases examined in this book, all of the successful niches developed under heads of state who were merely favorably disposed or inattentive. Because these types of political elite attention are empirically relevant and less theoretically well developed, this chapter will concentrate on those two types, and then return in the conclusion to discuss prior work on elite opposition and executive will.

FAVORABLY DISPOSED ELITES

Similar to damning with faint praise, heads of state may be merely *favorably disposed* to an organization succeeding in its stated operational goals. Instead of the gravity implied by "executive will," these are merely willing executives. These political elites are willing to allow the organization to accomplish stated goals. The organization's operational success could be beneficial, and political elites might be glad to take credit if it succeeds, but the organization accomplishing its publicly stated goals is not a high or existential priority. As such, operational orientation may be readily sacrificed to service a host of alternative political considerations.

BNDE Brazil: Vargas as a Favorably Disposed Elite Who Sacrificed Organizational Outputs

The BNDE case is a particularly illustrative case for understanding that formal legal autonomy can often be insufficient to grant true de facto discretion. It calls attention to the importance of the organizational and interpersonal work that is done to create greater spaces of discretion. This example leverages a within-case comparison between BNDE when it was founded under President Getúlio Vargas (1951–1954) to the later development of BNDE under President Juscelino Kubitschek (1956–1961). Vargas was favorably disposed to BNDE succeeding as a development bank. However, Vargas faced immediate political pressures. Despite the bank's seemingly strong legal autonomy, Vargas sacrificed BNDE's long-term organizational performance as a bank to political priorities, seeking to secure supporters through preferential bank jobs and loans. The early evolution of BNDE's discretion also provides evidence of the pivotal importance of discretion over personnel. When the bank finally achieved personnel discretion—in the hands of a small cadre of organizationally oriented leadership—that enabled the clustering of distinctive persons, after which transformative momentum and a distinctive sense of identification and orientation emerged quickly among the ranks.

The formal institutional arrangements for BNDE are regarded as politically insulated,[30] though as in many of the other cases, this position of formal de jure autonomy was considerably more complicated than it seems at first blush. BNDE had the official legal status of an *autarquia*. Relative to the mainline civil service organizations, *autarquias* officially had much greater control over financial and personnel decisions. *Autarquias* could cultivate their own streams of funding and apply their own systems for hiring and firing staff, including not being beholden to the civil service pay scale.[31] Moreover, to insulate the bank from congressional red tape or interference in lending decisions that could come with yearly congressional budgeting, the bank drew funding from a specially established Fund for Economic Rehabilitation (FRE).[32]

Despite all these formal organizational structures that limited control from the legislature, full de facto operational discretion was far from secure. As an *autarquia*, BNDE was protected from the congress but still dependent on the president.[33] The legal statutes governing the bank gave the executive considerable leeway over the finances, personnel, and—to a lesser extent— organizational tasks. Financially, the bank's FRE funds were disbursed by the minister of finance, whom bank managers often had to lobby directly for the release of funds.[34] Indeed, in the first years of its existence, BNDE was not merely organizationally located under the Ministry of Finance; it was also *physically* located within the Ministry of Finance building.[35] Top personnel were directly in the president's control: BNDE was headed by a board of directors and administrative council, all of whom were presidential appointees.[36] The president also held the power to summarily dismiss the organizational heads.[37]

Even though its status as an *autarquia* formally conveyed greater internal control over personnel, during the Vargas presidency that personnel discretion was significantly curtailed. Vargas did appoint qualified technocrats into key positions within BNDE's founding administration, including Ary Torres, Roberto de Oliveira Campos, and Glycon de Paiva Teixeira. However, Vargas appointed a close personal confidant with no technocratic skills—José Maciel Filho—as supervising director, with considerable organizational power over the technocrats. Maciel Filho famously resisted efforts to introduce competitive entry exams at BNDE, arguing that such exams would result in hiring "'ugly women and communists.'"[38] For a while, the BNDE technocratic management corps worked towards a skillful compromise with Maciel Filho, a form of "mixed meritocracy" where ideal-typical meritocratic criteria were coupled with alternative selection criteria, such as interpersonal connections to elites or, as in this case, ideological commitments aligned with elite views. Paiva Teixeira and Campos sought to recruit staff who were qualified and technically competent, but who were also acceptable to Maciel Filho because they shared his nationalist development ideology—which in the context of the time meant favoring restrictions on foreign capital and investments.[39] Despite these skillful compromises, in the last year of Vargas' presidency, many of the top-ranking technocrats—including Torres, Campos, and Teixeira— ultimately resigned over differences with Maciel Filho and the political interference with their technical vision of the bank.

In the two years between the presidencies of Vargas and Kubitschek, three different men would serve as Brazil's president. Each in his own manner sought to dismantle BNDE as a legacy of Vargas, or to cannibalize the bank to secure their own fragile hold on political power. Scholarship on BNDE broadly agrees that the bank emerged as a pocket of effectiveness under the Kubitschek presidency (1956–1961). Kubitschek came to power convinced that his political future depended on his ability to show concrete progress on his national development plan, famously promising "Fifty years of progress in five." The plan was manifest as a series of relatively concrete goals, reflected in the strangely apolitical title of Kubitschek's signature national development plan, which sounds like something only a technocrat or an engineer could love: *Plano de Metas* (literally: Plan of Goals). Led by Campos, a number of technocratic BNDE staff that had formerly resigned from the bank in protest then worked closely with Kubitschek during his campaign for president, helping Kubitschek design and formulate the *Plano de Metas*.[40] After Kubitschek was elected, those same BNDE staff who had been instrumental in its design would spearhead implementing the *Plano de Metas* in their reinstated positions at BNDE.

Thus, the disenfranchised BNDE technocrats worked to align the interests of the new President Kubitschek and the bank, cultivating trust, confidence, and a close relationship with Kubitschek before he came to power. Those same technocrats had also been primarily involved in the formation of the economic plan and were therefore particularly vested agents of its implementation. In turn, Kubitschek addressed the problems from BNDE's financial dependency on the executive that had come to the fore in the Vargas administration when BNDE had trouble getting Congress to allocate funds, and when a portion of those funds so allocated tended to be re-appropriated by the Ministry of Finance to cover deficits elsewhere.[41] Kubitschek instead created surtaxes that were collected and deposited directly with BNDE, which were never included in the federal budget and had only minimal initial approval by Congress,[42] thus endowing BNDE with significantly greater financial independence from both Congress and the executive branch. After Vargas' death, the BNDE technocrats gained greater discretion over BNDE personnel, as Campos was appointed director-superintendent in place of the problematic Maciel Filho.

Kenyan Tea Development Authority (KTDA): Kenyatta as a Favorably Disposed Elite Who Tolerated Success

The Kenya Tea Development Authority is a case that successfully developed into a pocket of effectiveness within the post-Independence Kenyan state, with high levels of achieved discretion affording shelter from neopatrimonial politics due to a personal relationship between the agency head and president. President Kenyatta appointed Charles Karanja, who was a close personal associate, as KTDA's director-general in 1970, after Karanja attracted attention for innovative ideas from within the organizational ranks.[43] Several scholars have claimed that KTDA's unusual success was due in large part to its internal control over financial resources and operational decisions.[44] However, in the intensely patronage-driven politics of post-Independence Kenya, Leonard argues that elite political connections were essential for any effort to gain such organizational discretion.[45] Even if a formal de jure declaration of organizational autonomy was obtained, de facto independence was not something obtained through a legal act, but rather a state of noninterference constantly maintained by nurturing personal connections to political elites. Where personal relationships dominate the formal exercise of state power, "This is a sign, not of the absence of politics, but of the presence of a very different form of politics. Power in African political systems is aggregated out of patronage networks, is highly personalized and generally is concentrated in the hands of the head of state."[46]

Karanja was a prime example of *mixed meritocracy,* whereby agency leaders have both personal connections to political elites *and* a sufficiently rare claim to expertise: Karanja was a credentialed civil engineer at a time in Kenyan history when university graduates were still quite rare.[47] KTDA was endowed with considerable discretion over personnel, tasks, and finances. In particular, KTDA received no ongoing funding from the government budget. KTDA was initially funded with large external loans, and was intended to finance itself by generating revenue capable of repaying loans and covering operational costs.[48] The primary formal organizational checks on KTDA were relatively few: Budgets were subject to audits by the controller and the auditor general, and the minister of agriculture technically had oversight although in practice a close relationship with the president limited the exercise of those formal oversight powers.[49]

Karanja gained and regularly defended considerable discretion over personnel staffing at KTDA. Although pressure to Africanize was intense, the KTDA retained a modest number of expatriate workers, all of whom had significant lived experience in formal organizations that endowed them with the know-how of *doing* bureaucracy. Even as late as 1978, there were still a handful of expatriates, strategically clustered not in the culturally sensitive farmer-interfacing roles of field officers, but rather in technical and engineering aspects of factory operations.[50] Initially, some portion of the staff for KTDA were seconded from their permanent positions at the Ministry of Agriculture. This secondment provided much-needed sector-specific experience in the early establishment of KTDA. But it also afforded an opportunity to evaluate those staff for hard-to-discern dispositions, such as incorruptibility and hard work: "The administrative control over the staff remained with KTDA which could ask the government to recall employees whose performance was found to be unsatisfactory."[51] Many, however, stayed with KTDA on long-term secondment, while others left their ministry post to officially join as KTDA employees.[52]

Even amid generally strong de jure formal autonomy, there were also significant moments of achieved control over personnel. Most notably, Kenyatta struck a nationwide deal with organized labor that would have permanently increased the number of employees by 10 percent and might have forced Karanja to accept new employees into KTDA who did not meet its performance standards. Instead, Karanja met the letter of the law while avoiding the potentially deleterious consequences by "transferring seasonal workers onto the permanent payroll without hiring new or additional labor in the KTDA or its factories."[53] Karanja was clearly explicitly aware that within the intensely neopatrimonial political environment wherein personalized exercise of power through networks reigned, formal declaration of semiautonomy would still require skillful action to become true de facto independence. Karanja observed "Though we have been set up as a semi-autonomous body, it is not difficult for the government to interfere if it wants to. We do not need government funds, but still require government support and facilities for many of our tasks."[54]

State-owned enterprises, such as KTDA, were a common tactic in the development aims of many post-Independence African states. Framed as ambitious efforts to launch African economies into manufacturing, a majority of state-owned enterprises ran at a net loss, sometimes running losses as a significant percentage of total country GDP.[55] In post-Independence Kenya, KTDA was one of thirty-two different public enterprises. With so many irons in the fire, President Kenyatta was a classic example of a merely willing executive: He would have been happy to capitalize on the organizational success of any of those enterprises but there is no evidence that Kenyatta was particularly invested in KTDA. KTDA took efforts to position the organization's goal—to foster commercially viable tea cultivation among small-scale farmers—as well-aligned with the interests of political elites in post-Independence Kenya. Because Kenya had a significant history of commercial agriculture by white settlers (unlike Ghana), "indigenization" of the economy was a high-profile post-Independence priority for President Kenyatta.[56] Moreover, given mounting political pressure about President Kenyatta's ethnic favoritism of Kikuyu elites, Kenyatta had an interest in being able to claim some success in elevating the economic well-being of black Kenyan smallholders. Thus, KTDA's official task of encouraging successful smallholder agriculture was politically advantageous for Kenyatta *but only after and because of KTDA's manifest success.* So long as KTDA was performing well, their success was a bulwark against political interference. Karanja noted, "Our focus has been on servicing the small farmer. [Kenyatta] is solidly behind us. This is a major source of strength."[57]

The Kenyan smallholder had been politically constructed as the epitome of social virtue, a morally unassailable character upon which legions of policies would be built,[58] much like Skocpol's analysis of the political construction of soldiers and mothers as morally unassailable in early American welfare policy.[59] In a political climate in which the small-scale African farmer was socially constructed as the epitome of social worth, the active support of the farmers was a significant guarantor providing KTDA shelter against deleterious political interference. KTDA also cultivated external support coalitions from other powerful players, particularly the Commonwealth Development Corporation (CDC) and the World Bank, both of which eventually became financially invested in the Kenyan tea development efforts. Karanja observed, "The presence of the CDC representative has been a positive influence on our autonomy. CDC is our major creditor and has no parochial interest. More recently, the involvement of the World Bank has reinforced the same trend."[60]

"You have to choose your battles": NAFDAC and Obasanjo as Merely Willing to Capitalize on Circumstance

Nigeria's NAFDAC is also a case of favorable disposition, demonstrating that organizations subject to favorable disposition are not necessarily doomed. There had been a series of highly public scandals surrounding low-quality and counterfeit drugs in the prior decade. However, when President Obasanjo came to power, he confronted a host of governance challenges clamoring for his attention, and there is no clear evidence that reforming NAFDAC was seen as an existential priority. He did not shower the agency with resources nor throw his considerable political clout behind selecting an "efficiency engineer." Indeed, the account highlights that even the president was frustrated by how difficult it was to find and discern candidates with strong reputations for effectiveness, suggesting scholars may have overestimated the extent to which even reform-inclined executives can merely exercise choice among a known menu of managerial options. Even when executives are willing to appoint leaders with skills and orientations to accomplish explicit organizational mandates rather than appropriate offices to nurture neopatrimonial relationships, executives can still face considerable scarcity and legibility problems.

In 1993 a new legislative decree gave birth to NAFDAC, replacing a moribund drug-safety organization that had existed since the 1970s. Throughout the 1990s, however, even with new formal autonomy and enhanced abilities on paper, NAFDAC languished, and counterfeiting flourished, suggesting those institutional changes alone were not sufficient to reform the performance of the organization. NAFDAC's initial formal legal founding coincided with considerable political turmoil. Shortly after its establishment, President Babangida resigned under pressure, appointing an interim president tasked with transitioning to democracy, Ernest Shonekan. But Shonekan's administration only lasted a few months before a palace coup once again introduced military rule under General Sani Abacha. Abacha's rule was characterized by some economic improvements, amid human rights abuses and rampant embezzlement. After his death, the Special Investigations Panel reported that

Abacha and a ring of confederates had embezzled at least $1,419 million USD and £416 million GBP, monies that were laundered through banks, businesses, and offshore accounts.[61] The U.S. Department of Justice would eventually forfeit $480 million USD in Abacha's funds that had been stashed in U.S. banks.[62] Some estimate that in the late 1990s, shortly before his death in office, Abacha was embezzling and misappropriating up to a quarter of the government's total budget.[63] Attention-diverting crises abounded.

Expert observers date the period of NAFDAC's transformation to 2001–2008, when Dora Akunyili assumed leadership of the organization.[64] Interestingly, however, Akunyili might never have been tasked with heading NAFDAC if not for a personal medical scare. While working for the Nigerian state's Petroleum Trust Fund (PFT) in 1998, Akunyili was diagnosed with a growth that doctors told her would require expensive surgery. The PTF allotted state funds for her to travel to the United States for a second opinion and to have the surgery. But doctors in the United States told Akunyili she had been misdiagnosed, that her ailment could be resolved with medication, and therefore did not require surgery. Akunyili returned to Nigeria and, to everyone's general astonishment, returned the £12,000 that PTF had given her for the now-unnecessary surgery.[65]

After the corruption and financial abuses of the 1990s, when many Nigerian government officials were devising means of siphoning illicit funds from the state, it was almost unheard of for someone to go out of their way to return funds that had already been legitimately issued to them. The story of Akunyili returning funds to the PTF made the rounds among senior state leaders. Shortly thereafter, the newly democratically elected President Obasanjo was seeking a new director-general for NAFDAC and asked his close confidants to identify "an honest Nigerian pharmacist" to head the agency. Stories of Akunyili's return of state funds conveniently presented itself as a solution to the otherwise high search costs of trying to discern "honesty" among the applicant pool. Obasanjo himself felt constrained, explaining he could not have reformed every agency of government because "there are political dimensions to reforms … you have to choose your battles."[66] Based on circulating stories of her honesty with the PTF funds, Akunyili was tapped to take charge of the ineffectual NAFDAC.[67] Just like the Ghanaian judges who felt acutely aware of being elevated beyond their seniority, the objects of outside scrutiny, and intensely dedicated to prove their selection had been wise, Akunyili's memoir reports: "Though lacking in experience, success on this job was crucial to me. The President of the Federal Republic of Nigeria had placed great trust and confidence in me by appointing me to the position, despite stiff political opposition."[68] NAFDAC suggests that favorably disposed executives may convey some shelter from the political interference of lesser political elites, but as Vargas demonstrates, do not necessarily protect the organization from their own operationally detrimental political interference.

ELITE INATTENTION

Political elite inattention is perhaps the most overlooked foundation for building organizational goal orientation. When organizations are neither supported by high-end political elites nor opposed, inattention can be surprisingly benevolent, providing shelter from the more sundry effects of being embedded in a largely neopatrimonial environment by minimizing elite interference in personnel or operational decisions. Elite attention is a finite resource, so heads of state and other influential political elites may be quite literally less interested in, and attentive to, some parts of the state. This may occur because attention is monopolized elsewhere—for example by insurrection or foreign war—or because particular parts of the state are socially or structurally undesirable for politicizing their operations or hiring. For example, some agencies may be less desirable for patronage because they are small, technical, offer few opportunities for illicit earnings, or require arduous and uncomfortable working conditions.[69] In this section I first examine the case of the Chinese Salt Inspectorate as a prototypical example of a bureaucratic niche emerging amid inattentive political elites. The Ghanaian cases were broadly similar, though less extreme, to the Salt Inspectorate in their trajectory to successful niche formation under inattentive elites. Therefore, rather than be repetitive, after examining the Salt Inspectorate the following section will employ comparable founding data on the Ghanaian niches, with briefer parallels drawn to the comparison niches, to address the question of what factors confer shelter from neopatrimonialism under merely willing or inattentive elites.

China's Salt Inspectorate: Distracted and Therefore Inattentive Elites

This case has both elements of favorably disposed elites and elite inattention, and is also a case where political and economic elites were riven with respect to the organization's goals. Political elites had fiscal interests aligned with enhanced revenue generation, while economic elites fought many of the organization's reform efforts because it decreased their own profits. Because taxation has been so central a sector in executive will explanations, it is important to note that in this case, political elites *did* face a sort of existential crisis that demanded revenue. However, despite that crisis they *did not* go to great lengths to give resources and protection to either the *Yanwu Shu* or the Salt Inspectorate. Why? Political elites would benefit from enhanced revenue. However, because reform efforts had previously failed, political elites did not *expect* that outcome and therefore did not act in ways to explicitly cultivate organizational capacities.

Because it involved the creation of an entirely new organization as a requirement of securing an essential foreign loan, Chinese political elites were clearly aware of the organization. However, political elites were significantly distracted by the turmoil of the era, and ultimately the diversion of their attention to more pressing problems elsewhere was the primary driver that enabled the organization to assert itself into new mandates and activities. Over time, political elites became favorably disposed in response to the organization's unexpected rise in revenue generation. That is, the shift from inattentive to favorably disposed political elites was a consequence of organizational performance, not its cause.

From its formation in 1913, the Chinese Salt Inspectorate was supervised by the Ministry of Finance—at least on paper.[70] The fledgling Republican central state painstakingly asserted itself as the sovereign equal to the foreign lenders in the loan agreement, specifying that the foreign participants were subordinate and advisory to their Chinese counterparts.[71] That claim on paper meant little in practice: The Salt Inspectorate had tremendous de facto financial, personnel, and operational discretion due to the inattention of Chinese central political elites, who were preoccupied by the turbulence of the era. This protective inattention was further enabled because when the Sino-Foreign Salt Inspectorate was formed Chinese political elites viewed maritime customs as their primary source of revenue and were less attentive to salt taxation. The Salt Inspectorate became so effective so fast that by the time Chinese elites realized how lucrative salt taxation could be, the foreign head had institutionalized layers of insulation, gained the trust of Chinese political leaders, and created financial dependencies on the revenues the Inspectorate generated. These all sheltered the organization from external political or patronage interference. During the Republican period, as the central government even struggled to control Peking (Beijing), the Salt Inspectorate was one of only two organizations that operated nationally and consistently transmitted revenue to the central government.[72]

Similarly, largely through accidental inattention, the Salt Inspectorate had surprising financial discretion. They collected revenue themselves and were not structurally dependent on political budgetary appropriations. The foreign loan that established the Salt Inspectorate included initial funds to modernize tax operations. More crucially, because both foreign lenders and Chinese political elites vastly underestimated how lucrative salt tax collection could become—and how quickly—no provisions were made to stipulate or cap the Salt Inspectorate's operational or infrastructural expenses. So long as the revenue collected remained plentiful enough to both service the foreign loan and provide Peking greater revenues, both sets of elites largely left the Inspectorate alone. In an interview, the Foreign Chief Inspector, Sir Richard Dane, noted, "At the close of 1915 the net sum turned into the government treasury by the new administration, *after the deduction of the cost of administration* [italics added], was $69,277,550.40 USD, an increase of almost 100 percent over that of the previous year."[73]

The Inspectorate had considerable operational discretion, and substantially expanded the scope of the organization's mandate. The Sino-Foreign Salt Inspectorate was initially authorized with a circumscribed organizational mandate: collect salt taxes and deposit them in a central account to service the foreign loan debt. It officially remained organizationally subordinate to the pre-existing *Yanwu Shu*, and the *Yanwu Shu* maintained official authority over all the other areas of the salt tax operations from production and transport to sale.[74] However, within the first four years of operation, under the stewardship of Sir Richard Dane, the Sino-Foreign Salt Inspectorate assumed a greater operational purview to manage its operational dependencies on the weak *Yanwu Shu*. Similar to the compensatory competence observed in the Ghanaian cases in chapter 4, the Salt Inspectorate simply assumed responsibility over auditing district offices, monitoring salt production, transportation, storage, and sale. Because the *Yanwu Shu* was organizationally weak, it could not resist these expansions. Moreover, Dane actively cultivated the allegiance of Chinese political elites, not only through economic dependency on revenues. Like the savvy framing to appeal to elite interests in Kenya, Salt Inspectorate field reports frequently appealed to the Chinese Republican state's concerns about regressive taxation that unduly fell on poor rural peasants.[75] Perhaps more important, the Salt Inspectorate positioned itself as a neutral arbiter in disputes between the Chinese government and the foreign lenders, building considerable trust with political elites in Peking.[76]

Shelter from Neopatrimonialism within Favorably Disposed or Inattentive Elites

How then do cases obtain shelter from neopatrimonialism under the conditions of merely favorably disposed or inattentive elites? This section uses the Ghanaian data, with brief parallels in dialogue with comparison cases, to identify three important means of attaining shelter from neopatrimonialism and increasing discretion over personnel and operations: (1) sponsored discretion granted informally by a powerful patron who is not a high-status political elite; (2) achieved discretion, through intentional and skillful maneuvering within formal constraints; and (3) accidental discretion, where structural conditions of the work filter patronage and influence because work within the niche is viewed by economic and political elites as undesirable.

SPONSORED SHELTER AND DISCRETION

Influential people exist at many layers of the state below high-status heads of state and legislators. Even if high-status political elites are inattentive or uninterested, shelter from neopatrimonial pressure can be obtained if a "big man" with status and social capital in the more-proximate organizational environment takes interest in cultivating a niche. Regarded as influential because of skill and charisma in attaining network positions, such "big men" may be lesser political elites beneath the head of state, such as ministers, but also include people who are particularly influential in kinship groups (*abusua panyin*), business, politics, or traditional chieftaincy.[77] A "big man" can therefore mobilize resources, especially social networks, to influence the outcome of power contestations.

Sponsorship may be a largely informal benefit that is not legally inscribed into the organization's status. The role of sponsorship in providing shelter from neopatrimonial influence can be seen clearly in the case of the Ghanaian Commercial Courts, though it is also present in several other cases, which will be discussed below. It was widely acknowledged that the creation of the Ghana Commercial Courts was the pet project of former Chief Justice George Kingsley Acquah.[78] Formally, the Commercial Courts had been internal to the Judicial Service and subject to the same hiring and operational procedures, differing only in that their court cases focused substantively on commercial litigation. However, the chief justice viewed the success of the Commercial Courts as a reflection of his own legacy and therefore used his influence to secure the human and material resources that would help the courts develop into a pocket of effectiveness. Chief Justice Acquah spearheaded the creation of the Ghana Commercial Courts, personally seeking funding, advocating for innovative infrastructural projects, and handpicking the founding justices and staff based on sterling reputations.

Chief Justice Acquah could not get the project funded through the Ghanaian government budget, and so he obtained a $4.7 million USD grant from Danida, the Danish development agency, for " 'structural reforms in service delivery and the establishment of a business law division in view of strengthening the responsiveness and efficiency of the legal and judicial environment for businesses in Ghana.' "[79] Danida's guidelines expressly prohibited using grant funds to build new infrastructure, but the chief justice travelled personally to the Danish parliament to advocate for special permission to use the funds to construct a new building with modern infrastructure. Similarly, although officially subject to the same hiring procedures used everywhere throughout the court system, as described previously in the second chapter, the chief justice took a personal interest in recruiting for the new Commercial Courts, personally investigating the reputations of every justice and high-level official placed in the court. He used his influence, not in classic clientelist fashion to hire people who were loyal to him, but rather to protect hiring appointments from patronage or politicalization, and to ensure that all those placed in the new court had strong reputations for unassailable integrity and hard work.

Lesser and apolitical state elites are important to distinguish analytically because they are not subject to the same democratic election or autocratic succession pressures, which can affect the fates of sponsored niches. Agencies that seem to flourish under the sponsorship of a head of state then subsequently wither when that patron is removed from power, as the new president dismantles the successes of his predecessor.[80] We saw this after Vargas's second term, as three different presidents over the next two years would each in different ways erode the capacity of BNDE before Kubitschek came to power. However, chief justices of the Ghanaian Supreme Court do not face the same existential calculus as elected heads of state. Chief Justice Acquah died in March 2007, when his pet project was only two years old. The former chief justice was dead and therefore no longer an active rival for the role, but more importantly chief justices serve in the position until death or voluntary retirement. The success of the Commercial Court as her predecessor's project was therefore not a significant threat to the new Chief Justice Georgina Wood's position, as it might have been for an elected elite.

Other Ghanaian and comparison cases had some less-direct or less-public forms of subelite sponsorship that likewise helped confer added shelter from neopatrimonial influence. Akunyili seems to have benefitted from good working relationships with ministers throughout the Nigerian federal administrative state, and in particular with reform-minded female ministers.[81] Several of the comparison cases feature external network connections to international organizations that served as a sort of sponsorship that muted local neopatrimonial interference by giving organizations cover to pursue more technocratic decisions—the Salt Inspectorate was a go-between to the state's significant foreign lenders, BNDE was a gatekeeper to local projects hoping to secure foreign loans, and the Commonwealth Development Corporation and World Bank were influential on the KTDA Board.

Sponsorship appears in the establishment of both PARD within the Ministry of Finance and the Monetary Policy Analysis Department within the Bank of Ghana. What eventually became known as PARD started because, as one official recalled, the minister at the time "thought there should be the need for more or less a think-tank division for the ministry." PARD began therefore as a handpicked collection of seven officials drawn from throughout the ministry. At the time, the Agriculture desk was considered "very strong ... and very hard working. So when PARD was created, that desk was taken to PARD." Another founding member was responsible for interfacing with the International Monetary Fund, and was also very trusted by and close to the Minister; one official explains that the man was "like a special assistant to the Minister" because he reported directly to the minister and "he was always moving around with the Minister." Another founding member of PARD worked on expenditures and was also considered very close to the minister. Three founding members came from agriculture, an important economic sector, and others came from functions throughout the ministry. I asked a senior member of the ministry if the work sector had been an important consideration for the selection of PARD's founding members. The official did not hesitate, "No. I think, I think they just took people who they thought were hard working." Similarly, the Monetary Policy Analysis Department of the Bank of Ghana was formed to be a nimble and responsive research arm for the Monetary Policy Committee—the board of high-ranking officials who actually set monetary policy for the country. The unit was created by Governor Paul Acquah, who selected a small group of officials drawn initially from existing divisions within the Bank of Ghana and supplemented with some promising young university graduates whom the Governor personally interviewed.

INFORMALLY ACHIEVED SHELTER AND DISCRETION

Many of the Ghanaian niches were subunits within the boundaries of larger formal organizations. The subunit scale means that most of the Ghanaian niches did not have formal legal autonomy from the larger ministry or agency of which they were officially a part. Full formal autonomy typically—perhaps exclusively—exists at the level of entire organizations. The Ghanaian cases are thereby particularly apt for illuminating the role of informally achieved discretion and shelter from neopatrimonial influence.

PARD is a subunit, existing within the Ministry of Finance and Economic Planning (MOFEP). As such, PARD is perhaps illustrative of how subunits manage to achieve greater personnel and operational discretion *despite* facing formal and environmental constraints. PARD cultivates greater discretion over personnel through a combination of strategic choices and leveraging political capital, employing tactics of refusal, poaching, or reassignment to informally achieve personnel autonomy. As part of a ministry, PARD is subject to standard civil service hiring and therefore illuminates how niches engage cultural and organizational work to accomplish greater discretion over personnel despite low formal autonomy.

Typically, the Ghanaian centralized Office of the Head of Civil Service hires new civil servants en masse and sends batches to all the ministries. Next, MOFEP's Human Resources Department circulates the list of new hires to department and division heads. As exemplified in the control case, and confirmed by a human resources manager from the ministry, typically department leaders do not control the distribution of personnel within the ministry. However, most directors regularly clamor for as many personnel as possible. Refusing available hires is uncommon in Ghanaian civil service and also in organizations generally. There is even a classic "law" of organizational theory —Parkinson's law—that argues supervisors always desire more subordinates, because subordinates increase status in the organization.[82] However, PARD preferred to take no one if recruits did not meet PARD standards. Mr. Mensah explains, "There are a number of people who finished their national service, they wanted to come to PARD, but I refused." Whether national service members placed in PARD or elsewhere within the ministry, Mr. Mensah would refuse to hire those who "did not perform up to expectations."

National service thereby affords probationary periods for observing difficult-to-discern characteristics, solving some of the search cost challenges discussed in the second chapter. PARD staff work hard to cultivate national service members placed into their division. Mr. Mensah explains that hardworking national service members who are performing well are even rewarded with international training courses: "We have some training programs in WAIFAL ... West Africa Institute for Financial Monetary Management in Lagos, which was set up by the English-speaking West African countries to build capacity. And we, we allow national service people to go there. In other divisions, they always argue: why national service people should be allowed to go to training? But we take them to be part of us." He repeats several times throughout his discussion of national service personnel "we take them to be part of us," underscoring how early cultivation through us-them boundary work begins. Recruiting from among national service placements affords potential new members a year to acculturate and be evaluated before officially being hired as civil servants.

As described earlier in chapter 2, PARD would also occasionally "poach" officers from elsewhere within MOFEP, another means of solving the search costs and informally gaining greater discretion over the composition of workers within PARD. Like national service, recruiting from elsewhere within the ministry provided an informal probationary period. Sanctioning through reassignment also afforded greater control over the personnel composition of the niche. Legal provisions and cultural norms make it exceedingly difficult to terminate a civil servant. Reassignment within the civil service does not violate those extensive labor protections, but is still remarkably rare, violating hegemonic administrative norms.

Though many of the comparison cases had some degree of legal formal autonomy or semiautonomous status, those cases nevertheless also illustrate the role of achieved discretion under merely willing or inattentive elites. For example, similar to PARD, KTDA also used probationary employment as an informal means of obtaining greater internal control over staffing. As discussed earlier, seconding staff from the Ministry of Agriculture allowed KTDA to either return staff if their performance was unsatisfactory or if staff were satisfactory, extend secondments long-term or poach workers by hiring them officially. Similarly, achieved discretion is also evident in the previous example of Karanja manipulating the status of existing employees to circumvent the edict to hire new employees. Operationally, much of the discretion and expansion of tasks in the Salt Inspectorate was first informally achieved despite formal legal mandates, and only later sanctioned.

STRUCTURAL FILTERING OF PATRONAGE PRESSURES

The types of shelter described above—subelite sponsorship and achieved discretion—work to filter neopatrimonial patronage and political pressures through intentional and strategic human action. Several of the Ghanaian and comparison cases also suggest that patronage pressures can be partly, or even primarily, filtered as a result of structural factors that make employment there less desirable to would-be patronage seekers. Those structural factors may influence human decisions in ways that ultimately result in fewer patronage seekers and professionally unmotivated candidates, even when such intermittent human choices were not intentionally or strategically oriented towards protecting a particular unit from patronage. This picks up on the idea, first introduced in the second chapter on recruitment, that states have a varied social topography.

Within the varied social topography of the state, some functions have proportionately less sector-based exposure to forces that enable corruption by street-level functionaries. Some state functions have, by virtue of their work, increased opportunities for unofficial income, which correspondingly enhances the attractiveness of those positions to candidates with fewer intrinsic professional motivations. Conversely, niches of the state that offer relatively challenging work with enticements that primarily appeal to the professionally oriented are likely to dissuade patronage seekers, resulting in a labor pool that skews towards organizationally oriented recruits. For example, work in Ghana's NCA field monitoring units required weeks of work out on the road, far from the comforts of home, while conducting detail-oriented and meticulous work monitoring the airwaves. This is the sort of thing that appeals enormously to a radio engineer who finds the work intrinsically interesting, but is not the first choice of work for the average patronage seeker. Similarly, recall from the last chapter that field postings—essential to moving up the ranks in the Chinese Salt Inspectorate—demanded long hours in the hot sun, uncomfortable travel, and physical exertion, all of which were considered beneath the Chinese upper classes, or as Chief Inspector Dane observed, "which are evidently very distasteful to Chinese gentlemen."[83] Selecting out socioeconomic elites best positioned to exert patronage pressures shifted the balance in the recruitment labor pool, helping to provide shelter from neopatrimonial influences.

Other features of a unit's work may lead to clustering distinctive persons —in this case selecting *for* merit rather than *against* patronage—without apparent coordinated or strategic effort to do so. For example, when I interviewed Junior Agyemang-Badu, a human resources officer in the Ministry of Finance, I observed to him that a lot of PARD members had international advanced degrees. Mr. Agyemang-Badu explained that civil servants were able to go for advanced schooling and then come back into the civil service, but that in departments such as Budget it was impossible to hold the position open and unoccupied while the officer completed a foreign degree program. Mr. Agyemang-Badu explained that Human Resources therefore sought to replace officials who went abroad for advanced degrees, filling their vacated posts as soon as possible. That meant that when the officials returned to the ministry after completing their education, they could not simply return to their old position. However, Human Resources had a sense that PARD's policy analysis work was 'very flexible.' Therefore, those officials returning from education abroad were staffed to PARD. I sought to clarify whether this was part of any intentional strategy to upgrade skills in PARD, which Mr. Agyemang-Badu dismissed entirely, explaining, 'No, no. Their work is so flexible, they can absorb the extra people.' Seemingly without strategy or intent, the perception that PARD's tasks allowed flexibility in scale of personnel resulted in the intensive and distinctive clustering of officials with advanced foreign degrees.

Situating the Framework within Prior Work: Elite Opposition and Executive Will

Across the range of Ghanaian and comparison cases, none of the niches faced substantial elite opposition. Prior work suggests active elite opposition may completely forestall initial efforts to build niche organizational capacity. For example, Johnson's work within Senegal convincingly demonstrates that donor efforts to build statistical capacity failed in the Ministry of Agriculture because donors' desires to enhance statistical capacity—and thereby render government more externally legible—directly conflicted with political elites' desire to obfuscate the extent to which programmatic agricultural resources were distributed according to political and patronage-based logics. Political elites therefore worked to actively undermine inchoate capacity-building efforts, starve the unit of resources, and insert a trusted patronage supporter into the key leadership structure.[84] Cumulatively, this suggests the *absence of opposition* from the head of state may be a necessary but insufficient condition for the initial emergence of an interstitial niche.

Thinking of active elite opposition as a subtype of elite attention also reframes Daniel Carpenter's brilliant work on agency autonomy in the nineteenth-century U.S. state.[85] His puzzle begins with agencies like the U.S. Food and Drug Administration (FDA) enacting new organizationally oriented programs and policies while in open conflict with the legislature. Carpenter argues that the agencies' autonomy—rendered methodologically clear precisely because they are acting in opposition to political elites' wishes—depended on a reputation for excellence with which they cultivated an external coalition of supporters. Unlike Senegal's agricultural statistical unit, I would argue the FDA thrived despite open conflict with political elites because it was *already* a pocket of excellence with demonstrably uncommon capacity to effectively administer programs in the public interest. Carpenter's work thereby gives insight into what we might anticipate concerning pockets that are already relatively well-developed, and the conditions under which such established pockets can survive open conflict with elites. Indeed, his accounting has substantial parallels with how the post-Kubitschek BNDE mobilized external coalitions around their technocratic reputation to grapple with subsequent presidents who sought to influence the distribution of BNDE loans for political gain. On balance, this suggests that absence of active elite opposition may be a necessary precondition for the early-stage emergence of a pocket of effectiveness, and that even well-established pockets may require cultivation of external coalitions of supporters to survive open conflict with political elites.

ELITE EXISTENTIAL PRIORITY AND ACTIVE SPONSORSHIP

Active presidential sponsorship has captured the most attention and is what is often meant by "executive will."[86] There is a prevailing sense, among scholars and development practitioners, that a head of state who is sufficiently committed to organizationally oriented reform is both necessary and sufficient for organizational reform and enhanced performance. For example, Ricks argues that the Philippine National Irrigation Administration developed surprisingly administrative strength—emerging as a "global leader in irrigation management"—because and only when the head of state faced the existential threat of domestic unrest and had too few financial resources to buy off protesters through less administratively arduous patronage gifts.[87] Vastly simplifying Charles Tilly's famous arguments about war as the stimulus to early European state capacity building in taxation, the argument can also be read as a case of heads of state facing critical existential crises and then willing into being the organizational capacity to tax.[88] Dan Slater also gives analytic pride of place to the elite's perceptions of urgent interests—here again I vastly simplify his rich historical detail—broadly arguing that in the Philippines the absence of urban, communal mass mobilization led to a low perception of threat among political elites and thereby ultimately resulted in low state capacities to tax.[89]

Executive will often appears as a deus ex machina account, seemingly self-evidently sufficient for organizational success without interrogating how it brings organizational capacity into being. Instead, I argue that successful agencies that arise out of executive will are just a particularly externally legible subtype of interstitial bureaucracy, arising through the same clustering distinctiveness mechanics. Understanding the framework and insights developed by observing cases of interstitial bureaucracies helps to illuminate how executive will operates to inculcate a niche of distinctiveness. Active executive sponsorship solves the dual problems of providing shelter from neopatrimonial operational and personnel pressures, and simultaneously provides motivation for orienting that space of potential difference to organizational goals. Within predominantly neopatrimonial environments, action is already habitually oriented to interpersonal networks mobilizing to fulfill the wishes of a "big man," whatever those wishes may be. Scholarly accounts suggest that executives face a host of choices when selecting ministry and organizational leadership appointments, some of whom are "consummate political brokers" while others have a reputation as "efficiency engineers," and elites select among available choices based on what they want the organization to accomplish, politically or operationally.[90] That is, executive will works to cultivate a pocket of excellence through the same *clustering distinctiveness* mechanics identified in this book, starting from the top down, and solving resource problems for chosen organizations. Executive will appears as an elegant explanation but is theoretically insidious because it elides the intervening mechanics and overshadows important alternative pathways.

Prior studies that emphasize executive will have often taken elites facing an existential crisis as both necessary and sufficient for the outcome, creating the impression that if executives are sufficiently motivated they will inevitably call into being the organizational capacity required to get the job done. Illuminating clustered distinctiveness as the mediating pathway to the organizational outcome is an important theoretical intervention even into cases of executive will because if elites face existential crises but are unable to cluster together the requisite personnel and skills—for example, because such people and skills are too scarce—the organizations will still fail. Ghana's first post-Independence president, Kwame Nkrumah, was acutely aware that he faced a genuine existential threat to his hold on power as the coffers of the state emptied and he was unable to provide the public services, economic development, and dreams of modernity he had promised to the newly independent country. Nkrumah actively feared the coup that would eventually force him out of power in 1966, and so clearly knew he was in an existential crisis. However, Nkrumah's seemingly sincere desire to see Ghana succeed at manufacturing and his executive will was not enough to bring into being a concentrated group capable of effectively administering to those ends, and thereby saving the state.

The Chinese case is particularly illustrative of how existential crisis without clustering distinctiveness can be insufficient for organizational reform. Salt was a convenient source of revenue because it was used amply in the Chinese diet, and the Chinese had taxed salt as far back as the seventh century BC.[91] However, the existing *Yanwu Shu* central salt tax agency had withered in size and organizational capacity. The Qing dynasty faced manifest existential crises in the form of internal revolts and foreign wars. Despite desperately needing revenues, Qing dynasty elites were unable to will into being the organizational capacity to collect them: Numerous attempts to reform the salt administration were made, but all failed. The evidence of these prior failures would later prove unexpectedly propitious for the formation of the Sino-Foreign Salt Inspectorate, as described above.

The cases herein demonstrate that executive will is not necessary for the emergence of a pocket of effectiveness, though executive will may still be a sufficient cause. In comparative logic, a cause like executive will may be sufficient but not necessary for an outcome if "presence inevitably leads to the outcome, though the outcome can occur through other means as well."[92] Indeed, the cases raise the empirical question of whether executive will is even the most common sufficient explanation for the outcome or whether, instead, it is more externally legible and therefore over-represented in cases of external attention because it is highly visible to observers outside the inner sanctum of state power.

Conclusions

The chapter has argued that scholars need to move beyond the contested and ambiguous concept of state autonomy to explain the rise of pockets of efficiency within the state, suggesting instead it is more fruitful to look at *shelter from neopatrimonialism* as a crucial condition for the emergence of bureaucratic niches. The presence of such shelter, in turn, depends on a wider array of variation in elite attention than prior scholarship has expected—not just whether political elites actively support or actively oppose a particular agency and its goals, but also whether political elites are merely willing or inattentive. Drawing particular attention to how shelter from neopatrimonial forces enables organization-level discretion over personnel and operations, the chapter identifies multiple pathways through which particular state agencies might obtain shelter even in settings of a benevolently tolerating or inattentive heads of state. These factors include sponsorship by certain subelites, achieved informal discretion through skillful tactics, or structural filtering of patronage attention resulting in discretion for some parts of the state without concerted human intention to do so.

Putting the Ghanaian cases into dialogue with the comparative historical cases suggests that prior scholarship may have over-emphasized the importance of full formal autonomy as a route to organizational effectiveness because such cases are relatively easier to observe from outside the state. Within the comparison cases, the modal means of discretion were formal declarations of organizational autonomy inscribed onto the official legal provisions governing the organization. NAFDAC, BNDE, KTDA, and the Salt Inspectorate were all formally autonomous or semiautonomous agencies with some supervisory relationship to a ministry, much like Ghana's NCA or central bank. Comparative historical cases of interstitial bureaucracy over-represent such obvious formal organizational autonomy, capturing fewer cases of sub-elite sponsored discretion, like Ghana's Commercial Courts, or PARD's informally achieved discretion. I argue that the bias of what gets recorded on the historical ledger renders fully formally autonomous agencies more externally legible, and has thereby led to the erroneous impression that full legal autonomy is necessary for the establishment of an interstitial niche. Cases of a subunit within a larger organization, like PARD, that informally achieve high degrees of operational and personnel discretion are very difficult to observe from arm's length and unlikely to leave clear marks on the historical record. From careful efforts not to offend when declining a bribe to the book's opening vignette about office lights burning bright, many interstitial niches intentionally tread lightly on their surroundings to avoid drawing too much attention to themselves, because such attention might incite sanction from neopatrimonial forces.

This chapter thereby helps further specify the scope conditions under which external support coalitions are important for agency success. Since Carpenter's masterful work on the American state, it has become the dominant position that bureaucratic autonomy depends on strong external coalitions that support the agency's work—perhaps benefit from it—and thereby act as a bulwark against political encroachment. *Patchwork Leviathan* puts that narrative in a broader context, suggesting that coalition-building comes after (and depends on) previously establishing organizational performance, and may be most important for niches whose unusually strong performance is very publicly visible and those who enter into open conflict with political elites. Because full formal autonomy is highly legible, even to outsiders, it may indeed be strongly correlated with powerful external coalitions supporting it. We see that not only in Carpenter's work, but also in the cases of BNDE after Kubitschek and in the Sino-Foreign Salt Inspectorate in the support from new elites created by expanding into nonhereditary salt licenses (see chapter 5). Of the Ghanaian cases, the Ghana Commercial Court was the most overt about cultivating a coalition of supporters from the business community. Not coincidentally, we might also observe that of all the cases, the Ghana Commercial Court was also one whose relative performance was the most externally legible: Judicial Service annual reports routinely published statistics from all the courts on caseload and time to completion, rendering the comparatively strong performance of the Commercial Courts starkly visible to all. The importance of coalitions might be overstated in part because coalitions have affinities with highly externally legible independence, which is also more likely to show up on the historic record and be legible to outsiders like foreign researchers. However, for many bureaucratic niches, avoiding overt outsider attention to their "rate breaking" performance—flying under the radar—may be an important sequentially prior, or continually alternative, strategy.

The cases also collectively shed light on long-standing interest in whether higher wages can cause greater organizational effort in otherwise weak institutional environments. One might note that NAFDAC, KTDA, and the Salt Inspectorate all had unusually high levels of financial independence— earmarked funding or directly collected revenues—which they used to pay their employees' wages and benefits that were different from those paid traditional public servants. Within the economic framework that so dominates modern life, higher wages seem to be the motivation par excellence. It can therefore seem intuitively logical that higher wages would enable organizations to recruit and retain the best people, improve productivity, reduce corruption, and enhance orientation to organizational goals.[93] This is often stated as a foregone conclusion, a self-evident relationship. For example, in explaining the institutional reforms of the Mexican tax administration, Portes explains, "Fiscal inspectors were placed on a salary scale above the rest of the official bureaucracy to bar corruption."[94] Indeed, scholars have argued: "One of the most important determinants of the effectiveness of the excise was high salaries, which made officials dependent on their positions."[95] However, prior research on whether raising public servants' wages improves organizational performance and reduces corruption is surprisingly mixed: Below-subsistence-level wages and dramatic decreases seem to correlate with corruption, but prior research generally finds that raising wages alone is insufficient to reduce established levels of corruption.[96]

Obviously, people must eat, and government workers deserve to be reasonably compensated for their daily labors. To be clear: On principle, I am glad to see people financially rewarded for a job well done, and I believe all people deserve a living wage. However, it is analytically important to acknowledge that the cases also demonstrate that highly effective niches can exist even without higher wages.[97] Members of PARD were paid the same as those elsewhere in the ministries. The justices and staff in the Ghana Commercial Courts were paid on the same scale as justices and staff throughout the judicial services. This evidence that higher wages are not a necessary condition for the establishment of a niche of excellence is good news to resource-strapped states hoping to improve organizational capacity.

Scholarship in social psychology and economics gives potential insight into why niche members may be so motivated despite having low pay, comparable to other public-sector workers. Wages sufficient for reasonable existence, but below comparable private-sector wages, may have an unexpectedly beneficial framing effect: None of the interviewed Ghanaian interstitial insiders said they were doing the work *because of* the money. It was far more common for insiders to say they were working for the state despite the pay, rather than because of it, which is coherent with increasing research showing that intrinsically motivated people often outperform those who are offered extrinsic rewards or punishments.[98]

If higher pay or financial discretion was not a feature of all the highly effective cases, why might prior work have given financial compensation such undue attention? Agencies that pay above conventional government pay scales tend to have financial autonomy, and those with financial autonomy also tend to have very high levels of personnel discretion. If all financially autonomous agencies using alternative pay scales also have personnel discretion, then given the taken-for-granted dominance of economic expectations about wage incentives, we may misattribute the effect of personnel discretion to the copresence of higher wages. Formal financial autonomy and separate pay scales are particularly rare in states and thereby command attention, overshadowing what I argue is the more significant influence of niche-level discretion over personnel. By contrast, niche-level discretion over personnel *was* present in all the high-performing cases and absent or diminished in their control cases. Control over personnel enables clustering distinctiveness, and through that, cultivating an organizational culture oriented to achieving organizational goals.

Finally, the cases speak to a scholarly interest in state autonomy, which came to the fore in debates in the 1980s about whether states constituted distinct actors from powerful interests in society, like capitalists. Later work further specified interest in whether the administrative body of the state could itself be autonomous from powerful political elites, like heads of state or congressmen. Autonomy has therefore long implied a sort of categorical distinction—agencies either are or are not, categorically, autonomous. Autonomy has then typically been defined as states (or agencies within states) acting in their own interests over or against the discernibly different interests of powerful social groups or political elites.[99] In part, that was a methodological necessity: Observing the aftermath of a decision, it was easiest to say that administrative agencies had acted in their own interests if the administrative interests were sharply distinctive from the interests of outside influence groups or political elites.

The Ghanaian and comparison cases paint a different picture. First, several of the cases made concerted efforts to reshape the perceived interests of political elites to align more closely with the organization's interests. This happened most notably when disaffected technocrats from BNDE actually authored President Kubitschek's development plan, giving BNDE pride of place in its subsequent administration. Elites' perceptions of their interests are, like their attention, imperfect and partially malleable. Scholarship typically thinks of political elites' interests and attentions as an external force acting on administrative organizations, not the other way around. Instead, these cases show that elites can shift their interest and attention in response to heightened organizational performance, as was the case in the Salt Inspectorate, and organizations can actively work to align elites' perceptions of interest with organizational goals. The alignment of those interests was a considerable organizational achievement that should not be overlooked as merely pursuing elite goals.

Second, despite having relatively high formal autonomy—including dedicated revenue streams—the comparison cases critically underscore that where the rule of law is fairly weak, de jure organizational autonomy does not assure de facto discretion. BNDE struggled considerably under the Vargas regime when its econometric ideals for evaluating loans clashed with Vargas's operational interference in lending decisions to secure his fragile hold on political power, and personnel interference in the ever-present person of José Maciel Filho. Even with formal autonomy, NAFDAC, KTDA, and the Salt Inspectorate all benefitted from aspects of sponsored, achieved, and incidental mechanics to ensure that they had autonomy, not only in law, but also in fact. I thereby join other scholars who have argued that autonomy is less a categorical condition and more a continuum of degrees of discretion. Completely full and unfettered legal organizational autonomy is rare, but more importantly: That level of autonomy—on paper—requires substantial maintenance and defense by the organization, particularly in weak rule-of-law contexts.

7

Dual Habitus and Founding Cadres: The Sociological Foundations of How Discretion Is Oriented to Organizational Achievement

How does clustered distinctiveness arise under conditions of merely willing or inattentive political elites? Why do some niches that are afforded operational discretion by willing or inattentive elites then come to be oriented towards achieving organizational goals, acting competently in the public interest? Discretion or insulation enables the *possibility* of difference from the larger institutional field. However, to borrow from Weber's characterization of the effects of bureaucracy, the effect of that discretion depends on "the direction which the powers using the apparatus give to it."[1] Organizations with high discretion could perpetuate practices of the larger neopatrimonial institutional field. Discretion could merely give officials greater insulation to advance personal or network interests at the expense of organizational and national goals.[2] Indeed, discretion has been famously enshrined by Klitgaard as part of the formula that leads to corruption.[3] Given such widespread expectations, it seems almost irrational that officials endowed with discretion—a potential license for personal enrichment—would instead turn that discretion to prosocial ends, sacrificing personal gain in the name of achieving organizational goals. Yet discretion may also be the organizational crèche within which novel and institutionally deviant rational, impersonal, and efficient bureaucratic practices are incubated. One might then wonder: Under what conditions is organizational discretion *bureaucratically* oriented towards achieving organizational goals? This is a particularly pressing question because, as the introduction observed, instilling the ethos of organizational orientation has seemed to be an intractable problem for would-be organizational reformers.

Do Leaders Matter?

I've earlier argued that some parts of the government may have advantages if they recruit from pools where the proportion of patronage pressures may be low relative to the rest of the state. Though this may facilitate the emergence of a bureaucratic niche, it is not a sufficient explanation because no correspondingly rapid change in the labor pool of tax collectors, pharmaceutical regulators, radio engineers, or judges can account for the rapid emergence of organizational orientation and effectiveness in the Salt Inspectorate, NAFDAC, NCA, or Ghanaian Commercial Courts, respectively. Likewise, there were not rapid changes in the extent to which the organizational sector was linked to capitalist interests, or served a pro-reform clientele. Empirically, the timing of those rapid transformations in previously ineffectual organizations or sectors coincided with the appointment of a new organizational leader. This chapter therefore synthesizes the Ghanaian and comparative cases to analyze some specific ways in which organizational leaders do (and do not) contribute to the cultivation of a bureaucratic interstice, a sociological approach to theorizing how leadership affects change in organizational ethos.

Sociologists are often justly skeptical of accounts in which organizational transformation hinges on the presence of a particular leader.[4] Explanations for organizational transformation and greatness can tend towards a cult of personality aggrandizing "great men"—this is certainly prominent in accounts of American corporations, for example. Attributing the transformative success of Apple® entirely to the stewardship of Steve Jobs would miss a host of deeply interesting sociological conditions, including the organization of work, demographic shifts in consumers, labor contract relations, or changing supply chain configurations emerging from the globalization of transportation and telecommunications, to name but a few.

To be clear, I will argue that leaders mattered, but this is not a story of *charismatic* leadership. There is little evidence that interstitial niches formed around charisma or particular personality types. Instead, the personality of leaders varied widely. Mr. Mensah, PARD's director, was certainly widely admired by his staff, but when describing himself explains, "I joke with everybody, but at the same time I can be very serious and ruthless with them [chuckles]. Ruthless and maybe, I don't know whether that is, that is a problem with me but [pause] people don't think I am diplomatic [chuckles]." By contrast, workers at the Bank of Ghana described the much-admired Governor Paul Acquah as "a quiet man of few words ... Overall, he is a very detail-oriented person who constantly focuses on how minute details connect to broad objectives." Dr. Frimpong, head of Monetary Policy Analysis unit, was also a precise and scholarly man who measured his words thoughtfully. By contrast, KTDA's Charles Karanja was "talkative, aggressive, ambitious, and shrewd in politics."[5] The Salt Inspectorate's Sir Richard Dane was described as speaking "testily" and having a personality that was "shaggy and blustering, with an immense capacity for concentrated work, and for making other people work."[6] BNDE's Ary Torres was a skilled social operator who moved easily among different groups,[7] but Roberto Campos was a polemical personality "firm to his convictions, eloquent in his speaking, consistent in his critiques and had an acute sense of humor," but also capable of "ignoring the presence of a friend sitting next to him in a plane, and ... going out with a brown sock in one foot and a blue one in the other."[8] The leaders of bureaucratic niches varied widely in their individual personalities and few could be described as charismatic in a classically Weberian sense.[9]

Yet sociological skepticism of leaders may also go too far. In reading accounts of distinctively high-performing organizations across a range of state functions, countries, and time periods, it is impossible not to be struck by how often the rise or transformation of an organization correlates closely with the tenure of a new leader.[10] In 2001 Dora Akunyili assumed leadership of a NAFDAC that had existed for roughly a decade but accomplished little; within a year there was a sense of a dramatically new direction in the organization and in the first two to three years they began to make remarkable reductions to counterfeit drugs in circulation.[11] Similarly, after years of declining salt tax collections under the moribund *Yanwu Shu*, there was an astronomical increase in salt tax collection beginning in the first year Richard Dane assumed leadership of the Salt Inspectorate. In the first year of operations, the net revenue skyrocketed from $11.4 million USD to $60.4 million USD.[12]

I accept the sociological skepticism about the essential role of any particular human being, and reject popular tendencies to attribute success to idiosyncratic qualities of a "great man." Instead, the chapter develops empirically grounded observations of the sociological characteristics and network positions that are comparatively common in leaders of interstitial niches. I will directly tackle the question of leadership in the founding of niches, bridging the extensive management literature on organizations with a sociologically grounded approach. I identify general sociological features and experiences characteristic of the kinds of people who have been the heads of successful pockets of effectiveness—in particular, the experience of *dual habitus* and *founding cadres.* I thereby take a sociological and relational approach that is an important corrective to typical managerial accounts that suggest that organizational transformation depends on idiosyncratic, heroic, or charismatic characteristics of a particular individual. The next subsection introduces a striking empirical pattern across the Ghanaian and comparison cases, explains how that observation helps address prescient actor problems, and fleshes out that argument by introducing quotes from interstitial insiders in Ghana.

Dual Habitus: A Cultural and Cognitive Approach to Changing Organizational Practice

The emergence of a bureaucratic ethos poses a "prescient actors" problem that plagues explanations of novel institutional change: We cannot explain the existence of an institution by the benefits it brings once it is fully established, because that would require the early pioneers to know the future.[13] I will argue organizational orientation takes hold in a sufficiently high-discretion niche of the state when a small cluster of people within that niche possess what I call *dual habitus*,[14] a duality of lived experience whereby they are deeply familiar with the local cultural and institutional environment but also deeply familiar with the habits and practices of doing formal rational bureaucracy, grounded in lived experience.[15] This concept draws on Pierre Bourdieu's idea of *habitus*, which Bourdieu defined as "A system of lasting, transposable dispositions which, integrating past experiences, functions at every moment as a matrix of perceptions, appreciations, and actions and makes possible the achievement of infinitely diversified tasks, thanks to analogical transfers of schemes permitting the solution of similarly shaped problems."[16] In a local environment wherein the bureaucratic ethos is not a common aspect of habitus, where aspects of rational formal organization are not scattered about the social landscape constituting a routine part of lived experience, how then do interstitial officials gain lived experience sufficient to formulate a dual habitus, including a robust alternative system of dispositions, perceptions, appreciations, and actions for doing bureaucracy?

I argue the answer lies in a striking empirical pattern: Ghanaian officials within the highly successful niches were similar to the control cases, and to Ghanaian college graduates generally, in almost every demographic way but one. Most people in influential positions within successful niches had a very distinctive educational profile: a first degree from a local university and an advanced or professional degree from a university abroad. The majority of Ghanaian niche insiders got their bachelor's degree at the University of Legon—the flagship university in Ghana. Some had bachelor's degrees from other Ghanaian universities; the Kwame Nkrumah University of Science and Technology was comparatively more common among those with engineering degrees. What differentiated officials in the successful niches from other college-educated civil servants was a distinctively high concentration of people who also had *advanced degrees from schools abroad*—most often from the United Kingdom or United States, but also from Norway, Ukraine, Russia, Japan, and Germany.

The same educational profile appears repeatedly in the comparison cases among the leadership ranks at the time when the niches were founded or re-formed. NAFDAC's Dora Akunyili was a professor who did her first degree in Nigeria and advanced degrees in pharmacology in London. KTDA's Karanja did some training in Canada before completing an engineering degree in Kampala. The same combinations are embodied in the founding fathers of BNDE: Torres, Teixeira, Lopes, and Campos. Torres was both a professor and a civil engineer who spent a year studying in technical research laboratories all over Western Europe, endowing him with lived experience of rational, technocratic, scientific orientation as practiced in those laboratories.[17] Teixeira was an engineer with experience abroad. Lopes was a professor of economic geography who worked closely with private-sector energy and mining engineers. Campos had a first degree from Brazil and advanced degrees in economics from two U.S. universities.[18] The Salt Inspectorate is the exception, or the inversion, that underlines the rule of dual habitus. The Inspectorate was transformed by Sir Richard Dane, who grew up in the U.K. but had extensive working experience in non-Western civil administration in India. When he first came to China, Dane gained the respect of the Chinese elites and workers, distinguishing himself from the racist condescension that prevailed at the time among Westerners. A few diverse expatriates from the U.K., the U.S., France, Germany, Russia, Japan, and elsewhere also occupied posts throughout the Inspectorate service working in partnership with Chinese locals holding the same position.[19] Like the Inspectorate, KTDA also included a small group of foreigners clustered in technical and engineering roles within factory operations.[20]

I argue that particular sequence and duration—local first degree, advanced degree abroad—is the "Goldilocks zone" of foreign exposure for cultivating dual habitus. Attending the flagship local university allows officials to build close personal networks with other college-educated Ghanaians—essential to successfully navigating the local cultural environment, which places strong emphasis on interpersonal relationships. A local first degree thereby gives officials valuable elite social and cultural capital in the local Ghanaian environment. Ghanaians who obtain their first degree abroad are often understood by other Ghanaians as too cosmopolitan and out of touch with local concerns and practicalities. Organizational reforms suggested by nationals who are perceived as too cosmopolitan can be perceived as outside imposition and met with resentment and "nationalist backlash."[21] Conversely, officials with a local first degree are typically received by other Ghanaians as authentically and thoroughly local.

Too little time in a bureaucratized environment is unlikely to have much of an impact. Experience in a bureaucratized environment can impart new networks, new skills, and an alternative organizational schema grounded in personal lived experience, but those things take time to cultivate and become habituated practices. However, *too much* time away can also be detrimental to the ability to innovate organizational practices that will be effective in the institutional environment of the home country. Long-duration time and experience abroad come, to some extent, at the expense of time and experience in the home country. Migrants living and working abroad for extended stays may find themselves increasingly out of touch with local practices, and peripheral to local social networks. In a sense, migrants who have spent too long away without regular deep engagement with their home context may come to approximate foreign organizational consultants: enamored of cutting-edge business practices from the United States or Europe but insufficiently thoughtful about how such practices might fit (or fail to fit) into the local environment. Even apart from changes to the Ghanaian expatriates' own thinking and dispositions, expatriates who spend too long abroad may be more likely to be subjectively understood by other Ghanaians as more *obrunyi*—foreign, especially Anglo—and less in touch with local sentiments. That subjective interpretation would also minimize return migrants' ability to impact local practices if others within the organization interpret a longtime expatriate Ghanaian as "them" not "us."

I am acutely sensitive that this empirical observation about foreign education runs dangerously close to sounding like a "great white savior" explanation, suggesting that normatively good things happening in Ghana are attributable to not the effort and ingenuity of Ghanaians themselves, but rather originate with Westerners. Many postcolonial societies have been subjected to decades of external condescension that frames Western ideas and solutions as innately better than local solutions—a tendency that is now increasingly and appropriately critiqued in scholarship. There are myriad normative critiques of the unreflexive export of Western ideals and models—such as neoliberalism—as the means and ends of development. Newer critiques are further grounded in practical concerns that such institutional exports rarely work well in the local context.[22]

By contrast, these niches have succeeded where Western global reformers have failed precisely because of the effort and ingenuity of a distinctive subset of local actors who have a foot in both institutional worlds—or more accurately, a brain in both worlds. These returning educational migrants embody *within one person* the blend of varied prior experiences that network scholars find typically characterize the most creative and productive teams.[23] In contrast to the failures of conventional cosmopolitan-led top-down statewide administrative reforms, this book has highlighted the localized emergence of the bureaucratic ethos within niches of the state, grounded in organizational practices that are tried and adapted to the local environment—for example, chasing—whose innovation has been shepherded by actors with dual cultural competency in bureaucracy *and* the local administrative environment.

International Education as Lived Experience with Bureaucratic Habitus

Dual habitus helps address the prescient actors challenge. People with positive lived experiences with bureaucratic comportment elsewhere need not have prescient knowledge to motivate their participation in establishing more bureaucratic comportment in their local environment. When people transpose cognitive models of bureaucratic practice to a new context (in which it is relatively novel), they transpose formerly observed benefits into *anticipated benefits*. Anticipated benefits are able to motivate actors, even if actors only imperfectly understand the eventual effects of the adapted institution after it is deployed locally in a new context.

Scholars who study higher education, even those focused on migration for university education, typically discuss the explicit knowledges that are the focus of educational programs, such as medical knowledge for doctors or the skills of econometric analysis for economists. Here, I argue that there are also a host of *tacit knowledges,*[24] orientations, practices, and motivations that international students from Ghana and elsewhere are exposed to through everyday lived experience abroad that provides a foundation for *doing* bureaucracy. Even a small starting concentration of people who fit the modal type of "local-bachelor's, international-advanced-degree" can thereby directly provide a foundation of people with proto-bureaucratic habits and dispositions. Inasmuch as that training profile serves as a signal to others of the predisposition to engage in proto-bureaucratic practices, and niches have discretion over recruitment to cluster even a small number of such people, that clustering can serve as a strong assurance signal to others that mitigates collective action concerns around conforming to locally unconventional bureaucratic practices.

My argument about lived experience as a foundation for doing bureaucracy is necessarily theoretical. There are considerable methodological challenges in attempting to "get into someone's head" to understand someone's cognitive orientations, schema, or habitus.[25] For example, the apparent correlation between international advanced education and organizational orientation could also arise from preexisting individual tendencies such as raw intellectual ability, strong work ethic, or an achievement orientation. Individuals with some intellectual ability or generalized achievement orientation may have a higher probability of obtaining advanced international education and also of exhibiting organizational achievement orientation. Several of the niche leaders had distinguished educational careers suggestive of raw intellectual prowess. Dora Akunyili, head of NAFDAC, distinguished herself as a top pupil from her earliest primary days, winning the award for the top student in her university, and garnering particularly high scores in the regional West African School Certificate results in the sciences.[26] Similarly, BNDE's founding president, Ary Torres, won multiple accolades as a student, graduating first in his class at the University of São Paulo. However, many other leaders of the Ghanaian and comparison cases did not have particularly distinguished educational careers. It is possible that the modal educational profile described above is particularly strongly associated with effective niches because concentrating such people affords multiple advantages to niche cultivation.

Ghanaian's Experience of International Education as Bureaucratic Habitus

While not disregarding the potential importance of some baseline intellectual ability and work orientation, the interview data from Ghana strongly suggests that lived experience within a well-functioning bureaucratic environment—typically but not exclusively experienced abroad—influences individuals. Their experience solidifies a taste for practicing "rational" formal organization. Their prior lived experience of the collective benefits of the systemic bureaucratic ethos appears sufficient to overcome individual free rider problems of bureaucratic comportment and explain the prescient actors puzzle. Below I quote at length from the reflections of Ghanaian officials with lived experience in both worlds, because I want the reader to be able to hear the Ghanaians in their own voices and see how their stream-of-consciousness reflections introduce and grapple with different ideas about organizational orientations spontaneously in response to basic questions about foreign experience. Their reflections highlight how international lived experience modifies the practices and orientations of Ghanaians in ways that are directly related to enhancing organizational orientation, and coupling individual effort to systemic outcomes by focusing on the more circumscribed space of the niche as a space of potential change wherein their individual efforts are more than a drop in the bucket.

Yao, a younger member of PARD, explicitly acknowledges that international travel is a distinctive experience in the broader Ghanaian context. While discussing whether he considers his childhood similar or different from a typical Ghanaian upbringing, Yao volunteers: "I would say I was privileged to gain travel experience [short pause] abroad." This is one indication that having travelled abroad is a recognized status signal marker, capable of signaling something distinctive and uncommon about the person with that experience. When I follow up by asking whether or not Yao thinks his time abroad has influenced him, he emphatically agrees, opening with "well, yes" in a tone that suggests this should be obvious:

YAO: Well, yes. Yes. Yes. Yes.

AUTHOR: How so?

YAO: In some ways because, let's call a spade a spade, okay? [He seems to think about phrasing.] Ummm, I have a reputation for good things. I have a reputation for a system that works smoothly and, you know, efficiently ... I would say my uncle abroad, he's a biochemist. Okay. And he's very hard working. So, it influenced. My dad is hard working. But the kind of system that is, is [trails off, short laugh]. That is a system that I wish we had in this part of the world. Okay? So, everything that I do, my work, the way I work, how I think, is geared toward making the system a better system. Yeah, like it is abroad. Yeah. I mean, I know, I know, I cannot do this alone. But in my own small way, I may be able to influence people one way or the other, somehow.

Yao immediately focuses on what he views as distinctive aspects of the organizational environment he encountered in the U.K. Those styles of organizational practice are cultural objects about which one can form a taste like any other cultural object, from styles of music to types of literature. Yao indicates that he has cultivated a taste for that style of work environment and draws an explicit connection between his personal action and that systemic outcome, such that now "everything that I do, my work, the way I work, how I think" is actively trying to cultivate within his Ghanaian organizational environment some of the features he sees as desirable based on his exposure and experience within the UK organizational environment.

When Ghanaians discuss their experiences abroad, they almost never focus first—or indeed, at all—on the explicit and job-relevant knowledges those degrees imparted. Instead they focus on the typically taken-for-granted aspects of doing and being in a formal organizational environment. For example, Martey is a Ghanaian official who obtained a degree abroad in Europe. Because Martey's experience was in a job-related educational environment, we might expect him to mention specific job-related skills he learned. Instead, Martey explains: "The time I spent abroad, actually even at [the European university] I had an opportunity to be a research assistant so I had some kind of experience which, which is helping me on my work. I mean, efficiency, punctuality, deliver on time, meeting deadlines." Observe that Martey could easily have mentioned the explicit knowledges and skills obtained from his international educational experience. He could have said he learned how to use pivot tables in Excel. He could have said he learned how to manage large data sets or run statistical analyses that he uses regularly in his role as a PARD official. But he does not. Instead Martey immediately and without pause explains: "I mean, efficiency, punctuality, deliver on time, meeting deadlines."

For many interstitial insiders, experience abroad affords a strong contrast through which officials endeavor to understand the systemic impediments to the rapid social development they so often desire for Ghana. Sedu obtained a degree abroad on a government scholarship. It is almost heartbreaking to hear his voice crack with emotion as he reflects on his experience, in which direct competition with European classmates forced him to grapple with the idea that individual ability to excel at the explicit knowledges and skills of his degree might not be enough, hinting at an awareness of a more systemic problem that he struggles to put into words:

> AUTHOR: How would you say your time abroad influenced you?
> SEDU: I look at things differently. My position of what we have in Ghana, or in Africa, sometimes makes me sad. I sit in class with those [Europeans], and I beat them in class. But their development is different from our development. So, the question is, where is the problem? It means we are not doing what is right. I sit with white boys not only from [that country], some from other [countries] and I sit in class. I didn't know any [of their] language; I went there and learned it in six months. I would sit in class, and I'd beat them. So, why? And the type of people like me, we are many, so much in this country. So, why do we—we can't solve national issues. We can't solve basic problems. We can't solve them, and it sometimes makes me sad. [pause] There's something else, which I don't know where it's coming from.

Like Sedu, Coblah also thinks through individual comparisons between Ghanaians and Americans that were illuminated in his time abroad, leading him to reflect on more systemic institutional differences in the environments. Coblah got his first degree in Ghana and then went on to obtain two advanced degrees abroad at prestigious American universities. As we have seen before, when discussing his experience abroad Coblah does not focus on explicit knowledges, like differences in subject-relevant education. Rather, he quickly focuses on aspects of work culture and comportment:

> COBLAH: One thing, the work ethic in the States, okay, is something that I won't experience around here. People *work* [vocal emphasis] and earn for their work. Umm, There was no … [trails off]. I had friends, both Americans and Ghanaians who had jobs. And they were very serious about being punctual at the office. Working the exact number

of hours. I won't say American workers don't cheat their employers, or they don't idle sometimes. But you will see that a majority of employees are doing their best to umm, fulfill their employment contract. Also they know that if they don't do well, they will be fired. So the work ethic is something that influenced me very much ... I believe that is what we need as a society ... I keep saying that it is the middle class in Africa or in Ghana that is lazy.

At the heart of his reflection, Coblah articulates the fundamental difference in comportment where the bureaucratic ethos is a widespread part of the habitus. He observes "People *work* ... you will see that a majority of employees are doing their best to umm, fulfill their employment contract." At times he can quickly name a feature, as when he says emphatically "people *work*" but other times he trails off or struggles to put into words the differences in the environment. I suggest that Coblah pauses several times precisely where he is working to put into words some of the taken-for-granted aspects of both environments. Such inarticulacy is a key cognitive sign of thinking using tacit knowledges.[27] First, Coblah's voice trails off as he seems about to characterize some of the negative aspects of the Ghanaian environment, instead shifting to focus on the system rather than individual characteristics by noting that while abroad he observed both American and Ghanaians who while in America were "very serious about being punctual at the office." He also carefully observes that the American system isn't perfect, noting that sometimes Americans too cheat their employers or idle. His measured speech stalls out again as he searches for the way to express what feels so different about the foundational orientation to work that structures conduct in American organizations, where "a majority of employees are doing their best to umm, fulfill their employment contract." I suggest Ghanaians with dual habitus have heightened reflexivity, wherein contrasting lived experiences in the two sharply distinct environments brings focused conscious attention to the typically tacit aspects of each, reflected as they endeavor to articulate otherwise taken-for-granted aspects.

Coblah goes on to explain that, in his view, rural Ghanaians are incredibly hardworking, detailing the long effort of a market woman who rises at dawn to buy fish, and works hard to sell them throughout the day to earn a living. By contrast, "the problem is with the middle class who sit around in offices like mine who just wait around, some of them even close at 3:00." His usually slow and measured speaking tone speeds up, as he goes on to describe his own personal work practices:

COBLAH: That is something that I have learned. I *work* [strong vocal emphasis]. I work, I mean seven days a week. I don't have closing time. The only time I close is when I am exhausted and mentally tired and I cannot proceed. That is for me one thing that I brought home from the States. Not that I was a lazy person before then, but it just reinforced my belief that working hard, working diligently can make a society succeed.

Coblah expresses the idea that he had some prior inclination to hard work "not that I was a lazy person before then" suggesting that as he makes sense of his own transformation, he concurrently identifies a particular ethos with the United States, going so far as to say it is something "that I brought home from the States" but claims that it was not orthogonal to his own understanding of himself previously. Rather, his lived experience in the United States reinforced a tendency that he believed to be already within him to some extent.

The accounts of these Ghanaians with practical experience in two institutionally different contexts give insight into the collective action problems that typically plague explanations of institutional origins.[28] The relative advantages of an institution *once it is widespread* do not explain how something initially novel and unfamiliar *becomes* widespread. If the effectiveness of a novel practice were the only explanation needed, we would all be typing on objectively more efficient Dvorak keyboards instead of the common QWERTY keyboards, which were designed to be intentionally inefficient to slow down typing and thereby avoid key jams on mechanical typewriters.[29] Instead we must wonder, how are multiple individuals enticed to collaborate together to build a new institution, given that the institutional outcomes are unknown in advance and the institutional vanguard may disproportionately pay the costs of the institution while others enjoy its diffuse benefits?

The key to addressing this challenge lies in how the interstitial subcultural structure reinforces in-group practices, already illuminated in prior chapters, and also in *how* locally unfamiliar ideas reach the niche. A critical mass of people in each niche had concrete, practical, lived experience in organizational fields outside of Ghana where a bureaucratic ethos pervaded. Ghanaians' experiences in a different organizational field afforded them concrete, grounded experience in the daily practice of doing bureaucracy. Through their lived experience, some bureaucratically exposed Ghanaians became both consciously convinced of the benefits of organizing and behaving in bureaucratic ways and also familiar with a host of implicit practices and dispositions for navigating rationalized organizational life.

Ghanaians with lived experience in hegemonically bureaucratized organizational environments had firsthand experience of the perceived benefits of a systemic bureaucratic ethos, which encouraged their individual willingness to act in ways that contributed to such a social system, forging a link between their individual micro-level practices and a now-desired future macro-level outcome. This sort of linkage is recognized when Coblah said, "It just reinforced my belief that working hard, working diligently can make a society succeed"; or when Yao acknowledged, "I know, I cannot do this alone. But in my own small way, I may be able to influence people one way or the other, somehow." Within the interstitial niches, such people experiment with their cognitive model of bureaucratic orientation and practice, transposing previously experienced and observed benefits into *anticipated* benefits. The motivation afforded by such anticipation is real enough, even if in retrospect people may only imperfectly understand the ultimate effects of the institution once it is transplanted, transposed, adapted, and adjusted.

Scholars and development practitioners often fetishize abstract knowledge but neglect the importance of "tacit knowledge" or "knowledge 'how,' "[30] the accretions of repeated lived, practical experiences that cultivate a sensibility or disposition, a taste for, and tendency toward certain practices. Ghanaians with a moderate amount of practical, lived experience in bureaucratized fields abroad acquire grounded, practical experience in both the local institutional and cultural field of Ghana and formal bureaucratic environments. Such actors have a three-dimensional understanding of the desired state of organizational practice—having experienced it firsthand—and a robust understanding of the local institutional and cultural environment within which they are operating. That duality of practical experience means that when problems inevitably appear, such actors are ideally positioned to make nimble and thoughtful responses. Actors with dual habitus are able to tinker and adjust specific organizational practices—the *means*—to bring outcomes ever closer to their envisioned *ends* of organizationally oriented, effective, bureaucratic administration.

With a foot in both worlds, interstitial insiders draw on a large repertoire of practical knowledge of *doing bureaucracy* grounded in their lived experience of the bureaucratic ethos elsewhere while remaining exquisitely sensitive to local Ghanaian tastes and grounded practicalities. They thereby arrive at novel solutions that go beyond merely applying abstract rules or procedures learned abroad. For example, as described in chapter 4, Ghanaian niches are often organized around intentional redundancy, duplicating knowledge and skill sets so that no one is indispensable—an imminently sensible response to local epidemiological, administrative, and cultural systems that may disrupt personnel with little notice. But this is also an adaptation that defies the taken-for-granted wisdom of Western organizations, one that you won't find recommended by Western organizational textbooks or cosmopolitan consultants.[31] Similarly, the Commercial Court justices demonstrated a particularly interstitial innovation grounded in dual cultural competency when they confronted initial resistance to alternative dispute resolution (ADR). With deft intersubjective understanding, the justices realized that ADR appeared less formal to lawyers and clients. They intuited that the perception of informality was leading to the legally incorrect but socially resonant interpretation that ADR lacked the legal weight of conventional courtroom procedures. In a solution one can scarcely imagine a cosmopolitan consultant suggesting, some justices experimented with wearing the white curled wigs common to British legal practice during mediations. Within interstitial niches, many officials express a desire to personally *be* more organizationally effective, and they nimbly deploy grounded practical experience in both the bureaucratic ethos and the local environment in an ongoing effort to bring that desire into being within the more circumscribed scale of the interstitial niche.

From Kenya to China: Dual Habitus in the Comparative Cases

Many people in key positions at KTDA, including Charles Karanja, had significant foreign or professional experience that gave them lived exposure to functioning formal organizations oriented towards efficiency. Karanja skillfully responded to political pressure to Africanize posts within KTDA, managing thereby to retain some expatriate experts for key positions that both required significant technical ability and would benefit from officials excluded from conventional power networks, which might otherwise pressure officials to cut corners or look the other way. For example, a European was the head of the Accounts Department until the mid-1970s, when a Kenyan of Asian descent was promoted from within.[32] Karanja was also known to concentrate expatriate experts in areas where the organization was expanding into new functions.[33] This allowed KTDA to borrow expatriate area-expertise in functions where there were no locally experienced staff, but it also meant that as the organization expanded, new staff were continuously added under the management of an expatriate with a thoroughly bureaucratic habitus. It was not until 1980, more than thirty years after its founding, that all senior positions in KTDA were filled with Africans.

In the Chinese Salt Inspectorate too, substantial experience in a functional bureaucratized environment abroad afforded lived experience doing bureaucracy. Indeed, of all the cases, the Salt Inspectorate is the one that has the most pronounced presence of actual foreigners in high-ranking positions within the organization. The Salt Inspectorate was conspicuously framed as a partnership between the multilateral Western lenders and the Chinese state. Sir Richard Dane was brought in by mutual agreement to serve as the first foreign chief director. Dane had years of experience in British colonial service working with the salt *gabelle* in India and was prevailed upon to forestall his retirement in order to help establish the Chinese Salt Inspectorate. Early in its establishment, Sir Richard Dane and other foreigners brought to the Salt Inspectorate their lived experience of bureaucratic habitus and models of organizational practice. Importantly, Dane also drew on his lived experience with salt tax administration in India. Although India was by no means a perfect simulation of China, that depth of prior exposure gave Dane lived experience in both a thoroughly bureaucratized context and in a largely nonbureaucratic environment, fostering understandings of both environments that were analogous to those of Ghanaians who received advanced education abroad.

Dane's reports are steeped in classically Weberian attention to record-keeping as a means of making the environment orderly, knowable, and predictable. To overcome the lack of record-keeping the Inspectorate had inherited, Dane and key officials conducted a nationwide tour of key salt production, transportation, and market locations to gain firsthand knowledge of staff and operational conditions. By compiling district receipts, interviewing officials, and direct observations at each site, they painstakingly constructed records of the expected production and receipts of each locale.[34] Based on those records, thereafter: "Bags of salt, amounts of revenue collected, and percentages of revenue spend on administrative costs could be (and were) duly counted and reported every year, district by district and station by station, thus leading to fairly efficient bureaucratization of most Inspectorate operations."[35]

Though some foreigners were employed, this is not a case of "nothing but" a significant foreign presence. The total number of foreigners employed in the Salt Inspectorate was relatively low—forty-six in total throughout the central and district offices.[36] Instead, the reform administration relied primarily on Chinese officials, something that was regarded by Westerners as unwise. In the racist language of the day—commingled with a strangely cheerful tone—one British news report observed that "many districts are wholly in the hands of Chinese without the faintest detriment, thus completely upsetting all traditional beliefs as to the impossibility of expecting the honest administration of public funds from the Chinese controlled."[37] In stark contrast to those racist perspectives held by other contemporaneous white foreigners, Dane had a reputation as a Westerner who respected and valued the Chinese and was in turn respected and valued by them. The trust and confidence Dane placed in the Salt Inspectorate's Chinese officials won him their admiration and enhanced their efforts in the field. Thus, foreign workers steeped in bureaucratic habitus who collaborated respectfully with Chinese coworkers paved the way for a bureaucratic ethos within this interstice.

From Great Men to Clustered Cadres: The Sociological Foundation for Organizational Change

Individual leaders espousing unconventional practices are just eccentrics unless they can cultivate the first few people who support and follow their example. These organizations were not so much run by singular individuals as by small, hand-picked, and tightly knit corps of senior staff who seem to de-fine the term esprit de corps. The early emergence of Ghana's PARD and Com-mercial Courts, China's Salt Inspectorate, and the transition to excellence of Kenya's KTDA, Nigeria's NAFDAC, and Brazil's BNDE, all share the early establishment of a cadre—a numerically small, interpersonally close, high-level inner circle of influential officials within the organization that were highly committed, professionalized, and drawn to participation by largely intrinsic professional enticements. That is, in all those cases, the small inner circle that founded or transformed the organizational unit were profession-ally motivated to participate in that *particular* organization, and not settling for one acceptable government job among many. For example, several mem-bers of the founding cadre at NCA's Spectrum and Frequency Management spoke with nostalgia about their childhood love of radio and described the great lengths they went to so they could obtain a degree in radio engineering abroad because they felt so passionate about working with radio. The critical factor was not *individual* great leaders atop organizations, but rather *clustered cadres* of shared distinctiveness in influential positions atop the organization. Leaders initially cultivate distinctive organizational orientation by clustering around them that first small and tight-knit cadre who shared that orienta-tion.[38] Those clustered cadres were the grit around which the pearl of organi-zational clustered distinctiveness would grow.

Named leaders are too easy to see, sometimes blinding us to more cru-cial but less legible social networks around them. Truthfully, I initially failed to notice this important comparative feature because so often the cadre are unnamed or mentioned only in passing. Only after multiple rounds analyz-ing the comparative cases—and in particular Brazil, where the cadre is most prominent—was I finally struck by the almost hidden similarity. I suspect many readers similarly missed these cadres even though they are mentioned when the comparative cases are introduced in chapter 5. The uncommonly successful organizations analyzed throughout this book were led by a clus-tered cadre of typically three to six officials with deep interpersonal bonds and a shared understanding or "vision" for the organization. One cannot speak of the founding of BNDE without speaking of Torres, Lopes, Teixeira, and Campos all in the same breath. At the Sino-Foreign Salt Inspectorate, Rich-ard Dane had a small cadre of other foreigners with shared bureaucratic back-grounds threaded throughout the organization. Both KTDA's Karanja and NAFDAC's Akunyili surrounded themselves early on with a cadre of high-ranking managers with strong interpersonal bonds who were highly compe-tent and dedicated to the organization's mission. Cadres also existed in the Ghanaian cases. Everyone within PARD clearly regarded Mr. Mensah as its director, but all likewise knew that Zakaria and Akosua were his "right hands" and at least four others within PARD worked closely and often with the director on complex projects. They formed a cadre with deep interpersonal ties and strong shared orientation. The Ghanaian Commercial Courts were widely understood as the pet project of the former chief justice, but their success depended on the founding cadre of six handpicked justices who had a shared orientation toward effective and efficient justice with resolute integrity.

Often these clustered cadres worked to cultivate dual habitus within ever-widening ranks of the organization. For example, after Akunyili and her close team of managers took control of NAFDAC, she sought training grants so that *every month* more than two dozen staff members went for international training. In addition to exposure to the explicit content of the training course, this meant that huge numbers of junior staff gained lived experience working in a bureaucratic system abroad. Other times organizational decisions unintentionally resulted in clustering junior staff with shared experiences of international education. For example, as described in chapter 6, human resources officials at the Ministry of Finance viewed civil servants going abroad for advanced education as a staffing challenge, because a "desk" (the colloquial term for a particular portfolio of tasks) could not be left unoccupied while officials were gone. Therefore human resources officials settled upon a solution: They would fill any desks left vacant when a ministry official went abroad for an educational degree. When officials returned to the ministry with their foreign degree, these returnees would be staffed to PARD, because the Human Resources department viewed PARD's work as flexible and therefore capable of absorbing returnees. This also afforded PARD a substantial cadre with dual habitus.

A founding cadre provides something more important than leadership: It provides highly visible followers. It is an act of deviance to be organizationally oriented in a predominantly neopatrimonial environment. When a radically new way of doing things emanates from a single person, even one in a position of formal leadership, he can easily be dismissed as eccentric. Subordinates may superficially comply, especially when being monitored, but fail to buy into the spirit. Conversely, the first few followers redefine the situation in subtle but critical ways: Followers lend credibility to novel alternative practices, transforming the social interpretation of the situation from an idiosyncratic whim to a movement. Without initial followers, the idea withers.[39] From strikes and riots to voting and migration, an individual's willingness to join can be critically shaped by how many others are participating.[40] Ultimately then, it is not the first-mover or leader who makes a movement, but rather the first-joiners. First-joiners legitimate what might otherwise be scorned as individual deviance. One shirtless guy dancing in a park is just an eccentric, but the first-joiners convert it into a flash mob with social momentum that draws idle observers into active participants.[41] Organizational reform efforts in many African countries are littered with examples of inspiring leaders, Ghanaians who succeeded in the private sector or big international NGOs, who are brought amid fanfare to reform intransigent state organizations but who leave quietly later, with little change accomplished. I argue this is because they failed to cultivate a cadre that legitimated their novel practices to catalyze diffusion more broadly within the organization.

The successful founding of a niche then does not depend exclusively on the presence of a leader. Instead, the emergence of a niche of administrative effectiveness depends critically on the presence of a founding cadre. If we peel back the earliest moments of distinctiveness we find an individual with distinctive dual habitus. But the earliest moments of *clustering* distinctiveness are found in the smallest unit of social action: a small group. Recall from chapter 5 that the scale of these organizations or subunits at the time of emergence as a bureaucratic niche typically ranged from a few dozen to around 150. Smaller group size at the time of niche emergence may be advantageous because it takes relatively fewer initial confederates to cultivate a critical mass of distinctiveness sufficient to reorient insiders' perceptions that the organizational culture is significantly differentiated from the broader state administrative culture.

SWEAT EQUITY

Interestingly, a number of these cadres had considerable sweat equity in the construction of the institution. BNDE was led by a cadre of managers with previous interpersonal ties and a shared vision for the organization that had been hashed out during their involvement in the joint commission that first formulated the plans, priorities, and incipient vision for a Brazilian development bank. Campos recalled, "Lucas, Glycon, and I were called the three musketeers. We maintained a long-standing relationship that had emerged at the Brazil-U.S. Commission [that laid the plans for BNDE]."[42]

These are a precious resource: honest brokers who feel invested in the system. Founding cadres with sweat equity are not merely being handed an organizational "tool" by international consultants and sold on its benefits. They are actively evaluating and creating with genuine voice in how the organization will operate. Their creative involvement gives them both better understanding of, and commitment to, the desired outcome.[43] They have a robust, three-dimensional understanding of the goal outcome and therefore when unanticipated problems crop up—as they inevitably do—the founding cadre is ideally situated to make nimble and thoughtful responses. Because they are a small group rather than a single individual, they are able to support each other in the difficult work of building the institution and defending it against the seemingly endless tides of the external environment. Their personal connection to critical decisions increases their personal investment in seeing the organization succeed.

The distinctive ethos that is first shared as a group style among the founding cadre, then through interpersonal contact, spreads out in concentric rings of small social groupings throughout the organization. Many of the observed interstitial niches were, in one way or another, composed of small teams, which resulted in common benefits of participating in a small, intimate group. Ghanaian interstitial niches used adaptive redundancy, where teams or individual workers possessed overlapping skill and knowledge sets and could substitute for each other with little notice. This helped the Ghanaians grapple with uncertainties arising from their embeddedness in administrative, epidemiological, and cultural systems beyond their control, but also fostered close interpersonal ties among small groups within the organizations. Akunyili similarly reorganized NAFDAC around teams. Roberto Campos early structured BNDE into small working groups that jointly issued recommendations on loans, which "reinforced the application of technical criteria and led to strong personal connections among personnel."[44] KTDA built their outreach into agricultural producers around small, team-like farmer committees that served as two-way conduits of information and also supervised the distribution of some resources among local participants.

Interpersonal interaction in niches was also enhanced by a notably common practice of niche leaders travelling, a particularly impressive accomplishment in cases with more geographically dispersed operations.[45] During the four years Dane headed the Chinese Salt Inspectorate, he constantly travelled around the country observing the various depots firsthand and writing reports on his observations and encounters. Likewise, KTDA's Karanja routinely travelled to the various production plants and NAFDAC's Akunyili travelled throughout the regions visiting various teams. But even on a more micro-scale, on any given day Mr. Mensah, PARD's director, could be found circulating through the PARD offices within the ministry. Mr. Mensah explains, "In fact, every day I go to some office." Regular face-to-face interaction with niche leaders and founding cadre members creates an interpersonal conduit for leaders and officials to observe and learn from each other.

Conclusion: Leaders and Small Groups as a Foundation for Learning to Do Bureaucracy

This chapter advances a sociological accounting for why leaders matter. Some prior scholarship on pockets of effectiveness has also highlighted leadership as a critical difference between highly effective agencies and their poor-performing peers, including excellent work by Merilee Grindle.[46] The critical importance of leaders is even evident in the scholarship of Judith Tendler, a classic book within the pockets of effectiveness literature that explicitly eschews theorizing leaders.[47] Nevertheless leaders played an analytically pivotal role in the success of her cases. Tendler brilliantly analyzed four particularly effective programs started in the Brazilian region of Ceará under reformist governor Tasso Jereissati. Governor Jereissati and a close-knit founding cadre were essential to many of the organizational performance reforms that Tendler details, but their role is minimized by attributing their actions to the depersonified entity of the state.

For example, Tendler found mass hiring for both the community health workers and emergency employment programs—typically ideal conditions for patronage—were remarkably merit based. How did merit come to a process long steeped in patronage? First, the governor retained the funds to pay salaries at the regional level, circumventing the tendency of both the Department of Health and municipal mayors to use the posts for patronage supporters. Second, a team of people working with the governor conducted hiring themselves, and *they* imposed merit selection criteria on the hiring process: "a nine-member coordinating team ran the program with an iron hand ... and traveled extensively throughout the interior to recruit agents through a rigorous selection program."[48] The involvement and presence of the governor's regional team provided essential support and protection from neopatrimonialism for the vast corps of street-level program administrators, it "made the most dedicated ones feel supported by the state government versus local politicians and other powerful personages who commonly diverted programs to their own ends. These workers now had an excuse to say no, and knew they would be supported for their stand."[49] Tendler recognizes that such protection is essential for enabling low-status workers to emulate an organizational orientation, observing, "The availability of this kind of 'protection' to public servants—or the lack of it—plays an important role in determining their accomplishments."[50] Readers who are curious about where Governor Tasso Jereissati got his bureaucratic habitus will find him again in the next chapter.

The present chapter takes Tendler's critique of highly individual characteristics seriously, analyzing instead the sociological features of leaders of bureaucratic niches that transcend contexts and specific people. The chapter makes a case for the importance of leaders, but *not* because they possess charismatic personalities or skills mere mortals cannot hope to emulate. Instead, those leaders matter because their dual habitus positions their skills as attainable and desirable to their subordinates. Leaders with dual habitus can use their position to model and encourage organizational performance-oriented practices that are well suited to the local environment, something addressed in more detail in chapter 3. Their position also theoretically enhances voluntary compliance: because leaders with dual habitus have deep cultural and social capital in the local environment, they are perceived by subordinates as authentically local, and so their solutions are not dismissed out of hand as a foreign imposition.

But a leader with dual habitus does not matter unless there is a founding cadre around the leader, essential first-followers who legitimize the leader's distinctive practices and provide mutual support. Thus the earliest foundation of clustered distinctiveness begins in clustering within the smallest unit of social action: the small group. The distinctive ethos that takes root among the founding cadre then spreads out in concentric rings of small social groupings throughout the organization, as cadre members both participate in recruitment of new members and cultivation of existing members. Many of this book's interstitial niches were, in one way or another, composed of small teams, which resulted in common benefits of participating in a small, intimate group. Interpersonal interaction in niches was also enhanced by a notably common practice of niche leaders and founding cadre members travelling, a particularly impressive accomplishment in cases with more geographically dispersed operations. Regular face-to-face interaction with niche leaders and founding cadre members created an interpersonal conduit for cadre members and officials to observe and learn from each other.

Small groups with high interpersonal contact innately afford the potential for mutual observation—what principal-agency theory might refer to as monitoring—which can forestall or better identify wrongdoing. But appreciating how small-group social dynamics operate empirically affords a critically different view on whether and how monitoring matters. Instead of a singular principal monitoring a corps of agents, the cases collectively highlight a more *distributed,* distinctively *personalized,* and *reciprocal* form of observation. As the NCA sign-in sheet or the Commercial Court staff members so ably illustrate, workers in team environments with strong, interpersonal connections know that particular named others on their team are aware of their presence, absence, and activities. They are thereby more motivated to work and more reluctant to shirk or sabotage, similar to observations that shoplifters are more reluctant to steal from a local mom-and-pop shop than from a nameless, faceless, corporate entity such as Walmart.

The foundations of dominant principal-agency theory are more sociologically impoverished, steeped in classic American managerial assumptions that workers are innately inclined to shirk. Those negative assumptions about workers inspire particular organizational solutions—technologically mediated, faceless mass surveillance coupled with carrot-and-stick incentives—that may have perverse effects, encouraging workers to game the system. Conversely, teams afford observation, but also (1) opportunities to emulate the behavior as when younger members learn how to tactfully sidestep ethically fraught gifts by observing experienced niche insiders and (2) the positive sense of mutual obligation to other people with whom you have a face-to-face relationship, and whose daily life suffers if you do not pull your weight. These observations about the foundations of the bureaucratic ethos within states thereby underscore increasing consensus about changing human behavior across a range of contexts: *Practice* is far more effective than punishment.

8

Long-Term Outcomes
in Pockets of Effectiveness

The book thus far has analyzed the characteristics that underpin the successful functioning of pockets of effectiveness within otherwise institutionally
weak and adverse environments. The book has also illuminated the challenging question of the conditions under which such pockets initially emerge by
bringing the Ghanaian cases into dialogue with a variety of comparison cases
drawn from around the world and across 100 years of history. Readers might
understandably be curious about what happens to such pockets of effectiveness over time. Are pockets of effectiveness within otherwise institutionally
weak states sustainable? If a leader and a founding cadre play a role in the
early establishment of bureaucratic niches, can the bureaucratic ethos endure
after the original founders leave? Can niches scale up, becoming a predecessor for the emergence of more general administrative competence throughout the state?

I discuss such questions here, because these questions are beyond the scope
of the primary analysis. Such questions emerge naturally from the theory-
building that the book lays out; however, the study was not designed to address such questions, and so a word of caution is in order. The original study
was designed to generate theory and comparative insight about a relatively
uncommon phenomenon, and so utilized a purposively sampled comparative
design of identified cases of effective bureaucratic niches contrasted with control cases to refine analytic focus. This design is fruitful for theory building,
with a comparative logic structured to both identify potentially necessary
conditions as well as eliminate potentially spurious conditions. However, because these are not a randomly sampled set of cases, they cannot definitively

tell us what *will* happen or even what is *likely* to happen as pockets of effectiveness within the state mature. They do however, sketch a range of future outcomes that are *possible*, laying a foundation for future research to analyze the conditions under which particular long-term outcomes do or do not emerge.

Can the Bureaucratic Ethos Endure after Founding Leaders Leave?

Since the Ghanaian fieldwork was originally conducted, there have been substantial changes of political elites running the state, elites at the apex of the organizations within which the niches functioned, and changes to the leadership of the niches themselves. Indeed most of the cases in this book had founding leaders who served for a relatively short period of time—Karanja's long oversight of KTDA being the prime exception. The Salt Inspectorate and KTDA have relatively well-documented, longitudinal performance measures that can give a more precise look at whether organizational performance changes upon the departure of a niche founder, which I examine briefly later. Overall the cases suggest that once a robust subculture of the bureaucratic ethos exists within an organization or subunit, it often successfully persists in the medium term beyond the departure of its founders.

Ghana has seen three new heads of state, and the ruling party in Ghana changed from the New Patriotic Party to the National Democratic Congress, and back again. At the top of the organizational pyramids, central bank governors, finance ministers, NCA directors, and even chief justices have changed several times, sometimes with little change to the niches within them and other times with serious consequences. When the central bank's governor Paul Acquah stepped down, Monetary Policy Analysis was disbanded by his successor and its staff reassigned elsewhere throughout the bank. The Commercial Courts still hear commercial disputes, though new justices are at the bench, because within seven years all the founding judges were promoted to the Court of Appeals and one now sits on the Supreme Court.[1] There have been two new directors general at the helm of the National Communication Authority, although Bernard Forson Jr. still serves on its board of directors. Within NCA, the engineering mobile units still make their regular but unpredictable pilgrimages to Ghana's farthest reaches, monitoring the nation's airwaves.

Within the Ministry of Finance and Economic Planning, PARD has been renamed and expanded to the Economic Research and Forecasting Division, which since 2013 has been under the stewardship of a well-respected PARD insider who previously worked very closely with Mr. Mensah. In 2018, PARD's much-loved Mr. Mensah left the ministry to take a position at a major international development bank, though he intends to return to government eventually to finish out his career. His informal second-in-command, Akosua, after many years of public service has likewise taken a post in an influential international financial institution. Other members of the inner circle close to Mr. Mensah have remained at the ministry and risen to new positions of influence. It is too early to say what their departure will mean for the bureaucratic ethos so carefully cultivated within PARD over the past decade. However, several of the comparison cases signal cause for optimism, demonstrating that it is possible for a robust meritocratic organizational culture and bureaucratic ethos to endure after the departure of the founding leader.

Dora Akunyili served as director-general of NAFDAC for only eight years before then-newly elected President Yar'Adua transferred Akunyili in 2008 to serve as the minister of Information and Communications. NAFDAC continues to do the work of reducing unsafe food and pharmaceuticals in the Nigerian market. As of 2017, NAFDAC was still evaluated by citizens as one of the five most effective government organizations in Nigeria, though the percentage of Nigerians agreeing with that statement in 2017 (61 percent) was lower than in the last year Akunyili served (74 percent).[2]

During its first decade of operation, the founding fathers of BNDE all took a turn as the president of the bank, but each served only for a year or two before moving on to other influential positions within and outside of government. Despite this revolving door of different leaders at the top, long after its establishment, BNDE remained a technocratic stronghold within the Brazilian state—eventually renamed BNDES when a social mission was appended to its mandate. Its combination of loans and effective technical advice is often credited with shepherding the expansion of major industries and thereby ultimately contributing to Brazil's rise as an economic powerhouse in Latin America.[3] Decades after its founding and unrelated to the early leadership succession, some individuals within BNDES would become implicated in a twenty-first century public corruption scandal, an issue addressed later in the chapter.

THE SALT INSPECTORATE

The history of the Salt Inspectorate is particularly useful for examining whether effectiveness changes upon the departure of a founder, because it has some of the best-documented and clearest outcome measures for organizational effectiveness to illustrate trends over time. Sir Richard Dane, first foreign chief director, was widely credited with establishing the bureaucratic ethos within the Salt Inspectorate upon its founding in 1913. Dane led the

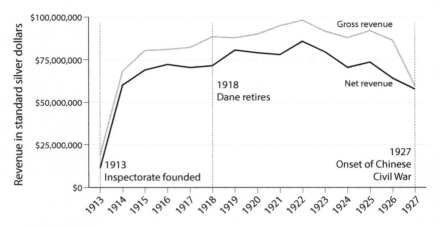

FIGURE 8.1. Salt tax collections by inspectorate over time. *Data Source:* Adshead 1970, p. 100

Inspectorate for only four years before returning to retirement. Yet as Figure 8.1 shows, there was no notable change in the effectiveness of the Salt Inspectorate upon Dane's retirement.

Dane's administrative successors in no way invoke dynamic or inspirational leadership. Instead, scholars describe subsequent chief inspectors as "a succession of colourless, faceless foreign chief inspectors whose assorted health problems, lack of 'vision,' and tendencies to focus narrowly on regulations, figures, and details [who] none the less seem to not have had a strongly negative effect on the organization as a whole."[4] The history of the establishment of the Salt Inspectorate suggests that the distinctive bureaucratic ethos instilled in those early years had become a taken-for-granted and valued part of the organizational culture of employees throughout the organization and thereby continued, even after the departure of those who first helped construct that sense of clustered distinctiveness. Dane and a founding cadre established locally innovative organizational practices and reforms oriented to achieving the organization's goals. Having cultivated and clustered a sense of distinctiveness within the organization that was contrasted with the prevailing administrative culture beyond the organization, employees came to strongly identify with the distinctive Salt Inspectorate way of doing things.

Indeed, the Inspectorate proved surprisingly robust in its first several decades, weathering the escalating warlordism of the 1920s. Then in 1927, in a symbolic move against the yoke of foreign oppression, the Guomindang abolished and then immediately reconstituted the Inspectorate, hiring back the prior staff.[5] The Salt Inspectorate entered a long period of decline during the Sino-Japanese War (1937–1945),[6] after which the new Communist state formed the analogous China National Salt Industry Corporation, a state-owned enterprise, in 1950. By the dawn of the twenty-first century, rapid Chinese industrialization meant that salt was no longer the important source of government revenue it had once been. In 2014 the Chinese state announced plans to phase out the government monopoly and open up salt production and distribution to private companies. Today the Salt Corporation remains an organization with over 31,000 employees that has received numerous awards for its performance.[7]

THE KTDA

The Kenyan case also provides well-documented outcome measures that suggest a niche of the bureaucratic ethos can persist beyond the departure of its instrumental founders, even when successors are not particularly gifted leaders. Charles Karanja is the organizational leader associated with KTDA's establishment as a pocket of effectiveness within the post-Independence state, but KTDA's organizational effectiveness outlived Karanja's stewardship. Karanja's ability to act with independence and impunity depended heavily on the interpersonal relationship with, and trust between, himself and President Kenyatta.

When Jomo Kenyatta died in 1978, for the first time Karanja and the KTDA were without the political protection of a powerful patron. Within politically ethnicized Kenya, Karanja and Kenyatta had shared the bonds of being co-ethics—both were from the powerful Kikuyu group. Kenyatta's successor, President Moi, was not a Kikuyu. However, after nearly fifteen years of success, Karanja "was so confident of the importance of the KTDA and of the quality of his management that he continued to act with the same independence and decisiveness."[8] Shortly before Kenyatta's death, Karanja leveraged his relationship with Kenyatta to push through a move to expand KTDA into factory management and tea processing over the opposition of other politically powerful elites. After Kenyatta died, Karanja found himself isolated from the new political elites forming around President Moi. Increasingly frustrated, Karanja began to lash out angrily at those who might otherwise have been cultivated as allies. Eventually he was pushed out of government on February 28, 1981.

Karanja's departure, however, did not significantly alter the organizational trajectory of the KTDA. Figure 8.2 shows a measure of the effectiveness of the KTDA over time, which was affected neither by the loss of Kenyatta as a protective patron in 1978 nor by Karanja's departure in 1981. This was not because another dynamic, firebrand visionary took Karanja's place. Instead, as with the faceless successors of Sir Richard Dane, Karanja's immediate successor lacked verve, dynamism, or political connections. As with the Salt Inspectorate, by that time staff members throughout the organization had already come to have a strong taste and preference for the distinctive

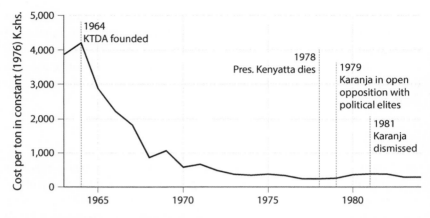

FIGURE 8.2. Production costs of Kenyan tea over time. *Data Source:* Leonard 1990, p. 131

organizational culture of KTDA: Leonard observed that there was "admiration and nostalgia" among senior staff for the Karanja period at KTDA.[9] Despite organizational successors who lacked any particular distinction as leaders, KTDA continued forward as a well-regarded pocket of effectiveness, suggesting its distinctive bureaucratic ethos was relatively robust once it had been thoroughly established.

Post-Karanja, KTDA continued to prosper and function well, and it continues to do so to this day. In the twenty-first century, a majority of Kenyan tea is still produced on KTDA farms, and in 2013 KTDA was the second-largest tea exporter globally. KTDA-produced tea continues to command average prices 12 percent above world market rates for tea. KTDA farmers receive more than three-quarters of the final tea price, a considerably higher amount than is paid to farmers in surrounding countries, and their compensation is sufficient to provide nearly all of their family income—a rare feat in rural Africa. KTDA continues to innovate programs to improve tea quality and yield. For example, it created 820 Farmer Field Schools around the country, offering training to farmers to increase productivity and quality. The organization has sufficiently high capacity to successfully acquire intricate and demanding international certifications, including Rainforest Alliance and Fairtrade Foundation. Amid a global wave of pressure to privatize even well-run state enterprises, the KTDA was privatized in 2000. More than half a million small tea farmers are now individual member-shareholders.[10] KTDA appears to be a case where early organizational effectiveness laid a foundation for long-term success. However, as I will discuss more in a later section, the Brazil case also illustrates that the tendency to persist in the medium term is no assurance that the bureaucratic ethos will persist unchanged in the longer time horizon of a half-century or more.

Can Bureaucratic Niches Scale Up or Diffuse?

Learning that effective bureaucratic niches exist as "bright spots" in otherwise administratively weak states often provokes curiosity about whether such niches can be the spark that spreads organizational capacity throughout the state more generally. Taken as a whole, the cases do not suggest that successful generalized scaling up is an inevitable or even likely outcome. For example, though the organizations persisted relatively effectively for years after the departure of their founders, there is no clear evidence that the administrative strength of the Salt Inspectorate or KTDA formed a foundation for more general expansion of effective bureaucratic administration within the Chinese or Kenyan states. It is possible that such a connection exists; however, available data makes no clear connection so this issue would be a matter for future research. Even if diffusion falls short of instigating generalized state transformation, several of the cases suggest that niches can foster some diffusion of the bureaucratic ethos through several paths: They can expand their own operational domain, can increase constituents' expectations for public service, become a template for emulation by other organizations, and become an incubator for circulating professionals.

First, I remind readers that some caution is required. The cases can only be suggestive in the sense of documenting some observed outcomes and mechanisms. The available data and research design cannot robustly analyze whether such outcomes are *likely* nor differentiate the conditions under which diffusion occurs. There are theoretical reasons to think that niches may not have a general propensity to spread their distinctive bureaucratic ethos throughout the state. Indeed, some of the very conditions that enable interstitial bureaucracy may also reduce their ability or incentives for diffusing. Interstitial bureaucratic niches feed off the mediocrity of others to build the sense of distinctiveness, fueling their own hyperperformance and enhancing in-group solidarity through a sense of relative superiority and pride. A number of the niches were also intentionally cautious, not flaunting their successes too flagrantly to avoid calling down attention on themselves as rate-breakers. Empirically, most of these niches were not overtly evangelical. Niches managed critical interdependencies that could impinge their own ability to function—PARD reverse-coopting the budget division, for example—but otherwise did not actively seek to spread their organizational culture of practice outside the niche boundaries.

DOMAIN EXPANSION

Some niches may expand the bureaucratic ethos by expanding their own operational domain, though there may also be some variation in how well-positioned niches are to do that work. BNDE, the Salt Inspectorate, and the KTDA all substantially expanded their operational domain, incorporating more tasks into their organizational mandate. BNDE rapidly expanded its purview from merely issuing loans to participating in the formulation and implementation of national development policies related to transportation, energy, infrastructure, and industry. BNDE employees created technical documents that guided governmental decisions, such as the Notes on the Program of Economic Restructuring, yearly reports offering assessment of, and suggestions for, Brazil's economic policies. Furthermore, the bank did not merely issue loans to public and private firms, but also assisted in executing invested projects, offering recipients comprehensive development management advice.[11]

The Chinese Salt Inspectorate had initially been authorized with a relatively small organizational mandate: collect the taxes and deposit them into a central account to service the foreign loan debt. Officially, it remained subordinate to the pre-existing *Yanwu Shu*, which was institutionally granted authority over all the other areas of the salt *gabelle* operations from production and transport to sale.[12] However, under the stewardship of Sir Richard Dane, within the first four years of operation the Sino-Foreign Salt Inspectorate assumed greater operational purview to manage their dependencies on the weak *Yanwu Shu*. Similar to the compensatory competence of the Ghanaian cases, the Salt Inspectorate simply began assuming responsibility over auditing district offices, monitoring salt production, transportation, storage, and sale. Previously, collecting salt taxes was not performed by the *Yanwu Shu* but outsourced to local powers through sale of licenses that were customarily treated like private property to be inherited or sold, a form of tax farming. The Inspectorate gradually expanded its purview over the distribution of licenses to incorporate market-like reforms that awarded licenses based on performance.[13] Because the *Yanwu Shu* was so organizationally weak, it was not in a position to resist these expansions. Eventually, the Inspectorate would also expand its operational mandate to include engineering tasks, developing new salt production techniques and building new infrastructure including roads, depots, and warehouses.

Like the Salt Inspectorate, under Karanja's leadership, the KTDA expanded its initial mandate of tea cultivation into related tasks of tea manufacture, warehousing, factory construction, marketing, and retailing.[14] Prior to 1973, multinational tea firms had managed the factories where KTDA-grown tea was processed and shepherded its entrance into the market. At first, to avoid the ire of powerful elites with a stake in the existing factories, KTDA gradually began assuming control over newly built factories. By gradually assuming control of some factories, KTDA was able to gain practical experience in the new domain. Importantly, because the factories performed functionally equivalent tea-processing tasks, KTDA could compare data on the performance of KTDA-operated factories to the contracted factories. Within the first six years, the KTDA factories were outperforming the others, and the KTDA moved to assume direct control of the previously contracted factories. To mitigate problems with construction companies inflating costs because they were paid a percentage of total costs, KTDA even expanded partially into engineering and construction of the factories themselves. By the time Karanja left KTDA, it controlled twenty-seven factories, with more under construction.

The characteristics of the cases that successfully expanded their operational domains suggest that not all central government organizations will be equally well positioned to engage in expansion. All three of these cases engaged in more extreme forms of compensatory competence that became formally institutionalized into their organizational purview. It is likely that their ability to expand into costly new domains, like infrastructural construction, was enabled by their extremely high levels of budgetary autonomy and the ability to generate their own revenue.

INCREASING CONSTITUENT EXPECTATIONS
AND TEMPLATES FOR EMULATION

A World Bank report observed that delays and generally low clearance rates were present in many of the automated and specialized courts in Ghana, with one notable exception:

> The only exception was the automated Commercial Court which had high case disposition rates. All the cases sampled in the Commercial Court reached one form of closure or other. There was greater efficiency in service of processes and case management in the Commercial Courts, thus obviating the delays that are caused by non-service of court processes on parties and poor case management leading to several adjournments for long periods of time.[15]

It is important to note that the automated courts in general were not performing much better than the unautomated courts, evidence that the distinctively high performance of the Commercial Courts was not purely due to a technological advantage.

The Commercial Courts in Accra suggest that highly visible and comparable effectiveness may fuel expansion of bureaucratic niches in more formal and publicly visible ways than the behind-the-scenes expansion via reverse cooptation or expanding organizational domain. Among the Ghanaian cases, the Commercial Courts were distinctive because they perform a function that is also performed by analogous units outside the Ghana Commercial Courts, which rendered their comparative organizational performance starkly legible. Importantly, the Judicial Service annually published results comparing the productivity of all the courts, allowing readers to directly compare the productivity of the Commercial Courts to other comparable High Courts. The Commercial Courts in Accra were so successful that there was pressure from the business community elsewhere in Ghana to spread the model and make specialized commercial courts available throughout Ghana's regions as well.

As of the 2016 annual report, the original Commercial Courts in Accra had been expanded from six to twelve justices, and there were commercial courts operating in six other regions beyond founding Commercial Court in Accra. The data available in annual reports paints a somewhat equivocal portrait of whether or not the regional courts have been able to successfully emulate the productivity of the original Commercial Court in Accra ... and indeed whether the original court itself was able to sustain its rate of hyperperformance over time. At points in time after their founding, all six regional Commercial Courts have had a rate of disposition over new and pending cases that is among the highest in any of the thirty-six High Courts, with disposition rates of 39 to 63 percent compared to an average of 28 percent for all High Courts.[16] But there are also some very high swings in the data from year to year, which raises questions about whether performance is highly variable or whether the underlying data are unreliable. Ultimately it would be a fascinating direction for future research to examine the expanded courts system more closely and rigorously.

The success of the Accra Commercial Courts diffused not only as a model for other Commercial Courts in the regions, but also as a template of particular practices that the Judicial Service attempted to spread more broadly throughout Ghana's courtrooms. There is now an Alternative Dispute Resolution Directorate, part of a policy directive from the new chief justice, Georgina Wood. As of 2016, sixty-seven different courts were utilizing ADR, suggesting a substantial spread of the practice. The available data, however, underscore that even within a sector in the same country, attempting to diffuse an organizational technology can be unsuccessful without also attending to the ethos or organizational culture within which that practice originally operated. Total cases mediated as a percentage of court caseload remain highly variant among the newer adopters of ADR, suggesting some courts may have adopted ADR as a form of superficial compliance rather than fully embracing the practice with the enthusiasm of the original Commercial Court justices, who had sweat equity invested in seeing ADR succeed as pioneers of the practice in Ghana. Moreover, even among those courts conducting mediation, some courts had much stronger settlement records, while others settled vanishingly few cases. For example, Amasaman settled 71 percent of the eighty cases mediated, while White House mediated a comparable eighty-five cases but settled only six cases (7 percent).[17]

INCUBATING AND SPREADING TRAINED PROFESSIONALS

The long and broad perspective on the Brazilian case offers both a caution-ary tale and the greatest suggestion that pockets of effectiveness may be able to gradually spread a bureaucratic ethos to other organizations across the state. First, the cautionary tale. The Brazilian case highlights the potential for threats to niches' bureaucratic ethos over time. Because BNDE was in a posi-tion to disperse very lucrative loans, from its birth politicians frequently tried to interfere in operations, hoping to secure their power by influencing the bank to give supporters favorable loans. For many years the bank managed to fight against this challenge innate to its function, attempting to hew closely to technical and econometric evaluations for whether loans should be given. In 1982 it added a social component to its mission, and to its name, becoming BNDES. By the mid-1980s it had begun investing in state privatization pro-grams, notoriously tempting for political patronage, and by the late 1980s had entered into markets with less clear econometric criteria, including social and urban development, and social inclusion.[18] In the 1990s President Cardoso pushed the bank to expand, claiming that expansion was a contribution to development. However, as it expanded, some felt the bank's reputation for efficiency was tarnished.

More recently the bank has also drawn corruption allegations. As part of the public-sector corruption investigation known as the "Car Wash Operation"— a wide-ranging money laundering and corruption investigation that began with construction project kickbacks—it was discovered that between 2003 and 2015 the bank had loaned at least $37.5 billion USD to entities implicated in the Car Wash investigation. The bank had a fivefold expansion over the past ten years of "soft loans" with heavily subsidized interest rates. Many of those loans appear to have been closely correlated with political contributions, arguably made more in service of politicians' friends than the national eco-nomic interest. For example, the CEO of JBS, the world's largest meat com-pany, claimed to have given the finance minister $61 million USD in bribes in exchange for subsidized loans from BNDES.[19] Some politically connected businesses became incredibly lucrative thanks to those subsidized loans, while other loans resulted in expensive business failures and bankruptcy.[20] Al-though BNDES still remains an active and economically well-regarded bank-ing institution, cumulatively, these developments suggest that there can be erosions in the sterling reputation of pockets of effectiveness over time.

On the other hand, of all the cases, the Brazilian case is also most sugges-tive that pockets of bureaucratic effectiveness can play a role in the broader expansion of generalized state capacity, particularly through the circulation of professionals. This is theoretically interesting because in the thirty-year rise of neoinstitutional theory as an explanation for institutional diffusion, the circulation of professionals is the vector that has received the least subsequent analytic attention. In the late twentieth century, Brazil moved onto the world stage, grabbing international prominence as one of a handful of formerly agrarian or "third world" countries to become a major emerging economy, one of the "BRIICS" of Russia, India, Indonesia, China, and South Africa. Brazil is therefore a very important case for scholars interested in understanding how states can contribute to large-scale economic development. At the same time, Brazil is also a key case for scholars interested in understanding the phenomenon of patchwork leviathans, because there is evidence that the Brazilian state was one of the first states in the world to explicitly understand itself as a state characterized by sometimes vastly uneven institutional quality, openly discussing pockets of effectiveness within the state as early as 1956.[21]

There is general consensus in the literature that the development of state capacities in Brazil emerged first within isolated pockets of the state.[22] The establishment of BNDE's bureaucratic ethos may have benefitted from an infusion of personnel already steeped in the bureaucratic ethos from their work in a prior pocket of effectiveness within Brazil: the Administrative Department of Public Service (DASP). DASP was created under the first Getúlio Vargas regime in 1938. DASP was a concerted and intentional attempt to create a meritocratic results-oriented agency within a state that operated under a clientelistic and neopatrimonial logic.[23] DASP was the brainchild of Luis Simões Lopes, a close confidant of President Vargas and also an ardent believer in scientific management principles, with which Lopes had become fascinated during his travels to the United States.[24] Through DASP, Lopes "sought to create a technical service with admission on a purely universalistic basis."[25] Despite Vargas being merely interested in merit reform, DASP successfully established a bureaucratic ethos through the efforts of Lopes and a close founding cadre who shared his vision. From 1938 until 1945 when Vargas was deposed, "a group of administrative technicians grew within the DASP, instilled with the ideas of neutral competence and scientific management. They constituted the administrative elite and the reservoir of technical knowledge of administration within the government."[26]

Much like the mythological Icarus, DASP is evidence of what can happen to bureaucratic niches that are forceful and public in their efforts to convert other parts of the state to their way of operating. Vargas supported the creation of DASP in part because of his close personal relationship with Lopes, and in part because DASP could help Vargas achieve an administration more capable of executing his developmental plans while redirecting away from the presidency itself the blame and tensions that merit-based reforms and oversight brought. DASP was tasked with reforming public service. It administered public service merit examinations, *concursos,* as a requirement for obtaining government jobs that had previously been given out more freely as patronage.

Thus, a zealous team steeped in the bureaucratic ethos sought to impose that way of operating throughout the state, which brought it into conflict with job-seekers, existing administrative personnel, and powerful politicians who benefitted from patronage appointments. Even with the protection of Vargas, DASP nearly came to blows with the Ministry of Finance when it attempted to wrest the power to formulate and administer the budget. Though legal decree officially gave DASP that power, arrangements were struck with the traditionally powerful Ministry of Finance that rendered DASP's legal budgetary authority only symbolic and retained the budget within the Ministry of Finance. Resentment against DASP simmered until Vargas was deposed, and thereafter DASP confronted a series of new regimes in rapid succession, each desperate to use patronage to cling to power and therefore eager to reduce DASP's influence.[27]

Facing political attacks that limited DASP's ability to pursue its mission, Luis Simões Lopes left the organization and founded the Fundação Getulio Vargas (FGV), along with numerous DASPians who shared his vision. FGV became a "talent bank" for the Brazilian state, a place where those with a taste for rational meritocratic administration in the public interest congregated, and a safe haven for such adherents when the winds of patronage blew too strongly through the state administrative apparatus.[28] It appears FGV, as an early pocket of effectiveness, may have over time scaled up to inculcate a broader bureaucratic ethos throughout the Brazilian state. However, this did not happen through changing institutional regulations in a sweeping state reform but rather in slow iterative change through the systematic training and circulation of professionals. FGV established business and public administration schools that served to inculcate its distinctive ethos in new generations of students:

> Within these schools the doctrine of scientific management was systematically taught, so that the early reformers, in effect, reproduced themselves. To a considerable extent the researchers, professors, and functionaries of the Foundation staffed a series of reform efforts during this entire period, while at the same time establishing beachheads within many of the state governments ... the perpetuation of professionalism in administration was the chief legacy of this entire period, even though its formal governmental reform strategies were a failure.[29]

I hypothesize that by systematically moving a critical mass of personnel, resources, and ideas across organizations, these actors built agencies with high levels of capacity and recognition, which managed to gradually create a new bureaucratic ethos within the Brazilian state more broadly. This picks up on one of the three originally theorized vectors of neoinstitutionalism—the circulation of professionals.[30] Throughout this period, FGV played a central role as a repository and incubator of a performance-oriented bureaucratic ethos.

For example, one of BNDE's first presidents—Lucas Lopes—was the cousin of Luis Simões Lopes, the founder of DASP and then FGV. BNDE drew a considerable number of its early recruits from DASP by way of FGV.[31] Alongside BNDE a handful of other pockets of effectiveness emerged in the mid-twentieth century Brazilian state, including the Superintendency of Currency and Credit (SUMOC, founded in 1945) and, later, several of the Executive Groups (Grupos Executivos) formed under Kubitschek (1956–1960).[32] Several leaders—and personnel—circulated among these pockets of effectiveness, a potential indication that developments within these agencies are connected to each other. FGV included actors who would be key to the development of future pockets of effectiveness, including Eugênio Gudin and Alexandre Kafka.

Earlier pockets of effectiveness seeded expertise in the later-founded Executive Groups. For instance, both GEICON (naval industrial construction) and GEIMAPE (heavy machinery) drew from BNDE, SUMOC, CACEX, and the Foreign Exchange Department of the Bank of Brazil.[33] Moreover, BNDE also provided training to managers of firms participating in the Kubitschek Targets Plan. Such training spread not only technical knowledge about compliance with bank loans in pursuit of the development plan objectives, but also the technocratic ethos for which the bank had become known. By training both public and private-sector organizations, BNDE helped diffuse its performance orientation to a broader Brazilian organizational field:

> Through its training programs of technically-oriented bureaucrats, the BNDES approach and perspective became disseminated throughout the federal government.... With a special eye to improving productivity in basic industries, it played a pioneering role in the introduction of modern managerial and production techniques in Brazilian enterprises still dominated by traditional management practices.[34]

Today, FGV remains a prominent center of excellence in policy research and education, not only in Brazil but globally. It is ranked the top think tank in Latin America and among the top ten worldwide.[35] FGV is also one of only a handful of Latin American universities to be ranked among the world's top universities, ranked slightly above American institutions such as the University of Michigan and the University of Virginia.

In the decades since its founding, FGV has graduated thousands of students, including among others a student named Tasso Jereissati in 1979. After his exposure at FGV, Jereissati would go on to be a widely acclaimed reformist governor of Ceará, at the epicenter of Judith Tendler's insightful work discussed in chapter 7. Jereissati was credited with the surprising transformation of the poor northeastern state by reducing corruption, improving transparency, and increasing meritocracy, while building programs that enhanced citizen well-being and the economy. Jereissati worked closely with a tight-knit cadre. For example, in imposing merit on emergency disaster relief programs, "a nine-member coordinating team [from the region] ran the program with an iron hand ... and traveled extensively throughout the interior to recruit agents through a rigorous selection program."[36] As with some of the rapid transformations observed at NAFDAC and the Salt Inspectorate, under Jereissati the state made surprisingly rapid gains in what had previously seemed to be intractable social problems. For example, within just a few years child vaccine coverage increased from 25 to 90 percent, and infant mortality had been reduced by almost half. As in the bureaucratic niches analyzed in this book, public servants working in the reformed Ceará programs had unusually high discretion, flexibly performed multiple tasks to compensate for what was externally lacking, felt intense pride in their accomplishments, and strongly identified with the mission of their organization.[37] Thus, the Brazilian case poignantly illustrates both some of the pitfalls and also the potential promise of long-term organizational efforts within patchwork leviathans.

Conclusion

Scholars and development practitioners increasingly realize that cosmopolitan organizational reform efforts in the Global South often fail because the organizational reforms are a poor fit for the local institutional environment.[1] Such reform efforts are predicated on an understanding of how states operate—what they are fundamentally like at an organizational level—that is grounded in the experience of Western states and organizations. Those models tacitly presume the bureaucratic ethos is a widespread part of the social environment. Typical global reforms thereby take for granted that orientations to abstract performance goals are "built into modern societies and personalities as very general values" such that "the building blocks for organizations come to be littered around the societal landscape; it takes only a little entrepreneurial energy to assemble them into a structure."[2] However, those "building blocks" are *not* widely available in many non-Western states, like Ghana.[3]

That so many well-funded reform efforts fail makes the book's opening narrative of PARD working late into the night all the more remarkable: PARD and the other cases in this book clearly exhibit the underlying bureaucratic *spirit* that is uncommon in the local public-sector environment, and so elusive in organizational reform efforts. Niche members strongly identify with, and feel an ethical commitment to, the office that transcends everyday commitments to kith and kin. They have distinctive ways of doing and being in the office that are oriented toward achieving rational, predictable, effective, and depersonalized administration. Decades of scholarship since Weber have emphasized that bureaucracy is defined by characteristics such as the hierarchical coordination of discrete jurisdictions, staffed by officials motivated by stable and financially secure employment throughout a lifelong career steeped in drudgery. By contrast, the Ghanaian interstices seemed almost the inverse. They had relatively high operational discretion, unusual organizational redundancy, spent inordinate effort managing external environmental disruptions, and were staffed by officials with nonfinancial motivations who did not anticipate or even desire stable life-long employment, but were *bursting with pride.*

What the Ghanaian niches do is paradoxical from the perspective of existing organizational scholarship, which largely expects organizations to adopt globally legitimated organizational models, but also anticipates "decoupling," whereby the actual practices may differ substantially from the outward façade, ultimately failing to produce the underlying spirit of reforms.[4] By contrast, bureaucratic interstices adopt practices that differ subtly but significantly from legitimated global organizational practices. I argue interstitial bureaucratic organizational characteristics differ from canonical Weberian bureaucracy because the adapted characteristics are strategic responses to the embedded-yet-distinct interstitial position. To cope with that structural position, interstitial niches employ distinctive organizational practices to cluster and cultivate resources that are not widely available, and manage disruptions arising from interdependencies with the adverse surrounding environment. In so doing, niches cultivate the underlying spirit of the bureaucratic ethos that so often eludes reform efforts.

Orientation to organizational goals was revolutionary, compared to historically prior organizational forms, because it radically depersonalized administration. Instead of personal economic interest or network ties motivating work in prebendalism or patrimonialism, bureaucratic officials were oriented to achieving goals on behalf of abstract collectives—the organization, "state," or "the people." From paperwork to rules and meritocracy, those characteristics were means for cultivating the bureaucratic ethos and reorienting individual action to collective goals. Ultimately then, bureaucracy inures not in the characteristic existence of "paperwork" but in what paperwork aims to accomplish: separation of personal and professional spheres, increased transparency, and more effective goal achievement based on analysis of documented patterns. Without the bureaucratic ethos, characteristic bureaucratic features like "paperwork" often fail to achieve the ends of rational, predictable, effective administration, instead becoming red tape that can be leveraged into a bribe. Conversely, in high-variation environments like Ghana, characteristics that appear nonbureaucratic according to Weber's classic typology actually support the bureaucratic ethos and ultimately achieve rational, predictable, effective, and depersonalized administration.

Argument Summary

Patchwork Leviathan traces the localized emergence of a bureaucratic ethos within niches of the state. Sufficient *shelter from neopatrimonial influence* mattered because it conveyed greater discretion over operations and personnel, enabling deviation from the status quo in the surrounding environment. For the effective bureaucratic niches in this book, shelter from neopatrimonial influence emerged under political elites who were *merely willing* or *inattentive*, a stark contrast to assumptions that organizational performance depends on executive will or, its inverse, full formal organizational autonomy. Niches achieved discretion through skillful manipulation within the constraints of the system, assistance from lesser elites, or structural filtering that made them unattractive for patronage hiring. Sheltered spaces emerged as bureaucratic niches when they were headed by a founding cadre of actors with *dual habitus,* lived experience in the local environment and in functionally bureaucratized environments elsewhere.[5] Such dual habitus was often, though not exclusively, the result of a local first degree—which gave them cultural and social capital that framed them as authentically local—and an advanced degree abroad—which gave them not only explicit professional knowledge but also practical lived experience in an environment where the bureaucratic ethos was common.

Those local actors with a foot in both institutional worlds were able to do what legions of cosmopolitan organizational reform consultants could not: cultivate locally adaptive practices that support organizational orientation among a corps of civil servants. A small founding cadre with dual habitus fostered a "cognitive subculture"[6] among a few dedicated actors who transposed, experimented, evaluated, tinkered, and created practices oriented to achieving the organizational mission but also well-fitted to the larger local institutional environment. Actors with dual habitus and discretion over personnel furthered *clustering* by recruiting people from the local labor pool with elective affinities for the bureaucratic ethos. They utilized a variety of strategies to mitigate the costs of searching for such an orientation, which is both difficult to discern and relatively uncommon in the labor pool broadly. In particular, recruiters actively sought to evaluate quasi-bureaucratic characteristics through direct observation and referrals. At the same time, the nature of work in some niches had costs that were balanced by benefits that disproportionately attracted already-professionalized applicants while discouraging applicants mostly interested in easy government pay or opportunities for lucrative illicit income.

Lived experience within the niche *cultivated* within insiders a taste for, and the practices of, being engrossed in work late into the night in one of those few offices where the lights still burn brightly into the Ghanaian night.

The clustered distinctiveness of the niche was deepened as niche members came to identify and conform with the standards that typified their distinctive work group—particularly along vectors that maximized out-group distinctions. The clustered distinctiveness provided members repeated practice with both conscious and tacit knowledges, a microcosm of lived exposure to the habits, practices, and dispositions of the bureaucratic ethos. Over time, this culminated in a subculture of bureaucracy that was *distinctive* from the surrounding neopatrimonial environment. That distinctiveness promoted within-group identification but also required active efforts to *protect* the niche by mitigating environmental vulnerabilities, which arose because the surrounding environment operated according to very different taken-for-granted rules of conduct. Niches protected their potentially vulnerable distinctive subculture by modifying internal practices and engaging in more ambitious projects of remaking the external environment. Ultimately then, *Patchwork Leviathan* argues that where the human, cognitive, and material resources of bureaucracy are rare, it matters critically how they are distributed.

I Know Why the (Iron) Caged Bird Sings: Pride and Public Service Motivations

Much scholarship following Max Weber has perpetuated the imagery of the increasing rationalization of modern society as a sort of "iron cage," an irresistible force of impersonal mechanization.[7] However, the book has shown that in many organizational fields the bureaucratic ethos is *still a socially deviant, uncommon, fragile, and ongoing project*. In niches where that is true, members often find their work and distinctive organizational culture to be a source of tremendous motivation and pride. This book's deep dive into the daily life of work in pockets of effectiveness supports growing scholarship that takes seriously the idea that people may have motivations that are vastly different from the rational self-interested actor seemingly at the heart of so many reforms to public-sector management.[8] The findings of this book suggest we need to reincorporate attention to intrinsic motivations and professionalism into our scholarship and the design of public policies aimed at improving public-sector performance.

Currently dominant approaches to public-sector reforms are grounded in assumptions that public workers are self-interested actors inclined to misappropriate benefits and subvert, shirk, or sabotage work whenever possible unless contained by monitoring.[9] Klitgaard, a hugely influential voice in anticorruption efforts, encapsulated this view when arguing that corruption occurs when the gains outweigh the probability of, and penalty for, getting caught. Klitgaard's approach demonized discretion in his famous pithy corruption formula: "Corruption = monopoly + discretion – accountability."[10]

Some of the lessons of this book suggest approaches to public-sector productivity that are grounded in professionalism, approaches that are starkly at odds with currently dominant approaches to state reform. Following Klitgaard, dominant approaches seek to limit discretion. By contrast, this book found that effective clusters emerged where leaders delegated enough authority to founding cadres, such that the initial cluster felt bonds of reciprocity and sweat equity in the institution-building process. Dominant approaches suggest simplifying tasks to limit discretion and better enable monitoring. By contrast, I join scholars like Judith Tendler in arguing that intrinsic motivation is best encouraged where varied opportunities for growth and intellectual creativity present professional enticements to effort.[11] Current approaches advocate for abstract monitoring systems that can monitor across large scales and at a distance, assuming only a pinnacle principal can be trusted to monitor his interests. However, scholarship on monitoring has increasingly found that people look to those around them to interpret cues about how a monitoring technology should be understood, often discerning that monitoring should not be taken seriously. When that happens, monitoring can create perverse incentives to game the system. By contrast, this book has highlighted the deeply sociological bonds of learning and emulation that took place within relatively small and generally face-to-face organizational settings, whether a few dozen workers of PARD or Dora Akunyili working to move around physically to routinely see everyone within the entire NAFDAC organization. To paraphrase Swidler's "give a man a fish" metaphor for development workshops, give an official a tool, and he nods and smiles and eats well for the duration of the international workshop.[12] This book suggests that if you let a small group of officials make important, consequential decisions about how a house will be built, they will defend it for a lifetime. We have been so fearful that public servants will live down to our worst fears of them that we have also robbed them of the discretion and agency that might enable them to rise to their own best hopes for themselves.

Professionalism may not be a silver bullet solution for all that ails states. Many of the moves toward increased monitoring were initiated in response to previous abuses of discretion and authority. However, the pendulum toward monitoring has swung too far and in so doing it may have created a lot of unappreciated harm while trying to stem the abuses of a few. Scholarship in a variety of fields raises concerns that extrinsic incentives—receiving personal financial benefits or escaping personal punishments—can "crowd out" intrinsic incentives, including a sense of moral obligation to perform a task well for the sake of the task and the broader benefit it brings.[13] This is especially relevant because a large literature in public administration research substantiates that many government workers are motivated by "public service motivation" or the intrinsic motivation for altruistic effort in the public interest.[14] This intrinsic motivation to do work that serves the public good is clearly evidenced in many cases of high-performing state niches, both within this book and in other scholarship on pockets of effectiveness, discussed below.

Implications for Development Practice

As I have contemplated ways that future work might further test and refine the findings laid out in this book, I have found myself sometimes frustrated. Answering some of the future questions with a high degree of causal certainty would likely require field experiments, including millions of dollars, relatively unfettered access to government programs, and the ability to explicitly tinker with how the programs were administered. In short, as an academic those conditions seemed like an unrealistic fantasy. Then one day I was on the phone with a friend who worked in a large global donor agency, who was desperately seeking any advice I might have on how to increase the capacity of government development partners. He explained that he was under a deadline to run a project, which meant that he had to spend millions of dollars, with close access to government agencies, and needed to make informed decisions about how those programs would be administered. What for me was an unreasonable fantasy scenario was for him the daily burden to act, despite an acute awareness of critical uncertainties about what was best.

The prevailing academic fashion is to criticize development practice; however, I have a lot of compassion for the structural position of development practitioners. To paraphrase a conventional dictum, academics' take on practitioners seems to be "Don't just do something, sit there and think" while practitioners' view of academics is "Don't just sit there thinking, do something." Too often academics offer criticism of the current state of affairs without putting our neck out to suggest what might be done better or differently. So below I will offer some lessons for development practice that might be garnered from the evidence in this book.

First, readers may understandably wonder if the model in this book constitutes a new set of "best practices" or a "Ghana model" that might be fruitfully diffused. I think the biggest takeaway of the book for development practice is that the particulars of what works well can be highly contingent on local environments,[15] which is why the specific content of organizational or technical strategies deployed by the various cases varied widely from country to country and sector to sector. What those innovations had in common was that they were driven by local agents with deep lived experience both in the local environment and in effective large formal organizations. Would a global best practices model based on Ghana be an improvement over exporting global best practices that are grounded in a hegemonically bureaucratic environment in the West? Yes, they might. But better still might be to empower local agents—perhaps especially those with dual habitus—to learn from what has worked elsewhere, not as pressure to conform as the primary way to demonstrate global legitimacy and secure donor funding, but merely as mental fodder to consider, allowing local agents more discretion to creatively borrow, repurpose, combine, or eschew what has worked elsewhere as guided by their local habitus.

In much of the field of development practice, the emphasis has been to think big and look for huge transformative interventions. The Gates Foundation, for example, laces the word "transformative" throughout its implementation missions, whether talking about "agricultural transformation" or "commercializing transformative sanitation technologies."[16] But after decades of trying, this approach has yet to regularly succeed despite millions of dollars in pursuit of top-down sweeping societal transformation. In contrast, I join other scholars who have argued for pursuing little, incremental wins.[17] In particular, working at a smaller scale may better harness the deeply social and interpersonal roots of how the productive niches emerged and flourished. Instead of an intervention weakened by its broad reach, we may instead try to make a big difference in a few more narrowly concentrated pockets within the state. To donors aiming for nothing short of social transformation that may seem like small potatoes. On the other hand, what in Brazil began as a few small potatoes grew into a few pockets of effectiveness within the state, which arguably over time spread into an archipelago of effectiveness within the state,[18] a seismic shifting over the course of fifty years in the capacity and effectiveness of the state. The third chapter on cultivation argued that the firsthand experience of even little wins was important for shoring up identification with the work and persistence in the face of subsequent challenges. Stringing little wins together may ultimately be a more effective means of generating genuine buy-in to those difficult-to-change social and behavioral aspects at the heart of "capacity building" goals.

Encouraging and then building on small wins calls for development practice to be more flexible and reflexive. In order to accumulate small wins, it may mean heeding the lessons of Ghanaian niches protecting themselves from disruptions that can derail organizational goals. Enabling small wins might therefore require incorporating more of the existing organizational wisdom on high reliability organizations and decreasing reliance on scholarship that emphasizes lean organizations. Similarly, being nimbly and thoughtfully *re*-active may be better than being boldly and incorrectly *pro*-active. Instead of going in with a five-year plan for the transformation one hopes to make, donors might instead seek to identify and support already existing pockets of excellence within the state, helping fledgling pockets become sustainable and perhaps even spread by supporting the innovative work of local agents in those pockets.

There is, for example, evidence of international institutions or donors playing some supporting roles for pockets of effectiveness in this book. Danida provided funding that enabled the Ghana Commercial Courts to construct a new building designed to enable justices to work closely with support staff, a building that set the Commercial Courts both physically and symbolically apart. Multilateral lenders were the impetus for the creation of the Sino-Foreign Salt Inspectorate in the Republican-era Chinese state. BNDE's position as a local guarantor required for development projects seeking international loans both placed it under political pressure and gave it a source of leverage through which it could discipline loan recipients. International donors belatedly helped finance the KTDA after the organization had established and given proof that tea farming could be locally viable, and donors on the KTDA board were sometimes important allies for the KTDA leadership that counterbalanced political motives of local politicians on the board. NAFDAC, the Bank of Ghana, and PARD all benefitted from donor-funded international training programs that helped their members learn new professional skills and also acquire lived exposure to bureaucratic habitus. Additionally, NAFDAC buffered its hiring operations from local patronage pressures by outsourcing the administration of a merit exam to an international consultancy group. Note that in all these cases the impetus did not originate with international donors who sought to create a pocket of effectiveness in a particular part of the state. Rather, in each case donors responded to already existing fledgling pockets of effectiveness driven on the ground by invested locals.

However, international donors seeking to intentionally foster pockets of effectiveness should heed a word of caution: there is a chance that lavishing donor attention on particularly effective parts of the state could have unintended negative consequences. As illustrated by the account of PARD's director recognizing others only through the few lights that were on late into the night, pockets of effectiveness often took pains not to call too much public attention to themselves, especially at early formative periods when their distinctive organizational ethos was still consolidating. By contrast, the attention and funding of multinational donors is unlikely to go unnoticed by elites or other civil servants. Attention drawn by donor support could call down the vitriol of other public servants, or have the perverse effect of making the agency a more attractive patronage target because of its close association with donor resources. Moreover, international donors are often symbolically understood as the antithesis of "local," such that plans that are interpreted as too closely aligned with global donors' desires may be rejected out of hand by other locals on whose cooperation and effort success depends.[19]

Donors cautious of unintended consequences might consider targeting to enable particularly inglorious, challenging, but necessary work within the state. Somewhere there are water quality monitoring units working in hot and undesirable conditions to produce important knowledge for public health and agriculture. Providing scientific equipment and new hip waders to that team would cost a fraction of the budget of the normal embedded technical assistance unit within the ministry, and would be unlikely to make the job substantially more attractive to a nonprofessional patronage hire, but would be a significant recognition and assistance to the dedicated professionals working there.

Appreciating the professional motivations of many of the workers in bureaucratic niches may also encourage donors to rethink the current approaches to capacity building, which typically have a dedicated team within donor agencies explicitly focused on capacity building who are decoupled from project delivery teams focusing on substantive areas, such as health, education, or agriculture. The current analysis suggests in part that members of effective niches are not motivated to engage in "honest" and "effective" work merely for its own sake, but rather because of deeply professional interest in the specific work itself. Economists at the Bank of Ghana are interested in, and proud of, their ability to manage the money supply effectively, and its indirect contribution to the economic prosperity of the country. Justices at the Commercial Court were deeply interested in the professional practice of expedient, effective, and just application of law in commercial cases, and went to great ends to ensure administrative effectiveness in service of those very substantive professional goals. This suggests that capacity-building teams should not be separate from substantive area teams working on things like health or agriculture, but rather should be embedded within those teams to continuously learn through evidence what works to better harness, enable, and build on public servants' area-specific intrinsic professional motivations to cultivate better administrative capacity.

Implications for Scholarship

EMBRACING VARIATION WITHIN STATES: A FOCUS ON POSITIVE DEVIANCE AND POCKETS OF EFFECTIVENESS

Patchwork Leviathan has argued that scholars need to examine within-state variation in administrative capacity, moving away from the unitary imagery of states both in how we theorize and measure them. *Patchwork Leviathan* thereby advances a research tradition of state-building largely based on historical analysis of premodern European states,[20] joining scholars who draw theoretical and empirical attention to within-state variation in capacity. Within-state variation is a significant empirical reality conditioning the organizational sociology of political bodies, particularly—but not exclusively—in many so-called developing countries. Broadly, it suggests that scholars reconceptualize states as patchwork composites of fractious subunits that may differ vastly not only in their organizational interests, but in foundational organizational capacities and the institutional rules of the game guiding their actions. This book joins a corps of growing scholarship deeply interested in the inner workings of the state as enacted by the human agents who comprise the administrative body of the state.[21]

In particular, *Patchwork Leviathan* has been motivated by *understanding what is working well* within states where the globally dominant narrative is that nothing works. As such, this book is a striking divergence from scholarly tendencies to analyze the *failures* of African states, a focus that predominates both among those whose scholarly proclivities point to the shortcomings of African states and politics as the sources of their own problems, as well as those who are inclined to see violent and extractive colonialism as the root of Africa's contemporary development challenges. Instead, this book is part of a growing movement calling for a concerted theoretical agenda for understanding "positive deviance" or "bright spots" within state administrative bodies.[22] We need greater explicit theoretical attention to the high end of the distribution of within-state capacities because, as the book demonstrates, outstanding administrative effectiveness depends on more than just the absence of conditions scholars have associated with corruption or administrative weakness.

Studying how some groups have more successfully grappled with a prevailing social problem has the potential to make sociology more relevant beyond the academy by highlighting ways to better solve problems everyday people care about, while also affording a perspective that is potentially powerful for the innovative sociological theorizing academics value.[23] Throughout the last fifty years, a small but growing number of scholars have been interested in understanding why some parts of the government managed to be effective in contexts where so many other agencies were not.[24] But until recently these efforts were largely individual, separated by scholarly geographic silos and varying terminology for the object of study. Scholarship in this vein has risen dramatically since the 1990s into a growing interdisciplinary scholarly agenda,[25] increasingly coalescing around the term *pockets of effectiveness*.[26] As this scholarly dialogue consolidates, future pockets of effectiveness research can move towards theoretically informed case selection to reform existing theory and test rival hypotheses. I suggest several exciting new directions for such work in the future research section later in this chapter.

My work advances a tradition within pockets of effectiveness scholarship that sees human actors and distinctive organizational culture as key to understanding how some government organizations manage to outperform their peers, joining august figures such as Judith Tendler and Merilee Grindle. Grindle's pathbreaking comparative study of twenty-nine organizations in six

countries found that "organizational mystique" was one of the strongest factors differentiating strong organizations from poor performers in her sample.[27] She describes organizational mystique as "well-defined missions that
were widely ascribed to by employees ... [which] amounted to a mystique
about the organization and the importance of the task it was performing.
Employees internalized the organization's goals and saw themselves as vital
contributors to its accomplishment."[28] Tendler observes a similar phenomenon among highly effective state programs in a poor region of Brazil, where
workers "demonstrated unusual dedication to their jobs" that was enabled by
government "creat[ing] a strong sense of 'calling' and mission around these
particular programs and their workers."[29] *Patchwork Leviathan* advances understanding of the organizational, sociological, and social psychological foundations for how workers come to identify so strongly with the organizational
mission, a transformation of attachments at the heart of the *bureaucratic ethos*.

Putting work in the pockets of effectiveness tradition into dialogue can
highlight important areas of theoretical agreement and differences that can
be productive for future theory refinement. To cite just one example, Tendler
credits public accountability of her street-level workers—community health
workers and agricultural extension agents wanting to "live up to the new trust
placed in them by their clients and citizens in general"—as the key to why
workers performed exceptionally well seemingly despite discretion and hazy
job requirements that might have enabled rent-seeking behaviors. Yet most
of the public servants I studied in Ghana, with the exception of the Commercial Courts, felt a similar obligation to perform well even though they did
not primarily interface directly with the public as program service providers.
This suggests a need for future research to better understand sociological
mechanisms of such discipline, and how sociological disciplinary motivations
might differ for parts of the state that directly provide services to the public
that citizens value (e.g., community health workers) compared to parts of the
state whose work is opaque to everyday citizens (e.g., central bankers) or for
whom faithful work in the abstract public interest may conflict with an individual citizen's short-term interests (e.g., tax collectors).

The detailed data of the book open up what is usually a macropolitical
black box. It argues organizational cultural work and practices are essential
parts of the explanation for why some organizations succeed in these inhospitable contexts, including how they build competence in the first place. In so
doing it also poses a theoretical challenge to the conventional understanding
that neopatrimonialism and the bureaucratic ethos are categorically distinct
and mutually exclusive. The data show that in midrange cases such as Ghana,
practices conceptually associated with neopatrimonialism and bureaucracy
may be intertwined, recombined, and repurposed, and may exist in varying
states of depth and institutionalization. For example, the book demonstrates

practices that may look curiously close to patronage hiring—like using social networks to find a job candidate—are repurposed by niches to search for difficult-to-discern proto-bureaucratic characteristics like work ethic. Instead of crisp categorically distinct concepts, the book's argument about iterative endogenous change re-envisions neopatrimonialism and the bureaucratic ethos as existing along a continuum of practice. More explicitly connecting this continuum argument to the detailed qualitative data of the Ghanaian cases thereby allows readers to see how sometimes small initial endowments of distinctive organizational practices or orientations come to be deepened over time, concentrated, and ordered into what becomes recognized distinctiveness.

The book has argued that organizational effectiveness depends on the foundation of establishing a bureaucratic ethos as the dominant organizational culture, which suggests a different interpretation for why the creation of parallel agencies has seemed to be more correlated with success than transforming existing agencies. Existing agencies come with established insiders and an existing organizational culture, which are often resistant to change from outsiders. By contrast, parallel agencies are established from scratch, which means there is no pre-existing organizational culture or entrenched insiders with which to grapple. The deck can be strategically stacked with clustered distinctiveness more easily. For example, it will be easier for a bureaucratic ethos to emerge as the most visible mode of interaction in the organizational environment if there is not a large population who is engaged in a coherent alternative interactional group style. This is a different way of thinking about why these organizations succeed: It suggests parallel agencies tend to be more performance-oriented, not necessarily because of their formal autonomy per se, but because their newness creates a blank slate for organizational culture and their discretion over personnel gives the bureaucratic ethos a fighting chance.

CONTRIBUTIONS TO POLITICAL SOCIOLOGY

Patchwork Leviathan contributes to political sociology by arguing for disaggregating "states" for analytic purposes, following in the footsteps of scholars such as Joel Migdal, Kimberly Morgan, and Ann Orloff. It thereby raises questions about bureaucratic variation in advanced industrialized countries as well. As Alejandro Portes so elegantly puts it, "It is possible that not all governmental agencies and other institutions in Nigeria are hopeless and that not all Dutch and Scandinavian ones are necessarily paragons of virtue."[30] Many U.S. and European civil servants have also been corrupt or inefficient, and administrative states in those regions have often exhibited the same challenges visible in places like Ghana, so we have reason to expect their bureaucrats have also had to figure out how to create different organizational cultures through selection, socialization, enforcement, and protection against external disruptions. The findings of this book thereby suggest approaches to rethinking state-building scholarship from early modern Europe to American Political Development to late twentieth-century developmental states in East Asia. In particular, the book calls for unpacking the organizational black box of administrative states, encouraging scholars to press more deeply into the organizations themselves to address *how* administrative capacity came to be vested within particular parts of the administrate states, and interrogating the adaptation of a bureaucratic ethos rather than taking it for granted.

For example, within developmental states scholarship, the 1990s occasioned a renaissance of scholarly interest in bureaucracy as scholars pointed to the critical role of states in shepherding the unprecedented economic growth of previously poor countries like South Korea and Japan.[31] At the heart of developmental states were nodal agencies performing the critical task of coordinating efforts among the diverse body of agencies comprising the central state, and between the state and private-sector partners—arguably the most famous of which was Japan's Ministry of Trade and Industry (MITI).[32] When the administrative strength of such nodal agencies is explained at all, explanations are usually brief and center on factors outside the organization, such as a reformist executive, or being highly sought-after employment for graduates of elite educational systems who have passed rigorous merit exams. Yet there is some evidence that clustering distinctiveness within MITI began *before* MITI had developed a particular public reputation for excellence that made it a professionally desirable post for elite university graduates. There are tantalizing hints that the very mechanics outlined in this book played a role. In 1925, the old Ministry of Agriculture and Commerce was set to be subdivided into two new ministries, one of which would go on to become MITI. A civil servant with dual habitus—a prestigious first degree from Japan and educational experience abroad in the United States and Europe—worked with a close-knit cadre. At the time of the ministerial division, they were strategically positioned where personnel matters were decided, and used that discretion over personnel to cluster distinctiveness: "Shijō and Yoshino sent all the stubborn and dull bureaucrats to the new agriculture ministry and kept in commerce all the flexible and bright ones."[33]

Incorporating meso-level organizational explanations for how administrative capacity comes to be vested in certain parts of the state also contributes to the field of American Political Development (APD). Historically, the U.S. state has also had pockets of effective and honest administration amid more general state administrative weakness, including long periods of its history during which the U.S. federal government operated openly under patronage politics whereby unqualified and unskilled people were given public-service posts as rewards for political support.[34] During the U.S. Jacksonian Era famed for patronage and rife with political scandal, and when federal science was still inchoate, the U.S. Coast Survey department emerged from a neglected and moribund agency to became "a world-renown scientific agency, doubtless producing the best known of all the scientific work sustained by the government."[35] Daniel Carpenter famously analyzed the administrative strength and autonomy of the United States Department of Agriculture (USDA) during the nineteenth century.[36] Even into the early twentieth century Theda Skocpol characterized the USDA as "an island of state strength in an ocean of weakness" demonstrating strong administrative capacities at a time when, in general, "the civil administrative capacities of the U.S. national state in the 1930s were weak and poorly coordinated."[37]

Most prior explanations of variation in agency strength within the U.S. state have focused extensively on what was going on outside of the agency, examining macropolitical factors and industry interests.[38] But it is of considerable theoretical and practical importance to question precisely how such external forces managed to occasion a disciplinary revolution within state agencies, and in particular, whether there were unobserved changes in the organizational ethos *within* agencies that were critical antecedents to their enhanced performance and engagement with outside interests.[39] Such an approach could, for example, build on Skocpol and Feingold's masterful analysis of the U.S. New Deal Agricultural Adjustment Agency, which was surprisingly successful administering interventionist policy despite a fragmented and querulous agricultural industry. They argue that interventionist government programs work better when they have state capacity: that is, when they "have or can quickly assemble, their own knowledgeable administrative organizations," and point to the Agricultural Adjustment Agency being nested within the already-competent USDA. More thoroughly analyzing the organizational mechanics of that transformation therefore has the potential not only to enrich American political development, but also to contribute to theoretical interest in how pockets of effectiveness can diffuse.

IMPLICATIONS FOR ORGANIZATIONAL SCHOLARSHIP MORE BROADLY

Many organizations, from central administrations in poor countries to public schools in America, would appreciate having people who take pride in their station, eschew laziness, circumvent incompetence from external agencies, and discipline recalcitrant colleagues. Typically, general institutional weakness overwhelms individual efforts, eventually discouraging future effort. Yet every polity, no matter how weak, possesses some baseline cadre of proto-bureaucratic potential recruits. However, where such people are never drawn into civil service, or spread too thin, or unable to shape the environment around them, these social agents will be unable to agglomerate a critical mass to establish an interstitial subculture of Weberian-style bureaucracy that is capable of acculturating newcomers and withstanding external pressures. Clustering provides a critical mass and subgroup support, while distinctiveness vis-à-vis the environment fosters a sense of pride, purpose, and disciplined capacity. Interstitiality underscores the critical importance of how particular social actors are distributed and clustered (or not).

In its emphasis on an ethos developing within small interpersonal groups, right down to the observation that feeling chosen can make people work harder, *Patchwork Leviathan* extends a classic body of organizational scholarship, emerging out of the Hawthorne experiments conducted in the 1920s.[40] Those studies highlighted that productivity at work was not merely mechanical but profoundly social, such that camaraderie, pressure, and interpersonal monitoring within working groups could be a powerful influence on workers' output—indeed often more powerful than the incentives of management.[41] These Hawthorne experiments are widely credited with spawning the creation of human relations departments within large corporations. *Patchwork Leviathan* reminds us, however, that those performance-enhancing social dynamics depend critically on being embedded within a group culture and interpersonal relationships with valued social others. Commercial Court justices felt honored to have been chosen personally by Chief Justice George Kingsley Acquah. Bank researchers felt honored to frequently interact with and provide analysis to Dr. Paul Acquah, the well-respected governor of the Bank of Ghana. Young PARD workers valued informal interactions with Mr. Mensah as opportunities to learn and observe. Those examples are quite different from the current state of human resources departments within large formal organizations, in which interactions are infrequent and formalized with human resources officials who are nameless, faceless, and of relatively low status.

Understanding how interstitial niches manage to cultivate clustered distinctiveness can shed light on organizational change more generally, including in private-sector organizations. Broadly, for organizational scholars this book advances understanding of large formal organizations as simultaneously unitary and composed of many more-or-less autonomous parts, which are still part of the whole. This inherent tension in many large formal organizations is important and undertheorized in organizational research, where dominant theories treat organizations either as coherent actors (e.g., principal-agent theory) or as loose networks. This work suggests that most organizations, including states, have properties of both, and that this duality affects organizational practice. For example, U.S. corporations likewise contain subunits that distinctively outperform the rest of the corporation.[42] Similar to cases in this book, ethnographic accounts suggest high-performing corporate sub-units are semiautonomous and characterized by a distinctive ethos and strong insider pride[43]—suggesting dynamics of clustered distinctiveness as a foundation for organizational cultural change may generalize to high-performing niches beyond interstitial *bureaucracy* in neopatrimonial settings.

Development practitioners working in low-income countries are not the only people looking to change the culture within organizations. To cite just one example, many people working with large North American corporations would like to make them more inclusive for women, people of color, differently abled people, and other under-represented groups. However, just as in the failures of top-down efforts to reform low-income states, organizational cultures that are, for example, inhospitable to women have proven very difficult to change, particularly with the typical tools of large one-day corporate mandatory training workshops. The research in this book suggests an alternative way to think about encouraging organizational cultural change as part of an ethos grounded in lived experience, which is made possible through clustered distinctiveness.

Here I will use the example of gender inclusiveness to suggest some implications for clustered distinctiveness as an approach to changing organizational cultures. (1) Appreciating the importance of habits of practice at the heart of an ethos suggests a targeted workshop or corporate education session in which the behavioral change (e.g., gender inclusiveness) is part of the explicit abstract teaching may not be as effective as concentrated lived experience in an immersive environment in which the targeted behavior is the dominant mode of interaction. This leverages the hidden wisdom of *how*, providing practice and observation of a positive model to emulate. (2) Change efforts may be better off working small with a few people who are intrinsically motivated to participate than working big with a ton of people who are being forced into it. Why? Because in each scenario the dominant small-group culture will be determined largely by the prevailing sentiment of either enthusiastic "all in" participation or withdrawn, even mock participation in the latter.

The study also has implications for what to do after training or exposure to different practices. If through good fortune or training an organization has six or ten people with strong prior experience in the targeted practice, what then should be done with them? Often in our eagerness to work transformatively or "at scale" we would have sent those six or ten experienced recruits back out into six or ten different units of the corporation, hoping that they would be ambassadors spreading change. Instead they become isolates who are overwhelmed by the already dominant contrary practices, just as described in chapter 2. Instead, to help an alternative ethos persist we need think about (3) how to keep the clustered distinctiveness after the training is done such that a substantial number of experienced people are all staffed together and can, like the Ghanaian civil servants, become the most visible small-group culture within a local niche, continuing to cultivate, support, and protect each other. This may mean establishing clusters within organizations that are relatively small to begin with—for example start-ups—or by doing symbolic boundary work to constitute a subunit within a larger organization as particularly distinctive such that the scale of the reference group for the dominant interactional style comes to be the smaller-scale subgroup rather than the larger organization.

Appreciating small-group interpersonal interactions as a foundation for organizational culture work has some implications, by extension, for whether it is desirable to encourage or discourage organizational cultural "contagion" between cohorts in programs, because each new cohort potentially represents a new opportunity for a distinctive interactional small-group culture. Theoretically, if you want to change the existing interactional small-group culture, it would be beneficial to create greater isolation between cohorts such that each cohort has the potential to establish a different interactional style as dominant within its smaller scale rather than to orient itself to the established mode of interacting. Conversely, if you want to perpetuate the existing interactional small-group culture, then you want to strategically encourage contagion between cohorts. For example, my university developed a program for adults who had already been professionally successful and wanted to return to the university to think about a second career, what is sometimes called encore education. Program designers felt the inaugural class had a great ethos, interacting with each other and engaging with the university in just the ways the program's designers had hoped. When they asked me what they could do to ensure that the next year's cohort had the same small-group culture, my first recommendation was to handpick a few of this year's cohort to carry over and have a second year. Thus on the first day of the next year, the most visible interactional style within the group would most likely be that of the alumni members from the previous year, and new members seeking to understand what it meant to be a good member of the group would be inclined to conform to that dominant style.

Thinking about expanding organizational subcultures or encouraging contagion across cohorts then raises fascinating questions about *how many* subcultural insiders it takes to "seed" a new environment or, conversely, how many newcomers an established organizational subculture can incorporate without disrupting their ethos. The precise numbers or percentages would have to be established in future research, but I would hypothesize that the model group could incorporate a larger number of new recruits if the new recruits were also intrinsically motivated but inexperienced, or could inculcate a smaller number of recruits who began as reluctant participants—perhaps a third the number of the established cohort. Moreover, because the importance is on establishing the most visible interactional style in a small-group setting, the proportions would likely also be sensitive to the probability that newcomers themselves shared a well-established alternative ethos, for example, a "bro" culture within technology fields that marginalizes or excludes women.

ADMINISTRATIVE STATES ARE ORGANIZATIONS, BUT THEY AREN'T JUST ANY ORGANIZATIONS

This book has offered a rare meso- and micro-level look at the inner workings of the people and organizations that comprise states such as Ghana, which are usually only examined at arm's length if at all. Too often states are presumed to be somehow purely political and we therefore overlook that they are deeply *organizational* entities as well. When scholars say that government workers are "bureaucrats" we seem to overlook that they are also workers in an organization. This book contributes to growing interest in "street level bureaucracy," which illuminates the microfoundations for how the state interfaces with everyday citizens through public-service provision.[44] However, *Patchwork Leviathan* is distinctive from this tradition both in that it attends to public servants outside Western states, and, importantly, in that the public servants in this book are for the most part *not* street-level agents who regularly interact with the public through public-service provision. Instead they walk the inner sanctums of state power and through their action (or inaction) inscribe the state as it exists in that vast organizational space between the streets and the elites.

Pushing back against the black box of the administrative state to illuminate its organizational dynamics suggests, among other things, actually looking at what is going on within state organizations as those organizations interface with political elites and the public. For example, accounts of public-sector reform grounded in social movements often place primary causal emphasis on what is going on *outside* of state organizations—the chanting in the street—and may thereby miss critical ways in which changes *within* public-sector organizations helped foment the social movement through strategic public outreach and laid the foundation for subsequent reforms to strengthen organizational capacity. I hope more work in the future that looks at forces affecting the state from outside will also look closely *within* the relevant parts of the state.

States are organizational entities, but this book also argues that the organizational sociology of states may differ critically from the capitalist organizations upon which most organizational wisdom is based. Many efforts to increase the administrative capacity and effectiveness of contemporary states are explicitly predicated on modeling not only what works in wealthy, Western, industrialized, democratic states, but also fetishize what works in the private sector. By helping to flesh out the understandings, concerns, and constraints of public servants whose work collectively comprises "the state" I hope this book helps further a discussion about ways in which states are distinctive organizational entities that may make the transposition of business models not merely ineffective, but sometimes result in perverse, unintended consequences.

Contrasting the organizational field of political administration with the private sector illustrates fundamental differences. Much organizational theory is based on the belief, grounded in the private sector, that organizations will become inevitably better because they are disciplined by competition. Over time, competition results in a field of ever-better organizations as superior organizations expand and inferior organizations die out (population drift) or, facing threat of annihilation, existing organizations adopt better practices, technology, or products (organizational change). Performance is particularly externally legible for publicly traded companies, which publish performance metrics that facilitate comparisons of interest to would-be investors. The private sector makes organizational performance externally legible: Even businesses producing vastly different products can still be compared according to profit, a fundamental outcome all capitalist businesses pursue.

This logic of comparability and competition fundamentally does not transpose to state administrative organizations. States are not organized such that agencies provide functionally equivalent, and therefore competing and readily comparable, services. Indeed, the very logic of discrete jurisdictions—a classic characteristic of bureaucracy—means that units within the state are almost never producing the same outputs or pursuing identical goals. Those discrete jurisdictions make it incredibly hard to compare organizational performance across ministries within a state, thereby making it difficult for politicians, citizens, and scholars alike to identify high-fliers or laggards purely by comparing outputs. How can even reform-minded political elites know whether the Ministry of Agriculture's progress on promoting fertilizer usage is a greater or lesser organizational accomplishment than the Ministry of Finance's reduction in budgetary overspending? If Agriculture is the only state entity promoting fertilizer usage, to whom should it be compared to understand whether it is as successful as it could be? This illuminates the often unspoken limitation of measuring organizational capacity. We can measure the capacity of a laboratory beaker apart from how much liquid it currently holds; however, when speaking of organizational capacity we typically cannot measure the potential maximum implicit in "capacity" apart from the present observed outputs.

Moreover, even if there is a general sense that a particular ministry is woefully underperforming, there is little that others elsewhere within the state can do about it. Comparison has a disciplining effect on organizations where performing poorly is a threat to organizational survival. This evokes one of Art Stinchcombe's overlooked classic organizational insights: Environments vary in "the degree to which the existence of an organization depends on its being better than its possible competitors."[45] Unlike the private sector, where organizations can discipline poor-performing partners by taking their business elsewhere, states are the example par excellence where organizational survival is decoupled from competitive performance. If the Ministry of Agriculture performs abysmally, there is no hostile take-over by the Ministry of Transportation. Nor does everyone shift their projects over to the *other* Ministry of Agriculture ... because of course that does not exist. The worldwide diffusion of legitimate structures for state administration means that state interstices are often inextricably tied to other organizations within the state administrative apparatus, critically dependent on other parts of the state to perform their core duties.

To be clear, I do not think making government more like the private sector is the panacea that so many privatization proponents presume, either in the form of restructuring states to operate more like private-sector organizations, or increasingly privatizing tasks previously done by the public sector. Indeed, there are many tasks of the state, from education to prisons, in which the "more widgets, lower costs" logic of the market offers at best a troubling alternative to public-minded state administration. Instead, I think it is time for organizational reforms to states that are grounded in the idea that states are fundamentally organizational entities, and that build a corpus of organizational theory of political entities that can better inform future reform efforts.

THE HIDDEN WISDOM OF DOING: TIME FOR A COGNITIVE TURN FOR STATES AND DEVELOPMENT

Patchwork Leviathan unpacks the microfoundations of a canonical institution —bureaucracy—calling attention to the cognitive and cultural elements of institutions that are embodied in what Weber called the bureaucratic ethos.[46] It thereby follows in the footsteps of scholars like Peter Evans, who points to esprit de corps, and Dietrich Rueschemeyer, who calls attention to the non-bureaucratic elements of bureaucracy.[47] It draws on advances in cognitive and cultural sociologies—absent in most macro-political sociology on states and institutions—to identify social foundations for how understandings and practices emerge, are shared, and stabilize within groups. This is consonant with institutional and organizational research seeking to "inhabit" institutions, situating institutions within human actors engaged in specific contexts.[48] Institutions like bureaucracy are not merely material manifestations such as written rules and regulations, but also a set of orientations, practices, and inclinations grounded in the lived experience of people. Some scholarship has examined the global diffusion of the outward material manifestations of bureaucracy, but I join others who argue we have been overconfident in the ability of the materials to cultivate the animating bureaucratic ethos.

From the perspective of conventional scholarship on states and development, the most theoretically radical assertion of this book may be that the bureaucratic ethos depends on a deeply cognitive underpinning: the tacit knowledge of doing bureaucracy. *Doing* bureaucracy depends on the implicit *cognition of doing* to a much greater extent than people typically realize—a relationship that most scholars of states and development have altogether missed. *Patchwork Leviathan* thereby challenges the assertion of the eminent anthropologist James Scott, who highlights bureaucrats following rules as the foremost example of social action that does not have mētis—his term for tacit knowledge of how to do something, which is acquired through practice and difficult to articulate.[49] This erroneous presumption that enacting bureaucracy does not require tacit knowledge has been perpetuated because so many have understood public-sector state workers only at arm's length, particularly in states like Ghana.[50] This ongoing oversight of the critical importance of tacit knowledge and experience for the cultivation of bureaucratic ethos has been at the heart of many of the failures of overly eager "transformative" top-down development efforts discussed earlier.

To address these shortcomings, the time has come for a cognitive turn in scholarship on states and development. Cognition matters because scholarship on states and development is often implicitly about attempting to understand change (or lack thereof) in patterns of human behavior. Cognition studies increasingly agree that the cumulative cognitive imprint of our prior life experiences profoundly shapes what we do, and do not do, as well as *how* we do things, through our everyday habits of practice.[51] People make sense of the world around them and pick up ways of doing and being from those whom they value and with whom they frequently interact. This is not only true of citizens in Ghana or Nigeria. Newcomers to Wall Street find themselves dressing, talking, and acting in the ways they see around them every day, even if it means making a huge deal that will hurt a client but save the company millions by off-loading a bad asset.[52] Men who fight wildfires for the U.S. Forest Service find themselves wrapped up in a rugged, individualistic masculinity that interprets fire as "not dangerous" if an individual understands fire well enough, reframing harm as an individual shortcoming not systemic risk.[53] So too, often without much conscious thought, justification, or reflection, state officials draw on the aggregation of their regular experiences in the social world to make some behaviors more or less available, including whether (or not) they seek a small gift for performing their job for a citizen.

Because development scholarship and practice have failed to appreciate the insights of cognition studies, we continue to approach efforts to change practices—including public servants accepting gifts—as though such practices are deliberated choices that can be shifted by rational arguments in awareness campaigns.[54] To borrow terminology from cognition, we are trying to solve a "type 1" problem with a "type 2" solution. Reform efforts tend to privilege type 2 cognition: explicit, deliberative, rationalized knowledge that people are aware of knowing and can articulate, like the rules for multiplication.[55] However, cognition studies demonstrate that much, perhaps most, of how people think draws on "type 1" *nondeclarative* cognition: dispositions and inclinations for how to think and act, which is developed slowly through associative learning via repeated exposures to composite general regularities.[56] This nondeclarative cognition has a taken-for-granted quality, a knee-jerk application that makes certain actions just *feel* correct without conscious consideration. If you have ever driven somewhere on "autopilot" without intending to, but nevertheless arrived without accident, you have glimpsed how powerfully nondeclarative cognition can affect action without deliberation or intent. Indeed, it is illustrative that when Vaisey gives an example of how nondeclarative, automatic cognition streamlines cognitive effort, he invokes an aspect of the bureaucratic ethos that he presumes to be a widespread experience: "Having a durable practical consciousness means that rather than having to weigh pros and cons on a daily basis (e.g., 'Should I continue to value hard work today?'), we can leave some things up to our habits of judgment and evaluation."[57]

Viewing nondeclarative cognition as essential to doing bureaucracy illuminates why interstitial niches succeed while most top-down reform efforts fail: Niches afford repeated exposures to practical lived experience for *doing* bureaucracy. As the third chapter on cultivation argued, one of the reasons interstitial niches are such powerful sites for reshaping the practices of public servants is that niches constitute a rich *prescriptive* model, grounded in lived experience of what *to do*—unlike the *proscriptive* "don't be corrupt!" messaging of most external interventions. It is incredibly challenging for people to figure out what *to do* based only on negative models of what *not to do*. This surprisingly common phenomenon afflicts would-be local reformers in neo-patrimonial contexts, as well as new fathers whose own fathers were distant and uninvolved,[58] medical students wishing to avoid the harried and dehumanizing practice of their supervising physicians,[59] or immigrant children who want to avoid the economic hardships of their parents but have no idea how concretely to prepare for college.[60] Condemning practices in the abstract and disembedded from context, such as accepting bribes or being lazy, offers only an incomplete template for action and crucially does not suggest *what to do instead*. By contrast, positive prescriptive models that are grounded in peoples' own lived experience combine a rich array of both declarative and nondeclarative knowledge, from which people can draw to navigate social situations with relatively less intentional cognitive effort.

A cognitive turn for development that better appreciates nondeclarative cognition would also shed new light on why institutional diffusion so often fails, and perhaps point the way toward how it might be done better. Top-down state organizational reform efforts often fail because "best practices" recommendations are necessarily an abstract compression of what the institution is like in its fullness and in context. These compressions inevitably privilege abstracted declarative knowledges and systematically omit the non-declarative cognition that may be essential to the motivation or means for successfully enacting those abstract rules. Perhaps this is why big sweeping attempts to comprehensively reform public administration have a long history of failing, even in supposedly rationalized administrative environments like the contemporary United States.[61] Declarative cognition is mentally tax-ing, especially when one does not have complementary nondeclarative habitus on which to off-load some cognitive effort. People tend to fill in the gaps—or bypass the rules entirely—based on their deeply ingrained habits of practice.

Typically, state capacity building and organizational reform efforts in-sufficiently capture tacit knowledges of the social environment in which the institution originated, and insufficiently understand or anticipate tacit knowl-edges about the local institutional context. Even when cosmopolitan reform-ers and local agents meet in earnest and mutually respectful efforts to build a better way forward, each person is hampered by their inability to articulate their own nondeclarative knowledges, or indeed to even be aware that such nondeclarative cognition exists and is relevant. Both remain catastrophically ignorant of their own and each other's unknown unknowns—the things we are not aware of not knowing. Because their distinctive wellsprings of non-declarative cognition are implicit and difficult to communicate, efforts to learn from successes elsewhere often go unintentionally awry. This further highlights why local actors with dual habitus are such a precious institutional resource: They quite literally have a brain in both worlds. Local actors with dual habitus are therefore perhaps uniquely positioned to understand pre-vailing nondeclarative cognitive tendencies of each institutional domain, and to implement creative and fruitful hybridizations that better account for the otherwise unknown unknowns.

Directions for Future Research

Even as *Patchwork Leviathan* answers many pressing questions, it raises a slew of new questions for future research. To name but a few of considerable interest to scholars and practitioners concerned with contemporary state capacity: How common are pockets of effectiveness in low-income states? Precisely how big must an initial cluster of distinctiveness be in order to initiate a reinforcing cycle of clustering distinctiveness? Are there patterns in which parts of the state have effective niches? What are the consequences of having a pocket of effectiveness in some parts of the state but not others? Can niches scale up and if so, how? How can these practices spread to other locations within the same state? The work also raises new questions for those working on states and organizations more generally, for example: Do these mechanics explain the emergence of the bureaucratic ethos within early European state-building? Within the private sector in Ghana? Do the same mechanics explain high-performing subunits within private-sector Western corporations? Niches of corruption within otherwise bureaucratic environments?

I love the outpouring of curiosity this research often engenders. Ultimately I hope the book begins as many new conversations as it answers. I believe such questions are an indication of the strength and intuitive appeal of the book, evidence that the framework advanced has the potential to open up new avenues of inquiry in a variety of fields, generating new research agendas in scholarship on development, states, and organizations. In this conclusion I point to some fruitful directions for future research and hypotheses that this work may generate for other areas of scholarship as well as development practice.

Future research could examine whether the framework of the book applies not only to public-sector organizations in states such as Ghana, but also to private-sector organizations. I did not conduct systematic data collection with Ghanaian private-sector companies, but based on my years of informal observation living in Ghana, I have reason to believe that the Ghanaian private sector does have its own patchworking, including substantial internal variation in organizational performance.[62] Perhaps more interestingly, some of the same underlying mechanics may help explain differences in private-sector performance. For example, I had a long discussion with the founder of a particularly successful local Ghanaian building firm. Like many of the niche leaders in this book, he had dual habitus, including a foreign degree. He spoke at length about how he had developed a taste for the style of work he experienced abroad and had experimented repeatedly with how to reduce lateness and absenteeism among his construction employees. Finally he decided to offer a filling traditional Ghanaian meal to every construction employee at the start of work, creatively fusing his interest in timeliness with his understanding of the preferences and constraints of his employees.

For scholars of politics and social movements, there is some excellent work on external coalitions of citizens or civil-society actors affecting the development of capacity within states, particularly across different regions.[63] Future work might seek to collect data directly on pockets of the government as well as on all their diverse constituents, which would be a fascinating future extension. Future work simultaneously examining developments within state organizations together with mobilization of outside actors would be an important corrective, because much prior work has tended to look at external coalitions without also investigating the conditions and actors within states. That creates the impression that external coalitions exist and affect change without state actors themselves, acting upon implicitly recalcitrant state agents rather than co-constituting change with state partners.

Other questions raised by this research would benefit from systematic quantitative analysis, which would require the creation of data that disaggregated administrative capacity at the level of ministries, departments, and agencies. Unfortunately, all current prominent cross-national indicators of "state capacity" offer a single measurement at the national level.[64] The qualitative case-comparative design of the present study is, for example, unable to assess factors that may have a moderate or mediated probabilistic effect on the formation and functioning of bureaucratic niches: for example, whether being in an economic sector increases the probability of niche formation even if it is not a necessary condition. Better assessing such arguments requires creating a cross-national and longitudinal quantitative data set that systematically measures organizational effectiveness of central state administrations at the level of ministries, departments, and agencies. Such a data set would be a transformative step forward in this research agenda, enabling comparisons both within and between countries, and over time. Longitudinal data would enable scholars to answer important questions about the potential for, and pathways of, positive contagion whereby effectiveness spreads among particular ministries, as well as whether effective bureaucratic niches erode over time, including how quickly increases or erosions in effectiveness emerge.

The book's arguments also illuminate ways that future lab or field experiments might help refine the theoretical roots of clustered distinctiveness. This book has identified a pattern of factors that were consistently present across cases of bureaucratic niches and systematically absent in less-productive control cases. For example, the second chapter argued that Ghanaians in bureaucratic niches oriented themselves toward organizational achievement while at work because they were acutely aware that people they respected had selected them because of their reputations for honest and effective work. Empirically in the available cases, having underlying merit and feeling aware of being selected for that reason appeared inseparably. It is a theoretically interesting and practically relevant question, however, to wonder whether a niche collectively oriented to organizational achievement could emerge where those factors were decoupled. Such questions could inform future laboratory experiments or randomized controlled field trials examining the performance of teams under different conditions. For example, studies could compare teams of objectively meritorious candidates who were *not* told that they were se-lected for merit, or conversely, objectively less meritorious candidates who *were* (falsely) told that they were selected for merit. Similarly, researchers could test for the effects of leaders with, and without, dual habitus, allowing them to compose their own teams and compare the performance both within and between groups.

Through new case analyses of pockets of effectiveness or large quantita-tive surveys, future research could move us closer to understanding precisely how common bureaucratic niches are within states. There may be many more niches than we are currently aware of because, as chapter 5 argues, unusually high performance within subunits of a larger organization is less visible to arm's length observers and leaves scant traces on the historical record. By the same token, the work of different parts of the patchwork state may be variously legible to different external audiences. Many citizens interact with doctors, teachers, or police and therefore have an informed perspective on whether or not they have been asked for a bribe. Conversely, few everyday citizens interact directly with state fiscal policy-making or field units in their trucks monitoring the airwaves.

Even organizations that interact frequently with state agencies may have low exposure to some parts of the administrative state, which could cause us to empirically undercount pockets of effectiveness and miss theoretically rel-evant instances of bureaucratic niches laboring away from public attention and the disciplining accountability it supposedly brings. Because I imposed rigorous standards on case selection for this study that required confirmation and consensus among state observers, I have thought often about the one that got away: a small group of public servants tasked with monitoring the quality of river water. The river water group was nominated as a pocket of excellence by one organization, who spoke glowingly and at length about their fast, thorough, high-quality work. Ultimately I did not select the river water group because I could not get any other state observers to corroborate the nomina-tion. This was not because anyone disagreed but because no other organiza-tion had interacted with them, or even heard of them. Later, I expanded the project to look at comparison cases in other countries and began reading about the physically demanding and socially undesirable postings of Salt In-spectorate officials in rural China or NAFDAC officials in Nigeria. I could not help but think of the river water quality monitoring teams in hip-waders col-lecting samples from potentially polluted or infested rivers throughout Ghana. It seems possible to me that there are many small pockets of effective-ness laced throughout state administrations, many of which are performing inglorious tasks that do not attract much attention. Nevertheless, they steadily and thanklessly serve the public without recognition, praise, or even an office light brightly burning to mark their distinctiveness.

METHODOLOGICAL APPENDIX

To select cases of central state organizations with reputations for effective administration in the public interest, I interviewed expert observers of the Ghanaian state from twenty-one organizations, including research institutes, universities, international nongovernmental organizations, industry groups, and donor organizations. Other selection interviewees included key actors inside the Ghanaian state, including high-ranking officials from the Public Services Commission, the Office of the Head of Civil Service, the Management Services Division, and other highly placed government officials. Selection interviews continued until saturation when no interviewees suggested expert observers or key stakeholder organizations that had not already been contacted. By cross-referencing public lists of organizations consistently invited to stakeholders' meetings by the government, I believe case-selection interviewees represent the near-universe of significant observers of the Ghanaian government. I interviewed expert observers about which organizations were most effective at accomplishing their mandate and about elements of Weberian bureaucracy (e.g., meritocratic hiring) least affected by inimical folk understandings associating bureaucracy with sloth. Selection began with interview participants spontaneously suggesting organizations or units and concluded by asking about the list of all organizations previously suggested, thereby eliciting prompted responses to specific organizations only as a secondary tool. I imposed a high standard on the case selection pool, requiring consensus and corroboration about an organization or subunit being a pocket of excellence, without dissent.

Based on results from diverse expert observers, I selected four public-sector organizations with the strongest and most-consistent reputations for organizational capacity. Some experts nominated large organizations while others specified particular subunits. Within nominated large organizations, I refined case selection to core organizational functions and selected subunits to study based on agreement between high-ranking internal members and external observers who mentioned particular subunits as noteworthy.

As part of the consent process, participants were told that the actual identity of selected organizational units would be disclosed but that individuals would be pseudonymous. Selected subunits include: (1) Monetary Policy

Analysis and Financial Stability Department (Monetary Policy Analysis for short), a Bank of Ghana department that prepares research for the Monetary Policy Committee; (2) the Policy Analysis and Research Division (PARD), a group within the Ministry of Finance and Economic Planning responsible for generating and researching fiscal policy initiatives; (3) the Ghana Commercial Courts, part of the High Courts—only the Appeals and Supreme Courts rank higher—dealing exclusively with commercial cases; and (4) the Spectrum and Frequency Management units, the field testing and monitoring units of the National Communications Authority (NCA), which is an organization that is responsible for licensing, regulation, and monitoring of communications. Individual interviews covered 60 to 95 percent of staff in the focal units and lasted at least one hour, though a number were over an hour and a half. With the respondent's permission, most interviews were audio-recorded and transcribed. Participants were given the opportunity to review their transcripts upon request, and several did, including Mr. Mensah. If respondents declined recording, I took written notes. Quotation marks indicate recorded verbatim transcriptions and material enclosed in apostrophes is from field notes or interview notes taken at the time (Lofland and Lofland 1995). I prefer to include full verbatim transcripts to give a sense of the verbal stalls or changes of direction in a participant's speech. The only exception is that I edited out word repetitions that occur only due to a stutter because those are not interpretively relevant and potentially identify participants. In the interest of the integrity of the words used, I prefer to draw from recorded interviews, particularly because the substance of the few interviewees who declined to be audio-recorded largely duplicates views expressed by others.

I also conducted limited fieldwork with comparison subunits within each larger organization to better understand the context and operations of the focal cases (see Table A.1). These were not pure negative cases—that is, not intentionally selected for absence of the outcome—but rather as minimal controls broadly representative of the larger organizations' operations and administrative culture. Practical constraints necessitated more limited fieldwork within controls: I interviewed five or fewer officials per case, and when possible included observations. To limit extraneous diversity, functionally analogous control cases were selected when possible (see Table A.1). Following the logic of comparative analysis, analysis focuses on characteristics shared across diverse primary cases, but generally absent in secondary control cases.

To select the comparative historical cases I conducted an extensive review of the existing pockets of effectiveness literature. Using purposive sampling, I selected cases that (1) had at least two scholars identify them as an unusually high-performing organization embedded in an environment that was inhospitable to those aims, and (2) provided sufficient depth of information in English, Spanish, or Portuguese language sources to enable evaluation

TABLE A.1. Overview of Selected Ghanaian Cases and Controls, by Organization

Organization	Bank of Ghana (BOG)	Ministry of Finance and Economic Planning (MOFEP)	High Courts of Justice	National Communications Authority (NCA)
Primary function:	Central Bank of Ghana. Generates monetary policy, issues & regulates currency, licenses & regulates banking and nonbanking financial institutions.	Ministry of Finance, responsible for fiscal policy, allocation, and management of government resources.	Third-ranking Superior Courts in the British-derived Ghanaian justice system, behind only the Supreme Court and Court of Appeals.	Licenses audible, visual, and data telecommunication systems, allocates, monitors and regulates use of frequencies, monitors quality of services.
Selected case:	Monetary Policy Research Unit (MPRU)	Policy Analysis & Research Division (PARD)	Commercial Courts (GCC)	Broadband Monitoring Units (BMU)
Primary function:	Research & report on economic impact of monetary policies proposed by the Monetary Policy Committee of the Bank of Ghana. Reports to the Monetary Policy Committee, composed of governor of Bank and other high-ranking govt officials.	Research & report on economic impact of fiscal policies proposed by minister of finance. Some policy generation around fiscal policy issues, e.g., expediting processing of government contract work or budgetary request approvals. Reports to minister of finance.	High Court specializing in commercial law cases.	Monitor and evaluate broadband audible spectrum usage around the country, including field testing with roving technical units, reporting on distribution of bandwidth and service quality.
Control case:	Banking Supervision Dept*	Budget Division	Regular High Court	Admin. Headquarters
Primary function:	Supervision and examination of banking institutions	Budgetary dispersals to ministries for operational and other expenses, including compensation of government contractors.	High Court hearing all civil and criminal cases referred to the High Court, including but not limited to commercial law cases.	Paperwork administration for licenses and regulations over telecommunications, human resources management.

*Expert observers indicated, and my observations broadly concur, that the Bank of Ghana as a whole was a pocket of effectiveness, so the control case in this organization exhibited more characteristics in common with the selected cases.

TABLE A.2. Overview of Selected and Control Cases by Country, Time, Function, Outcome, and Selected Alternative Explanations

Country	Organization	Time	Function	Executive will?	Sectoral vulnerability to corruption?	Outcome
Ghana	PARD	2008	Policy	Low	Low	POE
Ghana	Budget	2008	Budget Admin.	Low	Low	control
Ghana	Commercial Courts	2008	Justice	Low	High	POE
Ghana	High Court	2008	Justice	Low	High	control
Ghana	Monetary Policy Research Unit	2008	Policy	Low	Low	POE
Ghana	Banking Supervision	2008	Regulation	Low	High	control
Ghana	Field Monitoring Units	2008	Regulation	Low	Medium	POE
Ghana	Administration	2008	Regulation	Low	Medium	control
Nigeria	NAFDAC	2001–2008	Regulation	Med–Low	High	POE
Nigeria	NAFDAC	1990s	Regulation	Crisis but no assistance	High	failure
Brazil	BNDE	1956–1970s	Banking	Medium	High	POE
Brazil	BNDE	1952–1956	Banking	Medium	High	control
Kenya	KTDA	1964–1980s	Agriculture	Low	Medium Low	POE
Kenya	Special Crops Development Authority	1960–1964	Agriculture	Low	Medium Low	control
China	Salt Inspectorate	1914–1928	Tax	Crisis but no assistance	High	POE
China	*Yanwu Shu*	Pre-1914	Tax	Crisis but no assistance	High	failure

of all the theoretically salient organizational characteristics. In the interest of keeping the book more coherent, I also limited final case selection to (3) public-sector organizations (4) in predominantly neopatrimonial contexts. For example, I wrote entire case studies of the U.S. New Deal Agricultural Adjustment Administration and the U.S. corporate case of the NUMMI joint venture between Toyota and General Motors that were subsequently cut from the book to streamline its contextual focus. The book does not draw explicitly on those case studies nor the other cases from the literature review that were excluded because they lacked multiple scholarly accounts of excellence or sufficient detail on organizational processes. However, I refined the theoretical framework with these cases in the back of my mind, taking care that these excluded cases did not contain information that would contradict the approach. This is to say that on the aspects for which data was available, cases excluded for the four reasons above also appear to be well explained by the clustering distinctiveness framework developed within the book. All the selected pockets of effectiveness and their paired control cases are shown in Table A.2, which also shows the cases' values on alternative explanations discussed in the Introduction.

About Ghanaian Interstitial Insiders

Throughout the book I refer to participants using pseudonyms. Several high-profile organizational heads are referred to by their actual names when I draw on public information—notably Paul Acquah, the governor of the Ghanaian Central Bank; Chief Justice George Kingsley Acquah, who helped found the Commercial Courts; and Bernard Forson Jr. of the NCA. In the interest of maintaining the confidentiality of participants, I avoid disclosing sufficient personal detail in direct association with a given pseudonym; for example, I avoid using pseudonyms that would indicate a particularly distinctive religion or ethnicity if that would be numerically uncommon enough to identify a participant. Pseudonyms were generated from lists of common Ghanaian names and randomly assigned to participants by gender. However, to give readers a fuller sense of the breadth of backgrounds represented among the interstitial insiders, below I present a description of participants decoupled from their individual pseudonyms used throughout the text.

The staff are surprisingly representative of the range of demographics in Ghana generally—and closely track those of college graduates in particular. Like Ghanaians generally, most identify as Christian and a few identify as Muslim. Their close friends are primarily from church, their neighborhood, co-workers, and old classmates. When asked about friends, one warmly gushes, "My school days. Yes. They are my closest friends. We are like sisters, we're like a family." They come from regions across Ghana, from Volta Region and

234 METHODOLOGICAL APPENDIX

Eastern Region; from the Upper East, Upper West, and the Central Region. Accordingly, their ethnic backgrounds reflect their regional diversity, and, like Ghana broadly and the highly educated in particular, quite a few combine multiple ethnicities.

Their families of origin reflect a breadth of Ghanaian experiences. Echoing broader Ghanaian demographic trends toward smaller family sizes, younger members and those with more highly educated parents tend to come from smaller families. However, living with extended kin is extremely common. One grew up the youngest of ten siblings, her father a civil servant and her mother a seamstress, parents who were "strict, but they were humane about it. You couldn't just do anything." One was raised with eight siblings, and her father also has other children who live in different households. One younger official is the middle of three children. Another comes from a family of four children, but grew up in an extended kin household with up to twenty people at any given time. Another lives with his parents in a household he estimates at about fifteen members, including eight of his siblings, although the particular composition is "always changing." Most were raised with both their parents. One lost his father while still a child, and some have fathers who don't regularly live in their home even though their parents are still married. One was raised entirely by grandparents, and another grew up living in her grandmother's home together with both her parents. Like many Ghanaians living in Accra, it is not uncommon for younger members to live in an extended family home with their grandparents, parents, or siblings into their early thirties and beyond.

All of the staff have at least one college degree, except support staff personnel in the Courts and NCA headquarters (e.g., secretarial functions). Professionally, law, engineering, and economics degrees predominate in the Courts, NCA, and MOFEP or the Bank of Ghana, respectively. Like the college population generally, a number went to prestigious secondary schools that are well known in Ghana, like Wesley Girls' Senior High School and Adisadel College boys secondary school. Others went to lesser-known secondary schools and still others were scholarship students at Catholic schools. The vast majority got their bachelor's degree at the University of Legon—the flagship university in Ghana. In the successful niches, there is a distinctively high concentration of people with advanced degrees from international schools, many obtained through government sponsorship, something discussed in chapter 7.

Only a handful come from families influential and economically privileged enough to have included international travel in their childhood, relatives abroad, or families who could pay for them to get their undergraduate degree abroad. The parents of such families are more educated than Ghanaians generally, but their parental education is similar to those of university graduates.

Most participants have at least one parent who completed at least the equivalent of high school in Ghana. When one parent is more educated, it is typically the father. Sometimes the educational disparity between parents is very stark, by American standards. For example, one explains, "My mom was middle school leaver and my father was a [secondary school] graduate." This educational disparity is more common among older members, reflecting rapid changes in the Ghanaian educational system over the second half of the twentieth century. Even among older members, some have two relatively educated parents, for example a father who completed A levels, and a mother who completed O levels. A few of the younger members have two relatively highly educated parents. One has a father with a university degree and a mother with teacher training. Another explains "my mother has a first degree in history and English. My daddy has an MBA in finance."

But among them too are people from very humble socioeconomic backgrounds and economically disadvantaged regions. One older member comes from a region of "cattle and coconut" and had to negotiate with extended family to sell cattle in order to go to school. Similarly, one of the younger officials is the youngest of six children, who grew up in a very rural farming community in Ghana's far north. He rents a small place in Accra and tries to travel back to his hometown often. When asked about his parents' education, he explains, "Farmers, they haven't gone to school." Although he is barely thirty years old, when asked if he has anyone who depends on him for economic support, he counts "I think maybe about—my mother, I have another sister, my nieces and nephews. Let's say roughly about five." Most describe financially supporting their own children, some describe supporting or financially assisting a handful of others—typically younger siblings, nieces, or nephews. Having economic dependents beyond one's own children is more common among those who come from economically disadvantaged families—where the need is greater and those capable of helping fewer—and practically nonexistent among younger people who come from prosperous families.

Chapter 1. Introduction

1. Weber 1978: 958.
2. Evans 1995: 58.
3. Du Gay 2005.
4. Bratton and Van de Walle 1997; Eisenstadt 1973; Englebert 2000.
5. There are a number of thoughtful critiques available, including Erdmann and Engel 2007; Mkandawire 2015; Pitcher, Moran, and Johnston 2009. There is, of course, considerable internal variation on how such relationships are practiced and reasonable academic and popular debate about the issues of categorical labels; I acknowledge those important points; however, because it is not the core focus of this book for brevity I follow common scholarly practice and refer to such environments as neopatrimonial.
6. Englebert 2000.
7. E.g. Kopecký, Mair, and Spirova 2012; Rothstein and Varraich 2017; Van de Walle 2007.
8. E.g., Evans 1989; Helman and Ratner 1992.
9. Goldscheid, 1917 as cited in Schumpeter 1991: 100.
10. Colonial continuities are beyond the scope of the present project, but interested readers should see some of the excellent and voluminous scholarship on the topic, e.g., Mamdani 2018; Reno 1995; Young 1994.
11. Acemoglu, Johnson, and Robinson 2005; World Bank 2002, 2003; Woo-Cumings 1999.
12. Andrews, Pritchett, and Woolcock 2013.
13. Bromley and W. W. Powell 2012; Hallett and Ventresca 2006; Henisz, Zelner, and Guillén 2005; Weber, Davis, and Lounsbury 2009.
14. There have been efforts to deconstruct the monolithic interpretation of states since the 1980s (Hooks 1990; Migdal 2001; Morgan and Orloff 2017; Quadagno 1987). However, even scholars canonically associated with state-centered approaches have noted that "there may be insulation or contradictions among different kinds of state capacities" such that "possibilities for state interventions of given types cannot be derived from some overall level of generalized capacity or 'state strength'" (Evans, Rueschemeyer, and Skocpol 1985: 352–353). Advancing understanding of institutional change requires disaggregating "the state," viewing it instead as complex, inter-related systems of agents and agencies (Steinmetz 1999). This scholarship draws attention to variation within states, but stops short of considering how within-state variation is consequential for practices that can impact the effectiveness of organizations, that is, for precisely the content organizational reform efforts so frequently target.
15. Fischer 1975.
16. Goffman 1963.
17. For more on habitus, see Bourdieu 1977.
18. Because the book is not exclusively about Ghana but also traces similar contradistinction patterns in Brazil, Nigeria, Kenya, and China, here I use the term "local" in place of a particular

country name to gesture to the particular habitus of the area in which the organizational niche is physically and socially situated.

19. Lizardo 2016; Mukerji 2014; Reber 1989.

20. Du Gay 2005: 29.

21. Du Gay 2000: 4.

22. Du Gay 2005.

23. Weber 1978: 958.

24. Macaulay 1963.

25. Abdulai and Crawford 2010; Boafo-Arthur 2008; Kaufmann, Kraay, and Mastruzzi 2010; McDonnell 2016.

26. Fearon 2003; McDonnell 2016.

27. Young 2012.

28. Boafo-Arthur 1999; Ninsin 1987.

29. McDonnell 2016; Prah 2010.

30. McDonnell and Fine 2011.

31. Afrobarometer 2010.

32. "History—BNDES."

33. For institutions as 'rules of the game,' see North 1991.

34. Some scholarship has examined variation in organizational capacity but primarily views it as tied to different geographic locations and scales within national boundaries, attending to how levels of government—federal, regional, or municipal—have varying preferences and capacities Dobbin 1994; Singh 2015. Similarly, among scholars of non-Western statecraft, both "brown areas" (O'Donnell 2004) and "urban bias" (Bates 1981) highlight variation in the state's ability to enact and penetrate, but see that variation as fundamentally structured by geographic and social distances—e.g., rural peripheries or urban slums were more difficult to govern.

35. Morgan and Orloff 2017: 7. See also Gilbert and Howe 1991; Hooks 1993; Migdal 2001; Quadagno 1987; Steinmetz 1999.

36. Boone 2003; Dobbin 1992; Singh 2016.

37. Chibber 2002.

38. Binder 2007: 568. This also relates to a large and influential literature on "institutional logics" within organizational research (Dunn and Jones 2010 and Ocasio 2008).

39. Adams 2005; Ertman 1997; Tilly 1990.

40. Bensel 1990; Carpenter 2001; Skocpol and Finegold 1982; Skowronek 1982.

41. Bates 1981; Boone 2003; Herbst 2014; Migdal 1988; Scott 1999.

42. Skocpol 2016.

43. Rothstein 2011; Smith 2010; Teorell 2007; Johnston 2005; Teorell, 2007.

44. Armantier and Boly 2011; J. Davis 2004; Schulze and Frank 2003. For a fantastic review, see Borges et al. 2017.

45. Brehm and Gates 1999; DiIulio 2014; Dilulio Jr 1994; Watkins-Hayes 2009; Zacka 2017.

46. Morgan and Orloff 2017.

47. Hallett and Ventresca 2006; Lawrence, Suddaby, and Leca 2009.

48. Geddes 1996; e.g., Johnson 2015; Kohli 2004. Seemingly plausible for prominent cases like South Korea where executive will and rapid transformation coincide, such explanations fail to account for cases where equally fervent will fails to bring reform into being. At Independence, Kwame Nkrumah unambiguously had the will to transform Ghana into a political powerhouse capable of standing shoulder to shoulder with any nation on earth, but his executive will alone was not sufficient to bring that dream into being.

49. Ferreira, Engelschalk, and Mayville 2007; Flatters and Macleod 1995.

50. World Bank 1999.

51. World Bank 1999.

52. CDD-Ghana and World Bank 2000.

53. World Bank 1999.

54. World Bank 1999.

55. Carruthers 1994; Migdal 2001.

56. Migdal 2001: 57.

57. Carruthers 1994.

58. Andrews 2015; Bebbington and McCourt 2007; Daland 1981; Grindle 1997a; Grosh 1991; Hertog 2010; Paul 1982; Strauss 1998; Tendler 1997.

59. Barma, Huybens, and Viñuela 2014; Hickey et al. 2015; Johnson 2015; Leonard 1991, 2010; McDonnell 2017; Ricks 2017; Roll 2014.

60. See Leonard 2010; Roll 2014.

61. Bersch, Praça, and Taylor 2017; Grindle 1997a; Johnson 2015; Leonard 1991; McDonnell 2017; Strauss 1998.

62. Carpenter 2001; Matsuda 1998; Nunes 1984; Zaloznaya 2017. See also Grindle (1997) on personnel autonomy.

63. Barma, Huybens, and Viñuela 2014; Grant, Hudson, and Sharma 2009; Kjaer and Therkildsen 2013; Leonard 1991; Ricks 2017; Roll 2014.

64. Fjeldstad 2003; Grindle 1997a; Roll 2014; Zaloznaya 2017.

65. Leonard 1991; Ricks 2017; Strauss 1998; Tendler 1997.

66. Grindle 2007: 486.

67. Grindle 1997a; Grindle and Hilderbrand 1995.

Chapter 2. Recruitment

1. Ayee 2001; Chazan 1983; Price 1975.

2. See the methodological appendix for a more extended discussion of the backgrounds of participants.

3. Estimates range from 51 percent of currently employed for the 2008 report to 85 percent of economically active adults for the 2012 report.

4. Ghana Statistical Service 2008.

5. Ghana Statistical Service 2008. In July 2007, early in fieldwork, the Ghana cedi was redenominated 1,000 cedis = 1 cedi. This accounts for the difference in Kofi's reference to 1million per month and the government statistics here.

6. Bank of Ghana 2007.

7. Bank of Ghana 2007.

8. Evans 1995: 58.

9. Meyer and Rowan 1977: 345.

10. Doig 1997; March 1986.

11. March and March 1977: 405.

12. March 1986: 27.

13. See work on burnout: Hsieh 2014; Perlman and Hartman 1982; Schaufeli, Leiter, and Maslach 2009.

14. Ostrom and Basurto 2011: 319.

15. Piff et al. 2012.

16. Metropolitan Police Act 1839.

17. Michigan Penal Code 1931.

18. This combination of merit mixed with social connections is characteristic of the period in early modern European state-building transitioning toward more merit hiring (Fischer and Lundgreen 1975).

19. Adams 2005; Gorski 2003.

20. Leonard 1991; Chorev and Schrank 2017.

21. Abbott 1988.

22. Rueschemeyer 1986: 59.

23. This should not be read as nothing-but-professionalization. Economists, lawyers, and engineers—professional identities affiliated with the four niches—exist throughout public service and are not everywhere as successful where the rest of the interstitial mechanics are not present. Moreover, the extent of professionalization varies cross-nationally and by occupational field. This helps further explain the observation from the Introduction that there is not more cross-national consistency in which state functions emerge as highly effective interstitial niches.

24. Weber 1978: 958.

25. Weber 1978: 220.

26. Weber 1978: 959.

27. Rauch and Evans 2000.

28. Board interview was a practice during the recruitment of all interviewed members, but was later phased out.

29. Recently, but after the hiring of most of the current Monetary Policy Analysis members, the practice of a final round of interviews before the Board has given way to Board oversight and assent, without active interview. However, I would hypothesize that at this point the culture of meritocratic recruitment is so deeply entrenched within the bank, that reducing the number of rounds of recruitment from three to two is unlikely to roll back the practice of merit-based recruitment in the near term.

30. Anderson 1983.

31. Granovetter 1973.

32. Cofie 2007.

33. Bourdieu 1977; Sewell Jr 1992.

34. This is structurally similar to Tendler's observations of the disciplinary benefits of coopting those not hired to monitor the compliance of the lucky few given jobs (1997).

35. Granovetter 1973.

36. For example, Chibber (2002: 955) briefly observes that meritocratic recruitment "generate[s] a kind of esprit de corps within the bureaucracy: the knowledge that they belong to a highly select 'club,' with similar qualifications and rare skills, creates a corporate culture among functionaries, which, in turn, secures state cohesiveness." See also Evans 1995; Leonard 1991; Strauss 1998.

Chapter 3. Cultivation

1. Chibber 2002: 955.

2. Chibber 2002: 955; see also Evans 1995.

3. Henisz et al. 2005.

4. This is often called decoupling—meaning that the actual day-to-day conduct is not linked, or "coupled," to the official policy (Westphal and Zajac 1994, 2001).

5. Tilcsik 2010.

6. "Metropolitan Police Act, 1839."

7. Weber 1978: 958.

8. Macaulay 1963.

9. Kiser and Tong 1992.

10. Edwards and Roy 2017.

11. Dilulio Jr 1994: 281.

12. Haynie 2001.

13. The exception, as discussed in the Introduction, is the Bank of Ghana, where the bureaucratic ethos was organization-wide and so the control department within the bank was much more similar to the selected niche than were other controls.

14. Even where lawyers and companies may not wish for impartial or fair justice, because they stand more to gain from being able to manipulate outcomes, they may nevertheless support expedient results.

15. Lamont, Pendergrass, and Pachucki 2001.

16. Many august classical figures of social theory have been concerned with symbolic boundaries (Durkheim 1912; Elias 1982; Weber 1978). For a review of the history of symbolic boundaries and contemporary applications, see Lamont and Molnár 2002.

17. On entiativity, see Campbell 1958.

18. Levine 2008: 21.

19. Levine 2008: 86.

20. Levine 2008.

21. Adogla-Bessa 2017.

22. Buurman et al. 2012.

23. Selznick 1957: 40.

24. Weber 1956: 127.

25. Goffman 1963.

26. This is quite similar to what some scholars have characterized as a corporatist ethos, where community allegiance supersedes individual motives.

27. Leonardelli, Pickett, and Brewer 2010; Zuckerman 2016.

28. Leonardelli, Pickett, and Brewer 2010.

29. Lau 1989.

30. Ody-Brasier and Fernandez-Mateo 2017.

31. Bearman and Brückner 2001.

32. Abrams 2009.

33. Eliasoph and Lichterman 2003.

34. Wohl (2015) finds members of erotic arts clubs converge on a shared aesthetic of what is appropriate or inappropriate taste that helps to define group membership.

35. For the cognitive grounding on this see Lizardo and Strand 2010; Vaisey 2009.

36. This is a kind of positive deviance. We typically think of oppositional identity formation as associated with "negative" deviations. Argentine anarchists understand themselves to be contradistinctive from the police state. Hells Angels understand themselves to be contradistinctive from uptight, rule-abiding citizens. Interstitial bureaucracy turns these normative presumptions about subcultures on their head, yet the mechanics are very much the same. Insiders experience their niche as distinctive vis-à-vis the larger environment—in particular, offering a positive source of identity that sharply contrasts the "spoiled" identity of public servants broadly— which cultivates insider loyalty and shores up organizational boundaries against neopatrimonial logics.

37. Simon and Hamilton 1994.

38. Smith and Henry 1996.

39. Leonardelli et al. 2010: 78.

40. Leonardelli et al. 2010: 79.

41. Leonardelli and Brewer 2001.

42. Nelson and Miller 1995.

43. Azoulay, Liu, and Stuart 2017. For work on selection and influence within the public sector, see Oberfield 2011.

44. Simon 1982.

45. For example, research finds young postdoctoral scientists seek out mentors based on scientific specialty, geographic location, status, and interpersonal rapport, but are later also influenced by whether their mentor patented—and such students later go on to patent more themselves if their mentor happened to do so, even though it was not something the student had actively considered beforehand. See Azoulay et al. 2017.

46. Overmier and Seligman 1967.

47. Hiroto and Seligman 1975.

48. Maier and Seligman 2016.

49. Volpicelli et al. 1983.

50. Jones, Nation, and Massad 1977.

51. Being exposed to inescapable adverse events increases neurotransmitters that excite the dorsal raphe nucleus, which inhibits active escape and increases fear and anxiety. Repeated exposure to inescapable adverse events created sustained high neurotransmitter levels, affecting the sensitivity of neural receptors, and resulting in enduring effects for days afterward. Importantly, exposure to escapable adverse events also initially produced an increase in the same neurotransmitter. Perceived control over the situation made all the difference. Maier and Seligman, founding fathers of learned helplessness, observe: "the presence of control seems to be the active ingredient, leading to the inhibition of threat-induced changes in limbic and brainstem structures" (2016: 361). When another system in the brain simultaneously detected control over the situation, it inhibited that first reaction, which would have otherwise prevented active escape and increased anxiety (Maier and Seligman 2016).

52. Amat et al. 2006.

53. Maier and Seligman 2016: 362.

54. See Fine and McDonnell 2007.

55. Collett, Vercel, and Boykin 2015.

56. Du Gay 2005: 51.

Chapter 4. Protection

1. Lentz 2009.

2. Ghanaian Pidgin is simplified English coupled with local expressive conventions: e.g., Ghanaian pidgin when departing is "Eee Chale, I da go come." Chale is an expressive convention similar to "chap." "I da go come" is the literal translation of the Twi "Me kō na ba" (I go and come), used when departing.

3. Anderson 2000: 36.

4. Schniederjans, Schniederjans, and Schniederjans 2015.

5. Hamani 2014.

6. McDonnell and Fine 2011.

7. This might also be considered a specialized division of labor.

8. Sørensen 2015.

9. Weber 1978: 956.

10. Landau 1969.

11. Vaughan 1990.

12. Awumah, Goulter, and Bhatt 1991; Landau 1969.

13. For an example on public-sector service provision, see Miranda and Lerner (1995).

14. Scott 1985: 603.

15. Judicial Service of Ghana 2008.

16. This qualitative control selection is conceptually similar to regression discontinuity design, in which cases falling just above a threshold are compared to cases falling just below the threshold that are otherwise similar.

17. Selznick 1949: 13.
18. Taylor 1914.
19. Burawoy 1979.
20. Lindgren 1954.

Chapter 5. Comparison Cases

1. World Bank 1999–2007.
2. Pogoson and Roll 2014: 103.
3. Leonard 1991: 134.
4. This observation is confirmed by other studies of successful organizational reforms. Taliercio (2004a) provides an excellent detailed overview of staff composition changes at various revenue authorities undergoing organizational reforms. Organizational reforms at the Kenya Revenue Authority started with a noteworthy purge of "corrupt and ineffective employees" such that the purge for poor performance affected roughly 20% of total staff (p. 17). Between 1993 and 2001 the Ugandan Revenue Authority dismissed 647 employees, and of those, 257 were for "corruption" (p. 21). By contrast, the South African Revenue Authority did not employ a significant initial "retrenchment" dismissing a mere 1.5 percent of staff for misconduct between 1998 and 2001 (p. 19).
5. Goffman 1978.
6. Erhun, Babalola, and Erhun 2001.
7. Alubo 1994.
8. Taylor et al. 2001.
9. Akunyili 2012.
10. Pogoson and Roll 2014.
11. Akunyili 2012; Pogoson and Roll 2014.
12. Alubo 1994.
13. "World Development Indicators," World Bank Group, http://databank.worldbank.org/data/reports.aspx?source=2&country=NGA.
14. Akunyili 2012: 46.
15. Pogoson and Roll 2014: 103.
16. Pogoson and Roll 2014: 102.
17. Pogoson and Roll 2014: 104.
18. Akunyili 2012: 48.
19. Akunyili 2012: 335–37.
20. Paul 1982: 61.
21. Paul 1982: 62.
22. $185 versus $60; see Paul 1982: 61.
23. Wrong 2009.
24. Gertzel et al. 1969.
25. Branch 2011.
26. Alwy and Schech 2004.
27. Burgess et al. 2010.
28. Rothchild 1969.
29. Leonard 1991: 265.
30. Leonard 1991: 133.
31. Leonard 1991.
32. Leonard 1991: 133.
33. Leonard 1991: 141.
34. Leonard 1991: 134.

35. Leonard 1991: 138.
36. Paul 1982.
37. Paul 1982.
38. Selznick 1949.
39. Paul 1982.
40. Ochieng 2010.
41. Evans 1995.
42. Vargas served as head of state for two discontinuous periods: 1930–1945 and again from 1951 until his suicide in 1954.
43. Leonard 2010.
44. Numerous studies have attributed the success of this investment plan to the BNDE's standing as a pocket of effectiveness (Lafer 1970; see, e.g., Willis 1986).
45. Colby 2013: 122.
46. Hanley et al. 2016.
47. Willis 2014: 77. BNDES—social was added to its name and acronym—has recently been embroiled in a corruption scandal, an issue addressed briefly in the penultimate chapter.
48. Daland 1981: 354.
49. Geddes 1996: 65.
50. Daland 1981.
51. Daland 1981: 354.
52. Skidmore 1967; Ames 1995; Samuels 2002.
53. See also Schneider 1992.
54. Geddes 1996: 62.
55. Paiva 2012; BNDES: 24.
56. Geddes 1996: 62.
57. Daland 1981: 357.
58. Campos 1994: 195.
59. Willis 1986: 100.
60. Willis 1986: 224.
61. Willis 1986: 97.
62. Willis 1986: 222.
63. Willis 1986: 219.
64. Willis 1986.
65. Willis 1995: 652.
66. Lafer 1970: 128.
67. Lafer 1970: 129.
68. Geddes 1996: 64; Lafer 1970.
69. Lafer 1970: 132.
70. Pinto 1969: 55.
71. See Carpenter (2001) for a thorough argument about the importance of an external support coalition for sustaining autonomy.
72. MacMurray 1921.
73. "Foreigner Makes Millions for China" 1917.
74. Adshead 1970: 103; Dane 1917.
75. "Foreigner Makes Millions for China" 1917.
76. Sir Richard Dane in China 1919: 159.
77. Dane 1913, 1914; Dane and Von Strauch 1915; Strauss 1998.
78. Dane 1917: 3.
79. Dane 1917: 5.

80. Dane 1913: 9.
81. "Foreigner Makes Millions for China" 1917.
82. Dane 1914: 13.
83. Strauss 1998.
84. Strauss 1998: 73.
85. Strauss 2018.
86. Strauss 1998.
87. Dane 1913: 10.
88. Strauss 1998: 72.
89. Strauss 1998.
90. Strauss 1998: 73.
91. Strauss 1998: 74.
92. Strauss 1998: 74.
93. Strauss 1998.
94. Strauss 1998, 2018.
95. Strauss 1998.
96. Strauss 1998.
97. Strauss 1998.
98. Dane 1913: 11, 1914: 27.
99. Strauss 1998: 65.
100. Strauss 2018.
101. Strauss 1998.
102. Adshead 1970.
103. Adshead 1970.
104. Adshead 1970: 105.
105. "Foreigner Makes Millions for China" 1917.
106. "Foreigner Makes Millions for China" 1917: 355.
107. Dane and Von Strauch 1915: 30.
108. Strauss 1998: 72.
109. Leonard 1991.
110. Buurman et al. 2012.
111. The nineteenth-century American Coast Survey Department was likewise an agency that existed for years before exploding into global prominence rapidly after the appointment of Alexander Dallas Bache at the helm (Jansen 2011; Slotten 1994).
112. The staff count is central agency staff, excluding member farmers (Lamb and Muller 1982).
113. Pogoson and Roll 2014.
114. Dane and Von Strauch 1915.
115. "Foreigner Makes Millions for China" 1917.
116. Dane 1914: 2.
117. Dane 1913: 7.
118. "Sir Richard Dane in China" 1919: 159.
119. La Porta, Lopez-de-Silanes, Shleifer, and Vishny 19999.
120. Willis 1986.
121. Grosh 1991; Hertog 2010.
122. Garron Hansen (agricultural development specialist), personal communication, October 2, 2017)
123. Paul 1982: 61.
124. Paul 1982.

125. Leonard 1991; Paul 1982: 56.
126. Coser 1956; Simmel 1955.
127. Andrews and Seguin 2015; Bearman and Brückner 2001; Beisel 1998; McVeigh, Crubaugh, and Estep 2017; Tepper 2011.
128. DeSoucey 2010: 447.
129. Estep 2017.
130. Smith 1998: 91.

Chapter 6. Beyond Autonomy

1. Fukuyama 2013.
2. Geddes 1996; Robinson 2007.
3. Ann Swidler, personal communication (Seattle, WA: 2016). See also Geddes 1996: 58.
4. See Fukuyama (2013) on clientelism.
5. Hertog 2010.
6. Organizational scholars have long observed similar effects. Taylor's canonical study noted that "naturally energetic" men will nevertheless slow themselves down while at work to conform more closely to the pace of those around them (Taylor 1914: 6).
7. Grindle 2012.
8. Grosh 1991; Hertog 2010.
9. Polillo and Guillén 2005. See the introduction for a discussion of neopatrimonialism.
10. Moreover some scholars, particularly those emphasizing legal distinctions, view autonomy as more binary while others, especially those emphasizing how socialization can influence shared thinking, tend to emphasize degrees of autonomy (Carruthers 1994).
11. This was central to Marxist debates (Miliband 1969; Poulantzas 1973), but see also Carpenter 2001; Carruthers 1994; Domhoff 1996; Evans, Rueschemeyer, and Skocpol 1985; Hellman, Jones, and Kaufmann 2000; Hooks 1990; Migdal 2001; Mills 1956.
12. E.g., McAllister 2008; Strauss 1998.
13. Weber 1978.
14. Chibber 2002.
15. Grindle 1997b; Matsuda 1998, 2000.
16. Taliercio 2004b.
17. Leonard 1991.
18. Geddes 1996; Johnson 2015; Leonard 2010; Roll 2014.
19. Kjaer and Therkildsen 2013; Samatar and Oldfield 1995.
20. Lane 2000.
21. Schneider 1992: 82.
22. Pollitt et al. 2004.
23. DiMaggio and Powell 1983: 147.
24. Verhoest et al. 2004.
25. E.g., Schneider 1992.
26. Laking 2005; Robinson 2007; Therkildsen 2004.
27. Johnson 2015: 785. See also Geddes 1996; Grindle and Hilderbrand 1995.
28. Ocasio 1997; Simon 1947, 1972.
29. See Mahoney, Kimball, and Koivu (2009: 126) on SUIN causes: "A sufficient but unnecessary part of a factor that is insufficient but necessary for an outcome." In their terms, shelter from neopatrimonial influence is necessary but insufficient for a pocket of excellence; in turn, active elite support is only one of several alternatives, any of which are sufficient to grant shelter

from neopatrimonial influence, but which are not individually necessary for the outcome of pocket formation.

30. Geddes 1996; Nunes 1984; Willis 2014.

31. Colby 2013: 112.

32. Willis 2014.

33. Colby 2013.

34. Willis 1986.

35. Paiva 2012.

36. Geddes 1996.

37. Colby 2013.

38. Willis 2014: 84.

39. Willis 2014.

40. Geddes 1996: 64.

41. Geddes 1996; Pinto 1969.

42. Geddes 1996: 63.

43. Leonard 1991.

44. Lamb and Muller 1982; Paul 1982: 6.

45. Leonard 1991.

46. Leonard 1991: 258.

47. Kenya 1960.

48. Grosh 1991; Paul 1982.

49. Paul 1982: 56.

50. Paul 1982.

51. Paul 1982: 60.

52. Paul 1982.

53. Leonard 1991: 140.

54. Paul 1982: 60.

55. Grosh 1991.

56. Paul 1982.

57. Paul 1982: 60.

58. Branch 2011.

59. Skocpol 1995.

60. Paul 1982: 60.

61. Monfrini 2008.

62. "U.S. Forfeits More than $480 Million."

63. Lewis 2009.

64. Pogoson and Roll 2014.

65. This episode is reported in several Nigerian papers, and Akunyili includes a scan of the letter in the appendix to her book (Akunyili 2012: 322). When Akunyili died in 2014, Nigerian news sources reported that it was from ovarian cancer that had been correctly diagnosed in 1998 by Nigerian doctors, but then misdiagnosed in the United States when she was sent home without surgery (Ogundipe 2014).

66. Abah 2012: 258.

67. "The Life and Times of Prof Dora Akunyili" 2014.

68. Akunyili 2012: 42.

69. Schrank 2016.

70. MacMurray 1921.

71. MacMurray 1921.

72. Strauss 2018.

73. "Foreigner Makes Millions for China" 1917: 350.

74. Strauss 1998.

75. Dane 1913; Dane and Von Strauch 1915.

76. Strauss 1998.

77. Lentz 1998.

78. Cofie 2007.

79. Cofie 2007.

80. Geddes 1996.

81. Akunyili 2012; see also Roll 2018.

82. Parkinson 1955.

83. Dane 1913: 10.

84. Johnson 2015.

85. Carpenter 2001.

86. This perspective has also been critiqued as presenting too unified a conception of the interests of elites, with some scholars suggesting a need to focus on "elite settlements" or how power is structured among elites (Hickey et al. 2015; Khan 2010; Slater 2010).

87. Ricks 2017.

88. It might still be argued that the organization and micromechanisms through which executive interest led to improved taxation are underspecified in the masterful macro account of state building (Tilly 1990).

89. Slater 2010.

90. Schneider 1993: 83.

91. "Foreigner Makes Millions for China" 1917.

92. Mahoney et al. 2009: 121.

93. This is often just taken for granted in economics work, see Aidt (2003) and Besley and McLaren (1993).

94. Portes 2015: 30.

95. Kiser and Kane 2001.

96. Fjeldstad 2003, 2005; Foltz and Opoku-Agyemang 2015; Panizza, di Tella, and Van Rijckeghem 2001; Rauch and Evans 2000; Treisman 2007. Notably Van Rijckeghem and Weder (2001) are highly cited as evidence that wages do matter though their substantive effect is small; however, they find no significant effect when country fixed effects are included.

97. It is worth noting, however, that niches often had higher-than-average access to professional benefits, including things like international training short courses, which sometimes functioned as a reward for strong workers, and sometimes allowed niches to enhance training of weaker performers whose labor could be spared if performance pressures were too intense to release a strong performing member.

98. Gneezy and Rustichini 2000. Also see social psychological work on effort justification (Festinger 1962).

99. Carpenter 2001; Carruthers 1994.

Chapter 7. Dual Habitus and Founding Cadres

1. Weber 1978.

2. Discussing governance, Fukuyama (2013: 360) claims that on balance more autonomy is better than more subordination, but argues it depends on the agency's underlying capacity to administer: "In very low capacity countries, the opposite would be the case: one would want to circumscribe the behavior of government officials with more rather than fewer rules because

one could not trust them to exercise good judgement or refrain from corrupt behavior. This is why Robert Klitgaard coined the formula Corruption = Discretion – Accountability (Klitgaard 1988).... On the other hand, if the same agency were full of professional degrees from internationally recognized schools, one would not just feel safer granting them considerable autonomy, but would actually want to reduce rule boundedness in hopes of encouraging innovative behavior."

3. Klitgaard 1988.

4. In particular, see Tendler 1997.

5. Leonard 1991: 132.

6. Moreover, Dane looms large in the early founding of the Salt Inspectorate; however, after only four years he retired, "followed by a succession of colourless, faceless foreign chief inspectors whose assorted health problems, lack of 'vision', and tendencies to focus narrowly on regulations, figures, and details none the less seemed not to have had a strongly negative effect on the organization as a whole" (Strauss 1998: 78).

7. IPT n.d.

8. Luz 2002.

9. Early on I explored the possibility that the dynamics of leadership within these niches were a case of Weberian charismatic authority in various stages of routinizing into legal-rational authority. While I still believe there are interesting parallels, I became convinced that these leaders were not charismatic in the conventional Weberian sense, where charismatic authority is defined as a "certain quality of an individual personality, by virtue of which he is set apart from ordinary men and treated as endowed with supernatural, superhuman, or at least specifically exceptional powers or qualities. These are such as are not accessible to the ordinary person, but are regarded as of divine origin or as exemplary, and on the basis of them the individual concerned is treated as a leader" (Weber and Eisenstadt 1968: 48). There is much that could be explored here, but to be brief, these leaders were not "set apart from ordinary men" or seen as possessing exceptional qualities that were "not accessible to the ordinary person." On the contrary, these leaders were frequently so enticing to their staff because they served as a highly accessible model for staff to emulate by observing through frequent interpersonal interactions with leaders. What these leaders do comes closer to what Fligstein (1997: 397) calls social skill, "the ability to motivate cooperation of other actors by providing them with common meanings and identities."

10. For organizational scholarship that advocates for the importance of leaders, see especially Lawrence, Suddaby, and Leca 2009, particularly the chapter by Kraatz; Selznick 1957.

11. The nineteenth-century American Coast Survey Department was likewise an agency that existed for years before exploding into global prominence rapidly after the appointment of Alexander Dallas Bache at the helm (Jansen 2011; Slotten 1994).

12. Adshead 1970.

13. Pierson and Skocpol 2002.

14. For more on habitus, see Bourdieu 1977.

15. This is conceptually similar to the idea of the "amphibious" origins of some biotech firms, with founders who drew on prior experience as university-based scientists with collaborative labs, fusing that ethos with capitalist sensibilities for entrepreneurship (Padgett and Powell 2012).

16. Bourdieu 1977: 95; see also Lizardo 2004.

17. Brasil n.d.

18. Campos 1994.

19. Teichman 1938.

20. Paul 1982.

21. Babül 2012: 41.

22. Andrews, Pritchett, and Woolcock 2013; Evans 2004; Portes 2006.

23. Uzzi and Spiro 2005; Vedres and Stark 2010.

24. Mukerji 2014.

25. For a prominent and early version of this critique within cultural sociology, see Wuthnow 1989.

26. Akunyili 2012.

27. Mukerji 2014.

28. Pierson and Skocpol 2002.

29. Rogers 2003.

30. Lizardo 2016; Mukerji 2014; Reber 1989.

31. Sørensen 2015.

32. Leonard 1991: 138.

33. Leonard 1991: 263.

34. Dane 1913, 1914, 1917; Dane and Von Strauch 1915.

35. Strauss 1998.

36. "Sir Richard Dane in China" 1919.

37. "Sir Richard Dane in China" 1919: 159.

38. Ultimately then, the initial founding of a niche does not depend on a leader with objectively unassailable moral character. Rather, what matters is that subordinates subjectively perceive the leader as engaging in habits, orientations, and practices that are sufficiently distinct from the status quo. That perceived distinction upsets the default assumption that the status quo habits and practices will apply, opening up fertile cognitive ground for new practices.

39. For more on how followers are important for legitimating novel organizational "vision," see Kohles, Bligh, and Carsten 2013.

40. Granovetter 1978.

41. For a visual illustration of this, see Sivers 2010.

42. Campos 1994: 293, translation by Luiz Vargas.

43. Decades of laboratory experiments on "effort justification" have demonstrated across a wide range of situations that the more effort people put into something, the more they value it (Festinger 1962; Norton, Mochon, and Ariely 2012).

44. Willis 2014: 85.

45. Similarly, during the reform period of the nineteenth-century U.S. Postal Service, Postmaster Amos Kendall was known for "getting acquainted with all the officers and clerks and their respective assignments, visiting their rooms, examining their books and asking questions" and personally wrote to any postmasters reported to be behind in paying contractors (White 1954: 276).

46. Grindle 1997.

47. Tendler notes "I do not question the importance of leadership" but objects that "An explanation of good performance that stresses outstanding leadership emphasizes, by its very focus on individuals, the singularity of certain experiences, namely, their unlikelihood of being repeated.... This does not add up to much of a guide for action" (1997: 18).

48. Tendler 1997: 24. For those interested: the rigorous merit-based hiring program involved written applications and multiple rounds of interviews conducted in large public batches "to be chosen for the job of health agent, in sum, was like being awarded an important prize in public" (29). Those who were selected were told it would be "an immense 'honor'" and those who were not selected were converted into monitors, told they "must make sure that those chosen abide by the rules," rules which were elaborated repeatedly in public meetings (29–30).

49. Tendler 1997: 31.

50. Tendler 1997: 31.

Chapter 8. Long-Term Outcomes

1. As of 2013, five of the six founding justices of the Commercial Courts had been promoted to be among the twenty-four justices of the Court of Appeals. That rate of promotion was far above average: If promotion from the pool of High Court justices to appeals were random, a High Court Justice would have had approximately a one in ninety chance of being promoted, but five of six Justices from the Commercial Court division of the High Courts were promoted in the five years following the study period (Judicial Service of Ghana 2013). By 2018, the founding president of the Ghana Commercial Court had been promoted all the way to the Supreme Court (Judicial Service of Ghana 2018).

2. NOI-Polls 2017.

3. Willis 1986.

4. Strauss 1998: 78.

5. Julia Strauss, personal communication, November 8, 2018.

6. Strauss 1998: 65.

7. China National Salt Industry Group "About Us" http://www.chinasalt.com.cn/english /about/.

8. Leonard 1991: 257.

9. Leonard 1991: 175.

10. World Bank 2014.

11. Juvenal and Mattos 2002: 34.

12. Strauss 1998.

13. Dane 1914.

14. Leonard 1991.

15. Atuguba and Hammergren 2010: xv.

16. Dispositions calculated over civil cases only, as Commercial Courts do not hear criminal cases. Only Accra Probate and Winneba had higher rates of total disposition.

17. Judicial Service of Ghana 2016.

18. "The Brazilian Development Bank," BNDES, https://www.bndes.gov.br/SiteBNDES /bndes/bndes_en/Institucional/The_BNDES/history.html

19. Rapoza 2017.

20. Brazil Monitor 2017; Rapoza 2017.

21. Jaguaribe 1956 as cited in Lafer 1970.

22. Geddes 1996; Lafer 1970; Nunes 1984.

23. Nunes 1984.

24. Daland 1981: 356.

25. Daland 1981: 355.

26. Daland 1981: 357.

27. Graham 2014: 34.

28. Daland 1981.

29. Daland 1981: 358–359.

30. Babb 2001; Schneider 1992.

31. Geddes 1996.

32. There have been some excellent case studies on DASP (Graham 2014; Wahrlich 1983) BNDES (Willis 1995; Colby 2013), and Executive Groups (Lafer 1970).

33. Lafer 1970: 138–139.

34. Willis 1986: 258.

35. McGann 2018.

36. Tendler 1997: 24. For those interested, see endnote 48 for chapter 7 (250).
37. Tendler 1997.

Conclusion

1. Andrews 2012.
2. Meyer and Rowan 1977: 345.
3. I endeavor not to make universal normative statements implying that some ethos or socio-cognitive orientations are normatively or ideologically superior. What Westerners have too long labeled corruption and conceived of as sporadic instances of individual failings, would better be thought of as an alternative social order (Borges et al. 2017; Mungiu-Pippidi 2015; Rothstein 2011).
4. Bromley and Powell 2012; DiMaggio and Powell 1983; Meyer, Boli, and and F. O. Ramirez 1997; Westphal and Zajac 2001. There is a persistent belief in the literature that such decoupling is intentional and strategic, that it is situated in "outward" facing parts of the organization, such that the organization comes to have a front stage / back stage presence. It is important to emphasize that these states have not had the ability to call into being this type of disciplined civil servant in the past, even though they had persistent coercive isomorphic pressures from large and powerful third-party organizations and donors for decades, as well as considerable organic political will (see endnote 48 on p. 238, on Kwame Nkrumah at Independence). Also the positions of the book's niches are not particularly the parts of the state that mostly interface with powerful external actors—that would be the multidonor budgetary support unit of the Ministry of Finance, not PARD.
5. For more on this, see chapter 7.
6. For cognitive subculture, see Zerubavel 2009.
7. Weber [1930] 2012. For a famous example, see DiMaggio and Powell (1983). Note that Weberian scholars have some considerable debate, both about how the phrase was translated and about what it conveys, including the interpretation that the iron cage refers not to rationalization and bureaucratization but to consumerist imperatives in advanced capitalism (Charles Camic, personal communication, April 16, 2017; Swedberg and Agevall 2016; Weber [1930] 2012: 245).
8. Tendler 1997.
9. Brehm and Gates 1999; Lane 2000; Stiglitz 1989.
10. Klitgaard 1988: 75.
11. Tendler 1997.
12. Swidler and Watkins 2009.
13. Dickinson and Villeval 2008; Frey and Jegen 2001; Frey and Oberholzer-Gee 1997.
14. Buurman et al. 2012; Crewson 1997; Houston 2000; Jacobsen, Hvitved, and Andersen 2014; Vandenabeele 2007.
15. This is an argument others have also made. See, for example, Andrews, Pritchett, and Woolcock 2013; Evans 2004.
16. "Promoting Chinese Innovation/Transformative Sanitation Technologies," Bill & Melinda Gates Foundation, https://www.gatesfoundation.org/Where-We-Work/China-Office/Promoting -Chinese-Innovation/Transformative-Sanitation-Technologies
17. E.g., Andrews, Pritchett, and Woolcock 2013; Grindle 2004; Tendler 1997.
18. Bersch, Praça, and Taylor 2017.
19. Babül 2012.
20. Adams 2005; Ertman 1997; Tilly 1990.
21. Morgan and Orloff 2017. For African states, see particularly Bierschenk and de Sardan (2014).

22. Positive deviance has a long history in subcultural studies but has recently been popularized within political and organizational fields (Andrews 2015; Pascale, Sternin, and Sternin 2010). Markers of this also include CIFAR's Successful Societies program, co-directed by Michele Lamont and Paul Pierson ("CIFAR - Successful Societies") and Jennifer Widner's Innovations for Successful Societies Lab at Princeton (Widner 2018) and the summer institute on Organizations and their Effectiveness at Stanford (Powell and Gibbons 2019).

23. Prasad 2018.

24. Leonard 1991; Lafer 1970; Willis 1986; Geddes 1990; Grindle 1997a; Daland 1981; Grosh 1991; Uphoff 1994; Uphoff, Esman, and Krishna 1998; Strauss 1998; Israel 1987; Tendler 1997; Andrews 2015.

25. Barma, Huybens, and Viñuela 2014; Johnson 2015; Leonard 2010; McDonnell 2017; Owusu 2006; Peiffer & Armytage 2019; Roll 2014; Zaloznaya 2017.

26. For a current review, see McDonnell and Vilaça (forthcoming).

27. Grindle 1997a.

28. Grindle 1997a: 486.

29. Tendler 1997: 14.

30. Portes 2015: 27.

31. Evans 1995; Wade 1990; Woo-Cumings 1999; World Bank 1997.

32. Chibber 2002.

33. Johnson 1982: 95.

34. The Pendleton Act (1883) is often regarded as a pivotal moment in American political development as the state institutionalized a move away from the patronage staffing that had characterized the civil service.

35. Jansen 2011; White 1954: 490.

36. Carpenter 2001.

37. Skocpol and Finegold 1982: 271.

38. Gilbert and Howe 1991; Hooks 1990; Schumpeter 1939; Skocpol and Finegold 1982. Carpenter is a notable exception.

39. This is broadly commensurate with Skocpol and Feingold's analysis of the U.S. New Deal Agricultural Adjustment Agency centers on state capacity, arguing that interventionist programs work better when governments "have or can quickly assemble, their own knowledgeable administrative organizations" (1982: 260).

40. Mayo (1945) and Roethlisberger and Dickson (1939) are generally credited with spawning the fields of industrial psychology and human relations.

41. There are other interesting parallels between the Ghanaian niches and the Hawthorne results, but there is not room to fully explore them here. For example, the researchers identified a shared cultural ethic within the work groups, "a set of practices and beliefs which its members had in common" (Roethlisberger and Dickson 1939: 560). The Hawthorne researchers also found that feeling special and chosen enhanced productivity, while freedom, discretion, and a voice in the structure of work could increase commitment and discipline.

42. Sutton and Rao 2016.

43. Kunda 2009.

44. Lipsky 2010; Peter, Michael, and Buffat 2015; Tendler 1997; Watkins-Hayes 2009; Zacka 2017.

45. Stinchcombe 1965: 168.

46. For more on the bureaucratic ethos see the excellent theoretical work of du Gay (2005).

47. Evans 1995; Rueschemeyer 2005.

48. Battilana and Dorado 2010; Hallett and Ventresca 2006; Lawrence, Suddaby, and Leca 2009.

49. Scott 1999: 6.

50. Anthropologists specialize in close, in-depth studies, but even within anthropology, ethnographies of *state officials* remain relatively rare (Bierschenk and de Sardan 2014; Gulbrandsen 2012; Werbner 2004).

51. Lizardo 2016; Vaisey 2009.

52. Lewis 2010.

53. Desmond 2008.

54. T. E. McDonnell 2016.

55. Declarative cognition depends on the brain's working memory system; within the limited capacity of working memory, declarative cognition engages logical or hypothetical reasoning, supposition, and simulation, but also inhibition—including the ability to inhibit the pragmatic influences of nondeclarative cognition (Evans 2008: 262).

56. Evans 2008; Lizardo 2016.

57. Vaisey 2009: 1683.

58. Collett, Vercel, and Boykin 2015.

59. Rucker and Shapiro 2003.

60. Langenkamp and Shifrer 2018.

61. March and Olson 1983; Spillane, Reiser, and Reimer 2002.

62. Interestingly, a growing new body of institutional economics research has documented that there are persistent productivity differentials even among private-sector organizations in wealthy industrialized countries, differences in output that remain even after accounting for observable inputs (Syverson 2011).

63. Amengual 2016; D. E. Davis 2004.

64. E.g., Kaufmann, Kraay and Mastruzzi 2010; Transparency International 2018.

REFERENCES

Abah, Joe. 2012. "Strong Organisations in Weak States. Atypical Public Sector Performance in Dysfunctional Environments." Doctoral Dissertation, Maastricht University, Maastricht, The Netherlands.

Abbott, Andrew. 1988. *The System of Professions: An Essay on the Division of Labor.* Chicago: University of Chicago Press.

Abdulai, Abdul-Gafaru, and Gordon Crawford. 2010. "Consolidating Democracy in Ghana: Progress and Prospects?" *Democratization* 17(1): 26–67.

Abrams, Dominic. 2009. "Social Identity on a National Scale: Optimal Distinctiveness and Young People's Self-Expression through Musical Preference." *Group Processes & Intergroup Relations* 12(3): 303–317.

Acemoglu, Daron, Simon Johnson, and James A. Robinson. 2005. "Institutions as a Fundamental Cause of Long-Run Growth." In *Handbook of Economic Growth.* Vol. 1A, edited by Philippe Aghion and Steven Durlauf, 385–472. North Holland: Elsevier.

Adams, Julia. 2005. *The Familial State.* Ithaca, NY: Cornell University Press.

Adogla-Bessa, Delali. 2017. "1,373 Cases Mediated through ADR in 2016." *Ghana News.* http://citifmonline.com/2017/03/14/1373-cases-mediated-through-adr-in-2016/. Accessed July 24, 2017.

Adshead, Samuel Adrian Miles. 1970. *The Modernization of the Chinese Salt Administration, 1900–1920.* Cambridge, MA: Harvard University Press.

Afrobarometer. 2010. *Afrobarometer Round 4 Merged Data.*

Aidt, Toke S. 2003. "Economic Analysis of Corruption: A Survey." *The Economic Journal* 113 (491): F632–F652.

Akunyili, Dora Nkem. 2012. *The War Against Counterfeit Medicine: My Story.* Oxford: African Books Collective.

Alubo, S. Ogoh. 1994. "Death for Sale: A Study of Drug Poisoning and Deaths in Nigeria." *Social Science & Medicine* 38(1): 97–103.

Alwy, Alwiya, and Susanne Schech. 2004. "Ethnic Inequalities in Education in Kenya." *International Education Journal* 5(2): 266–274.

Amat, José, Evan Paul, Christina Zarza, Linda R. Watkins, and Steven F. Maier. 2006. "Previous Experience with Behavioral Control over Stress Blocks the Behavioral and Dorsal Raphe Nucleus Activating Effects of Later Uncontrollable Stress: Role of the Ventral Medial Prefrontal Cortex." *The Journal of Neuroscience* 26(51): 13264 –13272.

Amengual, Matthew. 2016. *Politicized Enforcement in Argentina: Labor and Environmental Regulation.* New York: Cambridge University Press.

Ames, Barry. 1995. "Electoral Rules, Constituency Pressures, and Pork Barrel: Bases of Voting in the Brazilian Congress." *The Journal of Politics* 57(2): 324–43. https://doi.org/10.2307/2960309.

Anderson, Elijah. 2000. *Code of the Street: Decency, Violence, and the Moral Life of the Inner City.* New York: W. W. Norton & Company.

Anderson, Paul A. 1983. "Decision Making by Objection and the Cuban Missile Crisis." *Administrative Science Quarterly* 28(2): 201–222.

Andrews, Kenneth T., and Charles Seguin. 2015. "Group Threat and Policy Change: The Spatial Dynamics of Prohibition Politics, 1890–1919." *American Journal of Sociology* 121(2): 475–510.

Andrews, Matt. 2012. "The Logical Limits of Best Practice Administrative Solutions in Developing Countries." *Public Administration and Development* 32(2): 137–153.

Andrews, Matt. 2015. "Explaining Positive Deviance in Public Sector Reforms in Development." *World Development* 74: 197–208.

Andrews, Matt, Lant Pritchett, and Michael Woolcock. 2013. "Escaping Capability Traps Through Problem Driven Iterative Adaptation (PDIA)." *World Development* 51: 234–244.

Armantier, Olivier, and Amadou Boly. 2011. "A Controlled Field Experiment on Corruption." *European Economic Review* 55(8): 1072–1082.

Atuguba, Raymond A., and Linn Hammergren. 2010. "Uses and Users of Justice in Africa: The Case of Ghana's Specialised Courts." Washington DC: World Bank.

Awumah, Kofi, Ian Goulter, and Suresh K. Bhatt. 1991. "Entropy-Based Redundancy Measures in Water-Distribution Networks." *Journal of Hydraulic Engineering* 117(5): 595–614.

Ayee, Joseph RA. 2001. "Civil Service Reform in Ghana: A Case Study of Contemporary Reform Problems in Africa." *African Journal of Political Science/Revue Africaine de Science Politique* 6(1): 1–41.

Azoulay, Pierre, Christopher C. Liu, and Toby E. Stuart. 2017. "Social Influence given (Partially) Deliberate Matching: Career Imprints in the Creation of Academic Entrepreneurs." *American Journal of Sociology* 122(4): 1223–1271.

Babb, Sarah L. 2001. *Managing Mexico: Economists from Nationalism to Neoliberalism.* Princeton, NJ: Princeton University Press.

Babül, Elif M. 2012. "Training Bureaucrats, Practicing for Europe: Negotiating Bureaucratic Authority and Governmental Legitimacy in Turkey." *PoLAR: Political and Legal Anthropology Review* 35(1): 30–52.

Bank of Ghana. 2007. *Issues on Wages & Labour Market Competitiveness in Ghana.* Accra, Ghana: Research Department, Bank of Ghana.

Barma, Naazneen H., Elisabeth Huybens, and Lorena Viñuela. 2014. *Institutions Taking Root: Building State Capacity in Challenging Contexts.* Washington, DC: World Bank Publications.

Bates, Robert H. 1981. *Markets and States in Tropical Africa: The Political Basis of Agricultural Policies.* Berkeley: University of California Press.

Battilana, Julie, and Silvia Dorado. 2010. "Building Sustainable Hybrid Organizations: The Case of Commercial Microfinance Organizations." *The Academy of Management Journal* 53(6): 1419–1440.

Bearman, Peter S., and Hannah Brückner. 2001. "Promising the Future: Virginity Pledges and First Intercourse." *American Journal of Sociology* 106(4): 859–912.

Bebbington, Anthony, and Willy McCourt, eds. 2007. *Development Success: Statecraft in the South.* New York: Palgrave Macmillan.

Beisel, Nicola Kay. 1998. *Imperiled Innocents: Anthony Comstock and Family Reproduction in Victorian America.* Princeton, NJ: Princeton University Press.

Bensel, Richard Franklin. 1990. *Yankee Leviathan: The Origins of Central State Authority in America, 1859–1877.* Cambridge, UK: Cambridge University Press.

Bersch, Katherine, Sérgio Praça, and Matthew M. Taylor. 2017. "Bureaucratic Capacity and Political Autonomy within National States: Mapping the Archipelago of Excellence in Brazil."

States in the Developing World Edited by Miguel Centeno, Atul Kohli, and Deborah J. Yashar, with Dinsha Mistree, 157–183. Cambridge, UK: Cambridge University Press.

Besley, Timothy, and John McLaren. 1993. "Taxes and Bribery: The Role of Wage Incentives." *The Economic Journal* 103(416): 119–141.

Bierschenk, Thomas, and Jean-Pierre Olivier de Sardan. 2014. *States at Work: Dynamics of African Bureaucracies*. Boston: Brill.

Binder, Amy. 2007. "For Love and Money: Organizations' Creative Responses to Multiple Environmental Logics." *Theory and Society* 36(6): 547–571.

BNDES. "History—BNDES." https://www.bndes.gov.br/SiteBNDES/bndes/bndes_en/Institu cional/The_BNDES/history.html. Accessed April 25, 2019.

Boafo-Arthur, Kwame. 1999. "Ghana: Structural Adjustment, Democratization, and the Politics of Continuity." *African Studies Review* 42(2): 41–72.

Boafo-Arthur, Kwame. 2008. *Democracy and Stability in West Africa: The Ghanaian Experience*. Uppsala, Sweden: Department of Peace and Conflict Research, Uppsala University.

Boone, Catherine. 2003. *Political Topographies of the African State: Territorial Authority and Institutional Choice*. Cambridge, UK: Cambridge University Press.

Borges, Mariana, Jordan Gans-Morse, Alexey Makarin, Andre Nickow, Monica Prasad, Vanessa Watters, Theresa Mannah-Blankson, and Dong Zhang. 2017. *Combatting Corruption Among Civil Servants: Interdisciplinary Perspectives on What Works*. USAID Research and Innovation Grants Working Paper Series. https://www.usaid.gov/sites/default/files/documents /2496/Combatting_Corruption_Among_Civil_Servants_-_Interdisciplinary_Perspectives _on_What_Works.pdf.

Bourdieu, Pierre. 1977. *Outline of a Theory of Practice*. Cambridge, UK: Cambridge University Press.

Branch, Daniel. 2011. *Kenya: Between Hope and Despair, 1963–2011*. New Haven, CT: Yale University Press.

Brasil, CPDOC-Centro de Pesquisa e Documentação História Contemporânea do. n.d. "TORRES, ARI." *CPDOC—Centro de Pesquisa e Documentação de História Contemporânea Do Brasil*. http://www.fgv.br/cpdoc/acervo/dicionarios/verbete-biografico/torres-ari. Accessed December 19, 2017.

Bratton, Michael, and Nicholas Van de Walle. 1997. *Democratic Experiments in Africa: Regime Transitions in Comparative Perspective*. Cambridge: Cambridge University Press.

Brazil Monitor. 2017. "Brazil's Bank BNDES Invested Billions to Finance the Corruption | Brazilmonitor.com." http://www.brazilmonitor.com/index.php/2017/04/29/brazils-bank-bndes -invested-billions-to-finance-the-corruption/. Accessed January 12, 2019.

Brehm, John O., and Scott Gates. 1999. *Working, Shirking, and Sabotage: Bureaucratic Response to a Democratic Public*. Ann Arbor: University of Michigan Press.

Bromley, Patricia, and Walter W. Powell. 2012. "From Smoke and Mirrors to Walking the Talk: Decoupling in the Contemporary World." *The Academy of Management Annals* 6(1): 483–530.

Burawoy, Michael. 1979. *Manufacturing Consent: Changes in the Labor Process under Monopoly Capitalism*. Chicago: University of Chicago Press.

Burgess, Robin, Rémi Jedwab, Edward Miguel, and Ameet Morjaria. 2010. "Our Turn to Eat: The Political Economy of Roads in Kenya." Manuscript, London School of Economics and Political Science, London.

Buurman, Margaretha, Josse Delfgaauw, Robert Dur, and Seth Van den Bossche. 2012. "Public Sector Employees: Risk Averse and Altruistic?" *The Great Recession: Motivation for Re-Thinking Paradigms in Macroeconomic Modeling* 83(3): 279–291.

Campbell, Donald T. 1958. "Common Fate, Similarity, and Other Indices of the Status of Aggregates of Persons as Social Entities." *Systems Research and Behavioral Science* 3(1): 14–25.

Campos, Roberto. 1994. *A Laterna Na Popa*. Vol. 2. Rio de Janero, Brazil: Topbooks.

Carpenter, Daniel P. 2001. *The Forging of Bureaucratic Autonomy: Reputations, Networks, and Policy Innovation in Executive Agencies, 1862–1928*. Princeton, NJ: Princeton University Press.

Carruthers, Bruce G. 1994. "When Is the State Autonomous? Culture, Organization Theory, and the Political Sociology of the State." *Sociological Theory* 12(1): 19–44.

CDD-Ghana and World Bank. 2000. *The Ghana Governance and Corruption Survey: Evidence from Households, Enterprises, and Public Officials*. Accra, Ghana.

Chazan, Naomi. 1983. *An Anatomy of Ghanaian Politics: Managing Political Recession, 1969–1982*. Boulder, CO: Westview Press.

Chibber, Vivek. 2002. "Bureaucratic Rationality and the Developmental State." *American Journal of Sociology* 107(4): 951–989.

China National Salt Industry Group "About Us" http://www.chinasalt.com.cn/english/about/. Accessed on February 15, 2019.

Chorev, Nitsan, and Andrew Schrank. 2017. "Professionals and the Professions in the Global South: An Introduction." *Sociology of Development* 3(3): 197–211.

"CIFAR—Successful Societies," https://www.cifar.ca/research/programs/successful-societies. Accessed on February 2, 2019

Cofie, Sandra. 2007. *Ghana: Establishment of the Commercial Court*. Washington, DC: International Finance Corporation of the World Bank Group.

Colby, Seth Stevens. 2013. "Searching for Institutional Solutions to Industrial Policy Challenges: A Case Study of the Brazilian Development Bank." PhD Dissertation, Johns Hopkins University, Baltimore, MD.

Collett, Jessica L., Kelcie Vercel, and Olevia Boykin. 2015. "Using Identity Processes to Understand Persistent Inequality in Parenting." *Social Psychology Quarterly* 78(4): 345–364.

Coser, Lewis A. 1956. *The Functions of Social Conflict*. Vol. 9. London: Routledge.

Crewson, Philip E. 1997. "Public-Service Motivation: Building Empirical Evidence of Incidence and Effect." *Journal of Public Administration Research and Theory* 7(4): 499–518.

Daland, Robert T. 1981. *Exploring Brazilian Bureaucracy: Performance and Pathology*. Lanham, MD: University Press of America.

Dane, Richard Morris. 1913. "Note on the Changlu Salt Administration." https://babel.hathitrust.org/cgi/pt?id=coo.31924023622651&view=1up&seq=8.

Dane, Richard Morris. 1914. "Note on the Administration of the Salt Revenue in Lianghwai District." https://babel.hathitrust.org/cgi/pt?id=coo.31924023622669&view=1up&seq=9

Dane, Richard Morris. 1917. *Note by Sir Richard Dane on the Government Salt Monopoly in Fukien, Chief Inspectorate, Peking, 23rd March, 1917*. Shanghai : Kelly & Walsh Ltd.

Dane, Richard Morris, and E. Von Strauch. 1915. *Notes by Sir Richard Dane, Associate Chief Inspector, and E. Von Strauch, Deputy Associate Chief Inspector, on the Szechuan Salt Revenue Administration, 1914–15*. Peking: Chief Inspectorate.

Davis, Diane E. 2004. *Discipline and Development: Middle Classes and Prosperity in East Asia and Latin America*. Cambridge, UK: Cambridge University Press.

Davis, Jennifer. 2004. "Corruption in Public Service Delivery: Experience from South Asia's Water and Sanitation Sector." *World Development* 32(1): 53–71.

Desmond, Matthew. 2008. *On the Fireline: Living and Dying with Wildland Firefighters*. Chicago: University of Chicago Press.

DeSoucey, Michaela. 2010. "Gastronationalism: Food Traditions and Authenticity Politics in the European Union." *American Sociological Review* 75(3): 432–455.

Dickinson, David, and Marie-Claire Villeval. 2008. "Does Monitoring Decrease Work Effort?: The Complementarity between Agency and Crowding-out Theories." *Games and Economic Behavior* 63(1): 56–76.

DiIulio Jr., John D. 1994. "Principled Agents: The Cultural Bases of Behavior in a Federal Government Bureaucracy." *Journal of Public Administration Research and Theory* 4(3): 277–318.

DiIulio, John. 2014. *Bring Back the Bureaucrats: Why More Federal Workers Will Lead to Better (and Smaller!) Government.* West Conshohocken, PA: Templeton Foundation Press.

DiMaggio, Paul J., and Walter W. Powell. 1983. "The Iron Cage Revisited: Institutional Isomorphism and Collective Rationality in Organizational Fields." *The American Sociological Review* 48(2): 147–160.

Dobbin, Frank R. 1992. "The Origins of Private Social Insurance: Public Policy and Fringe Benefits in America, 1920–1950." *American Journal of Sociology* 97(5): 1416–1450.

Dobbin, Frank. 1994. "Forging Industrial Policy: The United States, Britain." in *and France in the Railway Age.* Cambridge, UK: Cambridge University Press.

Doig, Jameson W. 1997. "Leadership and Innovation in the Administrative State." *International Journal of Public Administration* 20(4–5): 861–79.

Domhoff, G. William. 1996. *State Autonomy or Class Dominance?: Case Studies on Policy Making in America.* New York: Walter de Gruyter, Inc.

Du Gay, Paul. 2000. *In Praise of Bureaucracy.* London: Sage Publications.

Du Gay, Paul. 2005. *The Values of Bureaucracy.* Oxford: Oxford University Press.

Dunn, Mary B., and Candace Jones. 2010. "Institutional Logics and Institutional Pluralism: The Contestation of Care and Science Logics in Medical Education, 1967–2005." *Administrative Science Quarterly* 55(1): 114–149.

Durkheim, Emile. [1912] 2008. *The Elementary Forms of the Religious Life.* Oxford: Oxford University Press.

Edwards, Marc A., and Siddhartha Roy. 2017. "Academic Research in the 21st Century: Maintaining Scientific Integrity in a Climate of Perverse Incentives and Hypercompetition." *Environmental Engineering Science* 34(1): 51–61.

Eisenstadt, Shmuel Noah. 1973. *Traditional Patrimonialism and Modern Neopatrimonialism.* Vol. 1. New York: Sage Publications.

Elias, Norbert. 1982. *The Civilizing Process.* Vol. 1. New York: Blackwell.

Eliasoph, Nina, and Paul Lichterman. 2003. "Culture in Interaction." *American Journal of Sociology* 108(4): 735–794.

Englebert, Pierre. 2000. "Pre-Colonial Institutions, Post-Colonial States, and Economic Development in Tropical Africa." *Political Research Quarterly* 53(1): 7–36.

Erdmann, Gero, and Ulf Engel. 2007. "Neopatrimonialism Reconsidered: Critical Review and Elaboration of an Elusive Concept." *Commonwealth & Comparative Politics* 45(1): 95–119.

Erhun, W. O., O. O. Babalola, and M. O. Erhun. 2001. "Drug Regulation and Control in Nigeria: The Challenge of Counterfeit Drugs." *Journal of Health & Population in Developing Countries* 4(2): 23–34.

Ertman, Thomas. 1997. *Birth of the Leviathan: Building States and Regimes in Medieval and Early Modern Europe.* Cambridge, UK: Cambridge University Press.

Estep, Kevin. 2017. "Opting Out: How Political Context, Political Ideology, and Individualistic Parenting Contribute to Vaccine Refusal in California, 2000–2015." Doctoral Dissertation, University of Notre Dame, Notre Dame, IN.

Evans, Jonathan St. B. T. 2008. "Dual-Processing Accounts of Reasoning, Judgment, and Social Cognition." *Annual Review of Psychology* 59: 255–278.

Evans, Peter. 1989. "Predatory, Developmental, and Other Apparatuses: A Comparative Political Economy Perspective on the Third World State." *Sociological Forum* 4(4): 561–587.

Evans, Peter. 1995. *Embedded Autonomy: States and Industrial Transformation.* Princeton, NJ: Princeton University Press.

Evans, Peter. 2004. "Development as Institutional Change: The Pitfalls of Monocropping and the Potentials of Deliberation." *Studies in Comparative International Development* 38(4): 30–52.

Evans, Peter B., Dietrich Rueschemeyer, and Theda Skocpol, eds. 1985. *Bringing the State Back In.* New York: Cambridge University Press.

Fearon, James D. 2003. "Ethnic and Cultural Diversity by Country." *Journal of Economic Growth* 8(2): 195–222.

Ferreira, Carlos, Michael Engelschalk, and William Mayville. 2007. "The Challenge of Combating Corruption in Customs Administrations." In *The Many Faces of Corruption: Tracking Vulnerabilities at the Sector,* edited by J. Edgardo Campos and Sanjay Pradhan, 367–386. Washington, DC: World Bank Publications.

Festinger, Leon. 1962. *A Theory of Cognitive Dissonance.* Vol. 2. Palo Alto, CA: Stanford University Press.

Fine, Gary Alan, and Terence McDonnell. 2007. "Erasing the Brown Scare: Referential Afterlife and the Power of Memory Templates." *Social Problems* 54(2): 170–187.

Fischer, Claude S. 1975. "Toward a Subcultural Theory of Urbanism." *American Journal of Sociology* 80(6): 1319–1341.

Fischer, Wolfram, and Peter Lundgreen. 1975. "The Recruitment and Training of Administrative and Technical Personnel." In *The Formation of National States in Western Europe,* edited by Charles Tilly. 456–561. Princeton, NJ: Princeton University Press.

Fjeldstad, Odd-Helge. 2003. "Fighting Fiscal Corruption: Lessons from the Tanzania Revenue Authority." *Public Administration and Development* 23(2): 165–175.

Fjeldstad, Odd-Helge. 2005. *Corruption in Tax Administration: Lessons from Institutional Reforms in Uganda.* CMI Working Paper 2005:10. Chr. Michelsen Institute, Bergen, Norway.

Flatters, Frank, and W. Bentley Macleod. 1995. "Administrative Corruption and Taxation." *International Tax and Public Finance* 2(3): 397–417.

Fligstein, Neil. 1997. "Social Skill and Institutional Theory." *American Behavioral Scientist* 40(4): 397–405.

Foltz, Jeremy D., and Kweku A. Opoku-Agyemang. 2015. "Do Higher Salaries Lower Petty Corruption? A Policy Experiment on West Africa's Highways." Unpublished Working Paper, University of Wisconsin-Madison and University of California, Berkeley.

Foreigner Makes Millions for China. 1917. "A Foreigner Makes Millions for China: An Interview with Sir Richard Dane on the Reformed Salt Gabelle." *Asia and the Americas,* July, 349–357. https://books.google.com/books?id=D7A5AQAAIAAJ&pg=PA349&lpg=PA349&dq =A+Foreigner+Makes+Millions+for+China:+An+Interview+with+Sir+Richard+Dane +on+the+Reformed+Salt+Gabelle&source=bl&ots=xKQhAQo8Ln&sig=ACfU3U2Uh -_HLvkN9eM63DrAfmHqA8dPA&hl=en&sa=X&ved=2ahUKEwjq7t3rxojkAhUF5awK HakBBIEQ6AEwAHoECAkQAQ#v=onepage&q&f=false.

Frey, Bruno S., and Reto Jegen. 2001. "Motivation Crowding Theory." *Journal of Economic Surveys* 15(5): 589–611.

Frey, Bruno S., and Felix Oberholzer-Gee. 1997. "The Cost of Price Incentives: An Empirical Analysis of Motivation Crowding-Out." *The American Economic Review* 87(4): 746–755.

Fukuyama, Francis. 2013. "What Is Governance?" *Governance* 26(3): 347–368.

Geddes, Barbara. 1990. "Building 'State' Autonomy in Brazil, 1930–1964." *Comparative Politics* 22(2): 217–235.

Geddes, Barbara. 1996. *Politician's Dilemma: Building State Capacity in Latin America.* Berkeley, CA: University of California Press.

Gertzel, Cherry J., Maure Leonard Goldschmidt, Donald S. Rothchild et al. 1969. *Government and Politics in Kenya: A Nation Building Text.* Nairobi, Kenya: East African Pub. House.

Ghana General Legal Council. "List of Judges on the High Court." *General Legal Council, Government of Ghana.* http://www.glc.gov.gh/resources/list-of-judges/high-court/. Accessed April 11, 2017.

Ghana Statistical Service. 2008. *Ghana Living Standards Survey: Report of the Fifth Round.* Accra, Ghana.

Gilbert, Jess, and Carolyn Howe. 1991. "Beyond 'State vs. Society': Theories of the State and New Deal Agricultural Policies." *American Sociological Review* 56(2): 204–220.

Gneezy, Uri, and Aldo Rustichini. 2000. "Pay Enough or Don't Pay at All." *The Quarterly Journal of Economics* 115(3): 791–810.

Goffman, Erving. 1963. *Stigma: Notes on the Management of Spoiled Identity.* New York: Simon and Schuster.

Goffman, Erving. 1978. *The Presentation of Self in Everyday Life.* Woodstock, NY: New York Overlook Press.

Gorski, Philip. 2003. *The Disciplinary Revolution: Calvinism and the Rise of the State in Early Modern Europe.* Chicago: University of Chicago Press.

Graham, Lawrence S. 2014. *Civil Service Reform in Brazil: Principles versus Practice.* Vol. 13. Austin: University of Texas Press.

Granovetter, Mark S. 1973. "The Strength of Weak Ties." *American Journal of Sociology* 78(6): 1360–1380.

Granovetter, Mark. 1978. "Threshold Models of Collective Behavior." *American Journal of Sociology* 83(6): 1420–1443.

Grant, Ursula, Alan Hudson, and Bhavna Sharma. 2009. *Exploring "Development Success": Indicators, Stories and Contributing Factors.* London: Overseas Development Institute.

Grindle, Merilee S. 1997a. "Divergent Cultures? When Public Organizations Perform Well in Developing Countries." *World Development* 25(4): 481–495.

Grindle, Merilee S., ed. 1997b. *Getting Good Government: Capacity Building in the Public Sectors of Developing Countries.* Cambridge, MA: Harvard University Press.

Grindle, Merilee S. 2004. "Good Enough Governance: Poverty Reduction and Reform in Developing Countries." *Governance* 17(4): 525–548.

Grindle, Merilee S. 2007. "Good Enough Governance Revisited." *Development Policy Review* 25(5): 533–574.

Grindle, Merilee S. 2012. *Jobs for the Boys.* Cambridge, MA: Harvard University Press.

Grindle, Merilee S., and Mary E. Hilderbrand. 1995. "Building Sustainable Capacity in the Public Sector: What Can Be Done?" *Public Administration and Development* 15(5): 441–463.

Grosh, Barbara. 1991. *Public Enterprise in Kenya: What Works, What Doesn't and Why.* Boulder, CO: Lynne Rienner Publishers.

Gulbrandsen, Ørnulf. 2012. *The State and the Social: State Formation in Botswana and Its Pre-Colonial and Colonial Genealogies.* New York: Berghahn Books.

Hallett, Tim, and Marc J. Ventresca. 2006. "Inhabited Institutions: Social Interactions and Organizational Forms in Gouldner's Patterns of Industrial Bureaucracy." *Theory and Society* 35(2): 213–236.

Hamani, Oumarou. 2014. "'We Make Do and Keep Going!' Inventive Practices and Ordered Informality in the Functioning of the District Courts in Niamey and Zinder (Niger)." In *States at Work: Dynamics of African Bureaucracies,* edited by Thomas Bierschenk and Jean-Pierre Olivier de Sardan, 145–174. Boston: Brill.

Hanley, Anne G., Julio Manuel Pires, Maurício Jorge Pinto De Souza, Renato Leite Marcondes, Rosane Nunes De Faria, and Sérgio Naruhiko Sakurai. 2016. "Critiquing the Bank: 60 Years of BNDES in the Academy." *Journal of Latin American Studies* 48(4): 823–850.

Hansen, Garron. 2015. Personal Communication to Author. October 2, 2017.

Haynie, Dana L. 2001. "Delinquent Peers Revisited: Does Network Structure Matter?" *American Journal of Sociology* 106(4): 1013–1057.

Hellman, Joel S., Geraint Jones, and Daniel Kaufmann. 2000. *Seize the State, Seize the Day: State Capture, Corruption, and Influence in Transition.* Washington, DC: World Bank.

Helman, Gerald B., and Steven R. Ratner. 1992. "Saving Failed States." *Foreign Policy* 89: 3–20.

Henisz, Witold J., Bennet A. Zelner, and Mauro F. Guillén. 2005. "The Worldwide Diffusion of Market-Oriented Infrastructure Reform, 1977–1999." *American Sociological Review* 70(6): 871–897.

Herbst, Jeffrey. 2014. *States and Power in Africa: Comparative Lessons in Authority and Control.* Princeton, NJ: Princeton University Press.

Hertog, Steffen. 2010. "Defying the Resource Curse: Explaining Successful State-Owned Enterprises in Rentier States." *World Politics* 62(2): 261–301.

Hickey, Sam, Abdul-Gafaru Abdulai, Angelo Izama, and Giles Mohan. 2015. "The Politics of Governing Oil Effectively: A Comparative Study of Two New Oil-Rich States in Africa." Effective States and Inclusive Development (ESID) Working Paper series, No. 54. https://ssrn.com/abstract=2695723 or http://dx.doi.org/10.2139/ssrn.2695723

Hiroto, Donald S., and Martin E. Seligman. 1975. "Generality of Learned Helplessness in Man." *Journal of Personality and Social Psychology* 31(2): 311–327.

Hooks, Gregory. 1990. "From an Autonomous to a Captured State Agency: The Decline of the New Deal in Agriculture." *American Sociological Review* 55(1): 29–43.

Hooks, Gregory. 1993. "The Weakness of Strong Theories: The U.S. State's Dominance of the World War II Investment Process." *American Sociological Review* 58(1): 37–53.

Houston, David J. 2000. "Public-Service Motivation: A Multivariate Test." *Journal of Public Administration Research and Theory* 10(4): 713–728.

Hsieh, Chih-Wei. 2014. "Burnout among Public Service Workers: The Role of Emotional Labor Requirements and Job Resources." *Review of Public Personnel Administration* 34(4): 379–402.

IPT. n.d. "Personalidades IPT—Ary Torres." *IPT—Instituto de Pesquisas Tecnológicas.* http://www.ipt.br/institucional/campanhas/26-personalidades_ipt___ary_torres.htm. Accessed March 9, 2018.

Israel, Arturo. 1987. *Institutional Development: Incentives to Performance.* Washington, DC: World Bank.

Jacobsen, Christian Bøtcher, Johan Hvitved, and Lotte Bøgh Andersen. 2014. "Command and Motivation: How the Perception of External Interventions Relates to Intrinsic Motivation and Public Service Motivation." *Public Administration* 92(4): 790–806.

Jaguaribe, Helio. 1956. "Sentido e Perspectivas Do Governo Kubitschek." *Cadernos Do Nosso Tempo* (5): 11–12.

Jansen, Axel. 2011. *Alexander Dallas Bache: Building the American Nation through Science and Education in the Nineteenth Century.* New York: Campus Verlag.

Johnson, Chalmers. 1982. *MITI and the Japanese Miracle: The Growth of Industrial Policy, 1925–1975.* Palo Alto, CA: Stanford University Press.

Johnson, Martha C. 2015. "Donor Requirements and Pockets of Effectiveness in Senegal's Bureaucracy." *Development Policy Review* 33(6): 783–804.

Jones, Stanton L., Jack R. Nation, and Phillip Massad. 1977. "Immunization against Learned Helplessness in Man." *Journal of Abnormal Psychology* 86(1): 75–83.

Judicial Service of Ghana. 2008. *2007/2008 Annual Report.* Accra, Ghana: Judicial Service of Ghana.

Judicial Service of Ghana. 2013. *2012/2013 Annual Report*. Accra, Ghana: Judicial Service of Ghana.

Judicial Service of Ghana. 2016. *2015/2016 Annual Report*. Accra, Ghana: Judicial Service of Ghana.

Judicial Service of Ghana. 2018. *2017/2018 Annual Report*. Accra, Ghana: Judicial Service of Ghana.

Juvenal, Thais Linhares, and René Luiz Grion Mattos. 2002. "O Setor Florestal No Brasil e a Importância Do Reflorestamento." Rio de Janero, Brazil: BNDES.

Kaufmann, Daniel, Aart Kraay, and Massimo Mastruzzi. 2010. *Worldwide Governance Indicators*. Washington, DC: World Bank.

Kenya, Colony and Protectorate of. 1960. *Statistical Abstract*. Kenya: East African Statistical Department-Kenya Unit.

Khan, Mushtaq. 2010. "Political Settlements and the Governance of Growth-Enhancing Institutions." SOAS Research Paper Series on Growth-Enhancing Governance. SOAS. University of London.

Kiser, Edgar, and Joshua Kane. 2001. "Revolution and State Structure: The Bureaucratization of Tax Administration in Early Modern England and France." *American Journal of Sociology* 107(1): 183–223.

Kiser, Edgar, and Xiaoxi Tong. 1992. "Determinants of the Amount and Type of Corruption in State Fiscal Bureaucracies: An Analysis of Late Imperial China." *Comparative Political Studies* 25(3): 300–331.

Kjaer, Anne Mette, and Ole Therkildsen. 2013. "Competitive Elections and Agricultural Sector Policies in Sub-Saharan Africa." In *Developing Democracies*, edited by M. Böss, M. Jørgen, and S.-E. Skaaning, 116–136. Aarhus, Denmark: Aarhus University Press.

Klitgaard, Robert. 1988. *Controlling Corruption*. Berkeley: University of California Press.

Kohles, Jeffrey C., Michelle C. Bligh, and Melissa K. Carsten. 2013. "The Vision Integration Process: Applying Rogers' Diffusion of Innovations Theory to Leader–Follower Communications." *Leadership* 9(4): 466–85.

Kohli, Atul. 2004. *State-Directed Development: Political Power and Industrialization in the Global Periphery*. Cambridge, UK: Cambridge University Press.

Kopecký, Petr, Peter Mair, and Maria Spirova. 2012. *Party Patronage and Party Government in European Democracies*. Oxford: Oxford University Press.

Kunda, Gideon. 2009. *Engineering Culture: Control and Commitment in a High-Tech Corporation*. Philadelphia: Temple University Press.

Lafer, Celso. 1970. *The Planning Process and the Political System in Brazil: A Study of Kubitschek's Target Plan–1956–1961*. Ithaca, NY: Cornell University.

Laking, Rob. 2005. "Agencies: Their Benefits and Risks." *OECD Journal on Budgeting* 4(4): 7–25.

Lamb, Geoffrey, and Linda Muller. 1982. "Control, Accountability, and Incentives in a Successful Development Institution: The Kenya Tea Development Authority." World Bank Staff Working Papers Number 550. Washington DC: World Bank.

Lamont, Michèle, and Virág Molnár. 2002. "The Study of Boundaries in the Social Sciences." *Annual Review of Sociology* 28(1): 167–195.

Lamont, Michèle, Sabrina Pendergrass, and M. Pachucki. 2001. "Symbolic Boundaries." *International Encyclopedia of the Social and Behavioral Sciences* 23: 15341–47.

Landau, Martin. 1969. "Redundancy, Rationality, and the Problem of Duplication and Overlap." *Public Administration Review* 29(4): 346–358.

Lane, Jan-Erik. 2000. *New Public Management*. New York: Taylor & Francis US.

Langenkamp, Amy G., and Dara Shifrer. 2018. "Family Legacy or Family Pioneer? Social Class Differences in the Way Adolescents Construct College-Going." *Journal of Adolescent Research* 33(1): 58–89.

La Porta, Rafael, Florencio Lopez-de-Silanes, Andrei Shleifer, and Robert Vishny. 1999. "The Quality of Government." *Journal of Law, Economics, and Organization* 15(1): 222–279. https://doi.org/doi: 10.1093/jleo/15.1.222.

Lau, Richard R. 1989. "Individual and Contextual Influences on Group Identification." *Social Psychology Quarterly* 52(3): 220–231.

Lawrence, Thomas B., Roy Suddaby, and Bernard Leca. 2009. *Institutional Work: Actors and Agency in Institutional Studies of Organizations.* Cambridge, UK: Cambridge University Press.

Lentz, Carola. 1998. "The Chief, the Mine Captain and the Politician: Legitimating Power in Northern Ghana." *Africa* 68(1): 46–67.

Lentz, Carola. 2009. "Constructing Ethnicity: Elite Biographies and Funerals in Ghana." In *Ethnicity, Belonging and Biography*, edited by G. R. and Artur Bogner, 181–202. London: Transaction Publishers.

Leonard, David K. 1991. *African Successes: Four Public Managers of Kenyan Rural Development.* Berkeley: University of California Press.

Leonard, David K. 2010. "'Pockets' of Effective Agencies in Weak Governance States: Where Are They Likely and Why Does It Matter?" *Public Administration and Development* 30(2): 91–101.

Leonardelli, Geoffrey J., and Marilynn B. Brewer. 2001. "Minority and Majority Discrimination: When and Why." *Journal of Experimental Social Psychology* 37(6): 468–485.

Leonardelli, Geoffrey J., Cynthia L. Pickett, and Marilynn B. Brewer. 2010. "Optimal Distinctiveness Theory: A Framework for Social Identity, Social Cognition, and Intergroup Relations." *Advances in Experimental Social Psychology* 43: 63–113.

Levine, Robert N. 2008. *A Geography of Time: On Tempo, Culture, and the Pace of Life.* New York: Basic Books.

Lewis, Michael. 2010. *Liar's Poker.* New York: W. W. Norton & Company.

Lewis, Peter. 2009. *Growing Apart: Oil, Politics, and Economic Change in Indonesia and Nigeria.* Ann Arbor: University of Michigan Press.

Lindgren, Henry Clay. 1954. *Effective Leadership in Human Relations.* New York: Hermitage House.

Lipsky, Michael. 2010. *Street-Level Bureaucracy: Dilemmas of the Individual in Public Service.* New York: Russell Sage Foundation.

Lizardo, Omar. 2004. "The Cognitive Origins of Bourdieu's Habitus." *Journal for the Theory of Social Behaviour* 34(4): 375–401.

Lizardo, Omar. 2016. "Improving Cultural Analysis: Considering Personal Culture in Its Declarative and Nondeclarative Modes." *American Sociological Review* 82(1): 88–115.

Lizardo, Omar, and Michael Strand. 2010. "Skills, Toolkits, Contexts and Institutions: Clarifying the Relationship between Different Approaches to Cognition in Cultural Sociology." *Poetics* 38(2): 205–228.

Luz, Olavo. 2002. *Roberto Campos. Um Retrato Pouco Falado.* Rio de Janeiro, RJ, Brazil: Campus.

Macaulay, Stewart. 1963. "Non-Contractual Relations in Business: A Preliminary Study." *American Sociological Review* 28(1): 55–67.

MacMurray, John Van Antwerp, ed. 1921. *Treaties and Agreements with and Concerning China, 1894–1919: Republican Period (1912–1919).* New York: Oxford University Press.

Mahoney, James, Erin Kimball, and Kendra L. Koivu. 2009. "The Logic of Historical Explanation in the Social Sciences." *Comparative Political Studies* 42(1): 114–146.

Maier, Steven F., and Martin E. P. Seligman. 2016. "Learned Helplessness at Fifty: Insights from Neuroscience." *Psychological Review* 123(4): 349.

Mamdani, Mahmood. 2018. *Citizen and Subject: Contemporary Africa and the Legacy of Late Colonialism*. Princeton, NJ: Princeton University Press.

March, James C., and James G. March. 1977. "Almost Random Careers: The Wisconsin School Superintendency, 1940–1972." *Administrative Science Quarterly* 22(3): 377–409.

March, James G. 1986. "How We Talk and How We Act: Administrative Theory and Administrative Life." In *Leadership and Organizational Culture: New Perspectives on Administrative Theory and Practice*, edited by T. J. Sergiovanni and J. E. Corbally, 18–35. Chicago: University of Illinois Press.

March, James G., and Johan P. Olson. 1983. "Organizing Political Life: What Administrative Reorganization Tells Us about Government." *American Political Science Review* 77(2): 281–296.

Matsuda, Yasuhiko. 1998. "An Island of Excellence: Petroleos de Venezuela and the Political Economy of Technocratic Agency Autonomy." Doctoral Dissertation, University of Pittsburgh, Pittsburgh, PA.

Matsuda, Yasuhiko. 2000. *From Patronage to a Professional State: Bolivia Institutional and Governance Review*. Washington, DC: World Bank.

Mayo, Elton. 1945. *The Social Problems of an Industrial Civilization*. Boston: Graduate School of Business Administration, Harvard University.

McAllister, Lesley. 2008. *Making Law Matter: Environmental Protection and Legal Institutions in Brazil*. Stanford, CA: Stanford University Press.

McDonnell, Erin Metz. 2016. "Conciliatory States: Elite Ethno-Demographics and the Puzzle of Public Goods within Diverse African States." *Comparative Political Studies* 49(11): 1513–1549.

McDonnell, Erin Metz. 2017. "Patchwork Leviathan: How Pockets of Bureaucratic Governance Flourish within Institutionally Diverse Developing States." *American Sociological Review* 82(3): 476–510.

McDonnell, Erin Metz, and Gary Alan Fine. 2011. "Pride and Shame in Ghana: Collective Memory and Nationalism among Elite Students." *African Studies Review* 54(3): 121–142.

McDonnell, Erin Metz, and Luiz Vilaça. Forthcoming. "Pockets of Effectiveness and Islands of Integrity: Variation in Quality of Government within Central State Administrations." In *The Oxford Handbook of Quality of Government*, edited by Bo Rothstein, Monika Bauhr, and Andreas Bågenholm. Oxford: Oxford University Press.

McDonnell, Terence E. 2016. *Best Laid Plans: Cultural Entropy and the Unraveling of AIDS Media Campaigns*. Chicago: University of Chicago Press.

McGann, James G. 2018. "2017 Global Go To Think Tank Index Report." University of Pennsylvania.

McVeigh, Rory, Bryant Crubaugh, and Kevin Estep. 2017. "Plausibility Structures, Status Threats, and the Establishment of Anti-Abortion Pregnancy Centers." *American Journal of Sociology* 122(5): 1533–1571.

Metropolitan Police Act. 1839. London, U.K. Metropolitan Police Act.

Meyer, John W., J. Boli, G. M. Thomas, and F. O. Ramirez. 1997. "World Society and the Nation-State." *American Journal of Sociology* 103(1): 144–181.

Meyer, John W., and Brian Rowan. 1977. "Institutionalized Organizations: Formal Structure as Myth and Ceremony." *American Journal of Sociology* 83: 340–363.

Michigan Penal Code. 1931. The Michigan Penal Code Act 328. Vol. 750.

Migdal, Joel S. 1988. *Strong Societies and Weak States: State-Society Relations and State Capabilities in the Third World*. Princeton, NJ: Princeton University Press.

Migdal, Joel S. 2001. *State in Society: Studying How States and Societies Transform and Constitute One Another*. Cambridge, UK: Cambridge University Press.

Miliband, Ralph. 1969. *The State in Capitalist Society*. New York: Basic Books.

Mills, C. Wright. 1956. *The Power Elite*. New York: Oxford University Press.

Miranda, Rowan, and Allan Lerner. 1995. "Bureaucracy, Organizational Redundancy, and the Privatization of Public Services." *Public Administration Review* 55(2): 10–2307.

Mkandawire, Thandika. 2015. "Neopatrimonialism and the Political Economy of Economic Performance in Africa: Critical Reflections." *World Politics* 67(3): 563–612.

Monfrini, Enrico. 2008. "The Abacha Case." In *Recovering Stolen Assets*, edited by M. Pieth, 41–63. London: Peter Lang.

Morgan, Kimberly J., and Ann Shola Orloff. 2017. *The Many Hands of the State: Theorizing Political Authority and Social Control*. New York: Cambridge University Press.

Mukerji, Chandra. 2014. "The Cultural Power of Tacit Knowledge: Inarticulacy and Bourdieu's Habitus." *American Journal of Cultural Sociology* 2(3): 348–375.

Mungiu-Pippidi, Alina. 2015. *The Quest for Good Governance: How Societies Develop Control of Corruption*. Cambridge, UK: Cambridge University Press.

Nelson, Lori J., and Dale T. Miller. 1995. "The Distinctiveness Effect in Social Categorization: You Are What Makes You Unusual." *Psychological Science* 6(4): 246–249.

Ninsin, Kwame A. 1987. "Ghanaian Politics After 1981: Revolution or Evolution?" *Canadian Journal of African Studies / Revue Canadienne Des Études Africaines* 21(1): 17–37.

NOI-Polls. 2017. "NOI-Polls: Excerpts from the Results of the NOIPolls 2017 National Poll." https://www.noi-polls.com/root/index.php?pid=468&ptid=1&parentid=14. Accessed January 12, 2019.

North, Douglass C. 1991. "Institutions." *Journal of Economic Perspectives* 5(1): 97–112.

Norton, Michael I., Daniel Mochon, and Dan Ariely. 2012. "The IKEA Effect: When Labor Leads to Love." *Journal of Consumer Psychology* 22(3): 453–460.

Nunes, Edson de Oliveira. 1984. "Bureaucratic Insulation and Clientelism in Contemporary Brazil: Uneven State-Building and the Taming of Modernity." Doctoral Dissertation, University of California Berkeley, Berkeley, CA.

Oberfield, Zachary W. 2011. "Socialization and Self-Selection: How Police Officers Develop Their Views About Using Force." *Administration & Society* 44(6): 702–730.

Ocasio, William. 1997. "Towards an Attention-Based View of the Firm." *Strategic Management Journal* 18(S1): 187–206.

Ochieng, Cosmas Milton Obote. 2010. "The Political Economy of Contract Farming in Tea in Kenya: The Kenya Tea Development Agency (KTDA), 1964–2002." In *The Comparative Political Economy of Development: Africa and South Asia*, edited by B. Harriss-White and J. Heyer, 136–157. London: Routledge.

O'Donnell, Guillermo A. 2004. "Why the Rule of Law Matters." *Journal of Democracy* 15(4): 32–46.

Ody-Brasier, Amandine, and Isabel Fernandez-Mateo. 2017. "When Being in the Minority Pays Off: Relationships among Sellers and Price Setting in the Champagne Industry." *American Sociological Review* 82(1): 147–178.

Ogundipe, Sola. 2014. "How Misdiagnosis Killed Akunyili." *Vanguard News*. https://www.vanguardngr.com/2014/06/misdiagnosis-killed-akunyili/. Accessed March 9, 2018.

Ostrom, Elinor, and Xavier Basurto. 2011. "Crafting Analytical Tools to Study Institutional Change." *Journal of Institutional Economics* 7(3): 317–343.

Overmier, J. Bruce, and Martin E. Seligman. 1967. "Effects of Inescapable Shock upon Subsequent Escape and Avoidance Responding." *Journal of Comparative and Physiological Psychology* 63(1): 28.

Owusu, Francis. 2006. "On Public Organizations in Ghana: What Differentiates Good Performers from Poor Performers?" *African Development Review* 18(3): 471–485.

Padgett, John Frederick, and Walter W Powell. 2012. *The Emergence of Organizations and Markets.* Princeton, NJ: Princeton University Press.

Paiva, Márcia de. 2012. "BNDES: Um Banco de História e Do Futuro." Ministério do Desenvolvimento, Indústria e Comércio Exterior. São Paulo: Museu da Pessoa.

Panizza, Ugo, Rafael di Tella, and Caroline Van Rijckeghem. 2001. "Public Sector Wages and Bureaucratic Quality: Evidence from Latin America [with Comments]." *Economía* 2(1): 97–151.

Parkinson, C. Northcote. 1955. "Parkinson's Law." *The Economist.* November 19.

Pascale, Richard T., Jerry Sternin, and Monique Sternin. 2010. *The Power of Positive Deviance: How Unlikely Innovators Solve the World's Toughest Problems.* Cambridge, MA: Harvard University Press.

Paul, Samuel. 1982. *Managing Development Programs: The Lessons of Success.* Boulder, CO: Westview Press.

Peiffer, Caryn, and Rosita Armytage. 2019. "Searching for Success: A Mixed Methods Approach to Identifying and Examining Positive Outliers in Development Outcomes" *World Development* 121: 97–107.

Perlman, Baron, and E. Alan Hartman. 1982. "Burnout: Summary and Future Research." *Human Relations* 35(4): 283–305.

Peter, Hupe, Michael Hill, and Aurélien Buffat. 2015. *Understanding Street-Level Bureaucracy.* Chicago: Policy Press.

Pierson, Paul, and Theda Skocpol. 2002. "Historical Institutionalism in Contemporary Political Science." *Political Science: The State of the Discipline* 3: 693–721.

Piff, Paul K., Daniel M. Stancato, Stéphane Côté, Rodolfo Mendoza-Denton, and Dacher Keltner. 2012. "Higher Social Class Predicts Increased Unethical Behavior." *Proceedings of the National Academy of Sciences* 109(11): 4086–4091.

Pinto, Rogerio Feital S. 1969. "The Political Ecology of the Brazilian National Bank for Development (BNDE)." North Carolina, Department of Political Science.

Pitcher, Anne, Mary H. Moran, and Michael Johnston. 2009. "Rethinking Patrimonialism and Neopatrimonialism in Africa." *African Studies Review* 52(1): 125–156.

Pogoson, Aituaje Irene, and Michael Roll. 2014. "Turning Nigeria's Drug Sector Around: The National Agency for Food and Drug Administration and Control (NAFDAC)." In *The Politics of Public Sector Performance,* edited by Michael Roll, 97–127. London: Routledge.

Polillo, Simone, and Mauro F. Guillén. 2005. "Globalization Pressures and the State: The Worldwide Spread of Central Bank Independence." *American Journal of Sociology* 110(6): 1764–1802.

Pollitt, Christopher, Colin Talbot, Janice Caulfield, and Amanda Smullen. 2004. *Agencies: How Governments Do Things through Semi-Autonomous Organizations.* New York: Palgrave MacMillan.

Portes, Alejandro. 2006. "Institutions and Development: A Conceptual Reanalysis." *Population and Development Review* 32(2): 233–262.

Portes, Alejandro. 2015. "The Sociology of Development: From Modernization to the 'Institutional Turn.'" *Sociology of Development* 1(1): 20–42.

Poulantzas, N. 1973. *Political Power and Social Classes.* Trans. T. O'Hagan. London: NLB.

Powell, Walter W., and Robert Gibbons. 2019. "Organizations and Their Effectiveness | Center for Advanced Study in the Behavioral Sciences." Accessed April 7, 2019 (https://casbs.stanford.edu/projects/summer-institutes/organizations-and-their-effectiveness).

Prah, Kwesi Kwaa. 2010. "Multilingualism in Urban Africa: Bane or Blessing." *Journal of Multicultural Discourses* 5(2): 169–82.

Prasad, Monica. 2018. "Problem-Solving Sociology." *Contemporary Sociology* 47(4): 393–398.

Price, Robert M. 1975. *Society and Bureaucracy in Contemporary Ghana.* Los Angeles: University of California Press.

Quadagno, Jill. 1987. "Theories of the Welfare State." *Annual Review of Sociology* 13: 109–28.

Rapoza, Kenneth. 2017. "Brazil's New 'World Bank'-Sized Crisis." *Forbes.* https://www.forbes.com/sites/kenrapoza/2017/05/31/brazils-new-world-bank-sized-crisis/. Accessed January 12, 2019.

Rauch, James, and Peter Evans. 2000. "Bureaucratic Structure and Bureaucratic Performance in Less Developed Countries." *Journal of Public Economics* 75: 49–71.

Reber, Arthur S. 1989. "Implicit Learning and Tacit Knowledge." *Journal of Experimental Psychology: General* 118(3): 219.

Reno, William S. 1995. *Corruption and State Politics in Sierra Leone.* African Studies Series 83. New York: Cambridge University Press.

Ricks, Jacob I. 2017. "Sector-Specific Development and Policy Vulnerability in the Philippines." *Development and Change* 48(3): 567–589.

Robinson, Mark. 2007. "The Politics of Successful Governance Reforms: Lessons of Design and Implementation." *Commonwealth & Comparative Politics* 45(4): 521–548.

Roethlisberger, Fritz Jules, and William J. Dickson. 1939. *Management and the Worker.* Cambridge, MA: Harvard University Press.

Rogers, Everett M. 2003. *Diffusion of Innovations.* 5th ed. New York: Simon and Schuster.

Roll, Michael. 2014. *The Politics of Public Sector Performance: Pockets of Effectiveness in Developing Countries.* New York: Routledge.

Roll, Michael. 2018. "Gender & Corruption." Conference Presentation. Northwestern University Workshop on Islands of Integrity. Chicago. April 20, 2018.

Rothchild, Donald. 1969. "Ethnic Inequalities in Kenya." *The Journal of Modern African Studies* 7(4): 689–711.

Rothstein, Bo. 2011. "Anti-Corruption: The Indirect 'Big Bang' Approach." *Review of International Political Economy.* 18(2): 228–250.

Rothstein, Bo, and Aiysha Varraich. 2017. *Making Sense of Corruption.* Cambridge, UK: Cambridge University Press.

Rucker, Lloyd, and Johanna Shapiro. 2003. "Becoming a Physician: Students' Creative Projects in a Third-Year IM Clerkship." *Academic Medicine* 78(4): 391–397.

Rueschemeyer, Dietrich. 1986. *Power and the Division of Labour.* Redwood City, CA: Stanford University Press.

Rueschemeyer, Dietrich. 2005. "Building States—Inherently a Long-Term Process? An Argument from Theory." In *States and Development: Historical Antecedents of Stagnation and Advance,* edited by Matthew Lange and Dietrich Rueschemeyer, 143–164. New York: Palgrave Macmillan.

Samatar, Abdi Ismail, and Sophie Oldfield. 1995. "Class and Effective State Institutions: The Botswana Meat Commission." *Journal of Modern African Studies* 33(4): 651–668.

Samuels, David J. 2002. "Pork Barreling Is Not Credit Claiming or Advertising: Campaign Finance and the Sources of the Personal Vote in Brazil." *Journal of Politics* 64(3): 845–863.

Schaufeli, Wilmar B., Michael P. Leiter, and Christina Maslach. 2009. "Burnout: 35 Years of Research and Practice." *Career Development International* 14(3): 204–220.

Schneider, Ben Ross. 1992. *Politics within the State: Elite Bureaucrats and Industrial Policy in Authoritarian Brazil.* Pittsburgh, PA: University of Pittsburgh Press.

Schneider, Ben Ross. 1993. "The Career Connection: A Comparative Analysis of Bureaucratic Preferences and Insulation." *Comparative Politics* 25(3): 331–350.

Schniederjans, M. J., A. M. Schniederjans, and D. G. Schniederjans. 2015. *Outsourcing and Insourcing in an International Context*. London and New York: Taylor & Francis.

Schrank, Andrew. 2016. "Imported Institutions: Boon or Bane in the Developing World?" Conference paper, Harvard University. Workshop on Weak Institutions in Latin America. Cambridge, MA. May 9–10, 2016.

Schulze, Günther G., and Björn Frank. 2003. "Deterrence versus Intrinsic Motivation: Experimental Evidence on the Determinants of Corruptibility." *Economics of Governance* 4(2): 143–160.

Schumpeter, Joseph Alois. 1939. *Business Cycles*. Vol. 1. New York: McGraw-Hill.

Schumpeter, Joseph Alois. 1991. *The Economics and Sociology of Capitalism*. Edited by R. Swedberg. Princeton, NJ: Princeton University Press.

Scott, James C. 1999. *Seeing like a State: How Certain Schemes to Improve the Human Condition Have Failed*. New Haven, CT: Yale University Press.

Scott, W. Richard. 1985. "Systems within Systems: The Mental Health Sector." *American Behavioral Scientist* 28: 601–618.

Selznick, Philip. 1949. *TVA and the Grass Roots*. Berkeley: University of California Press.

Selznick, Philip. 1957. *Leadership in Administration: A Sociological Interpretation*. Berkeley: University of California Press.

Sewell Jr., William H. 1992. "A Theory of Structure: Duality, Agency, and Transformation." *American Journal of Sociology* 98(1): 1–29.

Siegel, Gilbert B. "The Vicissitudes of Governmental Reform in Brazil: A Study of the DASP." Ph.D. Dissertation, University of Southern California, 1966.

Simmel, Georg. 1955. *Conflict and the Web of Group Affiliations*. Trans. K. Wolff and R. Bendix. New York: Free Press.

Simon, Bernd, and David L. Hamilton. 1994. "Self-Stereotyping and Social Context: The Effects of Relative in-Group Size and in-Group Status." *Journal of Personality and Social Psychology* 66(4): 699.

Simon, Herbert A. 1947. *Administrative Behavior: A Study of Decision-Making Processes in Administrative Organization*. New York: Free Press.

Simon, Herbert A. 1972. "Theories of Bounded Rationality." *Decision and Organization* 1(1): 161–176.

Simon, Herbert Alexander. 1982. *Models of Bounded Rationality: Empirically Grounded Economic Reason*. Cambridge, MA: MIT Press.

Singh, Prerna. 2015. "Subnationalism and Social Development: A Comparative Analysis of Indian States." *World Politics* 67(3): 506–562.

Singh, Prerna. 2016. *How Solidarity Works for Welfare: Subnationalism and Social Development in India*. New York: Cambridge University Press.

Sir Richard Dane in China. 1919. "Sir Richard Dane in China." *The Nation*, February 22, 159.

Sivers, Derek. 2010."How to Start a Movement." Presented at the TED2010, February.

Skidmore, Thomas E. 1967. *Politics in Brazil, 1930–1964: An Experiment in Democracy*. New York: Oxford University Press.

Skocpol, Theda. 1995. *Protecting Soldiers and Mothers*. Cambridge, MA: Harvard University Press.

Skocpol, Theda 2016. Section on Comparative-Historical Sociology Invited Session. Honoring the 50th Anniversary of Barrington Moore's *Social Origins of Dictatorship and Democracy*. American Sociological Association Annual Meeting, Seattle, WA. August 20–23, 2016.

Skocpol, Theda, and Kenneth Finegold. 1982. "State Capacity and Economic Intervention in the Early New Deal." *Political Science Quarterly* 97(2): 255–78.

Skowronek, Stephen. 1982. *Building a New American State: The Expansion of National Administrative Capacities, 1877–1920*. Cambridge, UK: Cambridge University Press.

Slater, Dan. 2010. *Ordering Power: Contentious Politics and Authoritarian Leviathans in Southeast Asia*. New York: Cambridge University Press.

Slotten, Hugh Richard. 1994. *Patronage, Practice, and the Culture of American Science: Alexander Dallas Bache and the US Coast Survey*. New York: Cambridge University Press.

Smith, Christian. 1998. *American Evangelicalism: Embattled and Thriving*. Chicago: University of Chicago Press.

Smith, Daniel Jordan. 2010. *A Culture of Corruption: Everyday Deception and Popular Discontent in Nigeria*. Princeton, NJ: Princeton University Press.

Smith, Eliot R., and Susan Henry. 1996. "An In-Group Becomes Part of the Self: Response Time Evidence." *Personality and Social Psychology Bulletin* 22(6): 635–642.

Sørensen, Jesper. 2015. Personal Communication to Author. October 15, 2015.

Spillane, James P., Brian J. Reiser, and Todd Reimer. 2002. "Policy Implementation and Cognition: Reframing and Refocusing Implementation Research." *Review of Educational Research* 72(3): 387–431.

Steinmetz, George, ed. 1999. *State/Culture: State-Formation after the Cultural Turn*. Ithaca, NY: Cornell University Press.

Stiglitz, Joseph. 1989. "Principal and Agent." In *Allocation, Information and Markets*, edited by J. Eatwell, M. Milgate, and P. Newman, 241–253. London: Palgrave Macmillan.

Stinchcombe, Arthur L. 1965. "Social Structures and Organizations." In *Handbook of Organizations*, edited by J. G. March, 142–193. Chicago: Rand McNally.

Strauss, Julia C. 1998. *Strong Institutions in Weak Polities: State Building in Republican China, 1927–1940*. New York: Oxford University Press.

Strauss, Julia C. 2018. Personal Communication. November 8, 2018.

Sutton, Robert I., and Hayagreeva Rao. 2016. *Scaling up Excellence: Getting to More without Settling for Less*. New York: Random House.

Swedberg, Richard, and Ola Agevall. 2016. *The Max Weber Dictionary: Key Words and Central Concepts*. Redwood City, CA: Stanford University Press.

Swidler, Ann, and Susan Cotts Watkins. 2009. " 'Teach a Man to Fish' ": The Sustainability Doctrine and Its Social Consequences." *World Development* 37(7): 1182–1196.

Syverson, Chad. "What Determines Productivity?" *Journal of Economic Literature* 49, no. 2 (June 2011): 326–365. https://doi.org/10.1257/jel.49.2.326.

Taliercio, Robert. 2004a. *Designing Performance: The Semi-Autonomous Revenue Authority Model in Africa and Latin America*. Washington, DC: World Bank Publications.

Taliercio, Robert R. 2004b. "Administrative Reform as Credible Commitment: The Impact of Autonomy on Revenue Authority Performance in Latin America." *Part Special Issue: Island Studies* 32(2): 213–32.

Taylor, Frederick Winslow. 1914. *The Principles of Scientific Management*. New York: Harper & Brothers.

Taylor, R. B., O. Shakoor, R. H. Behrens, M. Everard, A. S. Low, J. Wangboonskul, R. G. Reid, and J. A. Kolawole. 2001. "Pharmacopoeial Quality of Drugs Supplied by Nigerian Pharmacies." *The Lancet* 357(9272): 1933–1936.

Teichman, Eric. 1938. *Affairs of China: A Survey of the Recent History and Present Circumstances of the Republic of China*. New York: Routledge.

Tendler, Judith. 1997. *Good Government in the Tropics*. Baltimore: Johns Hopkins University Press.

Teorell, Jan. 2007. *Corruption as an Institution: Rethinking the Nature and Origins of the Grabbing Hand*. Gothenburg, Sweden: The Quality of Government Institute.

Tepper, Steven J. 2011. *Not Here, Not Now, Not That!: Protest over Art and Culture in America.* Chicago: University of Chicago Press.

Therkildsen, Ole. 2004. "Autonomous Tax Administration in Sub-Saharan Africa: The Case of the Uganda Revenue Authority." *Forum for Development Studies.* 31(1): 59–88.

Thornton, P.H., and W. Ocasio. 2008. *"Institutional Logics" in The SAGE Handbook of Organizational Institutionalism,* edited by Royston Greenwood, Christine Oliver, Kerstin Sahlin, and Soy Suddaby, 99–129. London: Sage.

Tilcsik, András. 2010. "From Ritual to Reality: Demography, Ideology, and Decoupling in a Post-Communist Government Agency." *Academy of Management Journal* 53(6): 1474–1498.

Tilly, Charles. 1990. *Coercion, Capital and European States. AD 990–1992.* Cambridge, MA: Basil Blackwell.

Transparency International. 2018. "Corruption Perceptions Index 2018," https://www.transparency.org/cpi2018.

Treisman, Daniel. 2007. "What Have We Learned About the Causes of Corruption from Ten Years of Cross-National Empirical Research?" *Annual Review of Political Science* 10(1): 211–244.

Uphoff, Norman. 1994. *Puzzles of Productivity in Public Organizations.* San Francisco: ICS Press.

Uphoff, Norman, Milton J. Esman, and Anirudh Krishna. 1998. *Reasons for Success: Learning from Instructive Experiences in Rural Development.* West Hartford, CT: Kumarian Press.

Uzzi, Brian, and Jarrett Spiro. 2005. "Collaboration and Creativity: The Small World Problem." *American Journal of Sociology* 111(2): 447–504.

Vaisey, Stephen. 2009. "Motivation and Justification: A Dual-Process Model of Culture in Action." *American Journal of Sociology* 114(6): 1675–1715.

Vandenabeele, Wouter. 2007. "Toward a Public Administration Theory of Public Service Motivation: An Institutional Approach." *Public Management Review* 9(4): 545–556.

Van de Walle, Nicolas. 2007. "Meet the New Boss, Same as the Old Boss? The Evolution of Political Clientelism in Africa." In *Patrons, Clients and Policies: Patterns of Democratic Accountability and Political Competition,* edited by H. Kitschelt, S. I. Wilkinson, and P. of P. S. and I. A. S. I. Wilkinson, 50–67. New York: Cambridge University Press.

Van Rijckeghem, Caroline, and Beatrice Weder. 2001. "Bureaucratic Corruption and the Rate of Temptation: Do Wages in the Civil Service Affect Corruption, and by How Much?" *Journal of Development Economics* 65(2): 307–331.

Vaughan, Diane. 1990. "Autonomy, Interdependence, and Social Control: NASA and the Space Shuttle Challenger." *Administrative Science Quarterly* 35(2): 225–257.

Vedres, Balazs, and David Stark. 2010. "Structural Folds: Generative Disruption in Overlapping Groups." *American Journal of Sociology* 115(4): 1150–1190.

Verhoest, Koen, B. Guy Peters, Geert Bouckaert, and Bram Verschuere. 2004. "The Study of Organisational Autonomy: A Conceptual Review." *Public Administration and Development* 24(2): 101–118.

Volpicelli, Joseph R., Ronald R. Ulm, Aidan Altenor, and Martin EP Seligman. 1983. "Learned Mastery in the Rat." *Learning and Motivation* 14(2): 204–222.

Wade, Robert. 1990. *Governing the Market: Economic Theory and the Role of Government in East Asian Industrialization.* 2nd ed. Princeton, NJ: Princeton University Press.

Wahrlich, Beatriz. 1983. Reforma Administrativa Na Era de Vargas. Rio de Janeiro, RJ: FGV.

Watkins-Hayes, Celeste. 2009. *The New Welfare Bureaucrats: Entanglements of Race, Class, and Policy Reform.* Chicago: University of Chicago Press.

Weber, Klaus, Gerald F. Davis, and and Michael Lounsbury. 2009. "Policy as Myth and Ceremony? The Global Spread of Stock Exchanges, 1980–2005." *Academy of Management Journal* 52(6): 1319–47.

Weber, Max. [1930] 2012. *The Protestant Ethic and the Spirit of Capitalism.* Trans. Talcott Parsons. New York: Routledge.

Weber, Max. 1956. "Speech to Verein für Sozialpolitik." In *Max Weber and German Politics: A Study in Political Sociology*, edited by J. P. Mayer, 125–131. London: Faber and Faber Ltd.

Weber, Max. 1978. *Economy and Society: An Outline of Interpretive Sociology.* Berkeley, CA: University of California Press.

Weber, Max, and S. N. Eisenstadt. 1968. *On Charisma and Institution Building.* Chicago: University of Chicago Press.

Werbner, Richard. 2004. *Reasonable Radicals and Citizenship in Botswana: The Public Anthropology of Kalanga Elites.* Bloomington: Indiana University Press.

Westphal, James D., and Edward J. Zajac. 1994. "Substance and Symbolism in CEOs' Long-Term Incentive Plans." *Administrative Science Quarterly* 39(3): 367–390.

Westphal, James D., and Edward J. Zajac. 2001. "Decoupling Policy from Practice: The Case of Stock Repurchase Programs." *Administrative Science Quarterly* 46(2): 202–228.

White, Leonard. 1954. *The Jacksonians: A Study of Administrative History: 1829–1861.* New York: Macmillan.

Widner, Jennifer. 2018. "Innovations for Successful Societies." *Innovations for Successful Societies Lab.* https://successfulsocieties.princeton.edu/. Accessed April 7, 2019

Willis, Eliza J. 1986. "The State as Banker: The Expansion of the Public Sector in Brazil." Ph.D. Dissertation, University of Texas at Austin.

Willis, Eliza J. 1995. "Explaining Bureaucratic Independence in Brazil: The Experience of the National Economic Development Bank." *Journal of Latin American Studies* 27(3): 625–661.

Willis, Eliza J. 2014. "An Enduring Pocket of Effectiveness: The Case of the National Development Bank of Brazil (BNDE)." In *The Politics of Public Sector Performance: Pockets of Effectiveness in Developing Countries*, edited by M. Roll, 74–96. London: Routledge.

Wohl, Hannah. 2015. "Community Sense: The Cohesive Power of Aesthetic Judgment." *Sociological Theory* 33(4): 299–326.

Woo-Cumings, Meredith, ed. 1999. *The Developmental State.* Ithaca, NY: Cornell University Press.

World Bank. 1997. *World Development Report 1997: The State in a Changing World.* Washington, DC: World Bank.

World Bank. 1999–2007. *Governance and Anti-Corruption Diagnostic Survey Series.* Washington DC: World Bank.

World Bank. 2002. *World Development Report 2002: Building Institutions for Markets.* Washington DC: World Bank.

World Bank. 2003. *World Development Report 2003: Sustainable Development in a Dynamic World.* Washington, DC: World Bank.

World Bank. 2014. *Inclusive Business Case Study: Kenya Tea Development Agency Ltd.* Washington DC: World Bank Group.

Wrong, Michela. 2009. *It's Our Turn to Eat.* London: Fourth Estate.

Wuthnow, Robert. 1989. *Meaning and Moral Order: Explorations in Cultural Analysis.* Berkeley: University of California Press.

Young, Crawford. 1994. *The African Colonial State in Comparative Perspective.* New Haven, CT: Yale University Press.

Young, Crawford. 2012. *The Postcolonial State in Africa: Fifty Years of Independence, 1960–2010.* Madison: University of Wisconsin Press.

Zacka, Bernardo. 2017. *When the State Meets the Street: Public Service and Moral Agency.* Cambridge, MA: Harvard University Press.

Zaloznaya, Marina. 2017. *The Politics of Bureaucratic Corruption in Post-Transitional Eastern Europe*. New York: Cambridge University Press.

Zerubavel, Eviatar. 2009. *Social Mindscapes: An Invitation to Cognitive Sociology*. Cambridge, MA: Harvard University Press.

Zuckerman, Ezra W. 2016. "Optimal Distinctiveness Revisited." *The Oxford Handbook of Organizational Identity*, edited by Michael G. Pratt, Majken Schultz, Blake E. Ashforth, and Davide Ravasi, 183–199. Oxford: Oxford University Press.

INDEX

Italic pagination refers to figures and tables.

Abacha, Sani, 147–48
absenteeism, 110, 121–22, 225
Accra, 37, 45–46, 87, 93, 195–96, 234–35
Acquah, George Kingsley, 45, 152–53, 216, 233
Acquah, Paul, 40, 129, 154, 167, 188, 216, 233
Adisadel College, 234
Administrative Department of Public Service (DASP), 117–18, 198–200, 251n32
agriculture, 245n122; Brazilian National Economic Development Bank (BNDE) and, 119; ecological diversity and, 12; elitism and, 157; extension agents and, 212; fertilizer and, 220; Gates Foundation and, 208; Kenya Tea Development Authority (KTDA) and, 106, 112, 145–46, 155, 183; methodologies and, 232; Ministry of Agriculture and, 119, 145, 155, 157, 214, 220–21; Policy Analysis and Research Division (PARD) and, 153; subsistence, 26; U.S. Department of Agriculture (USDA) and, 141, 215; U.S. Food and Drug Administration (FDA) and, 13–14, 157–58; U.S. New Deal Agricultural Adjustment Agency and, 215, 233, 253n39; water quality and, 210
Akunyili, Dora: bribery of brother-in-law of, 110; death of, 247n65; dual habitus and, 169; education of, 169, 172; leadership style of, 167; National Agency for Food and Drug Administration and Control (NAFDAC) and, 107, 109, 111, 113, 129, 148, 172, 180–81, 183, 189, 206; reform and, 107
Alternative Dispute Resolution (ADR), 67, 99–100, 127, 177–78, 196
American Political Development (APD), 16, 214–15, 253n34
American Sociological Association, 32

Anderson, Elijah, 91
autarquias, 142–43
autonomy: binary, 246n10; Brazilian National Economic Development Bank (BNDE) and, 120, 161; bureaucratic ethos and, 8, 20, 213; bureaucratic niches and, 204; Carpenter on, 215; de facto, 136–37, 142–46, 155, 160, 164; de jure, 140, 142, 145–46, 164; elitism and, 8, 135–47, 154–57, 160–64; external constraints and, 137; Fukuyama on, 248n2; group style and, 83; interstitial niches and, 216–17; Kenya Tea Development Authority (KTDA) and, 115, 161–62; labor pool and, 30; National Agency for Food and Drug Administration and Control (NAFDAC) and, 161–62; neopatrimonialism and, 23; New Public Management and, 138; pockets of effectiveness and, 20, 195; Policy Analysis and Research Division (PARD) and, 161; Salt Inspectorate and, 161–62; use of term, 139

Bank of Brazil, 200
Bank of Ghana: Acquah and, 40, 129, 154, 188, 216, 233; comparison cases and, 110, 113, 129–30; cultivation and, 67, 241n13; dual habitus and, 167; elitism and, 136; leaders and, 167; methodologies and, 230, 231, 234; Monetary Policy Analysis and Financial Stability Department and, 12, 38, 129, 153–54; neopatrimonialism and, 136, 153–54; protection and, 103; recruitment and, 38–43, 51; reputation of, 38, 43–44; scholarship and, 209–10, 216
Belgium, 15
Benin, 18
best practices, 88, 127, 207, 224
Bolivia, 105

boundary marking: cultivation and, 61–70, 241n16; distinctive technologies as, 67–68; learned time culture and, 64–66; Policy Analysis and Research Division (PARD) and, 63; poor performers and, 68–70; symbolic time and, 61–64; technology and, 67–68; time culture and, 61–66

Bourdieu, Pierre, 24, 49, 168

Brazil, 237n18; comparison cases and, 106, 115–20; corruption and, 13, 116, 189, 197–98, 201; cultivation and, 62; dual habitus and, 169, 180, 182, 184; Kubitschek and, 115, 119–20, *141*, 142–44, 153, 158, 161, 163, 200; methodologies and, *232*; Ministry of Agriculture and, 119; Ministry of Public Works and, 119; neopatrimonialism and, 139, 142–44; pockets of effectiveness and, 189, 192–94, 197–201; private banks and, 13; scholarship and, 208, 212; slow pace of, 62–63; state-building and, 115–16; Superintendency of Money and Credit (SUMOC) and, 120; Vargas and, 108, 115–16, 118, 120, 134, 141–44, 148, 153, 164, 198–200, 244n42

Brazilian National Economic Development Bank (BNDE): administrative costs of, 116; Administrative Department of Public Service (DASP) and, 117–18, 198–200, 251n32; after loss of founding leaders, 189; agriculture and, 119; autonomy and, 120, 161; bureaucratic ethos of, 120; cadres and, 142; Campos and, 117, 143–44, 167, 169, 180, 182–83; clustering and, 117; comparison cases and, 106, 108, 115–20, 122, 130, 132, 134, 244nn44 and 47; corruption and, 244n47; Council of Development and, 120; cultivation and, 117–18, 132; domain expansion and, 193–94; dual habitus and, 167, 169, 172, 180, 182–83; education and, 118; elitism and, 142–44; exams and, 117, 122; Executive Groups and, 200; external opposition and, 132; Fund for Rehabilitation (FRE) and, 142; Getúlio Vargas Foundation (FGV) and, 118; growth of, 14; humanitarian aid and, 120; income and, 106, 116; incorruptibility and, 116; influence of, 116; leadership and, 167; as local guarantor, 209; Lopes and, 118, 169, 180, 198–200; meritocracy and, 117, 122; methodologies and, *232*; neopatrimonialism and, 141–44, 153, 158, 161, 163–64;

Paiva Teixeira and, 117, 143, 169, 180; patronage and, 13; Plan of Goals and, 144; pockets of effectiveness and, 21, 117, 134, 189, 193–94, 197–200, 244n44, 251n18; protection and, 119–20; Quadros and, 120; recruitment and, 117; reputation of, 116; return on assets of, 116; scholarship on, 143–44; spreading professionals and, 197; sweat equity and, 182–83; Torres and, 143, 167, 169, 172, 180; Vargas and, 108, 115–16, 118, 120, 134, 141–44, 153, 164, 198

bribery, 4–5, 10, 18–19, 41, 57, 59, 83, 108, 110, 161, 197, 203, 223, 227

Budget Division, 94–95, 101, *231*

bureaucracy: cognitive approach and, 6, 21, 25, 28, 105, 171, 177, 204–5, 221–24; corruption and, 6, 9, 15–16, 18, 22, 29, 38, 55, 70, 83, 105, 107, 109–10, 122, 128, 145, 162, 165, 201, 213, 223, 225; cultivation and, 53–57, 61, 63, 68, 70–83, 241nn13 and 36; distribution issues and, 6, 28–30, 34, 44, 105, 116, 139, 205; doing, 6, 8, 10, 54, 145, 168, 171, 176–78, 221–24; dual habitus and, 165–72, 175–86; interstitial, 6–7, 9, 14 (*see also* interstitial niches); labor pool and, 28; methodologies and, 229; need for more, 28; neopatrimonialism and, 138–39, 145, 149, 158–62; Nigeria and, 6; pockets of effectiveness and, 14, 187–201, 252n7; protection and, 85–91, 94–95, 98–110, 114, 116, 121–34; recruitment and, 27–31, 34–35, 38, 44–52, 240n36; reform and, 5, 8, 10–11, 16, 23–24, 54, 82, 107, 110, 126, 128, 134, 162, 166, 171, 179, 198–205, 214, 223; reputation of, 75; scholarship on, 202–27, 254n46; Weber on, 1, 9–10, 15, 35, 50, 54, 75, 83, 95, 102, 138, 165, 167, 202–5, 221, 229, 252n7. *See also specific organization*

bureaucratic ethos: absenteeism and, 110, 121–22, 225; after loss of founding leaders, 188–92; amplifying commonalities and, 77–80; autonomy and, 213; Brazilian National Economic Development Bank (BNDE) and, 120; clustered cadres and, 8; comparison cases and, 23, 104–6, 122, 126–29, 133; corruption and, 9, 16, 18, 22, 29, 55, 122, 128; cultivation and, 7–9, 22, 53–57, 75, 77–83, 241n13; dual habitus and, 166, 168, 171–72, 175–79, 186; education and, 127; group style and, 77–80; industrialized nations and, 10; ineffectiveness and, 5, 19, 28, 54, 93, 104, 128, 130, 135, 137, 220, 243; lived experience and,

8, 22, 54, 57, 83, 117, 168, 172, 176–77, 204, 217, 222; moral issues and, 4, 9; neopatrimonialism and, 6, 14, 212–13; niches and, 2–5; as ongoing project, 205; patchworking and, 6, 12, 14–17, 104, 225; patterns in, 18; pockets of effectiveness and, 24, 187–93, 197–201; protection and, 23, 86; recruitment and, 6, 22, 29–31, 52; reform and, 5, 8, 10–11, 16, 23–24, 54, 117, 126, 128, 166, 171, 179, 198, 202–5, 217; scholarship on, 202–5, 212–14, 217, 221–25, 254n16; self-comparison to, 9; subculture of, 6–7, 21–22, 31, 54, 56, 77, 106, 176, 188, 204–5, 218; sweat equity and, 182–83; tacit knowledge and, 8; variation in capacity and, 6; Weber on, 1, 9; work ethics and, 4

bureaucratic niches: agency failure and, 17–21; alternative foundations for action and, 7; autonomy and, 204; comparison cases and, 23, 104–5, 133–34; cultivation and, 6, 63, 81–82; diffusion of, 193–201; discipline and, 16, 23, 65, 85, 99–102, 227, 252–53, 253n41; dual habitus and, 166–67, 182, 184, 204; education and, 8, 24, 32, 90, 127, 168–72, 210; as interstitial niches, 21; lived experience and, 7–8, 22, 24, 54, 63, 78, 82–83, 168–72, 176–77, 204, 223; meritocracy and, 107; Ministry of Finance and Economic Planning (MOFEP) and, 2–3; neopatrimonialism and, 23, 139, 149, 160–62, 217; nonfinancial incentives and, 35–37; nonpecuniary motivations and, 37–38; organizational goals and, 2, 7–8, 22–24, 52, 83, 85–86, 127–28, 139, 159, 165, 208; as pockets of effectiveness, 21, 187, 193, 195, 197–98, 201; Policy Analysis and Research Division (PARD) and, 2–6, 12, 21, 202; protection and, 88, 103; recruitment and, 6–7, 22, 27–28; scale and, 193–201; scholarship on, 204, 210, 226–27

bureaucratic subcultures: clustered cadres and, 6, 22; comparison cases and, 13, 106, 119; cultivation and, 7, 22, 54, 56, 65, 74, 76–77, 131–33, 241n36; dual habitus and, 176; interstitial niches and, 2, 6–7, 13, 21–22, 31, 54, 56, 77, 106, 176, 188, 204–5, 241n36; organizational cultures and, 21; pockets of effectiveness and, 188; Policy Analysis and Research Division (PARD) and, 4; recruitment and, 31, 40; scholarship on, 204–5, 216, 218, 253n22

Burundi, 18

CACEX, 200

cadres: Brazilian National Economic Development Bank (BNDE) and, 142; clustered, 8, 24, 179–82; cognitive subcultures and, 204; dual habitus and, 7, 179–85, 204, 214; founding, 168, 180–87, 190, 198, 204, 206; pockets of effectiveness and, 187, 190, 198, 201; recruitment and, 215

Campos, Roberto de Oliveira, 117, 143–44, 167, 169, 180, 182–83

Cardoso, Fernando, 197

Carpenter, Daniel, 23, 139, *141*, 157–58, 161, 215

Car Wash Operation, 197

central banks: global economy and, 18; methodologies and, *231*, 233; neopatrimonialism and, 136, 161; pockets of effectiveness and, 188; recruitment and, 39–40, 42; scholarship and, 212. *See also* Bank of Ghana

charismatic authority, 20, 116, 152, 166–68, 184, 249n9

chasing, 3, 84, 86, 89–93, 102, 171

China, 237n18; bureaucratic ethos and, 6; comparison cases and, *106*, 107–8, 120–25, 131, 178–79; cultivation and, 55; dual habitus and, 169, 178–80; methodologies and, *232*; neopatrimonialism and, 6, 139, 149–51, 158; pockets of effectiveness and, 190, 198; Qing dynasty and, 120, 160; Salt Inspectorate and, 13–14 (*see also* Salt Inspectorate); scholarship and, 227; Sino-Japanese War and, 190; warlordism of, 13

China National Salt Industry Corporation, 190–91

Christians, 12, 233

civil service: *autarquias* and, 142; cultivation and, 64, 69; education and, 26–27, 32, 157, 169; ethnic issues and, 112–13; Kenya and, 112–13; neopatrimonialism and, 142, 154–55, 157; Office of the Head of Civil Service, 229; patronage and, 253n34; protection and, 92; recruitment and, 26, 30, 32, 37, 41, 47; reputation of, 11, 26–27, 57, 124, 229; salary issues and, 26–27, 57, 124, 142; scholarship on, 216

clientelism, 2, 128, 131, 152, 198

clustered cadres, 8, 24, 179–82

clustering: Brazilian National Economic Development Bank (BNDE) and, 117; comparison cases and, 23, 104–9, 113, 117, 122, 130, 133–34; cultivation and, 7–8, 53,

clustering (*continued*)
56–57, 61, 77, 79; distinctiveness and,
6–8, 19, 21–26, 38, 46, 53, 56, 61, 79,
85–86, 98–105, 117, 130, 133–34, 138–42,
156–59, 163, 165, 180, 182, 185, 190, 203,
205, 213–18, 225–26, 233; dual habitus
and, 24, 165, 168–71, 179–82, 185; education and, 8, 24, 30, 38, 157, 169, 171, 181,
214, 217; external projects of reshaping
and, 23, 85, 98–100, 102; group style
and, 22, 57, 77–80, 83, 106, 118, 183, 213;
influence effect and, 22, 54–57, 70, 79,
107; internal coping mechanisms and, 7,
23, 85, 89, 107, 125; interstitial niches
and, 77–80; Kenya Tea Development
Authority (KTDA) and, 113; labor pool
and, 30–31, 38, 204; lived experience
and, 8, 22, 24, 57, 117, 145, 168–71, 181,
217; meritocracy and, 113; neopatrimonialism and, 138–42, 145, 156–59, 163;
pockets of effectiveness and, 190; private
sector and, 109, 225; pro-bureaucratic
resources and, 6; protection and, 7–8,
85–86, 88, 98–103; pruning and, 7,
68–70, 107, 113, 123; recruitment and,
7–8, 21–23, 26, 28, 30, 38, 56, 86, 107,
109–10, 113, 117, 122–23, 171, 185, 204, 217;
Salt Inspectorate and, 122–23; scholarship on, 203–6, 213–18, 225–26; selection
effect and, 22, 34, 37–38, 55, 57, 70–74,
107, 122; subgroup support and, 216; tacit
knowledge and, 205
code switching, 89–92, 102
Cofie, Sandra, 45
cognitive approach: adverse events and,
242n51; bureaucracy and, 6, 21, 25, 28,
105, 171, 177, 204–5, 221–24; corruption
and, 252n3; cultivation and, 61, 79–80;
declarative cognition and, 223–24,
254n55; dual habitus and, 168–71, 175,
177, 250n38; in-group cohesion and, 133;
neopatrimonialism and, 141; pockets of
effectiveness and, 199; protection and,
102; recruitment and, 28–29; subcultures
and, 6, 204–5
colonialism, x, 4, 11, 14, 26, 112, 170, 178, 211,
237
Commission on Human Rights and Administrative Justice (CHRAJ), 46
Commonwealth Development Corporation
(CDC), 147, 153
communism, 53, 143, 190
comparison cases: Bank of Ghana and, 110,
113, 129–30; Brazil and, 106, 115–20;

Brazilian National Economic Development Bank (BNDE) and, 106, 108, 115–20,
122, 130, 132, 134, 244nn44 and 47;
bureaucratic ethos and, 23, 104–6, 122,
126–29, 133; bureaucratic niches and, 23,
104–5, 133–34; bureaucratic subcultures
and, 13, 106, 117, 119, 131–33; China and,
106, 120–22, 131, 178–79; clientelism and,
128, 131; clustering and, 23, 104–9, 113,
117, 122, 130, 133–34; corruption and,
105–10, 113, 116, 120–25, 128–31, 243n4,
244n47; cultivation and, 110–11; elitism
and, 108, 114, 116, 123–27, 132; external
opposition and, 131–33; Ghanaian Commercial Courts and, 127–30; hard work
and, 107–8, 111; innovation and, 115,
126–28; interstitial niches and, 106, 119,
127; Kenya and, 106, 112–13, 120, 127, 132,
178–79, 243n4; Kenya Tea Development
Authority (KTDA) and, 106–7, 112–15,
120, 123, 125, 127, 130, 132–33; Ministry
of Finance and Economic Planning
(MOFEP) and, 130; Monetary Policy
Analysis and Financial Stability Department and, 129–30; National Agency for
Food and Drug Administration and
Control (NAFDAC) and, 106–13, 122–23,
125–31, 134; National Communications
Authority (NCA) and, 113, 129–30; neopatrimonialism and, 105–7, 128, 138; new
insights from, 126–33; Nigeria and, 106,
108–11, 131; organizational goals and,
127–28; patronage and, 105–7, 112–13,
116, 120, 122–23, 125, 129, 132; pockets of
effectiveness and, 23, 105, 117, 134; Policy
Analysis and Research Division (PARD)
and, 113, 130; private sector and, 109, 114,
119–20; protection and, 111–12; public
interest and, 105, 111; recruitment and,
23, 107, 109–10, 113, 117, 122–23; reform
and, 107, 110, 117, 121–23, 126–34, 243n4;
reputation and, 106–7, 116–20, 124,
128–30; Salt Inspectorate and, *106*,
107–8, 120–25, 129; taxes and, *106*,
120–26, 129–31
competition, 112, 114, 174, 220
cooptation, 101–2, 115, 119
corruption: agency failure and, 18–21; Brazil
and, 13, 116, 189, 197–98, 201; Brazilian
National Economic Development Bank
(BNDE) and, 244n47; bribery and, 4–5,
10, 18–19, 41, 57, 59, 83, 108, 110, 161, 197,
203, 223, 227; bureaucracy and, 6, 9,
15–16, 18, 22, 29, 38, 55, 70, 83, 105, 107,

109–10, 122, 128, 145, 162, 165, 201, 213, 223, 225; Car Wash Operation and, 197; clientelism and, 2, 128, 131, 152, 198; cognitive approach and, 252n3; comparison cases and, 105–10, 113, 116, 120–25, 128–31, 243n4, 244n47; cultivation and, 55, 58–60, 70, 76, 79–80, 83; dual habitus and, 165, 248n2; embezzlement and, 147–48; Ghana and, 2, 5, 13, 15, 18–19, 22, 38, 105, 110, 113, 125, 130, 156, 213; income and, 105, 116, 156, 204; incorruptibility and, 22, 29, 79, 107, 116, 145; ineffectiveness and, 5, 19, 28, 54, 93, 104, 128, 130, 135, 137, 220, 243; Kenya and, 113, 243n4; Kenyatta and, 112; Klitgaard formula of, 205; larger environment and, 6; methodologies and, 232; Million Acre Settlement Scheme and, 112; money laundering and, 148, 197; monopolies and, 18, 126, 191, 205; neopatrimonialism and, 136, 145, 148, 156, 162; nepotism and, 4, 19, 41–42, 110; Nigeria and, 13; organizational goals and, 9; organizational subcultures and, 4; pockets of effectiveness and, 189, 197, 201; Policy Analysis and Research Division (PARD) and, 5, 59, 130; prescriptive model for, 223; racketeering and, 9; recruitment and, 38, 41–42, 46; rents and, 9; Salt Inspectorate and, 13, 19, 107, 122–25, 129, 156, 162, 201; scholarship on, 5, 20, 205, 211, 213, 223, 225, 252n3; Serious Fraud Office and, 46; state capacity and, 5; taxes and, 18, 120, 125, 129, 162; *Yanwu Shu* and, 121–22
cost-benefit analysis, 1, 22, 37–38, 97, 101, 176, 204
coups, 11, 147, 159
Court of Appeals, 188, 231, 251n1
cultivation: amplifying commonalities and, 77–80; Bank of Ghana and, 67, 241n13; boundary marking and, 61–70, 241n16; Brazil and, 62; Brazilian National Economic Development Bank (BNDE) and, 117–18, 132; bureaucracy and, 53–57, 61, 63, 68, 70–83, 241nn13 and 36; bureaucratic ethos and, 7–9, 22, 53–57, 75, 77–83, 241n13; bureaucratic niches and, 6, 63, 81–82; bureaucratic subcultures and, 7, 22, 54, 56, 65, 74, 76–77, 131–33, 241n36; China and, 55; civil service and, 64, 69; clustering and, 7–8, 53, 56–57, 61, 77, 79; cognitive approach and, 61, 79–80; comparison cases and, 110–11; corruption and, 55, 58–60, 70, 76, 79–80,

83; discipline and, 65, 68–71, 73; efficacy and, 80–82; ethnic issues and, 51; experienced efficacy and, 80–82; external opposition and, 131–33; Ghanaian Commercial Courts and, 60–62, 66–76, 79; Goffmanian approach and, 107–8; group style and, 77–80, 83; hard work and, 60, 62, 64, 66; influence effect and, 54–57, 70, 79; innovation and, 67–68; internal, 131–33; interstitial niches and, 58–65, 68, 70–71, 74–83; Karanja and, 114; Kenya Tea Development Authority (KTDA) and, 114, 131–33; learning by emulation and, 57–61; lived experience and, 54, 57, 72, 78, 80–83, 204–5; Ministry of Finance and Economic Planning (MOFEP) and, 59, 63; Monetary Policy Analysis and Financial Stability Department and, 68; National Agency for Food and Drug Administration and Control (NAFDAC) and, 110–11, 131; National Communications Authority (NCA) and, 58, 62, 65, 75; neopatrimonialism and, 56, 61, 68, 70, 78, 83, 241n35; organizational goals and, 55; pockets of effectiveness and, 42; Policy Analysis and Research Division (PARD) and, 57–65, 69, 75; pride in comparison and, 74–77; principal-agent models and, 54–55, 72; private sector and, 70; productivity and, 62–63, 69–70, 123; public interest and, 55; public service and, 57, 80; recruitment and, 56, 65, 68; reform and, 54, 66, 82; reputation and, 57–61, 65, 71, 75–76; Salt Inspectorate and, 123–24; selection effect and, 55, 57, 70–74; small-group acculturation and, 54–57, 71; sociological conceptualization and, 54–57; tacit knowledge and, 54, 82; technology and, 64–68, 70, 72, 81; time culture and, 61–66; Weber and, 54, 75, 83
customs, 5–6, 18, 87, 150

Dane, Richard: administrative costs and, 150; elitism and, 151, 156, 169; protection and, 121; Salt Inspectorate and, 121, 150–51, 156, 167, 169, 178–80, 183, 189–91, 194, 249n6
Danida, 152, 209
declarative cognition, 223–24, 254n55
decoupling, 203, 210, 221, 226, 233, 240n4, 252n4
democracy, 11–12, 147–48, 152, 188, 219
DiMaggio, Paul J., 138, 252n7

discipline: Brazilian National Economic
Development Bank (BNDE) and, 209;
bureaucratic niches and, 16, 23, 65, 85,
99–102, 227, 252–53, 253n41; comparison cases and, 104–5, 111, 115–16, 119,
125–27, 132; cultivation and, 65, 68–71,
73; protection and, 85, 93, 99–103; public
servants and, 9, 16–17, 21, 23, 252n4;
recruitment and, 35, 39, 240n34; scholarship on, 209, 211–12, 215–16, 220–21, 227;
social, 35, 65, 99, 105, 127
Dodoo, Francis, xii
drugs: counterfeit, 13, 106, 108–11, 131, 147,
167; illicit, 131; pharmaceutical, 14, 106
dual habitus, 23; Bank of Ghana and, 167;
Bourdieu on, 24, 49, 168; Brazil and,
167, 169, 172, 180–84; bureaucracy and,
165–72, 175–86, 204; cadres and, 7,
179–85, 204, 214; China and, 169, 178–80;
clustering and, 24, 165, 168–71, 179–82,
185; cognitive approach and, 168–71, 175,
177, 250n38; cognitive subcultures and,
204; corruption and, 165, 248n2;
cultural/cognitive approach to, 168–71;
discretion and, 165–66, 168, 171; education and, 168–81; elitism and, 165, 169;
Ghanaian Commercial Courts and, 166,
177, 180–81, 185; Goldilocks zone for, 169;
great men and, 166, 179–82; hard work
and, 173, 175–77; innovation and, 24,
170–71, 177, 248n2; interstitial niches and,
166–67, 177–78, 183, 185; Karanja and,
167, 169, 178, 180, 183; Kenya Tea Development Authority (KTDA) and, 167, 169,
178–80, 183; labor pool and, 166; leaders
and, 166–68; lived experience and, 8, 24,
168–81, 204; Ministry of Finance and
Economic Planning (MOFEP) and, 181,
188; National Agency for Food and Drug
Administration and Control (NAFDAC)
and, 166–67, 169, 172, 180–81, 183; National Communications Authority (NCA)
and, 166, 180, 185; nationalist backlash
and, 169–70; neopatrimonialism and,
24, 165, 181, 184; Nigeria and, 169, 180;
organizational goals and, 165–66; patronage and, 184; pockets of effectiveness
and, 167–68, 183–84; Policy Analysis and
Research Division (PARD) and, 166, 172,
174, 180–83; private sector and, 182;
public interest and, 165; recruitment
and, 171, 185; reform and, 8, 166, 169–71,
179–84, 250n45; sociological foundation
of change and, 179–83; sweat equity and,

182–83; tacit knowledge and, 171, 175, 177;
taxes and, 166–67, 179; technology and,
168, 185; Weber and, 165, 167, 179, 249n9

Economic Research and Forecasting
Division, 188–89
Ecuador, 18
education: Brazilian National Economic
Development Bank (BNDE) and, 118;
bureaucratic niches and, 8, 24, 32, 90,
127, 168–72, 210; capacity building and,
210; civil service and, 26–27, 32, 157, 169;
clustering and, 8, 24, 30, 38, 157, 169, 171,
181, 214, 217; degrees and, 8, 24, 26–27,
33–34, 39, 47, 101, 118, 122, 156–57,
168–74, 180–81, 204, 214, 225, 234–35,
248n2; dual habitus and, 168–81; elitism
and, 8, 90, 150, 169, 214, 220, 234–35;
encore, 218; Getúlio Vargas Foundation
(FGV) and, 118, 199–200; international,
170–78; learning by emulation and,
57–61; lived experience and, 171–72;
mentors and, 242n45; National Agency
for Food and Drug Administration and
Control (NAFDAC) and, 111, 127, 169;
parental, 234–35; Policy Analysis and
Research Division (PARD) and, 157;
protection and, 89–90; recruitment and,
26–27, 30, 32–33, 37–40; secondary
school and, 90–91; state administration
of, 221; university, 8, 26–27, 34, 36, 38,
90, 117–18, 145, 154, 168–74, 200, 214, 218,
229, 234–35, 249, 249n15; workshops
and, 1, 111, 127, 206, 217
efficacy, 80–82, 112
elitism: active sponsorship and, 158–60;
agriculture and, 157; attention and, 23,
135–57, 160–61, 164, 209; autonomy and,
8, 20, 135–47, 154–57, 160–64; Bank
of Ghana and, 136; Brazilian National
Economic Development Bank (BNDE)
and, 142–44; comparison cases and, 108,
114, 116, 123–27, 132; configurational
approach and, 24; Dane and, 151, 156,
169; dual habitus and, 165, 169; education
and, 8, 90, 150, 169, 214, 220, 234–35;
executive will and, 157–60; existential
priority and, 158–60; favorably disposed
elites and, 142–57; inattention and, 8,
23, 139, 141, 149–57, 160, 165, 204, 209;
Karanja and, 144–46; Kenya Tea Development Authority (KTDA) and, 144–47;
Kenyatta and, 112, 144–47, 191, 192; labor
pool and, 123, 156; landowners and, 116;

National Agency for Food and Drug Administration and Control (NAFDAC) and, 147–48; neopatrimonialism and, 135–64, 246n29, 248n86; opposition and, 157–60; pockets of effectiveness and, 188, 191–92, 194, 198; political, 18, 20, 23, 108, 114, 116, 132, 135–42, 145–52, 156–65, 188, 191–92, 204, 219–20; protection and, 136–40; salary issues and, 87; Salt Inspectorate and, 149–51; scholarship and, 8; system design and, 55; Vargas and, 142–44

embezzlement, 147–48

employee handbooks, 32, 42

esprit de corps, 20, 52, 80, 106, 118, 180, 221, 240n36

ethnic issues: cultivation and, 51; Ghanaian diversity and, 11–12, 20; group dynamics and, 2, 19, 51; Kenya and, 13, 112–15, 127, 146, 191; methodologies and, 233–34; neopatrimonialism and, 13, 106, 137, 146

exams, 117, 122–23, 198–99, 209

Executive Groups, 200

executive will, 17–18, 137, 139, 141–42, 149, 158–60, 204, *232*, 238n48

explicit knowledge, 30, 44, 171–74

external projects of reshaping, 23, 85, 98–100, 102

Feingold, 215, 253n39

Finland, 138

Forson, Bernard, Jr., 188, 233

founding cadres, 168, 180–87, 190, 198, 204, 206

France, 133, 169

Fukuyama, Francis, 248n2

Fund for Economic Rehabilitation (FRE), 142–43

Gates Foundation, 208

GEICON, 200

GEIMAPE, 200

gender, xi, 217, 233

General Motors, 233

Germany, 63, 169

Getulio Vargas Foundation (FGV), 118, 199–200

Ghana: Accra, 37, 45–46, 87, 93, 195–96, 234–35; bureaucracy and, 13 (*see also* bureaucracy); central banks and, 136; comparison cases and, 104–10, 113–14, 117–18, 124–30, 133; corruption and, 2, 5, 13, 15, 18–19, 22, 38, 105, 110, 113, 125, 130, 156, 213; cultivation and, 54, 57, 62–74,

77–78, 80; democracy and, 11–12, 147–48, 152, 188; demographics of, 12; diverse culture of, ix–x, 11–12, 20; dual habitus and, 166–83; economy of, 12, 27; elections in, ix, 12; hospitality of, 12; independence and, 11, 13, 26, 159, 238n48; international education and, 172–78; methodologies and, 17, 20–23, 229–36; neopatrimonialism and, 6, 136 (*see also* neopatrimonialism); pockets of effectiveness and, 188, 194–96; political sociology and, 16, 135, 213–15, 221; as presidential republic, 11–12; protection and, 84–95, 98–99, 102–3; Rawlings and, 11; recruitment and, 26–45, 49, 51; scholarship and, ix–xii, 2, 5–6, 11, 15, 17, 160, 170, 174, 202–4, 207–13, 216–19, 222, 225–27, 234; selection process in, 22, 34, 40, 45, 110, 148, 154, 229; slow pace of, 62–63; social context of, 4, 10, 42, 170; Supreme Court of, 45, 50, 153, 188, 230, *231*, 251n1; theory building and, 11–14; University of Legon and, 34, 38, 168, 234

Ghanaian Bar Association, 38

Ghanaian Commercial Courts, 19, 212; Accra and, 195–96; Acquah and, 45, 152–53, 216, 233; administrative effectiveness and, 210; after loss of founding leaders, 188; alternative dispute resolution (ADR) and, 67, 99–100, 127, 177–78, 196; Bannerman and, 44–46, 49–50; bribery and, 5; case load of, 12; comparison cases and, 127–30; constituent expectations and, 195–96; Court of Appeals and, 251n1; cultivation and, 60–62, 66–76, 79; Danida and, 152, 209; dual habitus and, 166, 177, 180–81, 185; group style and, 79; Judicial Services and, 45–46; leaders and, 166; neopatrimonialism and, 152–53, 161–62; pockets of effectiveness and, 188, 195–96; pride in comparison and, 74–77; protection and, 93–102; recruitment and, 36–38, 44–47, 50–51; reputation of, 44–47, 128–29; scale and, 130; selection effects and, 71–74

Global South, xii, 202

great men, 166–67, 179–82

Grindle, Merilee, 183, 211–12

group style, 22, 57, 77–80, 83, 106, 118, 183, 213

Guinea, 18

hard work: comparison cases and, 107–8, 111; cultivation and, 60, 62, 64, 66;

hard work (*continued*)
dual habitus and, 173, 175–77; incorruptibility and, 22, 29; neopatrimonialism
and, 145, 152–55; recruitment and, 29,
44, 46, 48; scholarship on, 216, 223
Hawthorne experiments, 216, 253n41
How to Write About Africa (Wainaina), ix
human capital, 93
human resources, 21, 29–30, 32, 34, 39, 41,
43, 49, 154, 156–57, 181, 216, *231*
human rights, 46, 147

income: average hourly earnings and, 27;
Brazilian National Economic Development Bank (BNDE) and, 106, 116; bribery
and, 4–5, 10, 18–19, 41, 57, 59, 83, 108,
110, 161, 197, 203, 223, 227; commissions
and, 122; compensatory competence and,
92–94; corruption and, 105, 116, 156, 204;
gap in, 36; Kenya Tea Development
Authority (KTDA) and, 112, 192; nominal,
27; poor countries and, 5, 35, 53, 105, 116,
135, 138–41, 217, 225; salary issues and,
20, 26–27, *28*, 57, 62, 87, 124, 142; unofficial, 156
incorruptibility, 22, 29, 79, 107, 116, 145
India, 169, 178–79, 198
Indonesia, *15*, 18, 105, 198
influence effect, 22, 54–57, 70, 79, 107
innovation: best practices and, 207; comparison cases and, 115, 126–28; cultivation
and, 67–68; dual habitus and, 24, 170–71,
177, 248n2; Kenya Tea Development
Authority (KTDA) and, 127–28; local
agents and, 207–8; National Agency for
Food and Drug Administration and
Control (NAFDAC) and, 127; neopatrimonialism and, 144, 152; pockets of
effectiveness and, 190, 192; protection
and, 100; reform and, 8; scholarship and,
211
insourcing, 92–94
institutional variation, 14–16
internal coping mechanisms, *7*, 23, 85, 89,
107, 125
International Monetary Fund (IMF), 18, 153
interstitial niches: autonomy and, 216–17;
as bureaucratic niches, 21; bureaucratic
subcultures and, 2, 6–7, 13, 21–22, 31,
54, 56, 77, 106, 176, 188, 204–5, 241n36;
clustering and, 77–80; comparison cases
and, 106, 119, 127; cultivation and, 58–65,
68, 70–71, 74–83; dual habitus and,
166–67, 177–78, 183, 185; ethos of, 6, 8,

14, 16, 22, 24, 75, 78, 80, 83, 86, 168,
176–78, 183, 185, 193, 203, 217; group
style and, 77–80, 83; interpersonal
environment of, 7; Kenya Tea Development Authority (KTDA) and, 112; lived
experience and, 7, 223; neopatrimonialism and, 7–8, 140, 157, 161, 217; operational discretion and, 106; as pockets of
effectiveness, 21; protection and, 22,
86–88, 96, 99–103; recruitment and,
27–28, 48, 50, 240n23; redundancy and,
203; scholarship on, 203, 216, 223; subcultures and, 241n36; tension of entanglement and, 20

Japan, 169, 190, 214
JBS, 197
Jereissati, Tasso, 184, 200–201
Jobs, Steve, 166

Karanja, Charles: cultivation and, 114; dual
habitus and, 167, 169, 178, 180, 183;
elitism and, 144–46; Kenya Tea Development Authority (KTDA) and, 107,
113–14, 144–47, 155, 167, 169, 178, 180,
183, 188, 191–95; mixed meritocracy and,
113; neopatrimonialism and, 144–47, 155;
pockets of effectiveness and, 188, 191–95;
recruitment and, 113
Kendall, Amos, 250n45
Kenya, 237n18; civil service and, 112–13;
comparison cases and, 106, 112–13, 120,
127, 132, 178–79, 243n4; corruption and,
113, 243n4; dual habitus and, 178–79;
ethnic issues and, 13, 106, 112–15, 127, 146,
191; independence of, 14, 112; Kikuyu
provinces and, 112; methodologies and,
232; Million Acre Settlement Scheme
and, 112; neopatrimonialism and, 13, 106,
139, 144–47, 151; pockets of effectiveness
and, 191–93
Kenya Tea Development Authority (KTDA),
x; after loss of founding leaders, 188,
191–92; agriculture and, *106*, 112, 145–46,
155, 183; autonomy and, 115, 161–62;
clustering and, 113; comparison cases
and, 106–7, 112–15, 120, 123, 125, 127,
130, 132–33; cultivation and, 114, 131–33;
dual habitus and, 167, 169, 178, 180, 183;
elitism and, 144–47; expansion of, 112,
114, 178, 191, 193–95; formation of, 14;
income and, 112, 192; innovation and,
127–28; international donors and, 209;
Karanja and, 107, 113–14, 144–47, 155, 167,

169, 178, 180, 183, 188, 191–95; leadership and, 167; meritocracy and, 107, 113; methodologies and, *232*; neopatrimonialism and, 141, 144–47, 153, 155, 161–62, 164; pockets of effectiveness and, 188, 191–95; protection and, 114–15; recruitment into, 107, 113; scale and, 130; success of, 112; technology and, 125; World Bank and, 13

Kenyatta, Jomo, 112, 144–46, 191, *192*

kinship, 87, 152

Klitgaard, Robert, 165, 205–6, 248n2

Kubitschek, Juscelino, 115, 119–20, *141*, 142–44, 153, 158, 161, 163, 200

Kwame Nkrumah University of Science and Technology, 168–69

labor pool: autonomy and, 30; bureaucracy and, 28; clustering and, 30–31, 38, 204; credentials matching and, 31–35; dual habitus and, 166; elitism and, 123, 156; *esprit de corps* and, 20, 52, 80, 106, 118, 180, 221, 240n36; incorruptibility and, 22, 29, 79, 107, 116, 145; March on, 29–30; neopatrimonialism and, 156; nonfinancial incentives and, 35–37; organizational practices and, 38–40; poor performers and, 68–70, 88, 113, 123, 183, 212, 221, 243n4; professionalism and, 22, 34–35, 37, 71, 180, 197–201, 204, 240n23; proto-bureaucratic experiences and, 28; public service and, 214–15 (*see also* public service); recruitment and, 28–30, *31*, 34–35, 38, 44, 51; skilled labor and, 36, 38–40, 44, 167, 199; stereotypes and, 2, 4, 11, 57–58, 63, 76–78, 80; sweat equity and, 182–83; talented, 38–40, 199; work ethics and, 48, 60, 62–63, 171–75, 213

Lagos, 155

learned helplessness, 80–81, 242n51

Leonard, David K., 144–45, 192

lived experience, 112; bureaucratic ethos and, 8, 22, 54, 57, 83, 117, 168, 172, 176–77, 204, 217, 222; bureaucratic niches and, 7–8, 22, 24, 54, 63, 78, 82–83, 168–72, 176–77, 204, 223; clustering and, 8, 22, 24, 57, 117, 145, 168–71, 181, 217; cognitive approach to, 222; context of, 207; cultivation and, 54, 57, 72, 78, 80–83, 204–5; declarative/nondeclarative knowledge and, 224; dual habitus and, 24, 168–81, 204; education and, 171–72; importance of, 25; interstitial niches and, 223; neopatrimonialism and, 145;

prescriptive, 82–83; recruitment and, 35, 117

Lopes, Lucas, 182, 200

Lopes, Luis Simões, 118, 169, 180, 198–200

Maciel Filho, José, 143–44, 164

Madagascar, 18

Malawi, 105

Management Services Division, 229

March, James, 29–30

mentors, 242n45

meritocracy: Brazilian National Economic Development Bank (BNDE) and, 117, 122; bureaucratic niches and, 107; clustering and, 113; exams and, 117, 122–23, 198–99, 209; Kenya Tea Development Authority (KTDA) and, 107; mixed, 113, 143, 145, 239n18; National Agency for Food and Drug Administration and Control (NAFDAC) and, 122; neopatrimonialism and, 143, 145; organizational goals and, 203; pockets of effectiveness and, 189, 198–99, 201; protection and, 119; recruitment and, 32, 34, 40–41, 44, 49, 113, 239n18, 240nn29 and 36; Salt Inspectorate and, 122–23; Weber on, 229

methodologies: agency failure and, 17, 19; agriculture and, *232*; Bank of Ghana and, 230, *231*, 234; Brazilian National Economic Development Bank (BNDE) and, *232*; bureaucracy and, 229; case selection and, 230–33; China and, *232*; consent process for, 229–30; corruption and, *232*; ethnic issues and, 233–34; interstitial niches and, 233–35; Kenya Tea Development Authority (KTDA) and, *232*; Ministry of Finance and Economic Planning (MOFEP) and, 230, *231*, 234; National Agency for Food and Drug Administration and Control (NAFDAC) and, *232*; National Communications Authority (NCA) and, 230–34; neopatrimonialism and, 233; Nigeria and, *232*; pockets of effectiveness and, 230, 233; Policy Analysis and Research Division (PARD) and, 230, *231–32*; reputation and, 229; sources for, 229; taxes and, *232*; Weber and, 229

Mexico, 63

Migdal, Joel, 213

Million Acre Settlement Scheme, 112

Ministry of Agriculture, 119, 145, 155, 157, 214, 220–21

Ministry of Finance and Economic Planning (MOFEP), 220, 252n4; Budget Division of, 94–95, 101; bureaucratic niches and, 2–3; comparison cases and, 130; cultivation and, 59, 63; dual habitus and, 181, 188; Human Resources Department of, 154; methodologies and, 230, *231*, 234; neopatrimonialism and, 143–44, 150, 153–56; pockets of effectiveness and, 199; protection and, 94, 103; recruitment and, 36, 40, 47–48, 50; reputation of, 18; Salt Inspectorate and, 150

Ministry of Trade and Industry (MITI), 214

Moi, Daniel arap, 191

Monetary Policy Analysis and Financial Stability Department: Bank of Ghana and, 12, 38, 129, 153–54; comparison cases and, 129–30; cultivation and, 68; neopatrimonialism and, 153–54; Policy Analysis and Research Division (PARD) and, 89–90, 93, 95–96, 99, 130, 153–54, 230; protection and, 89–90, 93, 95–96, 99; recruitment and, 38–40, 240n29

Monetary Policy Committee, 38, 154, 230, *231*

money laundering, 148, 197

monopolies, 18, 126, 191, 205

moral issues, 2, 4, 9, 17, 133, 146, 206, 250n38

Morgan, Kimberly, 213

Mozambique, 15

Muslims, 12, 233

National Agency for Food and Drug Administration and Control (NAFDAC): after loss of founding leaders, 189; Akunyili and, 107, 109, 111, 113, 129, 148, 172, 180–81, 183, 189, 206; autonomy and, 161–62; bribery and, 110; clustering and, 109–10; comparison cases and, 106–13, 122–31, 134; counterfeit drugs and, 13–14, 108, 111, 131, 147, 167; cultivation and, 131; Directorate of Food and Drug Administration and Control and, 14; donor funding and, 209; dual habitus and, 166–67, 169, 172, 180–81, 183; education and, 127, 169; elitism and, 147–48; exams and, 122; external opposition and, 131; innovation and, 127; international funding and, 209; leaders and, 166; meritocracy and, 122; methodologies and, *232*; neopatrimonialism and, 141, 147–48, 161–62, 164; Obasanjo and, 109, 147–48; pockets of effectiveness and, 134, 189, 201; protec-

tion and, 111–12; public interest and, 111; public service and, 131; recruitment and, 109–10; reform and, 107; regulatory endowment of, 111; reputation of, 13; Salt Inspectorate and, 14, 19, 122–23, 125, 127, 129, 141, 161–69, 180, 201, 209, *232*; scholarship on, 227; sociological learning and, 206; sweat equity and, 183; teams of, 110; water quality and, 108, 111–12, 127, 227; workshops and, 127

National Communications Authority (NCA): active role of, 12; comparison cases and, 113, 129–30; cultivation and, 58, 62, 65, 75; dual habitus and, 166, 180, 185; learning by emulation and, 58; methodologies and, 230–34; neopatrimonialism and, 156, 161; pockets of effectiveness and, 188; protection and, 97, 99; recruitment and, 36–37, 42–44, 51; Spectrum and Frequency Management and, 12

neopatrimonialism: active sponsorship and, 158–60; administrative culture and, 7; autonomy and, 23; Bank of Ghana and, 136, 153–54; Brazilian National Economic Development Bank (BNDE) and, 141–44, 153, 158, 161, 163–64; bureaucracy and, 138–39, 145, 149, 158–62; bureaucratic ethos and, 6, 14, 138, 212–13; bureaucratic niches and, 23, 139, 149, 160–62, 217; central banks and, 136, 161; China and, 6, 139, 149–51, 158; civil service and, 142, 154–55, 157; clientelism and, 152; clustering and, 138–42, 145, 156–59, 163; cognitive approach and, 141; Commonwealth Development Corporation (CDC) and, 147, 153; comparison cases and, 105–7, 128, 144–47, 155; corruption and, 136, 145, 148, 156, 162; cultivation and, 30, 56, 61, 68, 70, 78, 83, 241n35; dual habitus and, 24, 165, 181, 184; elitism and, 135–64, 246n29, 248n86; ethnic issues and, 13, 106, 137, 146; executive will and, 157–60; existential priority and, 158–60; Ghanaian Commercial Courts and, 152–53, 161–62; hard work and, 145, 152–55; innovation and, 144, 152; institutional variation in, 16; interstitial niches and, 7–8, 140, 157, 161, 217; Karanja and, 144–47, 155; Kenya and, 13, 106, 139, 144–47, 151; Kenya Tea Development Authority (KTDA) and, 141, 144–47, 153, 155, 161–62, 164; labor pool and, 156; legal-rational institutions and, 2; lived

experience and, 145; meritocracy and, 143, 145; methodologies and, 233; Ministry of Finance and Economic Planning (MOFEP) and, 143–44, 150, 153–56; Monetary Policy Analysis and Financial Stability Department and, 153–54; National Agency for Food and Drug Administration and Control (NAFDAC) and, 141, 147–48, 161–62, 164; National Communications Authority (NCA) and, 156, 161; New Public Management and, 138; Nigeria and, 6, 139, 147–48, 153, 247n65; organizational goals and, 139, 149, 159, 162–64; patronage and, 135–41, 144–45, 149–52, 156–60; as pejorative, 2; personal/professional inclusion and, 1–2; Policy Analysis and Research Division (PARD) and, *141*, 153–57, 161–62; politicalization and, 140–51; prebendalism and, 9, 203; private sector and, 162; productivity and, 162; protection and, 95; public interest and, 137, 158; public service and, *141*, 159; recruitment and, 30, *31*, 42, 49–50, 156; reform and, 135–37, 147–49, 152–53, 158–62, 223; reputation and, 152, 157–59, 173, 179; Salt Inspectorate and, 149–51, 156, 162; shelter from, 7–8, 138–41, 144, 149–56, 204, 246n29; subcultures and, 205; taxes and, *141*, 144, 149–51, 158–62, 248n88; technology and, 137; use of term, 2, 237n5; Vargas and, 141–44, 148, 153, 164; Weber and, 137–38
nepotism, 4, 19, 41–42, 110
Netherlands, 138
New Deal, 115, 215, 233
New Patriotic Party, 188
New Public Management, 138
Ngozi, Chimamanda, x
Nigeria, 237n18; bureaucracy and, 6; bureaucratic ethos and, 6; comparison cases and, 106, 108–11, 131; corruption and, 13; counterfeit drugs and, 14, 108, 131; dual habitus and, 169, 180; economy of, 109; fake products of, 108; Food and Drug Administration and, 19; methodologies and, *232*; NAFDAC and, 13 (*see also* National Agency for Food and Drug Administration and Control (NAFDAC)); neopatrimonialism and, 6, 139, 147–48, 153, 247n65; pockets of effectiveness and, 189; scholarship and, 213, 222, 227
Nkrumah, Kwame, 159
nondeclarative cognition, 223–24, 254n55

nongovernmental organizations (NGOs), xi, 35, 37, 182, 229
NUMMI, 233

Obasanjo, Olusegun, 109, 147–48
obrunyi (foreign), ix, 170
Office of the Head of Civil Service, 32, 154, 229
operational discretion, 23, 106, 143, 150–51, 154, 165, 203
organizational entities, 7, 20, 118, 120, 124, 219–21
organizational goals: bureaucratic niches and, 2, 7–8, 22–24, 52, 83, 85–86, 127–28, 139, 159, 165, 208; comparison cases and, 127–28; corruption and, 9; cultivation and, 55; dual habitus and, 165–66; employee leveraging and, 4; neopatrimonialism and, 139, 149, 159, 162–64; orientation to, 9, 16, 21, 24, 52, 118, 135, 149, 162, 166, 202–3; protection and, 7, 22–23, 85–86, 95; public interest and, 2, 16; recruitment and, 52; reform and, 8
Orloff, Ann, 213
Ostrom, Elinor, 31–32

Paiva Teixeira, Glycon de, 117, 143, 169, 180, 182
Parkinson's law, 154
particularism, 2, 124
patchworking, 6, 12, 14–17, 104, 225
patronage: Brazilian National Economic Development Bank (BNDE) and, 13; civil service and, 253n34; comparison cases and, 105–7, 112–13, 116, 120, 122–23, 125, 129, 132; credentials matching and, 31–35; dual habitus and, 184; extent of, 2; institutionalized, 13; legitimacy and, 32–34; masking of, 32–34; neopatrimonialism and, 135–41, 144–45, 149–52, 156–60; organizational practices and, 38–40; pockets of effectiveness and, 197, 199; recruitment and, 21, 27, 31–34, 37–44, 51–52; Salt Inspectorate and, 120–22; scholarship on, 204, 209–10, 213–15, 253n34; social topography of pressure in, 31–35; structural filtering of pressures and, 156–57
payrolls, 136, 146
pensions, 27, *28*
personnel discretion, 8, 122, 139, 142–43, 161, 163
Petroleum Trust Fund (PTF), 148

pharmaceutical industry, *106*, 108–9, 148, 166, 169, 189

Philippine National Irrigation Administration, 158

pockets of effectiveness: administrative capacity and, 25; autonomy and, 20, 195; Brazil and, 189, 192–94, 197–201; Brazilian National Economic Development Bank (BNDE) and, 21, 117, 134, 189, 193–94, 197–200, 244n44, 251n18; bureaucracy and, 14, 187–201, 252n7; bureaucratic ethos and, 24, 187–93, 197–201; as bureaucratic niches, 21, 187, 193, 195, 197–98, 201; bureaucratic subcultures and, 188; cadres and, 187, 190, 198, 201; central banks and, 188; China and, 190, 198; clientelism and, 198; clustering and, 190; cognitive approach and, 199; comparison cases and, 23, 105, 117, 134; constituent expectations and, 195–96; corruption and, 189, 197, 201; cultivation and, 42; domain expansion and, 193–95; dual habitus and, 167–68, 183–84; elitism and, 188, 191–92, 194, 198; Ghanaian Commercial Courts and, 188, 195–96; innovation and, 190, 192; as interstitial niches, 21; islands of integrity and, 20; Kenya Tea Development Authority (KTDA) and, 188, 191–95; long-term outcomes in, 187–201; meritocracy and, 189, 198–99, 201; methodologies and, 230, 233; Ministry of Finance and Economic Planning (MOFEP) and, 199; National Agency for Food and Drug Administration and Control (NAFDAC) and, 134, 189, 201; National Communications Authority (NCA) and, 188; Nigeria and, 189; patronage and, 197, 199; Policy Analysis and Research Division (PARD) and, 188–89; positive deviance and, 55, 210–13, 241n36, 253n22; pride of work and, 21; private sector and, 200; productivity and, 192, 196, 200; public service and, 189, 193, 198; reform and, 194, 198–201; reputation and, 197; Salt Inspectorate and, 201; scholarship on, 183–84, 205–13, 215, 225, 227; spreading professionals and, 197–201; state variation and, 210–13; taxes and, *190*, 194; technology and, 195–96; Vargas and, 198–99

Policy Analysis and Research Division (PARD): after loss of founding leaders, 188–89; agriculture and, 153; autonomy and, 161; boundary marking and, 62–63; bureaucratic niches and, 2–6, 12, 21, 202; chasing and, 3, 84, 86, 89–92; comparison cases and, 113, 130; compensatory competence and, 92–94; corruption and, 3–5, 59, 130; cultivation and, 57–65, 69, 75; dual habitus and, 166, 172, 174, 180–83; as Economic Research and Forecasting Division, 188–89; education and, 157; international funding and, 209; learning by emulation and, 57–61; Mensah and, 3, 47–48, 62, 65, 69, 101, 113, 155, 166, 180, 183, 188–89, 216, 230; methodologies and, 230, *231–32*; Monetary Policy Analysis and Financial Stability Department and, 89–90, 93, 95–96, 99, 130, 153–54, 230; Multi-Donor Budget Support team and, 3; neopatrimonialism and, *141*, 153–57, 161–62; poaching and, 47–49; pockets of effectiveness and, 188–89; protection and, 84, 87, 89–96, 99, 101–3; recruitment and, 26, 36–38, 47–51; reform and, 202; reputation and, 38; reverse cooptation and, 101–2; scale and, 130; sociological learning and, 206; subculture of, 4; success of, 18; time culture and, 61–65; wages at, 162

political sociology, 16, 135, 213–15, 221

poor performers, 68–70, 88, 113, 123, 183, 212, 221, 243n4

positive deviance, 55, 210–13, 241n36, 253n22

Powell, Walter W., 138

prebendalism, 9, 203

principal-agent theory, 17, 54–55, 72, 185, 216

private sector: clustering and, 109, 225; comparison cases and, 109, 114, 119–20; cultivation and, 70; dual habitus and, 182; neopatrimonialism and, 162; organizational entities and, 219–20; organizational performance and, 220–21; pay scale of, 27; pockets of effectiveness and, 200; political administration in, 220; productivity and, 114, 200, 254n62; recruitment and, 33, 36–37; salary issues and, 27, *28*; scholarship on, 25, 214

productivity: cultivation and, 62–63, 69–70, 123; increasing, 107–8, 162, 253n41; low morale and, 4; maximization of, 29; neopatrimonialism and, 162; pockets of effectiveness and, 192, 196, 200; private sector and, 114, 200, 254n62; professionalism and, 206; protection and, 87, 101; punishment for poor, 107, 123; recruitment and, 29; social context of, 216

professionalism, 22, 34–35, 37, 71, 180,
197–201, 204–6, 240n23
protection: adaptive redundancy and,
94–95; Bank of Ghana and, 103; Brazilian
National Economic Development Bank
(BNDE) and, 119–20; bureaucracy and,
85–91, 94–95, 98–110, 114, 116, 121–34;
bureaucratic ethos and, 23; bureaucratic
subcultures and, 85–86, 88, 98–103;
chasing and, 86, 89–93, 102; civil service
and, 92; clustering and, 7–8, 85–86, 88,
98–103; code switching and, 89–92, 102;
cognitive approach and, 102; comparison
cases and, 111–12; compensatory competence and, 92–94; discipline and, 85,
93, 99–103; discrete jurisdictions and,
94–95; disruptive environments and,
86–88; education and, 89–90; elitism
and, 136–40; external projects of reshaping and, 23, 85, 98–100, 102; Ghanaian
Commercial Courts and, 93–102; innovation and, 100; insourcing and, 92–94;
internal coping mechanisms and, 7, 23,
85, 89, 107, 125; interstitial niches and,
22, 86–88, 96, 99–103; Kenya Tea Development Authority (KTDA) and, 114–15;
meritocracy and, 119; Ministry of Finance
and Economic Planning (MOFEP) and,
94, 103; Monetary Policy Analysis and
Financial Stability Department and,
89–90, 93, 95–96, 99; National Agency
for Food and Drug Administration and
Control (NAFDAC) and, 111–12; National
Communications Authority (NCA) and,
97, 99; neopatrimonialism and, 95; organizational goals and, 7, 22–23, 85–86, 95;
Policy Analysis and Research Division
(PARD) and, 84, 87, 89–96, 99, 101–3;
problematic embeddedness and, 88–98;
productivity and, 87, 101; recruitment
and, 86; redundancy and, 94–98; reform
and, 88, 91, 98; reputation and, 87, 97,
100, 103; reverse cooptation and, 101–2;
Salt Inspectorate and, 125–26; taxes and,
96; Weber and, 95, 102
pruning, 7, 68–70, 107, 113, 123
public interest, 229; comparison cases and,
105, 111; cultivation and, 55; dual habitus
and, 165; individual interest and, 212;
National Agency for Food and Drug
Administration and Control (NAFDAC)
and, 111; neopatrimonialism and, 137, 158;
organizational goals and, 2, 16; pockets of
effectiveness and, 199; proto-bureaucratic

schema for, 44; working effectively for, 8,
11, 20
public service: Administrative Department
of Public Service (DASP) and, 117–18,
198–200, 251n32; cultivation and, 57, 80;
dysfunctional, 2; motivations for, 205–7;
National Agency for Food and Drug
Administration and Control (NAFDAC)
and, 131; neopatrimonialism and, 141, 159;
organizational mission and, 9; pockets of
effectiveness and, 189, 193, 198; recruitment and, 27, 28, 32–33, 36, 39, 51,
240n23; scholarship on, 20; street-level
agents and, 219; unskilled labor and,
214–15; Vargas and, 116
Public Services Commission, 32–33, 229
punctuality, 63

Qing dynasty, 120, 160
Quadros, Jânio da Silva, 120

Rawlings, Jerry, 11
recruitment: Bank of Ghana and, 38–43, 51;
Brazilian National Economic Development Bank (BNDE) and, 117; bureaucracy and, 27–31, 34–35, 38, 44–52,
240n36; bureaucratic ethos and, 6, 22,
29–31, 52; bureaucratic niches and, 6–7,
22, 27–28; bureaucratic subcultures and,
31, 40; cadres and, 215; central banks and,
39–40, 42; civil service and, 26, 30, 32,
37, 41, 47; clustering and, 7–8, 21–23, 26,
28, 30, 38, 56, 86, 107, 109–10, 113, 117,
122–23, 171, 185, 204, 217; cognitive
approach and, 28–29; comparison cases
and, 23, 107, 109–10, 113, 117, 122–23;
corruption and, 38, 41–42, 46; credential
matching and, 31–35; cultivation and, 56,
65, 68; discipline and, 35, 39, 240n34;
dual habitus and, 171, 185; education
and, 26–27, 30, 32–33, 37–40; Ghanaian
Commercial Courts and, 36–38, 44–47,
50–51; hard workers and, 29, 44, 46, 48;
influence effects and, 56–57; interstitial
niches and, 27–28, 48, 50, 240n23;
Karanja and, 113; Kenya Tea Development Authority (KTDA) and, 107, 113;
labor pool and, 28–30, 31, 34–35, 38, 44,
51; lived experience and, 35, 117; meritocracy and, 32, 34, 40–41, 44, 49, 113,
239n18, 240nn29 and 36; Ministry
of Finance and Economic Planning
(MOFEP) and, 36, 40, 47–48, 50;
Monetary Policy Analysis and Financial

recruitment (*continued*)
    Stability Department and, 38–40, 240n29;
    National Agency for Food and Drug
    Administration and Control (NAFDAC)
    and, 109–10; National Communications
    Authority (NCA) and, 36–37, 42–44,
    51; neopatrimonialism and, 30, *31*, 42,
    49–50, 156; nonfinancial incentives and,
    35–38; organizational practices and,
    38–40, 52; patronage and, 21, 27, 31–34,
    37–44, 51–52; perceptions affecting
    orientation and, 49–51; poaching and,
    47–49, 155; Policy Analysis and Research
    Division (PARD) and, 26, 36–38, 47–51;
    principal-agent theory and, 56; private
    sector and, 33, 36–37; productivity and,
    29; protection and, 86; public service
    and, 27, *28*, 32–33, 36, 39, 51, 240n23;
    reform and, 45; reputation and, 26, 38,
    43–49, 51, 226; selection effect and, 34,
    37–38; taxes and, 37; Weber and, 35, 50
redundancy: adaptive, 94–95; high
    reliability and, 97–98; individual, 95–97;
    interstitial niches and, 203; protection
    and, 94–98; uncertainty and, 97–98;
    unit, 97; zero, 94
reform, 237n14; administrative, 16–17, 117,
    171; agency failure and, 17–21; Akunyili
    and, 107; bureaucracy and, 5, 8, 10–11, 16,
    23–24, 54, 82, 107, 110, 117, 126, 128, 134,
    162, 166, 171, 179, 198–205, 214, 217, 223;
    comparison cases and, 107, 110, 117,
    121–23, 126–34, 243n4; cosmopolitan, 10;
    cultivation and, 54, 66, 82; democratic,
    11; dual habitus and, 8, 166, 169–71,
    179–84, 250n45; executive will and,
    18; Global South and, 202; innovation
    and, 8; international, 17; Jereissati and,
    200–201; Klitgaard and, 206; letter of
    the law and, 5; National Agency for Food
    and Drug Administration and Control
    (NAFDAC) and, 107; neopatrimonialism
    and, 135–37, 147–49, 152–53, 158–62,
    223; organizational goals and, 8; pockets
    of effectiveness and, 194, 198–201; Policy
    Analysis and Research Division (PARD)
    and, 202; protection and, 88, 91, 98;
    recruitment and, 45; Salt Inspectorate
    and, 129, 159–60; scholarship on, 202–6,
    211, 214, 217–24; South Korea and,
    238n48; tacit knowledge and, 224;
    top-down, 10–11; World Bank and, 5
religion, xi, 12, 19, 133, 233

reputation: assessing, 44–47, 51; Bank of
    Ghana and, 38, 43–44; Brazilian National
    Economic Development Bank (BNDE)
    and, 116; bureaucracy and, 75; civil
    service and, 26; comparison cases and,
    106–7, 116–20, 124, 128–30; cultivation
    and, 57–61, 65, 71, 75–76; Ghanaian
    Commercial Courts and, 44–47, 128–29;
    Ghanaian hospitality and, 12; learning by
    emulation and, 57–61; methodologies
    and, 229; Ministry of Trade and Industry
    (MITI) and, 214; National Agency for
    Food and Drug Administration and
    Control (NAFDAC) and, 13; neopatri-
    monialism and, 152, 157–59, 173, 179;
    pockets of effectiveness and, 197; Policy
    Analysis and Research Division (PARD)
    and, 38; protection and, 87, 97, 100, 103;
    recruitment and, 26, 38, 43–47, 51, 226;
    Salt Inspectorate and, 107, 124; stereo-
    types and, 2, 4, 11, 57–58, 63, 76–78, 80;
    through observation, 47–49
Revenue Commissioners, 46
Ricks, Jacob I., 158
rule of law, 15, 121, 164
Russia, 169, 198

salary issues, 20, 26–27, *28*, 35, 57, 87, 124,
    142, 162
Salt Inspectorate: after loss of founding
    leaders, 188–91; autonomy and, 161–62;
    clustering and, 122–23; comparison cases
    and, *106*, 107–8, 120–25, 129; corruption
    and, 13, 19, 107, 122–25, 129, 156, 162, 201;
    cultivation and, 123–24; Dane and, 121,
    150–51, 156, 167, 169, 178–80, 183, 189–91,
    194, 249n6; domain expansion and,
    193–94; elitism and, 149–51; exams and,
    122–23; external opposition and, 131–32;
    leaders and, 166; meritocracy and,
    122–23; Ministry of Finance and, 150;
    National Agency for Food and Drug
    Administration and Control (NAFDAC)
    and, 14, 19, 122–29, 141, 161–69, 180, 201,
    209, *232*; neopatrimonialism and, 149–51,
    156, 162; patronage and, 120–22; pockets
    of effectiveness and, 201; poor perform-
    ers and, 123; protection and, 125–26;
    reform and, 159–60; reputation of, 107,
    124; Salt Revenue Account and, 121;
    scholarship on, 227; taxes and, 14, 19, *106*,
    120–25, 129, 131, 149–51, 159, 162, 166–67,
    179–80, 194, *232*; technology and, 122,

125–26, 131; *Yanwu Shu* and, 14, 121–22, 125, 129, 134, *141*, 149, 151, 159, 167, 194, *232*

scholarship, 24–25; Bank of Ghana and, 209–10, 216; Brazil and, 208, 212; Brazilian National Economic Development Bank (BNDE) and, 143–44; bureaucracy and, 202–27, 253n22, 254n46; central banks and, 212; China and, 227; clustering and, 203–6, 213–18, 225–26; corruption and, 5, 20, 205, 211, 213, 223, 225, 252n3; directions for future research in, 224–27; elitism and, 8; Ghana and, ix–xii, 2, 5–6, 11, 15, 17, 160, 170, 174, 208, 216, 222, 234; hard work and, 216, 223; implications for, 207–13, 217–19; interstitial niches and, 203, 216, 223; lack of African, ix–xii; Nigeria and, 213, 222, 227; organizational, 215–19; patronage and, 204, 209–10, 213–15, 253n34; pockets of effectiveness and, 183–84, 205–13, 215, 225, 227; political sociology and, 213–15; private sector and, 214; public service and, 20; reform and, 202–6, 211, 214, 217–24; state variation and, 210–13, 237n14, 238n34; taxes and, 212, 224; Weber and, 202–3, 205, 216, 221, 252n7

selection effect, 22, 34, 37–38, 55, 57, 70–74, 107, 122

Selznick Phillip, 74, 75, 101, 115

Senegal, 158

Serious Fraud Office, 46

Sewell, William, 49

Shonekan, Ernest, 147

Sino-Foreign Salt Inspectorate. *See* Salt Inspectorate

Sino-Japanese War, 190

skilled labor, 36, 38–40, 44, 167, 199

Skocpol, Theda, 16, 146, 215, 253n39

Slovakia, 18

small-group culture, 6–9, 21–23, 54–57, 71, 85, 182–86, 217–19

social capital, 26, 90, 151, 185, 204

South Africa, 198, 243n4

South Korea, 214, 238n48

Special Crops Development Authority, 14, *232*

Special Investigations Panel, 147–48

Spectrum and Frequency Management, 12, 19, 97, 99, 129, 230

stereotypes, 2, 4, 11, 57–58, 63, 76–78, 80

Sub-Saharan Africa, 11, 112

Superintendency of Money and Credit (SUMOC), 120, 200

Supreme Court (Ghana), 45, 50, 153, 188, 230, *231*, 251n1

sweat equity, 182–83

Sweden, 138

tacit knowledge: bureaucracy and, 54, 82, 222; clustering and, 205; cultivation and, 54, 82; dual habitus and, 171, 175, 177; lived experience and, 8; reform and, 224

Taliercio, Robert, 243n4

taxes: cell phone, 37; comparison cases and, *106*, 120–26, 129–31; corruption and, 18, 120, 125, 129, 162; dual habitus and, 166–67, 179; methodologies and, *232*; neopatrimonialism and, *141*, 144, 149–51, 158–62, 248n88; pockets of effectiveness and, *190*, 194; protection and, 96; recruitment and, 37; Salt Inspectorate and, 14, *106*, 120–25, 129, 131, 149–51, 159, 162, 166–67, 179–80, 194, *232*; scholarship on, 212, 224; *Yanwu Shu* and, 14, 121–22, 125, 129, 134, *141*, 149, 151, 159, 167, 194, *232*

technology: boundary marking and, 67–68; bro culture and, 219; cultivation and, 64–68, 70, 72, 81; dual habitus and, 168, 185; Kenya Tea Development Authority (KTDA) and, 125; neopatrimonialism and, 137; organizational culture and, 127–28; pockets of effectiveness and, 195–96; political administration and, 220; reform and, 129; Salt Inspectorate and, 122, 125–26, 131; sanitation, 208; scholarship on, 206; social, 66; transportation, 122; Weber on, 137

Tendler, Judith, 184, 200–201, 206, 211–12, 240n34, 250n47

Thailand, 18

theft, 4, 147–48, 185

Tilly, Charles, 23, 139, *141*, 158

time culture, 61–66

Torres, Ary, 143, 167, 169, 172, 180

Toyota, 233

United Kingdom, 138, 169, 173

United States: American Political Development (APD) and, 16, 214–15, 253n34; business practices of, 63, 170, 176, 198, 224; corruption and, 2; development banking and, 118; education and, 169; election of 2000 and, ix; evangelicalism and, 133; expatriates and, 169; hospitals

United States (*continued*)
  and, 148, 247n65; influence of, 29, 176,
  198, 214; Jacksonian-era, 135; New Deal
  and, 115, 215, 233; punctuality and, 63;
  scientific management and, 198; sociological studies on, 16; telecommunications and, 129; welfare policy of, 146–47
universalism, 2, 198
University of Legon, 34, 38, 168, 234
University of São Paulo, 172
U.S. Coast Survey, 215, 245n111
U.S. Department of Agriculture (USDA),
  141, 215
U.S. Department of Justice, 148
U.S. Food and Drug Administration (FDA),
  13–14, 157–58
U.S. New Deal Agricultural Adjustment
  Agency, 215, 233, 253n39
U.S. Supreme Court, ix

vacations, 27, *28*
Vaisey, Stephen, 223
Vargas, Getúlio: Brazilian National Economic Development Bank (BNDE) and,
  108, 115–16, 118, 120, 134, 141–44, 153, 164,
  198; elitism and, 142–44; Getúlio Vargas
  Foundation (FGV) and, 118, 199–200;
  neopatrimonialism and, 141–44, 148, 153,
  164; official years of, 244n42; pockets of
  effectiveness and, 198–99; public service
  and, 116

Wainaina, Binyavanga, ix
Wall Street, 222
water quality, 108, 111–12, 127, 210, 227

Weber, Max, xi: on bureaucracy, 1, 9–10, 15,
  35, 50, 54, 75, 83, 95, 102, 138, 165, 167,
  202–5, 221, 229, 252n7; charismatic
  authority and, 249n9; classic typology
  of, 203; cultivation and, 54, 75, 83; dual
  habitus and, 165, 167, 179, 249n9; ethos
  of, 1, 9–10, 54, 75, 83, 203, 205, 221;
  general rules and, 10, 54; leadership and,
  167; life-order and, 9; meritocracy and,
  229; methodologies and, 229; moral
  issues and, 9; neopatrimonialism and,
  137–38; nonfinancial incentives and, 35;
  protection and, 95, 102; recruitment and,
  35, 50; scholarship and, 202–3, 205, 216,
  221, 252n7; technology and, 137
Wesley Girls' Senior High School, 234
West Africa Institute for Financial Monetary
  Management, 155
women, xi, 27, 77, 143, 217, 219, 233
Wood, Georgina, 153, 196
work ethics, 48, 60, 62–63, 171–75, 213
workshops, 1, 111, 127, 206, 217
World Bank, 5, 13, 15, 18, 106, 133, 147, 153,
  195
worldwide governance indicators (WGI), 15

Yanwu Shu: corruption and, 121–22, 129;
  organizational effects and, 121; pockets
  of effectiveness and, 134; protection and,
  149; salt police and, 121; taxes and 14,
  121–22, 125, 129, 134, *141*, 149, 151, 159,
  167, 194, *232*
Yar'Adua, Umaru Musa, 189

Zambia, 18

A NOTE ON THE TYPE

This book has been composed in Adobe Text and Gotham. Adobe Text,
designed by Robert Slimbach for Adobe, bridges the gap between fifteenth-
and sixteenth-century calligraphic and eighteenth-century Modern styles.
Gotham, inspired by New York street signs, was designed by Tobias Frere-
Jones for Hoefler & Co.